The Man Who
Would Not
Shut Up

Also by Marvin Kitman

The Number One Best-Seller

George Washington's Expense Account
(with Gen. George Washington)

You Can't Judge a Book by Its Cover

The Marvin Kitman Show: Encyclopedia Televisiana

The Coward's Almanac

I Am a VCR: The Kitman Tapes

The Making of the Prefident 1789

www.stmartins.com

Library of Congress Cataloging-in-Publication Data

Kitman, Marvin, 1929–
    The man who would not shut up : the rise of Bill O'Reilly /
Marvin Kitman.
        p.   cm.
    ISBN-13: 978-0-312-31435-4
    ISBN-10: 0-312-31435-3
    1. O'Reilly, Bill.   2. Journalists—United States—Biography.
I. Title.

PN4874.O73K58 2007
070.92—dc22
[B]

                                                            2006050577

First Edition: January 2007

10 9 8 7 6 5 4 3 2 1

The Man Who Would Not Shut Up

THE RISE OF BILL O'REILLY

Marvin Kitman

St. Martin's Press 🐾 New York

To William O'Reilly Sr. and the nuns at
St. Brigid/Our Lady of Hope in Westbury, N.Y, without whom
Bill O'Reilly would have been someone different.
And two long-suffering women: Maureen McPhilmy O'Reilly, for
having to put up with him; and Carol Kitman, for having read the
manuscript, edited it nine times, and for putting up with me.

CONTENTS

Part III The Meltdown

Part IV The Last Hurrah

Part V What Say You?

I frankly acknowledge to you my convictions, and I will freely lay before you the reasons on which they are founded. My arguments will be open to all, and may be judged by all.

—*Alexander Hamilton, as Publius in* The Federalist Papers

I wish I was as cocksure of anything as Tom Macaulay is of everything.

—*William Lamb (later to be Prime Minister, Lord Melbourne) about Macaulay, the famous British historian.*

PREFACE

You are about to read the first full-length biography of Bill O'Reilly.

It is a book by a liberal TV critic about a man who is widely perceived as a conservative television icon, a man about whom there is some difference of opinion. For some, he is a beloved voice of reason, a font of wisdom, a man who provides diversity on the airwaves. They love his passion and concern about what he reports on. For others, he is a semidemented TV talk-show host. He is, they say, an obnoxious, insufferable, rude, loudmouth whose views, according to the kinder analysis, are typical right-wing drivel. He has managed to win the enmity of liberals everywhere not only with the opinions he expresses but his style as well. Bill O'Reilly is unarguably the most loved and loathed media voice of the twenty-first century.

I am in a third group: guilty of liking him—with an explanation. I don't agree with much of what he says; but I like the way he says it, and what his success says about traditional television journalism, the most dysfunctional medium in the history of mass communication.

Most of the books praising O'Reilly are by O'Reilly himself, and they tend to be laudatory. The others are unmitigatedly negative.

Mine is different. It's fair and balanced. By that I mean it doesn't trash O'Reilly in the usual way. It is an even-handed, in-depth examination of the man through the prism of his work as a journalist.

Since 1996, Bill O'Reilly has become the most widely discussed—Google the words "Bill O'Reilly" and 6.5 million hits instantly appear—most misunderstood journalist in the history of TV news.

He is not an ideologue like Rush Limbaugh. I see him as an independent, a man who thinks things through and comes to conclusions, many of which are different from mine.

None of which matters to me, having grown up with the old-fashioned idea about the sanctity of free speech. In this day of polarization, it often seems that two fascist entities have joined together in the fight to squelch opinions they disagree with. I believe in the antiquated notion of fighting to the death for the right to say it. Whatever *it* might be. According to some people, the founding fathers would never have put that stuff in about the First Amendment had they known there would be an O'Reilly someday.

Approaching O'Reilly with an open mind was not easy to do. At best, he is dismissed by his enemies as an entertainer. While I find his performance on *The O'Reilly Factor* entertaining—when it doesn't make me climb the wall—he is not an entertainer, whatever his enemies say. He is a journalist, albeit a different kind.

He is a TV newsman, who is in the rare, envied position of being able to express his opinion while reporting and analyzing the news. He is a man who spent twenty-five years learning his craft before becoming a success. He had paid his dues, working at local station news, network news, and syndicated television magazines before finally becoming a success in cable news. He has the background and the credentials that make him more than just a shouting head on a cable network.

What attracted me to O'Reilly as a subject for a book is his idiosyncrasy as a TV journalist. Idiosyncrasy in TV news is an oxymoron. He is a man who is a nonconformist in a business that demands conformity as the price of success, a man who has risen to the top by not playing by the rules of broadcasting. O'Reilly's success in the modern age of journalism is a feat like that of a spawning salmon fighting its way upstream—in a can. His success is, in short, a miracle.

Not the usual pretty face, perpetually in trouble with management, O'Reilly still managed to become an overnight sensation in only twenty-five years.

The O'Reilly career is an adventure story about a climb to the top more perilous than either mountain climbing or social climbing. It's filled with news executives out to get him. Rebels in TV news, of whom O'Reilly is a paradigm, are viewed with suspicion and alarm. Usually, they get the hint early on that they are not wanted, and either leave the field or change to get with the program. O'Reilly defied the system by learning to give the public what it wants and thinks it needs. Happily for him, it coincides with his personal needs, allowing him to be consistent. He never needed news doctors to tell him what to say or do.

How he reached this amazing state of grace in a medium that grinds journalists down is my story. It's about all the things that led to the making of a Bill O'Reilly.

I am uniquely qualified to write a biography of O'Reilly. O'Reilly lives on Long Island. He grew up reading my column in *Newsday,* which I wrote for thirty-five years. His thoughts about TV journalism, what was wrong and right about TV news, were shaped by reading my five-times-a-week column, "The Marvin Kitman Show." He told me so himself. A kind of mentoring has been going on over the years, as he has assimilated my ideas with his own and put them into practice.

He agreed to tell me whatever I wanted to know for this book. He gave me twenty-nine interviews. They took place in restaurants, his favorite diner on Long Island, at Shea Stadium, in his home, but mostly in his office at the Fox News Channel.

On a clear and even smoggy day from O'Reilly's corner office on the seventeenth floor of Fox News Channel headquarters on the Avenue of the Americas in midtown Manhattan, you could see Secaucus across the river, the home of FNC's bitter rival in the cable news wars, MSNBC. Across the Avenue of the Americas is the GE Building, headquarters of NBC, where for ten years strategists have been trying to figure out what to do with its cable offspring MSNBC, mired in the outlet capital of America, built on the marsh grass and muck of the former pig farms. It was here that they invented *Countdown w/ Keith Olbermann,* O'Reilly's arch, and sometimes very funny, current rival in the nightly prime-time cable news wars.

Up the street from Fox, you can see CNN, at least the New York headquarters, where the storefront window studios of Paula Zahn and other journalism greats, like Connie Chung, labored in vain competing with O'Reilly in the Great Cable News War, the media's Hundred Years' War of the Roses.

Every third Tuesday or so, for thirty-one months, starting in the summer of 2001 and resuming in the spring of 2002, I sat down with him for about roughly a half hour carved out of his busy schedule. To have the full attention of the leading practitioner in the Attention Deficit Disorder school of journalism, on whose fast-paced show anybody was lucky to get five minutes without being interrupted or being on the verge of interruption, was unprecedented.

I would usually prepare a list of topics, questions that I needed answered for the biography I was planning to write someday. He would cast an eye on the day's list and throw it away.

"Anything you want, shoot."

Having a conversation with Bill O'Reilly is like trying to take a drink from an open fire hydrant. He would relax, kicking off his 12½D loafers, and talk at great length about his life and times, the good and bad, and the completely ridiculous in TV journalism, my special area of interest. Along the way I heard what was done to him, and what he had to do to climb to the top, doing things his way, despite everybody who told him it was the wrong way.

"We have all the time you need," he would say, looking at his watch. We both knew that between five-thirty and five-forty he would have to begin his final preparation for taping the TV show: putting in his contact lenses and brushing his teeth. And then the spigot would be turned off.

This is not an authorized biography. He did cooperate by giving me the names of friends, none of whom he asked not to talk with me. All in all, I had sixty-two interviews with O'Reilly's family, college professors and administrators, coworkers, local TV station general managers and news vice presidents, network news officials, and journalism superstars. They included friends as well as enemies, of which he has a few. He never asked to see what I had written for approval or tried to censor me in any way.

He gave me such access, because, having grown up reading my column, he said that he thought I was fair. By that, I came to realize, he meant that I hadn't attacked him as all my fellow members of the elite liberal media had been doing. In fact, I hadn't written about him at all.

My plan is to tell the story now without bias. I don't approach the subject from left or right, but through the politically neutral medium of TV news. The book will infuriate his fans as well as his enemies. I call them as I see them, based on thirty-five years of getting paid to watch the bad, the bemused, and the blond of TV news. I've lived through enough hair spray to have made a hole in the ozone layer.

As much as I admire how he has beaten the system that has ground down generations of equally competent and opinionated newsmen, he also has his faults and limitations that the faithful, starting with O'Reilly, are loath to concede. O'Reilly is not his own worst critic. I can be.

My liberal friends assure me that I am insane to have spent so many years on this book and still like O'Reilly. Listening to him makes my friends blow gaskets.

I have taken a lot of heat for not hating O'Reilly. But I don't care. I am a TV critic, and they're not.

I finished writing the book in 2003. Then I finished writing the book in 2004. I finished writing it again in 2005. It's not that I am more of a procrastinator than the average writer. The problem was O'Reilly. Every time he opened his mouth on some controversial issue, he made news. How could I send the book to press without including the latest fight that flooded the Internet, the newspapers, and, peculiarly, the rival cable network news shows? I apologize in advance for omitting other major parts of the story. I'm sure there will have been some beauts that befit a man who never shuts up.

—*Marvin Kitman*
Northern New Jersey
May 2006

The Man Who
Would Not
Shut Up

PROLOGUE

In the year 2004, a cataclysmic media event began taking place.

First, Tom Brokaw, sixty-four, cashed in his chips that October. Tom had been an anchorman for so long (since 1983) he had barnacles. The anchor of *The NBC Evening News with Tom Brokaw* was taking early retirement to return to his home on the range in Montana, where the deer, antelope, and his cows roamed.

In November, Dan Rather, seventy-two, startled the media world by announcing that he, too, was stepping down at *The CBS Evening News*, due to circumstances beyond his control. Rather's producers had failed to recognize that documents about George W. Bush's Vietnam War service in the Air National Guard, featured in his reporting on *60 Minutes I* and the nightly news, were composed on a typewriter using a typeface not available until long after the service might or might not have taken place, damaging Rather's credibility.

On April 5, 2005, Peter Jennings, sixty-seven, announced on the air that he had lung cancer. In a raspy voice that saddened the TV journalism world, Jennings told *World News Tonight* viewers he would begin chemotherapy that week. He did not return to the air. Jennings died August 8.

In November 2005, Ted Koppel left ABC News. After twenty-five years, the dean of late-night news retired as host of *Nightline*, an institution that for your above-average informed viewer had become a going-to-bed ritual like putting the cat out at night.

The loss of our four gods at the same time, in terms of TV journalism, can only be described as the same way the dinosaurs bought the farm one day 65 million years or so ago. A meteorite or something hit, and pow, the oceans swamped them, or the gases killed them, and that was it.

A revolution had already been taking place on the Fox News Channel about the way news was being presented on TV. Bill O'Reilly has been the spearhead in that radical movement, masterminded by Roger Ailes, chairman of Fox News.

Since 1996, Bill O'Reilly has been the executive producer and anchorman of *The O'Reilly Factor,* an hour-long cable network nightly news/analysis program in which he gets to report on what he considers the day's important and interesting news, while giving his opinion about the issues he believes are bugging the American people or him on any given night. Besides the news, the program is a complex mix filled with self-references, obsessions, and updates on his latest crusades, causes, fights with institutions, individuals, and other enemies. In ten years, the program has not lost its ability to delight and enrage viewers.

At fifty-seven, O'Reilly, an alpha male, testosterone-plus, hard-driving, in-your-face, seemingly terminally pissed off individual is the self-acclaimed discoverer of a previously unknown virgin territory called *The No Spin Zone.* He works for the Fox News Channel, whose parent, Rupert Murdoch of News Corporation, owns the *New York Post* and other papers on three continents, Fox Entertainment television networks and movie companies. Fox News, of course, is the cable news network that hails itself as "Fair and Balanced. We Report. You Decide." And Bill O'Reilly, his enemies have decided, is the most unfair and unbalanced of them all, a first-class pain to everybody he finds fault with, especially the purveyors of what he decided was political and social hokum.

The year the mediarite hit, the loss of TV's top four anchormen caused a seismic shift in broadcast news. The coming apocalypse in commercial network news actually began appearing in 1982 with the retirement of Walter Cronkite from the *The CBS Evening News.* Commercial network newscasts had for years been the sick old men of journalism, their foundations cracking from old age and old ideas, their audience and influence melting like the ice cap. The overall viewership ratings for three commercial nightly newscasts by 2005, according to the Project for Excellence in Journalism, had declined by 34 percent in the past decade, nearly 44 percent since 1980, and 59 percent from their peak in 1969. While the shows declined in prestige and viewership, the age demos were rising. It was a race to see whether the audience or the shows died first.

The network news model was dead. Not only weren't people watching the six-thirty news the way they used to, they were often not even home from work yet or they had heard all the news on the car radio or read it on the Internet at work. Basically, they didn't learn anything different from the old, established network news. It was always the same story. If you saw the snail-darter story on Dan, you knew you were going to see the snail darter on Tom or Peter. It was the same stand-ups, same polls, same terrible natural disaster, all of which you already knew all about.

Technologically, with satellites, video phonecams, and other high-tech toys, the network news was coming to us faster than ever. The one thing that was always missing was what did it all mean? Why was everything so crazy in this insane world?

O'Reilly is radical for TV journalism in that he he thinks he knows what it all means. You may not agree with his analysis, point of view, or value system, but you always know where he stands. And he never shuts up.

Many people love him for his outspokenness. Perhaps because the public doesn't have time to think. People are busy working two jobs, watching their 401(k)s disappear, adjusting to lower standards of living. Where are all the shootings happening and why? Not just drive-by shootings where the drug deal-ers live in the inner cities, but the ones in rich suburbia with two parents work-ing, ignoring what the culture is doing to their kids. There's no effort to explain all of this on the network news. O'Reilly has answers.

He seems to enjoy weighing in fearlessly on difficult moral issues, where the news never goes. He looks down on the world from moral heights, scaled only by O'Reilly, as he would have it. His diatribes about pet hates are stimulating, whether it was John Ashcroft, unprotected borders, celebrities as political pun-dits, the secular war against Christmas, or newspapers, especially *The New York Times* and, seemingly, any other paper with the last word *Times* on its masthead [Los Angeles, St. Petersburg].

O'Reilly and his opinionated news and analysis today dominate cable news as much as Walter Cronkite dominated broadcast news when CBS News was in its prime. Before O'Reilly, cable prime-time news often seemed like Punch and Judy shows. They usually gathered people from both sides to discuss the big story of the day, wound them up, and watched them start shouting at each other. The one in between is an "immoderator," as Ben Wattenberg of the old PBS show *Think Tank* used to label the moderators, "giving the illusion of bal-anced discourse."

What they practiced in these media mud-wrestling contests is what I call yeller journalism. They yell the news. In the terms of actual news content, the cable networks seem like a big jukebox. Somebody pushes E5 (the Peterson murder case) or D7 (the latest shark attack in Florida), and they all play E5 and D7, as veteran news-watcher Doug Johnson put it.

O'Reilly was different from the others. He didn't scream as much. Prince Charming, he's not. He is evenly balanced—by that I mean he has a chip on both shoulders.

His standard approach to guests is a don't-bullshit-me, defender of the downtrodden voiceless, huddled, masses in the TV dens. On any *subjet du jour*, O'Reilly's thing is to be the man of the people, "the folks," as he calls them, their primary if not only true representative. It's sometimes hard to see how a true populist can favor the elimination of the estate tax, as he stood on a big issue in 2002, a cruel and unusual punishment imposed solely on the wealthiest, including media mogul Rupert Murdoch or O'Reilly himself.

Members of the punditocracy travel back and forth between politics and the media, like the Grand Central Shuttle. The unique thing about O'Reilly is that he never boarded that train. He wasn't, for example, like Chris Matthews on MSNBC.

After years of working for Speaker of the House Tip O'Neill and the Carter White House, Matthews joined the motormouth brigade in 1987. "His first move," explained Howard Kurtz in *Hot Air*, "was to sign on as Washington Bureau chief of the *San Francisco Examiner*, a job that basically involved writing a twice weekly column."

"He needed to be a journalist to have the kind of respectability to be on TV," Larry Kramer, the former *Examiner* editor who hired Matthews, told Kurtz.

Tony Snow, host of *Fox News Sunday*, joined the Bush administration as press secretary in 2006, George Stephanopolous had been communications director in the Clinton administration before joining ABC News. Over the years, David Gergen was a paid propagandist for four presidents, working for both George Bush and Bill Clinton, an ideological coup. Mark Shields, a fixture on the *News Hour with Jim Lehrer*, and the host of *The Capital Gang*, was a Democratic campaign operative for Bobby Kennedy, Henry Jackson, and Morris Udall before launching a new career as a talking head. Tim Russert studied under Pat Moynihan and Mario Cuomo. Pat Buchanan worked so often at the White House he hummed "Hail to the Chief" in the shower. John McLaughlin, George Will, John Sununu, Mary Matlin, James Carville are among the dozens of prominent prognosticators who have feet in both worlds of media and partisan politics.

Prior to coming to Fox News in 1996, O'Reilly's entire career has been in journalism, moving from market to market, perfecting his craft, and irritating people. He earned his chops, as I was to find.

Television is a form of limited democracy in which an electorate consisting of the twenty-five thousand families in Nielsen metered homes vote for the rest of us. Nielsen families who take cable sit on their couches in their TV dens and vote with their remotes every night. The folks are the average hardworking Americans, the ordinary Joes and Janes, who are the heroes in O'Reilly's view of the world, especially since they are the people who watch him. He believes he speaks for the folks when he cuts through what he feels is the standard interview of newsmakers on TV. Regardless of class, what unites the O'Reilly voting bloc is seeming to be mad as hell about the way things are going but not knowing what to do about it—except listen to their Bill every weekday night at eight. The folks have made him the most popular newsman in the history of cable news.

By March 1, 2006, full-page newspaper ads by Fox News were proclaiming *The O'Reilly Factor* had been "#1 for 226 weeks . . . and counting." He had almost three times as many viewers as his eight o'clock rival on CNN, Paula Zahn, ten times as many as the MSNBC opponent, Keith Olbermann.

"You know, we're just so far ahead," said O'Reilly. "We win by the biggest margins, I think, in the history of television. Competitively, there's nobody close. These numbers are an overwhelming reality that Americans favor my kind of a presentation over the politically correct stuff they get on the other networks. Period. There's no other analysis. They can't spin it any way. In every category, every night, every way, that's it."

What really makes this snarling, barking man so successful on TV?

Michael Kinsley, then editorial page director of what O'Reilly calls "the far-left loony" *Los Angeles Times,* now a columnist at the *Washington Post* and a serial O'Reilly antagonist as the editor of *Slate* and the former near-left contributor on *Crossfire,* understands O'Reilly's appeal. "He's a thug, and appeals to the thug in other people."

Richard Leibner, the superagent whose wife, Carole, is O'Reilly's agent, knows why, by the spring of 2003, he was getting as many as 4,675,000 people a night:

"He is successful because he's been to school, the school of hard knocks for twenty-five years. He has had seven jobs before his big success. He understands broadcasting. He can deal with six subjects a night, and he goes in and out of those six subjects like a perfectly greased wheel. He writes his own stuff and is a master performer. Besides being superconfident and having his own ideas and not being afraid to express them. It's the saying what's on his mind, not what somebody else wrote and that he's reading off the TelePrompTer. His show is over in what seems like ten minutes. It's so compelling. You find when you put it on you stay with it. You're sucked right in."

Stephen Chao, founder of Fox News at the entertainment network, when the Fox News Channel on cable was a gleam in Rupert Murdoch's dreams, says O'Reilly wouldn't have been possible if not for the news establishment. "Look at the stand-up reporters on networks or on prime-time network news magazines. They're so molded. It's always the same thing. It's like how do they all dress? The same. How could they all have the same hair guy and makeup guy? It's just remarkable. If you break down news into every category . . . the hiring of the people . . . the way the shows are formatted . . . weather at this minute, sports at another . . . and the type of stories . . . it's like, wow! There is a conspiracy, for sure. The same thing goes for the casting of personalities. And there's the same opportunity, which is, you put in somebody, you know, a little different and a little original. And a little good. You have a good shot."

O'Reilly has a more simple answer. "There are a heck of a lot of people out there who want to hear the truth, as I tell it."

Roger Ailes had another theory about why O'Reilly has been so successful. "He's smart," Ailes said, "smarter than people think. Most television people are idiots. O'Reilly is not an idiot.

"The beauty of Bill O'Reilly is this: It isn't like some people say, 'Well, I don't care what people think about me.' Bill deeply doesn't care what anybody thinks about him," Ailes said, laughing. "You know when that feeling is really that deep it allows you to do and say things that other people would probably check themselves for saying. He's absolutely fearless. I've never seen him be afraid of a subject or a topic or a booking or anything."

One day in its second year, when *The O'Reilly Factor* began getting traction, O'Reilly asked his boss, "What do you think the success of my show is?"

"I said people in cable like authenticity," Ailes recalled. "I have a particular eye for finding authentic things. Shep Smith is a very good field reporter and he's authentic. He's an authentic television guy.

"I said, 'Bill, you're authentic. You are an authentic prick. It's just not on the air. Like you're a prick to your staff, you're a prick to management. You're a prick to your family. You're authentic. You're actually a prick. And that has allowed you to become very successful. You know, I always looked at people, and said, 'If I wake them up at three in the morning, will they be consistent?' Yes, you'll be a prick, it wouldn't matter what the time was. I can tap you on the shoulder in church on Sunday, you'd be a prick. That's the secret to your success. I have a certain knack for spotting that sort of thing. And that's why people work on television."

How did Bill O'Reilly get to be so authentic? That's what this book is about.

Part I

The Making of an O'Reilly

Chapter One

In the Beginning

———•—•———

Opa-Locka is a small town in Florida, which sounds as if it is located in the deepest, swampiest Everglades but is actually a suburb in the northwest corner of Miami with a Miami zip code (33054). The name Opa-Locka is from the Seminole Indian word "Opa-tisha-woka-locka," meaning "a dry place in the swamp covered with many trees." Obviously this would not readily fit on a letterhead and be rather difficult to pronounce, the official Opa-Locka city guide Web site explains. "Hence it was shortened to Opa-Locka."

Opa-Locka was invented by aviation pioneer Glenn H. Curtiss, builder of the famed World War I Curtiss Jennies. Some people still believe Curtiss flew the first airplane successfully, not the Wright Brothers. He designed and built the first flying boat in 1911 and the first car trailer/motor home, "The Aerocar," in his factory in Opa-Locka. He built a flying school and airports including the Opa-Locka Airport, used by the Graf Zeppelin, the second-largest airship, as a regular stop on its Germany–Brazil–United States–Germany run. Amelia Earhart took off from Opa-Locka on her last flight. A millionaire from his aero inventions, Curtiss went on to become a real estate developer founding the cities of Hialeah and Miami Springs, but his crowning glory was inventing Opa-Locka.

Founded in 1926, during the Florida land boom, Opa-Locka was Curtiss's dream city, his "magical fantasy," based on the stories from *The 1001 Tales of the Arabian Nights*. Architect Bernhardt E. Muller designed for Curtiss the largest single collection of Moorish revival architecture in the United States. Opa-Locka's skyline is an Islamic motif of old domes, minarets, horseshoe arches, crenellated parapets, building textures that resembled adobe, glazed tiles, stucco crescent moons and stars applied to the face of buildings, distressed brickwork, and faded earth tone colors. The town has street names like Ali Baba Avenue, Caliph Street, Sharazad Boulevard, Sultan Avenue, and the original Sesame Street. It is no wonder that Opa-Locka is called "the Baghdad of Miami-Dade County."

In the summer of 1971, a lanky and pale-faced, twenty-one-year-old man with long hair, sideburns, and a New York accent walked into this 4.2-square-mile Scherezadian Disneyland. It was Bill O'Reilly in Opa-Locka to start what could be the fulfillment of his father's dream by becoming a teacher at Monsignor Edward Pace High School.

William James O'Reilly Jr. was born on September 10, 1949, at Columbia Presbyterian Hospital in the Washington Heights section of Manhattan, the elder of two children of Irish Catholic parents, William and Winifred Angela O'Reilly. William O'Reilly Sr. was a Brooklyn native, tall (six-three), handsome, blond-haired, loquacious, with a keen Irish wit and an anger-management problem. Known as Ann, Mrs. O'Reilly was from Teaneck, New Jersey, a suburb of New York. She graduated as a physical therapist from Sargent College of Health and Rehabilitation Sciences in Boston. After marriage and the birth of her son, she became a homemaker.

O'Reilly's father had gone to Lafayette High School in the Bensonhurst section of Brooklyn, then to St. Francis, a workingman's college in downtown Brooklyn. His father and grandfather were cops, and that was his vocational plan. The war changed his career path. Enrolled in the Navy's V-12 program during World War II, Mr. O'Reilly was sent to Holy Cross College. Lieutenant (JG) O'Reilly was on the way to invade Japan when they dropped the atom bomb.

During the occupation in Japan, Lieutenant O'Reilly had major responsibilities serving as an adjutant to the admiral in charge of dismantling the Japanese Manchurian army when it came back from China a month after the surrender. When he returned home in 1946 he took a job at an oil company. William O'Reilly Sr. was a low-level accountant in the currency department at Caltex, commuting to a Madison Avenue office in Manhattan, and never moved up or left for another challenge, even though he hated every minute of it. Educated and capable of more, he was frozen in a dead-end job by his fear that he would make a mistake, his son told me. "So he stayed where he was and took the crap that they regularly dished out there. He did not express himself through his work; he was simply unhappy. He was stuck." His fear and frustration also shaped the way he ran his family.

A subjugated, unfulfilled man, who thought he could have done big things, he had a deep sense of failure, always feeling he had been shortchanged by life, and he was angry. "He'd get into a fight at the drop of a hat," an elderly neighbor recalled about Mr. O'Reilly Sr.'s mercurial nature. The favorite target of his rage was his son.

"Billy," as he was called to differentiate Bill Junior from Bill Senior, spent his first two years in a crowded apartment across the river in Fort Lee, New Jersey. In 1951, the O'Reillys moved to a small house on Long Island built by William Levitt, one of the 17,447 homes on a thousand lanes originally in the Levittown development on 7.3 square miles of former potato fields, a mass-produced subdivision that was to become a synonym for the New Suburbia that spread like crabgrass in the post–World War II period of American history.

All a prospective buyer needed to buy one of the original Levitt "ranch" · houses, sales priced at $7,990, was a $90 deposit and payments of $58 a month. Mr. O'Reilly bought the house on Page Lane by himself. His wife didn't even see the house. She was told that was where they were going to live. And that was it. All the decisions in the O'Reilly home were made by Mr. O'Reilly Sr.

Mr. O'Reilly ran a tight ship, exercising control over the spartan life in the house on Page Lane. He had his four tailored-by–Robert Hall suits hanging in the small closet of the two-bedroom, one-bathroom, thirty-two-foot-by-twenty-five-foot Levitt house. He believed in the annual two-week vacation, the nightly having a cold one in the living room while reading the paper, and direct communication. "You're having meat loaf and shut up about it, all right?"

"My father was an autocrat," O'Reilly wrote in his first best-selling book, *The O'Reilly Factor: The Good, the Bad and the Completely Ridiculous.* Mr. O'Reilly had a mean temper; his mother, O'Reilly thought, was a bit ditzy, but "kind of nice." He saw to the used cars, and she prepared the Yankee-Stadium-style food. Both said, "You will do what I say," but his mother was slower on the trigger finger. "Sometimes she even felt sorry for our mistakes and offenses and tried to hide them from my father. This wasn't license; it was always a reprieve. It was something like the poet Robert Frost once said: "The father is always a Republican toward his son, and his mother is always a Democrat." Mr. O'Reilly Sr. was a rock-ribbed, knuckle-scraping Republican with William Jr.

The O'Reilly house on Page Lane was not a home where children were encouraged to express their opinions. More Mussolini than Montessori, Mr. O'Reilly Sr. believed in the shut-up-you-idiot school of child-rearing: this is the way it is, boyo, don't ask questions. The problem was that young Bill Junior would never shut up.

Billy and his friends were, as O'Reilly calls them, fiends. That was considered the normal childhood state growing up on the streets of Levittown. There were fifteen to twenty kids on the block, recalled his sister Jan, younger by two years. They ran around doing things, creating havoc, from the adults' viewpoint. Billy was the fiend-in-chief, being the tallest and most outspoken.

"We weren't hoodlums, but little cutups," explained gang member Justin McDevitt, "smashing pumpkins at Halloween. We always kind of went out of our neighborhood to do the pumpkin thing. That way we wouldn't be blamed for what went on in our neighborhood."

But Billy got blamed anyway.

Mr. O'Reilly Sr. went from zero to sixty in five seconds. "If Bill did something, broke a pencil or something, it would just set him off," Jan remembered. "He was on him twenty-four/seven. He got very red in the face. He had this look, and you knew it was coming."

"One more time, and you'll be sorry," Bill O'Reilly told me, was one of his father's favorite sayings. "One more time" was not an empty threat. "He didn't like what you said. Or, say, you were a wiseguy to him, or wising off. You know he would just whack you. He'd just give me a shot in the arm or something. It was like boom, boom, boom, and that was that."

"I expected only one thing from my dad," O'Reilly said. "Leave me alive to celebrate my next birthday."

O'Reilly admits he was a pain. "If I didn't want to eat my potatoes," he explained, "I wouldn't eat them, you know, that kind of thing. I wasn't Wally Cleaver, okay. I mean, I was annoying, and he didn't want to be annoyed. I didn't go out of my way not to annoy him."

O'Reilly still apologizes for his father's bad temper. "He did the same thing to me that his father did to him. My father wised off to my grandfather, a New

York City cop who walked a beat in Brooklyn and carried a billy club, he'd get a blast, and that was it. There was, like, no diplomacy. It was like, do this, and shut up."

The tiny Levittown house was also occupied by Barney, a big brown bad German shepherd. Barney played an important role in O'Reilly's adolescent years at home. On Fridays, the O'Reillys always had fish for dinner. Because in the fifties and the early sixties you couldn't eat meat on Friday, O'Reilly explained. He could never figure that one out, why Catholics couldn't eat meat. "So we had these horrendous fish sticks. I said, 'Look, if you can show me in the ocean where there is a fish shaped like that, I'll eat it.'"

Mr. O'Reilly Sr. didn't see the humor in it. "Eat the fish sticks."

"Fine, fine, I'll eat the fish sticks."

Barney loved the fish sticks.

Barney would eat anything, including human beings. "Which is why my father liked Barney, because, believe me, nobody would ever come into that house without permission because of Barney. Barney wouldn't bite you unless you made some threatening move, but he was loud, and it looked like he would bite you."

A popular movie in Billy's childhood developmental period was *The Wild Ones* with Marlon Brando. Billy didn't know anything about *The Wild Ones*, and what they were so wild about, but he had gotten hold of a motorcycle cap he liked. "And I walked into the house with it, and my father just took it and ripped it right in half. [Making a ripping noise.] He goes, 'You're not wearing that.' And I had no idea. I thought it was just like a little sailor cap or something really sharp, you know, a military-type thing, and he just went [making the ripping noise again]—gone!"

Life with Dad O'Reilly wasn't like *Ozzie and Harriet*, a favorite TV show of Billy's.

Since the early eighteenth century, the O'Reillys had lived in County Cavan, equidistant between Belfast and Dublin. O'Reilly was a Kennedy on his mother's side. O'Reilly's father's mother's name was McLaughlin. His mother's maiden name is Drake. The Drakes—his grandfather on his mother's side—are from Northern Ireland.

"So I'm one hundred percent Irish, which is very unusual, you know, for an

American this day and age," O'Reilly told me. "My bloodline is all Celtic, which is frightening. I mean, you know, you have all of those Irish tendencies, the blarney, which has really served me well, though, I must say."

O'Reilly's people began coming to America during the Famine, between 1848 and 1858. At one time, the O'Reillys owned all the land in Cavan. They were very wealthy, fief landholders, until Oliver Cromwell took it all for the crown in the mid–seventeenth century. His grandparents were the newly emerging Catholic lower-middle class, which had been pushed off the tenant farms of their ancestors, many of whom crowded into cities like Dublin before emigrating to the United States. It was a bad time for tenant farmers, working on the vast lands of their new lords of the manor. "There wasn't a history of accomplishment or power in the family after Cromwell," O'Reilly told a reporter for *Irish America* magazine. "It was a working class [*sic*] family and it stayed that way for a hundred years."

O'Reilly's early people were cops and firemen and laborers and a couple of teachers. One of his grandfathers pounded the pavements as the patrolman in Brooklyn; the other was a train conductor in New Jersey. His mother's mother was a telephone operator, and his uncle was a fireman. His sister became a nurse. He was expected to become a teacher or, if he got lucky, a lawyer. What his mother feared was that her son would become "a nonconformist in the nineteen seventies."

"She would not rest until I wore a leisure suit," O'Reilly remembered.

"Play it safe. Play it safe, don't make any waves, take what comes, a little fatalistic, little afraid," O'Reilly told Niall O'Dowd of *Irish America* magazine of his parents' attitudes about life. The upbringing that O'Reilly had in Levittown, Long Island, was like the upbringing an Irish kid would have had in South Boston or Woodside, Queens, or Dublin or Galway.

It was very basic, O'Reilly told me. "It was tuna. It was hot dogs and beans. It was steak on Saturday night. It was spaghetti. It was secondhand sports equipment, movies now and then." When his family went out to eat, O'Reilly recalled, it was a rare treat. "We didn't waste money on appetizers, if only because we didn't go to the kind of restaurants that offered appetizers. Typically the pasta dish was spaghetti, and that was it. No linguine, fettuccine, *etceterine* to confuse the issue."

O'Reilly once looked over the menu at the only place his father would go to— Savini's in East Meadow—and told the waiter he would have the veal. His father said, "You'll eat the spaghetti and shut up." The veal was a dollar fifty more.

Mr. O'Reilly Sr.'s respect for the dollar was extreme. O'Reilly never received an allowance growing up. It was not considered one of the basic necessities of life. "I never asked him for a nickel," he says of his father. "I always worked, always doing something."

He started at age nine, washing cars, mowing lawns. First, with a hand-propelled reel mower. Mr. O'Reilly Sr. did not object to buying a luxury power mower because he had to cut his own lawn when O'Reilly wasn't around. "I remember that sucker. You could never start it, which was the problem with the rope. I use to kick the damn thing. It used to drive me crazy, try and turn it over."

At eleven, he was making money shoveling snow. At twelve or thirteen, he started to babysit. He also earned money by selling firecrackers to other kids on the block. His first real job at age sixteen was at Carvel on Old Country Road. He worked there while in high school, making sundaes, earning a dollar an hour and all the ice cream he could swallow. He put a lot of hours into his job at Carvel, sister Jan remembers. "We had a freezer full of Flying Saucers for years. They were everywhere when you opened it. He took the job very seriously. There was no fooling around. He was there on time. He worked hard, and he wore the hat proudly."

O'Reilly's early earnings didn't go to help support the family but for things like movie tickets and buying baseballs and bats. "We're always breaking baseball bats. I mean, it would drive me crazy because we had the wooden bats, they weren't aluminum."

At seventeen, during the summer, he went into his first business, painting houses with some of "my thug friends." Some weeks they cleared as much as $200 each. His partner, Jeff Cohen, remembered painting the outside of one Levitt house when a can of paint fell on an azalea bush while the owners were away. O'Reilly solved the problem by cutting down the bush, which went unnoticed by the customers.

Mr. O, as Billy's friends all called Mr. O'Reilly, was ecstatic about his son's early entrepreneurial skills. Billy was never going to meet him at the front door with his hand out asking for cash. "I'm not sure he could believe his good fortune," said O'Reilly.

He didn't care about money growing up, O'Reilly said. "I wasn't envious because nobody else had anything, either. You see, if there had been a rich kid in the neighborhood, he'd be walking around with a lot of stuff, maybe I would have had some envy. But everybody else had what I had. You know, a broken-down bike, and, you know, secondhand this, taped-up that. I never had any interest in material things, ever. I didn't say why didn't I have this, why don't I have that? I didn't do that. I think it was because nobody else had anything, either."

O'Reilly was about five when he realized he was a leader. "I was always the guy that wanted the action, organized the guys, thinking about what we are going to do next. 'Okay, what are we going to do?' the guys would ask. And I said, 'Well, we're going to do this,' and they'd go, 'Okay.' And then we'd all go do it. That was always my role in the neighborhood."

His guys were basically up for anything. "I'd just have to figure out what we wanted to do on any given day," said O'Reilly. "And I was good at it. I just, you know, always wanted to be doing stuff when I was a little kid. We played 'Davy Crockett' or we'd play 'Army' or we'd play 'hide-and-seek' or 'ring-a-levio' or something like that. They looked to me to provide the agenda for the day."

If it snowed, it would be army forts made out of snow. Very sophisticated forts with tunnels, built on sound military principles. Summer was baseball, fall was football, and winter was hockey. Since the pond didn't freeze until December, Billy's agenda also included roller hockey. And in the springtime, they would play stickball.

Justin McDevitt was a charter member of the original O'Reilly gang. "My first sort of dealings with Bill, when we were about thirteen, was going to Saturday matinees at the Westbury Theatre on Post Avenue. He was a lot taller than us, and we were still able to get in for, you know, children's age prices, for like twenty-five cents."

It was Billy's idea to have Justin McDevitt's brother, Davy, age ten, buy him a kid's ticket, and there he'd be, six feet tall, going up to a doorman. He would give Billy an extended look: "How did the cashier sell you a . . . ?"

Eventually, O'Reilly came up with a more practical solution. Little Davy was paid to buy a ticket to go in and open up the exit door. The sunlight would fill the theater. "As soon as the door opened we're charging in," said Jeff Cohen, another charter member of the O'Reilly gang. "Shutting the door so it's dark, we're running to all four corners. And, of course, the matrons in the starched white dresses were trying to find out what's happening, you know, and we're causing havoc with water pistols, and throwing jawbreakers down the aisles and things like that. It's typical crazy kid stuff. But that was before the lady caught O'Reilly, and we were all banned from the movie theater forever."

One weekday night, Mr. O'Reilly Sr. wanted to take Bill Junior to the Westbury movie theater to see *The Longest Day*. "Bill is trying to use some excuse about he can't go, homework, and this and that," Jeff Cohen remembered. "So, anyway, they go to the theater, and O'Reilly's kind of keeping his head down while Mr. O is buying the ticket. There's a lady stopping Bill and Mr. O. 'It's okay,' Mr. O said. 'He's with me.'

"The matron said, 'You mean to tell me you're the father of this boy?'" She immediately starts to describe how each Saturday he and his friends cause havoc. He's banned. He can't come in here. Mr. O is going, 'I'm so embarrassed,'" said Cohen. "He's furious with the whole thing."

Mr. O'Reilly assured the management he would deal with it in his own way. He hit Billy on the spot.

As Billy and his friends matured, they went beyond the streets and the local movie theater in search of cultural enrichment. As teenagers, O'Reilly & Co. used to go to the Westbury Music Fair. In those days, they'd have headliners like The Supremes as the opening act, then Stevie Wonder as the main act. O'Reilly figured out a way to catch the shows on a limited entertainment budget.

"They never checked tickets," Justin McDevitt recalled, "when you were going back in after intermission. So you might miss The Supremes, but if the place wasn't sold out, you could kind of get in and watch Stevie Wonder."

One night O'Reilly tried to convince an older guy named Stu Solomon to get in on it, and Stu objected, "Billy, that's kind of juvenile stuff." Stu thought it over and decided to give it a try. Stu was still skeptical even after O'Reilly and his entourage got to the Music Fair. "I don't know, Billy," he said, "I don't like the setup." And Billy, to encourage him, just kind of patted him on the back, and said, "Come on, Stu, once we get in there, you'll thank me."

"So we got inside, and it worked like clockwork," McDevitt recalled. "We found nice seats to sit down in front, and Stu is just raving. He's just so happy they did it. He says, 'I don't know why I gave you such a hard time about this, Billy, I'm sure glad we got in.' O'Reilly is shaking his head in disbelief. And Stu goes, 'What's the matter, Billy?' And O'Reilly says, 'To tell you the truth, Stu, I don't know how you got in.' And Stu says, 'What do you mean?' And O'Reilly pulls a sign off Stu's back that says, 'Catch me, I'm sneaking in.'

"And the poor guy is beside himself. 'How could you do this to me, O'Reilly?'"

You could divide the neighborhood into two groups: those who liked him and those who didn't, a pattern that was to be repeated in his professional life. "This is going to be a shock to you," said another gang member, John Blasi, "but some people, and I know it's hard to imagine, had a problem with his ego even as a kid."

There was a gap between how O'Reilly saw himself and how others saw him. Typically it would end up in a discussion with people saying, "Oh, really, O'Reilly?" "He'd wind up in a fight, just because some people got tired of the ego, being bossed around," Blasi said.

Mostly it was shouting matches. They might take a couple of swings, but if there was a fight, it deteriorated into a wrestling match pretty quickly. O'Reilly had the weight on most people, and he had the height, but he got his comeuppance more than once, McDevitt said. "He was a big guy, but he was not physically aggressive. His language got people more upset with him than any bully-type tactics, and he paid for it. More than once I remember him being on the short end of some of the fights he got himself involved in."

O'Reilly felt obligated to demonstrate his power on the block. He would claim nobody could tackle him. "One day, he boasted to this guy, Joe Dalton, this was the case," Justin McDevitt recalled. "And we huddled on my front lawn on Patience Lane, where O'Reilly used to like to hang out. And I said, 'Joe, you hit him high and I'll hit him low.' We crashed into him, and he went down like a sack of potatoes. But he jumped back up and says, 'Well, it took you long enough.' You know, he always had that bouncing-back quality with an explanation: 'Hey, you guys tackled me, but it took you all of two and a half seconds to do it.'"

O'Reilly remembers his days as one of the most gifted debaters on the streets of Levittown. Verbal dexterity was required for the leadership role. "You had to be fast on your feet. This sounds stupid, but it's absolutely true. One of the reasons that I'm so glib and so quick on the air is because when I was a kid growing up we had something called 'ranking out.'"

You got ranked out when somebody would insult you faster and better than you could insult him. You didn't want to be ranked out. "So you learned to get quick like Don Rickles with the one-line zingers," O'Reilly said. "And you learned to listen and then capitalize on whatever your opponent was doing wrong or stuttering or anything like that. It was every day, you know, insults flying back and forth. Out on the street, you'd be going, 'Ah, your shoes are this or that . . .' 'Your hair's cut . . .' And it was pum pa pum pa pum, and everybody would go, 'Oh, he ranked you out.' That was huge. And a lot of them were ethnically based insults, which at that point was like standard procedure. Nobody got offended we'd call you a 'Mick' or a 'Wop' or something like that. You had to be glib in my neighborhood. You couldn't be shy. You couldn't say, 'Wait a minute, I got to get my writers in here.'

"It's the same way now in the ghetto. These rappers are unbelievable. If you listen to these guys, how they speak and how quickly they speak, its pum pa pum pa. I mean it's street lingo. But very few people can do it. You have to train yourself to do that. And I swear to God that made me, that rank-out stuff."

If you were ranked out, you were humiliated. And if you started fisticuffs, then you lost worse. Then people would go, "Oh, look at him, he's a jerk." O'Reilly said. "I mean, even if you were a tough guy with your fists, it was better to be a quick guy with your mouth."

Billy was about thirteen or fourteen, and he was arguing one day with an adult, a schoolteacher, Mr. Oberwagger. According to McDevitt, "Bill said, 'You know, Mr. Oberwagger, I probably have a higher IQ than you do.' And to Bill's astonishment, Mr. Oberwagger said, 'I grant you that, you probably do.' And Bill was, like, he had nothing more to say. He took away his power of speech because the guy was agreeing with him."

O'Reilly thought he was a good chess player. Davy McDevitt had gotten very good, Davy's bigger brother Justin told me. So they went inside the McDevitt house to play chess, and Davy came out two minutes later. He did the Muhammad Ali thing: "It's all over guys, it's all over." Nobody wanted to go inside and watch two guys play chess, McDevitt said. "So after Davy was doing his Muhammad Ali thing, we all go inside, and there's Bill still sitting in my living room pondering how Davy beat him in eight or nine quick moves."

Billy decided that the match should be seen by everybody, and the only way that could happen was if they played in the middle of the street. They were sitting there with a soapbox and the chessboard on Patience Lane, and the same thing happened. "I could still see him just amazed that my little brother actually beat him so easily," McDevitt recalled.

. . .

Billy's father had a great fear that his son would grow up like Billy Joel, a contemporary of Billy who lived a few streets over on Meeting Lane. Joel and his gang were always hanging out at Levittown's Village Green stores, wearing black pointy shoes and smoking cigarettes. O'Reilly Senior didn't want his son to become a hood.

It would have been impossible for O'Reilly to be a hood. "I couldn't slick back my hair the way Billy Joel and his friends did, the big pompadour coming down, wear the black pointy shoes, which if you kicked somebody with they really hurt. Couldn't have done that. He wouldn't have permitted it." Young Billy never thought he was in danger of winding up with the Billy Joel guys, anyway, because he played sports. But his father didn't want to take any chances.

Billy was the tall one in the class of sixty, starting school at St. Brigid/Our Lady of Hope Regional School at 101 Maple Avenue in Westbury on September 12, 1955. Sixty first graders, all wore green uniforms: white shirts, green trousers, clip-on bow ties for the boys. They were all scared speechless by the woman who stood in front of them. Dressed almost entirely in black was a small woman, who did not look at all happy: Billy's first teacher, Sister Claudia.

They all knew the drill from elder siblings and in the street: it was the Lions versus the Christians in the Coliseum in Rome. The kids were about to be thrown to the nuns as junk food.

O'Reilly was not the worst student in St. Brigid's 150-year history. "I think I was the second worst ever to go that school," he said modestly. "I think they still got my picture up: DON'T LET THIS KID NEAR THE BUILDING."

His problems at St. Brigid's began the first morning with his name card. It said "William O'Reilly."

"I figured someone screwed up," he explained in a 1988 magazine piece celebrating the twenty-fifth anniversary of his graduation, "because my name was Billy. I had never heard of this guy 'William.'" So he proceeded to cross out "William" and pencil in "Billy." It was the first of many mistakes. "Sister Claudia was on me with the quickness of a puma. She grabbed one of my earlobes and pulled like a bell ringer on speed. I can't remember her exact words, but I did get the gist of the one-way conversation: My name was William."

Sister Claudia's teaching technique was definitely hands-on. "That is, hands on your head, neck, and upper body," O'Reilly said. "She was terrifying to me, and I was a rowdy little kid. Some of my more timid classmates were rendered almost catatonic."

Each of his teachers left her mark on Billy. "I can give you the nuns I had," he said, rattling off their names for me forty years later like catechism. "I had Sister Lurana in third grade . . . I had Sister Caroline in fifth grade . . . Sister Thomas in seventh grade and Sister Martin in eighth grade."

Mrs. Boyle in the sixth grade actually liked him, remembered his sister Jan. "She thought he was a very misunderstood child. Sister Martin in the eighth grade didn't like him." The worst of them was Sister Thomas in the seventh grade, according to O'Reilly. "She was just a harridan, you know, brutal."

Some of the nuns "wouldn't just verbally reprimand you," said Jan O'Reilly, two grades behind her brother. "They'd give us a bop in the head."

"It wasn't just with a ruler. Anything they can get their hands on, anything that wasn't, you know, tied down," O'Reilly said.

In the second grade at St. Brigid's, Billy had been initiated into the sacrament of Penance. It took about two weeks for Billy and his friends to figure out the deal. If you had to confess your sins, Father Ellard was the man to see. A kindly old gentleman, Father Ellard did not care what a second grader did. Whatever your sin, he gave the same penance: say one Hail Mary. "This was a great deal," O'Reilly recalled, and the line to get to Father Ellard was nine blocks long.

Father Tierney, on the other hand, believed that throwing an eraser was a felony. He was not exactly sought out, O'Reilly said. "The nuns, however, forced some of us over to Father Tierney, who proceeded to give out such sentences as 'pilgrimage to Lourdes' as penance."

Billy would always try to go to confession immediately after his friend Clement Simonetti. No matter what he did wrong, he knew it would not even come close to what Clement was telling them. "You did what?" Father Tierney's voice was heard echoing through the church one day. A few moments later, Clement emerged smiling from the confessional. It was a sin to tell anyone but a priest your sins, but Clement confided in Billy that Father Tierney was particularly upset when Clement told him he had hung his little brother upside down from an oak tree.

Sin was a major subject in the curriculum at St. Brigid's in the fifties, where many of O'Reilly's basic ideas about life were hammered into him. The other major topic of discussion as the years went by was sex. "Young love by the eighth grade made the nuns panic," O'Reilly recalled. "The sight of blossoming young girls and semibarbaric boys slow dancing together simply drove the good sisters crazy. Cheek-to-cheek dancing was forbidden. "We had to 'leave room for the Holy Ghost.' Why the Holy Spirit would want to position himself between the two sweaty adolescents was a mystery to me."

"Sex for me," O'Reilly recalled, "was 'the talk' my father gave me when I turned thirteen. It was awkward for both of us, as the Irish aren't exactly known for their Dr. Ruth–like candor in these matters. 'The talk' was also somewhat unnecessary. I already knew the basics from seminars with my friends, using *Playboy* magazine as text. And my father's words were highly theoretical, because the reality was I had about as much chance of landing the great white whale as I did of having sex. Teenage girls want to date smooth guys. I was a barbarian. But I gave my father points for trying."

Billy's basic recurring sin at St. Brigid's was talking in class. "I just wouldn't shut up. I was bored. I didn't want to read about Dick and Jane. Who were these people anyway? I wanted character development."

In parochial school in the late 1950s to early 1960s, recalled classmate John Blasi, when you wanted to answer, you raised your hand, and the teacher would ask you to answer it, or she would pick you out. You'd stand up, your hands at your sides. Then you'd sit down. "People might get excited to answer," said Blasi, "and they'd be raising their hand, or waving their hand, saying 'Sister, Sister,' you know, 'pick me, pick me,' but that's about it. So it couldn't be like you just shout out your answer."

Young Billy felt constrained by this pedagogical method.

What Billy was famous for was having discussions with the nuns. Not necessarily on theological issues. Some might call them arguments. "He might not fess up to something," Blasi said, "and then it might be back and forth about who did it and didn't do it, those kinds of things. But you wouldn't stand there and have an argument with the nuns."

"There weren't a lot of discussions," Blasi added. "They came down the aisle, and bam, bam, bam, out in the hallway, down to the principal's office. You could be sent outside in the hallway pretty quick. You'd be slapped around, you open your mouth. There wasn't a whole lot of tolerance for what Bill thought it should be."

By the third grade, the faculty was beginning to understand Billy. "William, you are a bold, fresh piece of humanity," Sister Lurana bellowed, as Billy recalled. "And she was right. I was a little hooligan. While others submitted to the iron wills of the nuns, I rebelled. I was on the fast track to hell, or at the least, facing a long stretch in purgatory."

One sister told him he wasn't going to go anywhere. He was going to wind up in the state penitentiary.

What O'Reilly couldn't figure out was why they never got it. "No matter how many times you hit me, it ain't going break my spirit. Because it's just going to make me more resistant to whatever you're trying to sell there, lady. And they never broke me. There were three or four of us, you know, caused trouble, and no matter what they did we would continue to cause trouble. It was like a badge of honor."

He graduated: June 1963. JFK was in the White House, Martin Luther King was in the South, the Beach Boys were Surfin' USA, and those frightened first graders were cocky eighth graders about to bid farewell to their alma mater. St. Brigid's faculty was glad to see him graduate. So was Mr. O'Reilly Sr.

A lively debate broke out in the summer of 1963 about where Billy would continue his education. William O'Reilly Sr. voted for Chaminade High School, a fancy college-preparatory school in Mineola with a reputation for high educational values and strict discipline. Billy voted to attend W. Tresper Clarke in the East Meadow school district, one of the four public high schools where Levittown kids were parceled out.

Billy wanted to go to Tresper Clarke because it was the school to which all of his closest friends were going. Clement Simonetti was going to Westbury High, but O'Reilly was not eligible to go there because his house was not in the Westbury school district. Tresper Clarke's bussed kids returned home at two-forty-five. The bus from Chaminade in Mineola didn't get back to O'Reilly's street until three-thirty in the afternoon. Forty-five minutes of valuable game time would be lost, five days a week. If he went to Chaminade, who else could decide which sport would be played on any given afternoon?

"We were always waiting on the street corner for Billy," recalled Jeff Cohen, a friend who went to Tresper Clarke. "He'd come running over, and the first thing he would do is throw the football at the light on the street, knocking it out, and just go, 'I'm great.'" The town's lighting repair bills dropped when O'Reilly went off to college.

The argument in favor of his going to Chaminade was that his father wanted him to go there. The debate was short-lived.

The nuns who told Billy he was going to hell for his sins at St. Brigid's were right on target. Chaminade was, at least, his teenage purgatory. Father Tierney's words about his penance must have been: "Forget Lourdes, go to Chaminade."

O'Reilly—nobody called him "Billy" after St. Brigid's—gained entrance to this new upmarket prison without taking the rigorous entrance examination. His father had a friend who was a Chaminade guidance counselor. He pulled a couple of strings, because O'Reilly didn't have the grades or the jack, as Mr. O'Reilly Sr. called money, to get into the pricey private school.

O'Reilly had been a handful at St. Brigid's, but was no problem at Chaminade. Those Marianist Brothers were tough guys, O'Reilly said. "They punch you in the arms, they'd give you a shot. You mouthed off to these guys, you got blasted. You don't want to be fooling around over there. That's what the people paid for. I didn't cause a lot of trouble there. Unlike St. Brigid's, where I caused *beaucoup* trouble all the time. Because I was bored. My father was so smart to impose that kind of academic discipline on me because I didn't have it coming out of grammar school."

He had hours and hours of homework, sister Jan said. "By high school, his room was above mine. When we were very little we shared this teeny-tiny room. When we got older, they finished the attic, and he went up there. But I remember as a kid, I can hear him banging on the wall with his foot, and it got louder and louder as the hours went on. I mean, I really thought he suffered up there. I think he was just so frustrated and so mad. He would be up there literally until ten or eleven at night banging on the wall."

At Chaminade, Billy ran into traditional authority figures, the faculty, but also something new to rebel against, the class system. His introduction to it came as quite a shock.

On his block, in the cramped classrooms of St. Brigid's, everybody lived in the same modest circumstances, had the same limited amenities and luxuries, same cars, same uniforms in school. Everybody was equal.

At Chaminade O'Reilly discovered the other world.

O'Reilly says he had no clue to what was going on his first two or three months at Chaminade. "It was supercompetitive, the kids were all very well dressed, very expensive clothing. I had two sports jackets—neither of them exactly Armani. They were from Modell's. And they were cheap pieces of junk, the ugliest jackets, but I didn't care."

At Chaminade, a jacket and a tie were required. O'Reilly only had a clip-on tie then. He didn't have a single silk tie. "And these guys at Chaminade were mocking my clothes. It took me, like, three weeks to figure out what they were mocking. And then I said, 'Wait a minute, these guys are mocking the way I dress,' and that led to some physical altercations at the school. Because they all had five or six cashmere coats. They were rich kids. That was the first time I ever saw the difference between what we had then and what Garden City and more wealthy Long Islanders had. Believe me when I tell you that I couldn't care less at that point in my life about any of that stuff. Who cares about the dopey jacket and the clip-on tie? I mean, because I was growing fast, my pants were always too short, you know, and that kind of thing. I wasn't stylish, and I wasn't interested in that. But come high school, it started to sink in that there was a fairly big difference between me and them."

One day in his freshman year, O'Reilly was at his locker, and two boys from his class came up to him. He was facing his locker. "One guy pushes me," O'Reilly remembers. "So I turn around, and there's these two guys standing there, okay? They're going, you know, 'We don't like the way you dress.' So my reply was 'stuff it,' something like that.

"So the guy goes like this . . . I can remember, I looked away and I went . . . bang! I hit him right in the face. The guy dropped like a top. I mean, right to the floor, okay. And then I turned to the other guy, and he ran."

Walking down the hallway toward O'Reilly was a brother. He saw the whole thing. "Now this other guy is on the floor, his nose is bleeding, whatever, and the other guy just bolted. The brother kicks me, grabs the lapels of my cheap jacket—I thought it was going to rip, all right—throws me up against my own locker, and said, 'We don't do that at Chaminade. We don't fight at Chaminade.'

"I said, 'These guys, they pushed me, Brother. They started with me.' He said, 'Don't you back sass me.'

"Oh, I want to tell you I was that close to decking the guy, that's how angry I was, you know. I was debating in my mind. I didn't really care whether I got expelled or not. I didn't like Chaminade. Maybe I should drop this guy. That would get me expelled. I go back to my friends in public school. But I didn't, all right."

O'Reilly went home. He didn't say anything about it to anybody. His punishment at school was detention. "At Chaminade, for some stupid thing, they give detention. I mean, from fighting in the hallway to whatever. In hindsight, I understand you can't have fighting in the hallways, and this guy didn't want to hear what happened. And that was the problem with Chaminade. They didn't want to understand what the dynamic was within the school. And they were blind to it, that there was this elitism . . . you were supposed to, like, kiss up to these kids. It was like there was favoritism going rampant."

O'Reilly adjusted to it. "I adjusted to the school in the sense that I was smart enough to realize what the score was." His father said, "Look, you know, if you get expelled, you flunk out, I'm just going to send you to another structured environment. You're never going to Tresper Clarke. You're never going there, so get it out of your mind. You get out of this, I'm sending you somewhere else."

That was what was good about his father, O'Reilly says thirty-eight years later. "My dad knew that if I got through that place with its strict code of behavior, there'd be a chance I wouldn't wind up in Sing Sing, a situation my grammar school teachers had predicted." He realized that if his son didn't get this kind of discipline, structure, that he was going to go the way of a lot of his friends in Levittown. "I was going to be a thug. You know, going to go the Billy Joel route, hanging at the stores and all of that. And with Chaminade, they really didn't give you an opportunity to do that, all right? I had to go on a bus to Mineola; I had to come back. I had a few hours to fool around after school, but I didn't have a lot of time to get into a lot of trouble. So it worked, as much as I despised the school. I hated it for the four years I was there."

"I remember my brother was fascinated in the early sixties with color television," said his sister, Jan. "He just wanted to get on the television, he kept saying when he was nine or ten, and we kept saying, 'Well, what do you want to do that for?' He said, 'Oh, I just want to tell people what I think, you know.'"
But what he really wanted to do when he grew up was play baseball.

O'Reilly was a rookie sensation in the Levittown Little Leagues during the 1956–65 seasons. At age seven, he began considering himself a star. For some reason, at age sixteen, his option wasn't picked up to play in the Levittown Babe Ruth Leagues. There were two Levittown Babe Ruth teams, A & B, in the Central Nassau League. There were tryouts for the team. "I'm doing what I always do, throwing the ball eighty-five miles an hour. I'm a pitcher, and I can hit. So I didn't think there was any problem at all. You know, I'll make the team. I always made the teams."

And he didn't make the team. He was stunned. "I mean, I'm not going to play ball? I was furious, I mean, absolutely furious, because every guy on the team said, 'This is outrageous. This is an outrage. You're much better than these guys. What was going on here?"

It was all politics. The reason he didn't make the teams, O'Reilly was convinced, was because the team managers had sons who were pitchers, and they didn't want him in the mix. They wanted their kids to be pitchers. "I would have even taken a relief role at that point."

O'Reilly's father didn't do all the political things that get you on the all-star team. Mr. O'Reilly Sr. wasn't one of those fathers who went to Little League games. He commuted to New York City with his car pool, which left around six-thirty in the morning and didn't get home at night until about seven, or later if he was taking the LIRR. That didn't bother young Bill. "Most of the kids in the Central Nassau Little League would want their fathers to show up. I didn't want him to come because I was so competitive. It was an intense game. And he would kind of, like, say, 'How come you're not having more fun?'"

Son and father would get into fights. "Just enjoy it, just relax," he would say to his son. "And me, my idea is to win. If I didn't, I was teed off. That served me well in television because I mean you gotta win."

O'Reilly went home after the Babe Ruth snub. "I think I came in and broke six bats over my head. I was really mad. My mother didn't say anything, didn't say a word." He went upstairs to his small room in the attic, lay on his bed, and kicked the wall, his way of anger management as a teenager. He came down for supper. His father came home from work. "He goes, 'What's the matter with you?' and I say, 'Aw, you know.' My father wasn't engaged at that level. He didn't care as long as I wasn't in jail."

About a week went by. O'Reilly went to school, came home, stewed in his room. And one day his mother said to him, "I got you on the team at St. Raphael's."

"What the hell is this?" O'Reilly said.

She goes, 'Well, I have a priest friend and he called over. They have a CYO team over there, sixteen to eighteen.'"

St. Raphael's was in the next town, East Meadow. A different parish. It was

Catholic Youth Organization. The CYO league was at the same level of competition as Babe Ruth. They had better fields. They had dugouts. They had lights. They had everything. The uniforms were great.

"So I go over. The guys give me a uniform, bang, bang, bang, and I'm the ace in the league. I played all summer for those guys, and I was the best pitcher on the team and, you know, I hit about .300 and had a great time."

O'Reilly says he will never forget what his mother had done. She is not an aggressive woman. At that time, Ann O'Reilly was working as a physical therapist at the Holly Patterson, an old-age home in Nassau County. She was busy all day, and she took it upon herself to make it happen, said O'Reilly. "I think she realized that was my outlet. Because there were a lot of thugs in the neighborhood. A lot of guys hanging out. You know, a lot of guys using drugs, a lot of guys doing this, doing that. And I think my mother was smart enough to know you get him into this. He enjoys it, he's competitive in it, he's good at it, and you keep him away from that. Because it was there. All you got to do is go out of the door, walk up to the stores and there it was. So I mean my mother and the Babe Ruth thing was definitely a turning point for me.

"I'm sure I thanked her, but I don't think I ever thanked her enough. It meant a lot to me that I could continue to play baseball because I didn't want my career to stop at age sixteen."

When he wasn't playing baseball, young O'Reilly was going to Shea Stadium. "I remember between ten and fourteen, we'd take the Long Island Railroad. They used to have Midget Mets. We're so politically correct now they took the 'midget' out of there. That's too offensive. It's Future Mets now. But, anyway, when I was growing up it was Midget Mets, and every game they have a bunch of kids who get in free, courtesy of the Mets. Well, me and my friends from Levittown, we'd just get on the line and we'd get into every single game for free. Just walk in the line because there are always thirty, forty kids. They didn't know who you were, walk right in, Midget Mets. 'Hi, how you doing?' And then we'd split from the Midget Mets. You know, they were sitting in the cow pasture, and we'd go down to the box seats and sit there. It was great. And I did that for, like, five years. Saw every Mets game, and the players got to know us. 'Boy, you must have a lot of money, man.' They'd go, 'What do you do? How much you making? Where you getting all this money?' What a scam. We snuck in, we snuck in. It was so much fun."

.   .   .

Chaminade was a football powerhouse in the New York metropolitan area, the Notre Dame of private schools on Long Island.

He wanted to play football, sister Jan O'Reilly says, remembering her brother kicking the wall in the attic while he was going to Chaminade, "and for some reason they didn't want to let him play football." O'Reilly had been the star quarterback, passer, and punter for the Caddy House Favorites, the team O'Reilly had founded at Caddy House Field in Eisenhower Park, several blocks from his home on Page Lane. O'Reilly seemed to be banned from playing football because of his personality, rather than athletic ability, as he saw it.

"The football coach at Chaminade wouldn't let me go out for the team," O'Reilly recalled in an interview. "Chaminade was a football factory and remains so to this day. They recruit their teams from junior high school, Pop Warner, and things like that. I mean, they're serious, these guys."

When he showed up as a freshman at Chaminade, their freshman team was already picked. O'Reilly didn't know it. "So I go, hold it. How do you even know these guys? We're all freshmen. They knew everybody, all right, nobody had a shot. Very few walk-ons, unless you were six-eight in basketball. They had all the guys they needed for every sport, not just for football. They had guys scouted in grammar schools and all of that."

In his senior year, O'Reilly thought he was so good and so much better than what they had at the Chaminade football factory, he decided to push it, going out for the team. "We were playing flag football in Phys Ed, and I was just, you know, throwing the ball eighty yards down the field, kicking it sixty yards. And the Phys Ed teacher said, 'How come you're not playing football?' I said, 'Because Coach Thomas won't allow me to come out for the team.'

"The Phys Ed teacher, who wasn't a bad guy, said, 'Well, that doesn't seem right.' I said, 'Well, you know, that's the way it is.' So then the next day, he says, 'I got you a tryout.'" The teacher had talked to Joe Thomas, who had been there for what seemed to O'Reilly like fifty years.

O'Reilly showed up after school. He was a quarterback, but they had their quarterback, so he decided just to go out as a kicker. "I was so much better than what they had, you know, it was ridiculous. I mean, it was absurd. I remember the punter they had was kicking them, you know, thirty . . . forty yards. Boom!

I rocket them out sixty—boom! Like this. And everybody was like . . . and then we were going for field goals. I could kick field goals forty-five and in. And here's what they did; this epitomizes Chaminade. The holder, you know, the guy he takes the snap. Okay, he was intentionally turning the laces into me, because he didn't like me, didn't want me on the team."

The first time he did it, O'Reilly gave him the benefit of the doubt. He kicked it up, and it went through anyway. "Second time he did it, I stopped and looked at the guy. I looked at Coach Thomas. I said, 'I need another holder here.' He said, 'Well, that's the regular holder, that's the holder guy.' I said, 'Well, that's the regular holder you got, there's a problem because those laces are supposed to be handled the other way.' The whole team now is listening to this, and I'm staring at this guy Thomas. I knew what the hell was going on. So he goes, 'Well, we only have one holder, so you have to use him.' So I said, 'Are you going to let me do it the right way or what? If not, I'll dropkick it, all right. I don't need a holder.'

"You know, that's how arrogant I was. So the guy did it the right way and boom! It was a *tour de force*. And after the tryout, Thomas comes over to me, and goes, 'Well, I think I'm going to suit you up.' Which means you get a jersey, and I was happy. Why, I don't know. I should have known it wasn't going to work out right.

"He goes, 'Come in and get fitted for your pads,' and all of that. So the next day after school I come in and I go to the equipment guy, again another guy that has been there for years. I said, 'Well, Coach Thomas told me to come down and get fitted for my gear.' And he goes, 'Well, we don't have any left.'

"You know, at that point I was playing hockey; the football season was parallel. I just said to myself, is this worth it? And it was not. So I decided screw this I'm going to play ice hockey. So the bottom line of the story is I never got a shot at playing football for Chaminade."

"I made the varsity hockey team," O'Reilly said. He spent most of his time playing hockey from October until April. "That was good, because it just got me out of the general population and got me into, like, a club." The few friends he had at Chaminade were on his hockey team.

Hockey was a big sport at Chaminade. Everybody knew O'Reilly was the goalie. The team won games. There was prestige attached to playing for the

Chaminade Flyers. The public school didn't have a team. So that was a good thing about Chaminade.

O'Reilly didn't skate very well in the beginning, which was not a major problem for a goalie. He also cut a peculiar figure on the ice.

"I didn't have enough money to get the equipment that I needed to be a hockey goalie, all right, the pads and everything. So I said to my father, 'Look, you know, I'm pretty good and I'm going to start on the varsity hockey team here.' He just went like this . . . He goes, 'Look, you know, the jack.' So what I did was I got a baseball catcher's chest protector from a friend. I got a first baseman's mitt. And I had my mother sew a pad that covered my arm. I got an old lacrosse mask that had been thrown away by the Tresper Clarke High School lacrosse team. And then I had to buy leg pads. I bought secondhand leg pads, you know, leg pads that had been around since Gump Worsley's day. When I didn't have the pads, I played in jeans. And I just looked like, you know, what the hell is this? Because all the other goalies had everything. I remember in our league Emile Francis, who was the Rangers coach, his kid played in our league. Ricky Francis, he played for Long Beach High. And most of these kids were pretty affluent kids. So they had everything. And I come out and look like this, you know, monster from outer space playing goalie. But I was so tough. I mean I would do anything just to not let that puck go in the goal."

O'Reilly still has his Chaminade jersey. Chaminade #1.

By O'Reilly's senior year at Chaminade, Mr. O'Reilly Sr. had decided his son would go to Marist College, a small liberal arts school of sixteen hundred undergraduates on the Hudson in Poughkeepsie, New York. Given his son's view of his football talents, it should have been Notre Dame. Why Marist?

There was the Marianist (Society of Mary) connection. St. Brigid's and Chaminade were Marianist institutions. In the United States, the brothers and priests of the Society of Mary run three universities, eighteen high schools, and six elementary/middle schools, as well as eleven parishes, and, as its mission statement explains, are "dedicated to educating and nourishing the mind, the body, and soul."

O'Reilly's father also had picked Marist, founded in 1929 by the Marist Brothers, because he considered it a safe place for his son to go to college. A large percentage of its student body had blue-collar roots. Tuition was moderate for college of that day: $1,000, plus $1,000 for room and board. Not only was it affordable, Mr. O'Reilly Sr. also had relatives in Wappinger Falls, a few miles to the south of the campus, who might keep an eye on the boy.

Mr. O'Reilly Sr. didn't want his son getting a swelled head. "It was basically, 'Hey, we're here, this is it, you know, make the best of it,'" O'Reilly said. "It wasn't like, 'Hey, you can go to Harvard and be a big television star.'"

At Marist, O'Reilly majored in football, as he liked to think, with a minor in history. His roommate, Joe Rubino, was not a jock. An English/journalism major, he had been an editor at the Marist newspaper, *The Circle.* By their senior year at Marist, they had done everything together, coconspirators in numerous campus and off-campus hijinks. Inseparable companions, Rubino was about five-nine, and Bill was six-four. "I think he's been six-four since he was born," Rubino said.

Rubino wore long hair, a beard, construction shirt, white painters' pants. He looked like the ultimate Haight-Ashbury guy. O'Reilly was extremely debonair, in Rubino's opinion. He could have appeared on the *CBS Sports Sunday* golf show. He was into plaid pants, the Continental pants without a belt, and the Banlon shirts. He had Clint Eastwood sideburns. Dirty Harry was O'Reilly's cultural hero in his college days.

His friend would always brag about his Nordic good looks, Rubino remembered. "He was always very very very very pale. I tan in ten minutes. Bill burns even before he gets any color. He is as white as a slice of white bread. So it was quite a contrast: this pale Nordic-looking guy with the long Clint Eastwood sideburns, the combed hair and me walking around like I was Charlie Manson."

O'Reilly also was a little different-looking on the football field at Marist. He had asked for and got number 12 on his football jersey. It just happened to be the number of O'Reilly's football hero, Joe Namath of the Jets. Marist teammate Ed Fogarty also remembered the Namath long hair. He went out in his sophomore season and bought the white shoes that Namath made famous. No one had that in 1968. "Okay, they are going to hate me," O'Reilly told teammate Gerry Tyne. "They might as well really hate me." "I think he did that just to cause controversy," Tyne said. It worked.

Marist today is a Division III school in football. Back then, they didn't have varsity football; Marist played club football. They played Manhattan, Fordham, St. John's, Albany State (now SUNY Albany), Sienna, Fairfield of Connecticut. Marist had a good club football team. "On a performance basis, we probably had the best record of any school our size," said Ron LeVine, football head coach during that period of Marist football history. In the years O'Reilly was at Marist, they never had a losing record. In one of those years (1971), O'Reilly's final season, Marist was undefeated in the regular season until they lost in the big Metropolitan Bowl game. "In the four years O'Reilly was at Marist," Coach LeVine said, "the school went undefeated twice in the regular season, and won two of its four Metropolitan Bowl games. "We were forty-eight and two in regular-season play. Bill was on three of those teams." It was the Golden Age of Marist football.

Not that O'Reilly would have much to do with the won-lost record. The unacclaimed Levittown jock made the varsity as a freshman. He was the second team quarterback. Also arriving at the school the same summer were several players from the Chaminade High School varsity. "They kind of had it in for him," said Gerry Tyne, a sophomore end on the team at the time. "Spread the word to their buddies, and they gave him the business."

"Why? Because he was a ball-breaker, quite frankly," Tyne said. He also was smarter than they were. They would get frustrated because he usually came out on top when it came to a match of wits.

They made life miserable for him as the second team quarterback, Tyne recalled. In the early practice sessions, the first team defense would tell the second team offense to lie down when O'Reilly was the quarterback, and they would just come in and kill the poor guy. "And he'd be looking out of his ear hole," Tyne said, "because absolutely naked he would get hit." One scrimmage O'Reilly actually got knocked off the field. The side practice field was kind of elevated. He got knocked out into a little gully, and you couldn't even see him. Finally, he crawled back up. "But he just wouldn't give in," recalled Tyne. "He never said a word. I admired the fact that he wouldn't back down. He just wouldn't give in to them. That showed his character even back then."

There wasn't anything unusual what the first team was doing to the second-string quarterback, in the eyes of the Marist coaching staff. "He played scouting team quarterback," said Coach LeVine, "whenever the team we were going to play had a passer. He took his lumps with everybody else and made a real contribution."

O'Reilly was taking his lumps, which Gerry Tyne considered "a beating," all season. "And, of course, he came right back at these guys," Tyne said, "mostly off the field and intellectually, he was just far superior to them, and I think that just ignited them more."

O'Reilly had the chance to hone what was to be his ongoing fight against authority figures at Marist. The figure who was most in his face on the football field was his coach, Ron LeVine.

"He hates me," O'Reilly said during our taping sessions thirty-one years after his graduation. "Why? Well, he is about five-four."

Coach LeVine remembered his first impression of O'Reilly as his rookie second-string quarterback. "He showed up basically as Joe Namath. I didn't like the white shoes, no. I was a Vince-Lombardi-type person. I thought that Joe, Joe Namath, had the right to wear whatever color shoes he wanted.

"He was very self-confident. He wasn't a bragger in that particular period of time. I'm sure there were guys on the team who felt that they'd give him a lesson or a licking, whenever they got an opportunity to do it on the field. But he fit in real well. I mean, as in any group of sixty guys, you're not best friends with everybody."

In the Levittown sporting community, young O'Reilly might have been the tallest kid on the block, but he wasn't the most fleet of foot. Actually, he was slow. "God, was he slow," said Gerry Tyne. "Those little skinny legs, they couldn't support him at all." Running was definitely not his thing as a kid, either. Flash O'Reilly, as they used to call him on the block, did not like to run, neighborhood friend John Blasi recalled: "You will never see O'Reilly on a tennis court. Racquetball would not be his game."

By the time O'Reilly came to Marist, he had acquired another nickname.

Before Pete Gogolak—in the 1960s the New York Giants place-kicker and another O'Reilly gridiron hero—everybody in professional football was a conventional kicker, approaching and kicking the ball straight on, leading with the toe. Gogolak revolutionized kicking by approaching the ball from the side, and kicking with the arch and in-step, soccer-style.

O'Reilly revolutionized extra point and field goals at Marist by kicking them soccer-style in the manner of Gogolak. On campus, they were calling him Gogo O'Reilly.

· · ·

Football wasn't the only thing on Gogo's mind at college. There were girls. He was the world's worst date until his midtwenties, O'Reilly says. But he had an excuse. Since being enrolled in an all-boy Catholic high school, after St. Brigid's, he said he was clueless. "I was as far away from the action as Lawrence Welk," O'Reilly remembered.

It would be years before he learned to slap on a little Brut aftershave and get that double-knit shirt collar to fit just right, the keys to success, as he considered at the time. It didn't help at all that Marist also was an all-boys college. It wasn't until his junior and senior years that a few girls showed up on campus as day students.

As a teenager, O'Reilly had his wandering eye on Sharon, he writes of his first crush. "But I was hopelessly shy."

Sharon Patterson lived on Patience Lane, around the corner from the O'Reillys on Page Lane. The Pattersons were close friends with the O'Reillys. Mr. O'Reilly Sr. was Sharon's brother's godfather. She called him Uncle Bill. In and out of each other's kitchens, Sharon and Billy, as she still calls him, were constantly put together because of the families. They were classmates at St. Brigid's. While O'Reilly was at Chaminade, she was at St. Mary's in Manhasset. He would be at the Chaminade dances, Sharon recalled, not dancing but observing. "He felt he was too awkward," sister Jan said.

"I played ball with her brother, and I thought she was kind of cute," O'Reilly told me. "But I was a barbarian. I mean, nothing ever came of it."

Sharon told me she was surprised to learn she was O'Reilly's first crush, not being aware of it until she read about it in his book.

"I grew up with all these guys in the neighborhood, but the dynamic was a little different when he asked me out to dinner. This was a date. I think I was nervous. I wasn't quite sure exactly what all this meant. Bill always had an air of confidence, so if he was nervous I didn't detect it."

Sharon didn't know where they were going in O'Reilly's used maroon Mercury Comet until he pulled up at the old Millridge Inn in Hicksville. "It was a very nice date. We talked. He talked a lot about movies. He was a regular Mr. Movie Man, always reviewing and describing movies he had seen. He was a perfect gentleman, very good company, very entertaining, and very funny. So he took me back home. We said good night, and that was it."

He had no moves at all as a teenager, O'Reilly confessed. "Count them: zero. So far as boy/girl interaction was concerned, I was pathetic. So were all of my friends, for all of the same reasons. So we played a lot of football and got very good at it. And we kept reading those *Playboys*."

By the summer of 1968, he was on his way to becoming what he called "a dating lunatic." When working as a lifeguard and swim instructor at a pool in Babylon, Long Island, he asked a student to a movie. She suggested a drive-in. He got to second base by the end of Annette and Frankie's second adventure and was steaming into third when the game ended. His date's parents had a nonnegotiable strict curfew.

He always kept his mouth shut about his romances. His Marist classmate Ed Fogarty remembered him once dating a cheerleader. "And he did that on the sly," said Fogarty. "He didn't make a general announcement that he was dating this girl. But I caught him. Her name was Judy. I remember him taking her out to dinner—which was unusual. When we were seniors, a date would be going somewhere with a group or something. He did it a little differently. Because he was different."

Another social handicap Gogo had in his college days was that he didn't drink. O'Reilly wasn't carousing at all hours, unlike fellow students at Marist. "Even as a teenager he didn't drink," sister Jan said. "Never touched it." He was already a confirmed nonalcoholic in high school. "I went to a party at a friend of mine's house, a guy named Miles McLaughlin," O'Reilly said. "We were hockey players together at Chaminade. He threw a big party when his parents went out of town and everybody got drunk and started throwing up. And I said, 'You know, what is this? Why do I want to get drunk and throw up? I don't like throwing up.' So I never had an inclination to do that anyway. And that pretty much reinforced the foolishness of it all."

At the Rathskeller, the campus hamburger joint, the center of Marist social life, O'Reilly was the one who was hitting a bottle of soda. He still drinks his favorite brew, Dr Pepper, although he will knock back a few root beers from time to time. Ed Fogarty remembered O'Reilly was antidrinking at college, "although he didn't preach it for anyone else. He practiced it, and I think was upset by the excesses at the school. He was the one person I could say I never saw take a drink in four years. I can't name another."

What confused people was that O'Reilly's saying "no" to alcohol didn't fit his personality. He was such a life-of-the-party kind of guy, always carrying on. Many people equated that behavior with drinking.

He never did drugs in college. "Never smoked a marijuana cigarette,"

O'Reilly said. "The only time I ever used tobacco was when I was, like, twelve, a little punk. Everybody was smoking in the neighborhood, you know. I tried a couple of cigarettes, but I never inhaled. I just didn't like it. It was one of the few times I was really ahead of the game and said this is just stupid, and I'm not doing this."

Rubino said O'Reilly was so antidrug at Marist he used to bust his chops about it all the time. He decided to play off that one day.

They were sitting around the dormitory, and Rubino said, "O'Reilly, I have to tell you the truth, buddy, I have a little pot in the room."

O'Reilly looked at him. "What did you say, Rubino?"

"O'Reilly, I have a little pot in the room."

He said, "You're kidding, right?"

Rubino said, "No, O'Reilly, I have a little pot."

And O'Reilly said, "Better get it out of here right now."

Rubino said, "It's just a little pot."

"I don't care if you're my best friend. You know how I am. If you don't get it out of here, I'm going to call the police."

"O'Reilly, you would call the police on me? I'm practically your brother, your best friend."

"I don't want drugs around me."

Rubino dragged out "it's just a little pot" for ten minutes. O'Reilly was getting angrier and angrier. "He kept threatening to call the police," Rubino remembered. "He was trying to decide what jurisdiction. The Poughkeepsie police? The county police? I mean, he's really going to turn me in."

Rubino walked over to his dresser, opened the bottom drawer, and picked up a little stainless-steel saucepan, and held it up. "O'Reilly, I told you it was just a little pot.

"Oh, my God, his face. I mean, oh, my God, he just went nuts. Anyway, I told that story a million times, and people on campus just goofed on him, you know, later on holding up little pots, saying, 'I got a little pot.' And I'm thinking, like this guy was really going to turn me in."

Not only was O'Reilly marching to his own glockenspiel in substance abuse in college, but he was different from his classmates in his musical tastes. Most of the people in their dorm either listened to The Doors and Jimi Hendrix, or Bob Dylan and other protest music. But O'Reilly was listening to Motown, like Jay and the Techniques. And O'Reilly didn't just listen to music, he would always sing along with it. He fancied himself a lounge act, like a singer in a band. "He wouldn't just sing, like, sitting in a chair." Rubino recalled his being amazed when they became roommates. "He would actually stand at the window overlooking the Hudson River, as if he was looking out at an audience. And he would actually hold his hand up to him like he had a microphone in his hand. And then he would, you know, bob up and down, like he was the lead singer, like dancing in place, singing *a capella*."

Many of his friends got together in the Levittown years and formed bands, O'Reilly said of his musical career in the days of the Beatles craze. "Some parents became concerned when their kids adopted Cockney accents. A few guys even began calling each other 'bloke.' The neighborhood was awash in bowl haircuts." The Mersey Sound didn't affect O'Reilly. "I am proud to say that even early on I was a contrarian, and Beatlemania did not affect me." He was a Beach Boys kind of guy, he said, when he wasn't doing his Motown thing.

O'Reilly met Rubino in his freshman year at Marist. Rubino was editing a spin-off of the college newspaper aimed at freshman. A mutual friend came to Rubino, and said, "Listen, Joe, there is this jock, a football player, who is a very funny guy." He thought the paper could use him. "He looked like a giraffe on roller skates," Rubino said of the way he walked into his dorm room with a sample of his writing.

Rubino sat there reading, looking at the page and looking at the guy. "It was very funny, tongue-in-cheek," Rubino said, "like Dave Barry—just getting started. This humor did not match the guy. You pictured some cowlick-haired nerd, sitting in a corner banging his head at a typewriter." In person, O'Reilly was totally out of sync with that image. It was such an incongruous thing, because he is in a college full of protestors, Rubino said, "And he's, like, he should be on the third tee at the Augusta National. I mean, he looks like Tom Weiskopf or something, and he's standing there in his polished loafers, with fashionable socks, and his Continental pants, his Banlon shirt."

In 1968–9, there were two groups on campus. One was marching in peace marches, and the other guys were drinking down by the river. O'Reilly didn't jibe with either of those groups. He didn't have many acquaintances who hung out with him or would even sit with him at the cafeteria table.

One who didn't appreciate O'Reilly was the editor in chief of the school paper, a Brooks Brothers kind of guy who wore tweed jackets and Buster Brown shoes. He didn't like O'Reilly. He thought he was too sarcastic for a very stately college newspaper, so O'Reilly didn't get much ink in his freshman year.

By their sophomore year, Rubino had become an editor on *The Circle* and made it possible for O'Reilly to get some pieces into the paper. He could pick his topics, but Rubino would have to edit him. "Bill was very raw, a very bright guy, extremely articulate, but he was not the greatest wordsmith in the world."

English major Rubino had an extensive vocabulary. Whenever he would use a word like "pith," O'Reilly would say, "What are you talking about? You just made the word up." Rubino would explain.

Later on, Rubino used the word "opine." O'Reilly didn't believe him and accused him of making it up. "It's the verbal form of opinion," his mentor explained. Every time Rubino would use a word he didn't know, O'Reilly would question it, then it would show up in his vocabulary. "Keep it pithy," he now opines on his TV show.

O'Reilly admits he wasn't fully formed as journalist. When you look at some of his early writing, it's surprising how much the Bill O'Reilly voice of today is already there in the Marist columns, which he called "Attitudes Outrageous." One of his more outrageous columns involved a black student at Marist. The student had meandered into O'Reilly's class in a course with a teacher whom the campus rumor mill had given a reputation as doing her bit for the civil rights movement by marking on a curve. Any black student who enrolled in her class was guaranteed at least a "B+." This proved her sensitivity to the race question.

On the first day of class, the student sat down next to O'Reilly. "I knew who he was, and he was definitely not a good citizen. In fact, [he] was a campus 'badass,' well-known in some quarters, feared for his intimidating behavior and his trafficking in drugs." He gave O'Reilly a special a kind of scowl, and that was the extent of their relationship. He never reappeared. He cut the entire semester after that first class.

When grades were handed out at the end of the term, the rumor was the student had somehow garnered a "B" from what O'Reilly called "this unusually understanding teacher."

"I guessed he missed the "+" because he had so openly done bubkus." O'Reilly also got a "B," even though he actually attended the classes.

O'Reilly went to the student and asked about his rumored grade.

" 'Shiiiit, man, that jive ass course don't mean, nothin' to me,' he said. 'So I got a "B." You got a problem with that?' "

O'Reilly explained this curious situation in his newspaper column, suggesting this teacher was guilty of reverse racism and doing a disservice to hard-working students, regardless of race or color. It brought attention to a problem that had been an open secret on the campus.

The column circulated in the dorms and created an uproar. "Attacks on me were personal," said O'Reilly. "While some kids thought I was wrong and others that I was just stupid, there were others who accused me of being a racist just for bringing up the subject. Once that charge is raised, it's a hard one to beat. In fact, in the heat of the battle, I was called every racial name in the book and some the book had never heard of."

This was part of O'Reilly's higher education, valuable preparation for his coming broadcasting career.

"In the end, though, I won the battle," he says. "Too many people on campus knew what was going on. Now that it was out in the open, the teacher could not defend the grade. The student later dropped out of college. According to O'Reilly, "Soon afterward he murdered a policeman."

There were not many people who really got Bill O'Reilly. "They were still just a minority of us," said Rubino. "So it was a little tough for Bill. But he didn't care. He was never afraid of anything. He knew that a lot of people just didn't care for him. He knew it, and he kind of thrived on it."

By the end of his sophomore year, Gogo realized he was not going to make the pros. He was tired of his rebellion against Coach LeVine. He was not thrilled by being the number two or third-string quarterback. It was time to expand his horizons.

His father was deeply upset by young Bill's decision to quit football. He objected when Bill Junior told him he was going to study abroad during his third year. "You could be the starting quarterback in your junior year," he had told Bill. "You're going to stay at Marist."

Where O'Reilly came from, kids didn't get Beemers for high school graduation presents but hand-me-downs when their folks bought later-model used Rambler station wagons, if they were lucky. They took the Greyhound bus to Miami for the family's annual two-week vacation rather than fly, and their kids didn't go to Europe for cultural enrichment. "He didn't want me rocking the boat or getting a big head," said O'Reilly.

Brother Bellinger was the chairman of the French Department at Marist, and director of the Third Year Abroad Program. He also didn't want O'Reilly to go abroad for his junior year.

"Because I was a hooligan," O'Reilly said. "He wanted cultured guys."

"The administration wasn't too thrilled with Bill," explained Edgar Royce, a basketball player who also had applied for the program, a model Marist student, as far as Brother Bellinger was concerned, whose only flaw was being a friend of O'Reilly since freshman year. "O'Reilly had his own mind," Royce said. "He did some things with the paper, the radio station occasionally. I'm sure that's what got the administration worked up. So I think Brother Bellinger was a little nervous about turning Bill loose in Europe."

"The fact that he said I couldn't go meant that, of course, I was going to go. I had the grades to go," said O'Reilly, an honors student by now majoring in history.

Brother Bellinger turned him down, anyway. "The first time he turned me down, I said, 'Look, I'm going. You want to do this, I'll raise holy hell here, because I'm qualified to go, academically qualified.' Emotionally, I wasn't qualified to go anywhere. I wasn't qualified to go to Hicksville, all right. I couldn't go to the Mid-Island Mall."

Brother Bellinger had spent years establishing academic links with the University of London and was proud of its unblemished record of sending UOL Marist's finest. He may have feared that all his hard work building the bridge from Poughkeepsie to London was about to be blown up by a Long Island loose cannon.

"Bellinger pulled a fast one. He said, all right, you can go, but we don't have a spot for you in any of the dorms. You've got to find a place on your own. Which he thought was going to dissuade me, but, of course, it didn't. So I said, all right, fine, I'll go find a place to live on my own, which was insane, but I didn't know that."

O'Reilly and his classmate Royce went over in the summer of 1969. "Nine days on this rotten, rickety vessel," O'Reilly said. "I don't remember the name, but it was awful. Just one of these little things rocking and rolling."

"You know, when you're a college kid you don't care," Royce said. "You don't realize that you're only a floating cork in the middle of the Atlantic, and it was a nine-day party. There was a band playing every night, you know, you sleep half the day, get up, and dance with the girls at night, and do it again the next day."

Opus Dei had built a college dormitory, called Netherhall House in west central London. "It was a beautiful dormitory, only in its first year of occupancy, marble here and terrazzo there," Brother Bellinger told me. "Glorious, you know. Opus Dei had money. I mean, they're rich. They're known to be catering to the rich. That's why they got the Queen Mother to dedicate it. I mean, not too many student halls are dedicated by the Queen Mother."

One of the first students to enter the newly opened hallowed dorm was Bill O'Reilly. It wasn't anything Brother Bellinger planned or even imagined in his worst nightmare.

"So we get to London," O'Reilly recalled, "and Edgar had a spot at this place called Netherhall, which was just first-class. It was terrific, but they didn't have any room for me. Sold out. I'm staying at a bed & breakfast across the street from where he's staying. I guess I could have lived in that B&B, but it was a little expensive."

The deal was his father would pay the tuition. O'Reilly would pay living expenses. It was money that he had earned during the summer. "I made a lot of money in the summer painting houses. I had a grand or two, and every month he would wire me, and I'd go pick it up at the bank in Berkeley Square. I remember that like it was yesterday."

The B&B got to be a strain on O'Reilly's budget. So he went to the University of London housing office. There was a room in a place called Clapham Common. O'Reilly went down there to look at this room.

"Every Arab you had ever seen was living there, like eighteen guys to the room. I walked in there, and I'm sorry, I just said there is no way. Besides, it was way down south London. You know, I have nothing against Arabs. I've been to lots of Arab countries, and I enjoyed myself, but this was too much for me."

He got back on the tube, Northern Line. By now, he is a little troubled. "What the hell am I going to do? I went to church, St. Paul's, and lit a little candle, and said, 'Look, you know, it's pretty tough here.'"

The next day he met Edgar for lunch, and Edgar said, "Hey, you ought to check this out. I heard that one of these guys from Czechoslovakia couldn't get a visa to come here, and I think there might be a room open. The guy couldn't get out of Prague."

Bing! His prayers had been answered. "The room opened up," said O'Reilly. "They let me in. It was great. And so I was in the same dorm as Edgar, top-of-the-line dorm, all meals, perfect."

O'Reilly asked Edgar not to tell Brother Bellinger anything about what had happened. "I was mad at Bellinger now because he made me sweat," O'Reilly said. "I had a friend in the Peace Corps in India, a guy named Stu Solomon. So I sent Stuie a letter. Enclosed in the letter was a postcard written to Bellinger: 'Dear Brother Bellinger, I couldn't find a place to live in London, so here I am in India. Please call my parents and tell them I'm all right.' And instructions to Stuie to mail the card to Bellinger, from Bangalore, India.

"So, of course, he does. Then I wrote another letter to my roommate at Marist, Joe Rubino, the editor of the newspaper, and I said, 'Rubino, I want you to ask Bellinger what the hell O'Reilly is doing in India, and if this is the way he runs his Third Year Abroad Program, threatening to do a big exposé.' Of course, I'm not in India, but he thinks I am because I mailed this card to him, all right? What a scam this is, this is the greatest scam ever."

Stuie mailed the card. Rubino went over with his little notebook, and asked, "Is it true, O'Reilly's in India? What the hell is he doing in India?"

The upshot was that Bellinger sent an emissary to London to find out what was going on, and nobody knew he was coming. Jeb Lanigan just showed up. Brother Lanigan's instructions were to make sure O'Reilly wasn't wandering around the world somewhere and to observe how O'Reilly was burning the midnight oil to study and enrich himself as a student in his junior year.

O'Reilly and Royce were both taking classes at the University of London. Royce was at the London School of Economics (LSE) and O'Reilly was taking classes at Queen Mary College. University of London is somewhat like CUNY, a collection of independent colleges run under one umbrella. "You got a college here," Royce said, "a college there. All over London. Whichever one O'Reilly went to, he didn't go to a lot of classes, I can tell you that."

As far as Brother Bellinger knew, O'Reilly was going to class approximately seven, eight hours a week. He was expected to write papers and read in the libraries. His papers were submitted to a tutor who individually assigned to him essays, generally about one thousand to two thousand words.

"He'd spend some time in the library," Royce remembered. "History was his best subject. He was always reading biographies, not historical novels, but *The Rise and Fall of the Third Reich* or something, something a lot of college kids wouldn't be picking up for light reading. But he was really into that kind of thing. And then, you know, he'd sit down and knock out a paper. Writing was what he was good at. What do you need class for? That's the way he looked at it."

O'Reilly liked to stay out all night in London. "We saw every show, then bomb around in Piccadilly Circus, or something, and you know I get back to the dorm around one, one-thirty and then I read a little bit, go to bed around three, and get up around eleven, eleven-thirty. That's my lifestyle in London, all right. So, anyway, I hear a knock on the door about ten-thirty. Everybody knew nobody disturbs me until eleven-thirty. I'll be up for lunch, all right. I hear a knock on my door, boom, boom, boom, boom, and I go, 'Hey, get out of here, what are you doing?' Boom, boom, boom, boom.

"So I get up out of bed, and I rip the door open, like this. I thought it was one of the guys just giving me a hard time. And there's Lanigan standing there. And he looks at me, and I go, 'I'm sick HAAAAGH' [does a cough].

"He says, 'What's the matter with you?' I said, 'ACK, ACK, ACK' [makes funny noises, like he is dying]. 'I don't know,' I finally said. He just stands there as I'm coughing. I mean, how am I going to explain I'm in the sack at ten-thirty in the morning. I'm supposed to be at school going to these classes, you know.

"Anyway, Lanigan couldn't pin it on me. I mean, what is he going to say, you're not sick? I mean, take my temperature? So basically he stayed for a couple of days, you know, and he's going, 'Well, I want to go to your class with you."

O'Reilly agreed to take Brother Lanigan to one of his theoretical classes. "There was this giant lecture hall," O'Reilly said about this great moment in Anglo-American pedagogy. "Some English guy who is ninety-five going on about some dynasty. There were 150 kids in the class. The teacher didn't know who the hell you were or whether you were there or not. Who cares? I mean, I sized that up right away. I didn't have to go. Nobody knew.

"And that was, like, the only time that I ever went to these classes."

From time to time, O'Reilly would do things that tweaked Brother Bellinger. "He got about five of us together one night, and we took a picture next to five bikes," Royce recalled. "So it looked like we were a motorcycle gang, you know, us with our motorcycles, like five of these thugs. And he sent it to Brother Bellinger."

The early signs of O'Reilly's Dirty Harry obsession were exhibited in his Third Year Abroad. Among the principle cultural shrines the Marist student chose to visit on the Honda 125 motorbikes he and Edgar Royce rented was the area in Spain where Clint Eastwood's spaghetti Westerns were shot.

"Somewhere along the line," said his travel companion Royce, who had been following O'Reilly's directions riding their Hondas through Portugal, Spain, and a ferry trip to Marrakech and the Kasbah in Morocco, "we went through some mountainous area. It was freezing, and I asked, 'Where the hell are we go-ing?' It's like we could be on the moon. And he said, 'I want to see the towns where these Clint Eastwood movies were filmed.' We got there, and it really was interesting, because in the middle of nowhere in Spain it looked like you were out in the Midwest."

Finding a couple of these little towns where the Clint Eastwood movies were made was an emotional experience for O'Reilly, like paying homage to the Get-tysburg battlefield.

As usual, there were two schools of thought about O'Reilly. He had a simple way of classifying the student body at the dorms: those who liked him and those who thought he was a barbarian.

The only British students he saw regularly were the ones he saw in the dorm, since he didn't go to class that often. When O'Reilly came into the Opus Dei dorm, he stood out like a six-foot-four-inch sore thumb, as Royce recalled, "which never bothered Bill." O'Reilly quickly formed an alliance with what he considered the good guys, the ones who liked him, the ones who would eat with him. "They considered us just very funny. They thought we were great, and they loved to hang out with us."

The bad guys were the majority. "A lot of the upper-crust English. They just looked down their noses."

So O'Reilly decided to teach those chaps a thing or two.

"Oh, that was the worst," O'Reilly said gleefully, looking at his watch to see if there was enough time to do justice to the story. "And I feel guilty about it to this day. It happened at the end of the school year, you know, after this horren-dous London winter where you never see the sun. It's May, and we're about fin-ished. And I thought it was time to give the people who thought we were barbarians something to remember us by. So with about two weeks to go we de-cided to take care of these guys by the old American college trick of filling up garbage cans full of water. By leaning them against the door and knocking on the door. When the guy opens it, gallons of water go into his room.

"So we got this coordinated plan," O'Reilly said. "We're going to take care of these guys, and that's what we did. We'd filled up the water in the bathroom, and we put the things there, and simultaneously we knocked on ten doors, and they opened the doors and the water came in. So these guys were really mad because they all had rugs, and, you know, they all got red in the face and all of that rot. So they decided to get revenge.

"Anyway, a giant water fight ensued, which had never been seen in England since Henry VIII. I mean, the guys are running around the dorm with buckets of water. The next day, when the provost of the dorm came in, he was furious. "I mean, they didn't see the humor in this at all. I couldn't believe how serious they were."

The authorities started their interrogation of who did it and who started it. "And, of course, we all lied. We all said, we don't know who started it. I mean, we were just walking down, somebody threw garbage cans filled with water at us, blah, blah, blah, blah.

"Everybody knew I did it, everybody knew I was the instigator, but nobody would tell. No, because if you told, you were going to get kicked out. I mean, they weren't going to give you a second chance. Everybody just said, who knows? Nobody knows. They knew it was me. And I felt quite bad, because they did me a favor by letting me in here. But for the long run it was just water, I mean so what? Nobody got hurt. It wasn't anything else."

When he spoke to me in 2003, Brother Bellinger did not remember O'Reilly giving him any grief.

Among O'Reilly's memorable extracurricular activities, one that lives in the annals of Marist College hijinks was the Ed McMahon Coup of 1971.

Brother Tarcissus on the Marist campus, in his eighties or nineties, was too old to teach, so he had a job running the print shop in a little building on campus that most people didn't know about. Rubino knew because he was editing the newspaper. Rubino was the press lord, the Rupert Murdoch of Marist, at the time. "To this day, we don't know if Brother Tarcissus actually spoke," said Rubino. "We would just bring this material in. He would smile, look at us, and he would print it."

O'Reilly and Rubino got the idea they could get into places free if they had press passes. So they had Brother Tarcissus make them press passes for the Intercollegiate Press, an AP for college papers. They brought the brother their pictures and the Intercollegiate Press logo and asked him to make business cards. "And, gosh darn, if the guy didn't make Bill O'Reilly and Joe Rubino legitimate press passes," Rubino said.

As accredited Intercollegiate Press correspondents, O'Reilly and his room-mate were able to get in "everywhere." "Every time we wanted to get into a club, we would say we're doing a review of the club. We were getting into games free, everything free."

Their senior class was trying to decide whom to get for their senior speaker at graduation. The list was boring to O'Reilly. He decided the class should get Ed McMahon to be their speaker.

"For no other reason than Ed was like a symbol," Rubino said. "Here's a guy who does not drink, O'Reilly, but he realizes that Ed McMahon is like the patron saint of college students. Because for all the guys he is known for drinking Budweisers. The legend supposedly was he had a swimming pool with the Bud logo. The Odd Couple are sitting around the table at lunchtime and announced they are going to get him. All the others guys at the table started laughing at them. So they said not only are they going to get Ed McMahon to be their speaker, they're going to be on *The Tonight Show* that night.

O'Reilly and Rubino hop into the car, drive to New York City to NBC at 30 Rockefeller. They flash their press passes and get past security. The two students go up to Ed McMahon's office, and say, "We want to speak to Ed McMahon. We want Ed to be our commencement speaker."

"You guys are out of your mind, you know," McMahon's assistant said. "Go downstairs and get in line with everybody else. Maybe after the show we'll talk about it."

Getting into *The Tonight Show* was a first-come, first-served deal. People line up for tickets. Marist's two musketeers decided they were not going to get into the line. They believed that if you walk as if you know what you're doing, people think you're supposed to be there. They found another elevator and came out right in front of *The Tonight Show* studio door. They used Ed McMahon's assistant's name with the security guard. They flashed their press passes again and went inside.

The two boys knew that Joey Bishop was going to be on the show that night as the replacement for Carson. O'Reilly used to watch *The Tonight Show* a lot, and he knew that Joey Bishop didn't have a monologue like Johnny did. He started off every show by roaming through the audience and talking to studio guests. That was the way Joey Bishop always killed the first twenty minutes. O'Reilly knew that Joey was not going to go to the first row. When he went into the audience, he always walked up a few steps to talk to somebody. So they sat in row seven. O'Reilly took the aisle seat. *The Tonight Show* started, and Joey Bishop did his thirty-second monologue, then headed for the audience. As he walked up the steps, O'Reilly stood up.

He didn't wait for Joey Bishop to call on anybody, he just stood up. Joey Bishop, who's about five-three, stood next to O'Reilly, six-four. He did his facial thing: "Oh, my God, look at the size of this guy." He now had to interview O'Reilly, who started doing a parody of a college student. It was the day before St. Patrick's Day, March 16, 1971. O'Reilly, who didn't drink, pretended that he was a student in town to get drunk on St. Patrick's Day. Their conversation went back and forth with the usual TV nonsense. O'Reilly said, "By the way, I have my friend here," and Rubino stood up.

Bishop asks Rubino, "And are you Irish?" And he replied, "No, I'm Italian." A few people applauded.

When Joey started to walk away, O'Reilly asked, "Hey, don't we get a free dinner?"

"And Joey, like, looks at us, looks at O'Reilly," Rubino explained.

"We were not shy," O'Reilly says, using the editorial "we" in his account of the Joey Bishop *Tonight Show* caper in the first volume of his autobiography. "When we lost the game of 'Stump the Band,' we demanded a free dinner certificate anyway. A perspiring Bishop reluctantly gave in and handed over the certificate."

O'Reilly spared readers a few of the details. According to Rubino, "Well, O'Reilly just asked for a free dinner. Joey is embarrassed. So he looks at the audience and goes, 'Well, folks, what do you think, should I give these boys a free dinner?' And the audience applauds. So he goes, 'Okay, these boys are getting a free dinner.'"

After the show, the boys go to the pickup window where people pick up things they won during the course of the show, and there's no dinner from Joey Bishop. Rubino was just for blowing it off but not O'Reilly. Bishop told him he's giving them a free dinner, he wants that free dinner. He goes to the dressing room and finds Joey Bishop. This is a twenty-year-old college student, who brasses his way on the TV show, now he wants his free dinner. He finds Joey's dressing room and busts right in. Joey is so annoyed, he opens his wallet and takes out a five-dollar bill. He gives O'Reilly the five. He goes, "Here, buy your own dinner with this."

They drove like madmen from the taping in Manhattan back to Poughkeepsie, roughly a two-hour drive. "We march around like heroes," said Rubino. "You remember now the show's taped at four-thirty and goes on at eleven-thirty that night. So we are telling everybody that we are going to be on *The Tonight Show*. They're going, 'What? You're really on TV? Baloney. You mean you're in the audience.' And we said, 'We're on TV.' We knocked on every door in the dorm and got everybody to stay up and watch us on TV. It was, like, unbelievable."

They never got Ed McMahon as a speaker, but at least they showed them they could get on TV.

O'Reilly remembered another part of the stunt. "We ran around the campus betting everyone we saw that we would appear on the Carson show, which would air at eleven-thirty that evening. The whole campus turned out to watch in the college auditorium. When Bishop told us to stand up, the crowd went into an uproar. We won hundreds of dollars in addition to the dinner extorted from Bishop. You can't make stuff like this up. My roommate and I were immortalized at Marist."

O'Reilly didn't play baseball at Marist, the other sport he considered a potential profession after graduation, since they didn't have a baseball team. Coming back to school after his Third Year Abroad the summer of 1969, the nineteen-year-old O'Reilly, who had spent one summer being a ball boy for the New York Mets, took the next step on the road to Shea Stadium and his beloved Mets, playing semipro ball on Long Island with a Brooklyn-based team called the New York Monarchs. The Monarchs played in Oceanside, a town on the south side of Nassau County. Oceanside was their home field. Don't ask how the New York Monarchs, based in Brooklyn, got to Oceanside, but that was where O'Reilly had to go to keep his baseball career alive. They played double-headers on Sundays in Oceanside, or one of the other south side parks.

O'Reilly knew guys playing for teams in the league. The Monarchs were looking for pitchers. Friends gave him the name of the manager, whom O'Reilly remembers as Solly. "He said come down and throw for us. Which I did. And they gave me a uniform, and that was that. I didn't have to convince too many people."

"It was pretty nice," O'Reilly said about what he called "a glorious career" with the Monarchs. "I was the only white guy on the team. I would tell the manager, 'Look, I'm not pitching the first game.' They were all hungover from Saturday night. We would lose the first game. I said no way I'm getting out there the first game. In the second game, they sobered up, and they were much better. They were the best ballplayers I've ever seen. Unfortunately, half of them were heroin addicts, but they were still great ballplayers. I mean, by the fourth inning the captain would be running off. 'I got a headache.' So it was really a lot of fun."

It also was what O'Reilly called his first "race relations deal." "I was never brought up with any black guys. I went to all-white schools; my neighborhood was Jewish, Irish, Italian. There were a few black guys on my college football teams, but they were middle-class guys, not really ghetto guys. These were hard-core ghetto guys."

He was known as "White Boy." That was his name. It wasn't "Bill" or "O'Reilly." " 'White Boy, you better get that ball over the plate. I gotta get out of here.' I mean, I was more afraid of my team than the opposing team. And that's why I did so well. I mean, I walked more than two guys, and my guys are like . . . They were so funny. We'd sit in the dugout and the way they would heckle the other team, especially if the other team was white. They'd try to imitate the walk of the white guys, and say polite things like, 'Oh, how are you?' "

They were about his age. He was almost twenty at the time. "How old are you?" they'd ask. 'Twenty? My kids are older than you, motherfucker.'

"But they kind of liked me, sort of a curiosity. They'd say, 'Don't be looking at my woman.' I never had so many laughs in my life." He hasn't kept in touch with his former teammates. "They're all in jail. I mean, they were a tough crew."

O'Reilly was scouted by the Mets. Bubba Jonnard saw him pitch a game, and brought him to Shea Stadium. He went into the right field bullpen. It was an off day, and they had a radar gun or whatever passed for one back then. O'Reilly threw for him. "I'll never forget it, because another guy walked out onto the mound next to me. You know, the guy didn't even warm up. And his first pitch was a rocket. It was like bang!" It was Tom Seaver. By the end of that 1969 season, Seaver won 25 games and the National League Cy Young Award, and led the Mets to their First World Series championship.

"So, anyway, Jonnard said, 'Look, you know, we like you, keep in touch.' "

Then O'Reilly went back and told his father the potentially good news. "Look, there's a chance they'll give me a little contract to go to West Virginia to play in a rookie league," O'Reilly explained. "And he said, 'You're not going to

West Virginia. You're not going to some stupid summer camp. You're going back to college, that's where you're going, and shut up.'

"I knew in my heart that I just didn't have the stuff that was going to take me into the big leagues. I mean, I just knew I wasn't good enough. And it was fine with me. I gave it my best shot. I did very well at baseball, and took it as far as I could take it. And then it was realistic to know I didn't want to waste my time in something that wasn't going to happen."

Chapter Two

Man About Miami

———————————

L ike many red-blooded, macho young men from Long Island, O'Reilly had grown up with sports and girls on the brain, the latter interests being in a state of arrested development thanks to the nuns and brothers in his parochial school education. At twenty-three, he was your above-average—nothing O'Reilly did was average—confused bright young man who did not fit into his father's or family's image or gene pools. He has spent his early years trying to figure out what to do with his life. He could not focus on which career path he would take.

His early aspirations were to be a *somebody* in sports. "He always picked high-risk positions," Marist football teammate Ed Fogarty said. "Pitcher in baseball, goalie in hockey, quarterback and kicker in football. High success or high failure rate. He liked the pressure."

In whatever sport, he was always the guy who controlled the action. He was in the hot center, a predilection we will see acted out in later career choices. All eyes had to be on him in whatever he would eventually choose to do. Whatever he was going to be in life, he had to be seen. Everybody had to know that Bill O'Reilly was the star. He also had to be calling the shots. "I think early on O'Reilly saw that he was at his best," his childhood friend John Blasi observed, "when he was surrounded by people that he could direct, where he could do the thinking and do the execution, and have everybody else just follow out his orders. He was happiest when he was in the driver's seat."

When O'Reilly was growing up, he didn't have any practical career aspirations. He came from a lower-middle-class family, which he likes to think is blue-collar, even though his father was white-collar, an accountant with a big oil company who eventually was making $35,000 a year ($92,000 to $100,000 in today's dollars, O'Reilly's enemies will point out) when ulcerative colitis, which had affected him for the prior three years, forced him to retire at fifty-two.

His father encouraged him to get a middle-class job, something that was secure. He advised him to become a cop or something like that. "Because we came from a long line of cops," O'Reilly said. "And firemen. That's what the O'Reillys were since they came over in 1858. And I never really questioned it, you know. I figured I'd be a baseball player. But I wasn't good enough.

"I didn't get a lot out of my father. And as far as shaping me as a journalist, there really wasn't anything along those lines. I wasn't born into the Peter Jennings family where his father was president of the CBC [Canadian Broadcasting Corporation]. That was expected of him. I was just like a barbarian that got involved because I finally figured out what I was good at. Or could be at it."

There was only one thing O'Reilly was good at, in his opinion. He had the blarney. "I could speak," he said. "I was always a good public speaker."

In sixth grade at St. Brigid/Our Lady of Hope Regional School Bill O'Reilly discovered he had a talent for extemporaneous expression. "I found that out in Mrs. Boyle's class," O'Reilly said. "I was an obnoxious little kid, you know, and I was always making fun of her. I would always just mock her. I mean, it was just something I did." One time she said, "Okay, you have so much to say, William, why don't you get up here in front of the class and say it?"

"Boom. I slip out of my chair, you know, like a clown that I was, and I walk up to the front of the class, and she goes, 'Why don't you tell us about who you favor in the next election?'

"And it happened to be the Kennedy/Nixon election in 1960. I said, 'Okay, Mrs. Boyle. I favor Richard Nixon, because I think . . .' And I just made it up. I just blathered on about why I favored Nixon. I had no idea about who he was. I mean, I knew he was the vice president with Eisenhower, and I knew he was running for something. I mean, I didn't know why, I didn't know what for. I just made stuff up, just off the top of my head.

"And the class was, like, mesmerized. O'Reilly is such a dumb jerk, how is it he knows all about Richard Nixon? And I'm going, you know, he's from California, and he's forward-looking, and he's got new ideas, he could revitalize the economy. I didn't know what I was talking about. I had no idea what I was talking about, but it was just like coming. I was, like, Stevie Wonder. I was just hearing the tune in my head. And I'll never forget it. That was the first time. I said, 'Jeez, I was pretty impressed.'

"After that, I figured I always loved public speaking. So that was always ingrained in me."

Willie Mays was O'Reilly's childhood baseball idol. He treasured his autograph and it still hangs in his house today. His favorite hero in fiction is Dirty Harry Callahan. "I admired individuality," O'Reilly said. "I admire the guy who swaggers in Clint Eastwood–like, takes over. He doesn't really care what people think about him. My heroes were guys who just were individuals who did what they want to do even if it made them enemies." His pantheon of heroes in real life are Jesus of Nazareth, Mother Teresa, Abraham Lincoln, George Washington, Winston Churchill, Eliot Ness, Paul Newman, and Nathan Hale. The political figure he most identifies with is Robert F. Kennedy.

"There have been very few politicians in the contemporary era that I had any respect for, very very few. Because most of them are interested in themselves. It's public service, okay, it's supposed to be for the public. Bobby Kennedy was the exception. He had the fire of a reformer and the determination to get things done. He was one of the few politicians who actually got angry at social injustice. He took unbelievable risks to get people that his family didn't want him to get, you know. Why are you doing this, it's going to hurt us, leave him alone. He was just teed off that the Mafia was doing this and the idiot Southern politicians were doing the Jim Crow stuff. He was personally offended. I mean, that's the way I am."

O'Reilly saw teaching as a worthy contribution to society, as well as fulfilling his need to be the center of attention. He could be the center of attention in the classroom, and it would give him control for an hour or so, and he'd have impact, shaping lives of his students.

O'Reilly arrived in Opa-Locka, Florida, in that summer of 1971 to begin his career as a high school teacher with his closest college buddy, Joe Rubino, who also decided to teach. Marist had an arrangement with Monsignor Pace,

O'Reilly told me. "It was a slave labor thing," he said. "They paid me like five thousand dollars a year to go down there. It wasn't a student-teaching program. They just took us on as regular teachers. You know, those Catholic schools, they just wanted cheap labor. As long as you weren't committing a mortal sin on campus, they didn't care." The school's philosophy was, O'Reilly said, "Poverty is good because Jesus was poor. Unfortunately, poverty was one of the few things Jesus and I had in common."

The Marist Brothers were a teaching order, focused primarily on preparing young men for secondary school teaching level, explained Shaileen Kopec, Marist's vice president for college advancement. "So it may have been natural for the Marist graduate O'Reilly to feel a sense of commitment to teach at a Marist high school."

Joe Rubino had a somewhat different spin on how O'Reilly became the Mr. Chips of south Florida. "Neither of us knew what we wanted to do when we graduated," Rubino said. "But we did have one thing that we knew what we wanted to do, and that was meet beautiful women. We didn't know where, we didn't know how, but we wanted to do that."

While they waited for further revelation about their ultimate vocations, the solution came to them as if an epiphany. Rubino had two words for it: Girls. Miami.

"Somebody had come to us," Rubino reminisced about the decision, "and said, 'You know, there are some Marist high schools affiliated with our college you could teach at.' And they gave us a list. Scotch Plains, New Jersey? We looked at each other, like, you're joking. And then they said there also are some in Pango Pango, Pago Pano, whatever they call it. Bill and I look at each other, and we're saying, 'You mean the island on the other side of the world?' And they said, 'Yeah.' We said, 'Oh, my God, give us this book.'

"Bill and I start going through this book that had all these Marist schools. It's listed alphabetically. All of a sudden we hit the Ms and there it was in little print at the bottom of the page: MIAMI. We looked at each other like we had just struck the pot of gold at the end of the rainbow. We said, 'Oh, my God, Marist has schools in Miami. This is like better than winning on Monty Hall [*Let's Make a Deal*]. This is like unbelievable.'"

Rubino and O'Reilly went down to Miami on senior break. They did what every senior did, partied and had a great time, but they also interviewed. One school wanted to hire only one of them but they wanted to stay together. The second school, Monsignor Pace, hired them on the spot. "Because we told them we'd work cheap," Rubino recalled. "We even said to the principal, we're going to live together, we'll give you a discount. Whatever you pay for teachers, we'll work for less.

"And the principal actually got out his calculator and started adding up, and thinking, like I'm going to save, like, three thousand dollars on these guys."

Back in those days, teachers only got paid $6,000–7,000. "Bill and I agreed to work for less than five thousand dollars. They were paying us like we were members of a religious order." The newly hired teachers drove back to Marist, graduated, and moved to Florida.

The Odd Couple roomed together. "We're pooling our money," Rubino said. "I mean, gas was twenty-three cents a gallon, but still we didn't have much to live on. How could we live on a hundred dollars a week?"

Sister Jan O'Reilly, who was in Florida at a college an hour and a half away, said she didn't know how her brother survived that year. "On pineapples and bananas, I guess."

What they did was look in the newspaper to find out all the bars that had happy hours with a free buffet. "We found a different bar for happy hour seven nights a week," Rubino said. "What we would do is go to a bar. I would order a beer, Bill would order a Coke, you know, big spenders' night. And we would sit there with a seventy-five-cent beer and a fifty-cent Coke, and have our only meal of the day. After a while the bartender would say, 'Are these the guys that buy one drink, gorge themselves, and leave?' So we had to keep finding new places."

Another page from their survival guide: "We accepted dinners at our students' houses and things of that nature." Said Rubino, "We lived by our wits."

Their press credentials from college were a big help, too. There was a faculty meeting on August 23, 1971, their first day as teachers. Everybody introduced himself. In the course of the conversations, somebody pointed out that next door to Monsignor Pace was Biscayne College (now St. Thomas University), where the Miami Dolphins were holding their summer training camp.

Nineteen seventy-one was a big year—the Dolphins went to the Super Bowl.

Don Shula was like a God, one of the most famous coaches in the country. He had coached the Baltimore Colts in the Super Bowl. In the Florida sports time line, this is before the Miami Heat, before the Florida Marlins, before the Florida Panthers. The Miami Hurricanes college football team was terrible. The Dolphins were the only game in town.

During lunch at the Monsignor Pace faculty get-together, O'Reilly and Rubino sauntered over to Biscayne College. They tried to go to the cafeteria. Security said, "You can't go in there, you got to have press passes." So they whipped out their Intercollegiate Press cards. They had to be cleared by Charlie Callahan, the famous former publicity director of Notre Dame, then working for the Dolphins. "Would you believe Charlie Callahan gives us press credentials," Rubino said, "and he gives us season tickets to the Dolphins? And he says if you guys are hungry, go on into the cafeteria."

They walked into the cafeteria, flashed their credentials, were seated at the press table. Who came over to the press table and plopped his tray down next to the Intercollegiate Press journalists? Don Shula.

"So O'Reilly and I look at each other," Rubino says. "We're in town, we're in Miami for six hours, we have press credentials to the Dolphins, we have season tickets to the Orange Bowl, and we're having lunch with Don Shula. Shula is like the Pope in Miami. We look at each other . . . we couldn't believe it."

O'Reilly wanted to look good. So he asked Don Shula a question, pretending he was a reporter. Like how many quarterbacks are you going to keep, two or three? The other reporters at the table asked the boys what paper they were from, and they answered Intercollegiate Press, "And they're going, what? What is that? We're sitting there with Channel 10 and Channel 7, the *Miami Herald* and the *Florida Sun-Sentinel* and we're from the Intercollegiate Press, which, of course, no one's ever heard of, and now they're trying to find out what interest does the Intercollegiate Press have in the Miami Dolphins?"

Their answer, of course, was free tickets. They ended up going to the Dolphins' cafeteria whenever they wanted, having lunch with Don Shula. They got to go to every Dolphin home game, either staying in the press box or on the field. They also ended up getting tickets to the University of Miami games and the Floridians in the old American Basketball Association.

The Floridians were so bad that O'Reilly and Rubino didn't even go to the games. They just went for halftime, because that was when the press buffet opened. The way the two journalists from Marist covered the game: They showed up halfway through the second quarter, sat down, and cheered the Floridians on. At halftime they would go into the press lounge. "We'd have all the food, and everything," Rubino said, "and then we'd leave."

And the girls?

This was the interesting part of the story, according to Rubino. "The guy who hired Bill and me, immediately a lightbulb went off in his brain. This guy has hit a bonanza with us. If I can duplicate this deal with about six or seven more guys, we have a lot more bingo money. So Bill and I show up the first day of class in August 1971, we are two of about eight brand-new never-taught-before twenty-one-year-old teachers."

The word went out among the female alumnae, the women who graduated in 1970, 1969, that there were all these handsome young teachers at Monsignor Pace. All of a sudden at the basketball and football games, groups of beautiful women who weren't students were in the stands, loyal Pace alumnae coming back to meet the new teachers.

"So Bill and I each started dating. We obviously had no shortage of women."

It turned out to be what the two liberated boys from Poughkeepsie agreed was an incredible year. "You talk about living the dream," Rubino said of their second year of teaching at Pace. The fall of 1972 through the spring of 1973, they found a bachelor-type apartment in a place called Miami Springs. Miami Springs is on the north side of the Miami Airport. It was the time when Miami was the capital of the airline industry. Eastern, National, and Pan Am had bases in Miami.

"And our area was stewardess row," Rubino said. "I mean, they weren't just living there, they were hanging from the balconies." Thirty-two years later, Rubino still doesn't know how they managed it. "We lucked out or something. We got the apartment first floor, next to the swimming pool. Every day there was a volleyball game going on with the stewardesses. All we had to do is open the door, and I mean stewardesses were tripping and falling into our apartment. It wasn't like we did anything bad or immoral, but it was just we were the most popular guys on the planet. Everybody wanted to visit us, every male friend was dying to come over to our house."

The two guys were like sultans in the Long Island version of the *Arabian*

Nights with their harem. "We have girls from Marist," Pasha Rubino said. "We have stewardesses. We have other guys who live in the building knocking on our door, saying what do you guys got in there that everybody's in there. I mean, I swear to God, one time we had so many people in our apartment that we ran out of silverware. So I had to run down to a couple of guys who lived down the end, and I said, 'Bill and I have a few guests, we ran out of silverware, can you help us out? Do you have any extra forks and knives?' And the guy says to me, 'Well, if you guys will send some girls over, I'll give you my whole damn kitchen drawer.'"

There is more to being a Catholic high school teacher than having hot and cold running stewardess. There are the students. Classes. Faculty. Principals.

O'Reilly was teaching sophomore English, history, and a couple of other subjects, including one he called "Contemporary Problems."

Prior to O'Reilly's arrival, Monsignor Pace High School had been a constitutional Catholic school, which meant it was coeducational, except the girls were on one side and the boys were on the other side of the school. It was evolving from a strict Catholic high school tradition. In those days, as a freshman you had to wear a white shirt, a necktie, and it was discipline with a capital "D." Some of the teachers were clergy, some lay teachers.

O'Reilly was tough on the kids. Some took to him, some didn't. He still keeps in touch with some of them. Mike Dutko was one of O'Reilly's students. He was a football player who went on to become a cop, then a lawyer. O'Reilly's kind of student.

"O'Reilly showed up with this swagger and style that was a little different than what we were used to," Dutko reminisced when I reached him in his Fort Lauderdale law office. "His style intimidated many of the students, and I think most of the teachers. I thought he was funny. I think he appreciated an audience. The fact that I found his irreverence entertaining sort of created a friendship between us."

O'Reilly as a teacher was less like Mr. Chips than Mr. Kotter. His classes were like *Welcome Back, Kotter*. "He was a wisecracker," Dutko said, "but there was no question that he was really, really bright. He knew what he was talking about."

. . .

"The room buzzed with excitement, as is normal for a class of fifteen-year-old girls awaiting their first day of sophomore English. We wondered who our teacher was going to be and what the year had in store for us. It was assumed that a Theresian nun would be making an entrance at any moment. Suddenly, to our surprise, a tall, blue-eyed *MAN* walked into our room. A collective audible sigh could be heard as this person informed us that he would be our new English instructor."

So Alicia Gonzalez Grugett wrote of her first memory of Bill O'Reilly as a teacher.

"It's been twenty-three years since you walked into my English class," wrote Jennifer King Carnes in her critique of O'Reilly's style as a teacher at Pace, "and began to unlock my mind and open my eyes. And just in the nick of time. Years of Catholic school and a strict disciplinarian father almost turned me into a 'Stepford' woman."

"In addition to the planned curriculum," Carnes continued, "you tried to teach us other things such as being an 'effective' person. You told us to make sure the things we do make a difference—that our message was clear and understood—that our deeds brought the results we intended. Another thing that made an impression was your comments about the stupidity of getting drunk or 'high.' Most authority figures just said, 'No, don't drink. It's illegal.' You said, 'Why do you want to go out with friends and not be yourself? Why act stupid?' It made sense to me, and it broke through all the 'dont's' I was hearing."

O'Reilly former student Gloria Garcia wrote, "With your charm and your gift of eloquence, you prompted us to question and not to assume that others would be acting in our best interest."

O'Reilly's classroom at Monsignor Pace was a discussion-intensive zone. "The first time I remember consciously searching for Truth was in your class," wrote student Ana Ortiz Cooper. "You exposed me to the following ideas:

- There are many sources for Truth—not just one.
- There's a big world out there to learn from, so get out there and keep learning.
- Fight for what you want—you can have it.
- Always keep high standards.
- It's important to express yourself well.

"You've heard of 'the gift that keeps on giving.' To me your class was 'the class that keeps on teaching.'"

Twenty years later, some think he still stands for these things.

O'Reilly was a student-friendly teacher. He organized intramural games, always faculty against students. He would goad the students into playing the teachers. He would look at a bunch of students in a gym class, and say, "You know, it's too bad you guys don't have a touch football team because me, Mr. Rubino, and other faculty members will kick your ass."

And they would jump up and say, "Yeah, you wait and see." And the next thing you knew, there would be a game, and it'd be six sophomores against O'Reilly, Rubino, and four other teachers. As a result, O'Reilly and Rubino developed relationships with students. Every day they'd have a game after school. These students started visiting at the apartment.

Monsignor Pace was not exactly a football powerhouse like Chaminade. If you could run, you were expected to be on the football team. If you could run fast, you were expected to start.

O'Reilly was one of the football coaches at Monsignor Pace—sort of. Traditionally, football coaches are there every day. They work hard every afternoon. "O'Reilly would be there for some practices," said Mike Dutko, who was a varsity wide receiver, a running back, and defensive back, "and would kind of hang out with the quarterbacks and tell them how he could throw the ball better and that kind of thing. He never threw a bad pass in his career, apparently. There were many that weren't caught, but it wasn't his fault. The receiver ran a wrong pattern, he didn't run fast enough, he didn't run slow enough."

But he never missed a game. He would show up on game days and stand on the sidelines next to the head coach and cheer on the football team.

"And, frankly, I wondered if the reason he showed up for the games was because he wouldn't have to pay the admission," Dutko said. "You got to stand on the sidelines. You didn't have to pay to get in. Because he was famous for that sort of thing."

O'Reilly's reputation for frugality was to follow him.

Dutko, who became a boon companion in Miami, recalls one night on the town with O'Reilly. They were at the Playboy Hotel. It had no cover charge in its nightclub, but a two-drink minimum. "If you had a drink in your hand," said Dutko, "they weren't hitting you to buy another drink, right? I remember being behind him the first night, thinking, what the hell are we doing here? I am following him walking in, and we walk near a table, and he says, 'Dutko, pick up that glass.' And I turned. There was a table people had left. He'd pick up a glass; I'd pick up a glass. He said, 'Hang on to that.' I said, 'Why?' Frankly, I wanted a drink. He said, 'They won't hit you up as long as they think you're drinking.' And we walked around thirty minutes holding these glasses. And I was, like, you know, it's fun, and funny, but I'd like a beer. But for him it was the sport of it."

"It was also typical of O'Reilly, a classic case of how he wasn't going to spend a nickel he didn't have to, either," Dutko added. "But guess what? I suspect that today he would do the same thing."

There have been many jokes over the years about O'Reilly's football career at his expense. Whenever anybody mentioned football, O'Reilly was saying, "Football? Who wants to play football?" They would soon be playing touch football in a schoolyard or anyplace. "It was kind of a corny thing," said Dutko, the ex-jock. "But then once everybody was there and having a good time, you were like, 'I am glad somebody thought to do this.' And he has always been the guy who organizes stuff like that."

It was such a Kennedy thing. "Over the years," said Dutko, "anytime he would come down to Florida, it was kind of like a social event for him. Where some people might say, 'Hey, let's get together and go to dinner at such and such,' or 'Hey, let's have a cookout,' O'Reilly always wanted to organize a touch football game. And every time he would come into town, it was pretty much he expected we were all going to get together, the same group of guys, and we would play football. And most often, if I recall correctly, O'Reilly and I were on the same team, and we won."

O'Reilly's other favorite pastime, next to playing football and getting things for free, was challenging authority. He looked for ways to impose his will on the school authorities and found them.

Several of the buildings at Monsignor Pace were the old-style Florida architecture, designed to have open windows and an open door, thus creating a breeze. This was energy-efficient and good for the environment, and worked fine, except when there was no breeze, and the temperature rose. Florida is known to get hot. The newer buildings had air-conditioning but not the older ones.

With the bad luck of the draw, O'Reilly taught every one of his classes in a classroom that was non-air-conditioned. He appealed to the school to install air-conditioning, and his requests were denied.

"He got really pissed off about that," Rubino said. O'Reilly went to a department store and priced out an air conditioner. It was going to be about $400. Then he counted up all the students that were going to be in his class during the course of the day, divided that number into the air conditioner's cost, and decided if every kid gave him some number like $1.75, he could buy an air conditioner.

"Well, sure enough, he took the collection from every kid in his classes," Rubino remembers, "and damn if they didn't buy an air conditioner. And he tipped the maintenance man to install it."

So O'Reilly got his cool air. All the other teachers couldn't believe O'Reilly. Anybody else would have just given up. But he refused. He wanted air-conditioning, and he found a way to impose his will and get somebody else to pay for it.

O'Reilly liked being a teacher. "I felt I helped some students and kept the rest awake. I always prepared for class because I didn't want to waste their time or mine. But the school's dictator of a principal took a different approach. He was perfect for the totalitarian state that is American education," O'Reilly says in the first volume of his autobiography, "laying down foolish rules and ignoring important things. I mocked him at faculty meetings." But that kind of behavior is a dead end, O'Reilly eventually realized. Nothing was going to change. The principal had no respect for students or teachers. He just wanted to keep a lid on things.

A major subject at the school during O'Reilly's tenure (1970–2) was sex. Drugs and rock and roll were minors. As a young teacher, O'Reilly was more relaxed talking about sex than his father or the nuns had been. "But I was careful. Students have a way of misquoting any provocative comments, and that can lead to big trouble in a Catholic high school. Some of my students as young as fifteen were having sex, and almost everyone in the school knew about it. I encouraged the use of contraceptives for any American who did not want to become a parent."

The dictatorship at Monsignor Pace did not like O'Reilly's approach. "They were determined to control the sexuality of the students by threatening them with various punishments for risqué behavior," O'Reilly said. "This, of course, was insane. The more you just say 'no,' the more enticing certain kinds of behavior."

In Florida, Friday night high school football games are big social as well as athletic events. Since the weather in south Florida is hot until Thanksgiving, many of the high school girls were going to the games dressed, as O'Reilly writes, "like Anna Nicole Smith in full seduction mode, hot pants and skimpy halter tops topped the dress hit parade." Many teachers were appalled.

The dictator called a faculty meeting to discuss the menacing problem. One of the teachers asked what proper attire actually was for football games? O'Reilly courageously rose to answer the question. "Okay, proper attire for a football game," he said earnestly, "begins with shoulder pads, a helmet, knee and thigh pads and spiked shoes, but never high heels."

A few of the male teachers actually laughed out loud, but were silenced by the dictator principal's stern glare. Most of the female teachers were aghast that he could be taking this situation so lightly.

The meeting went on for hours. O'Reilly says he headed for the men's room and never returned. The next day he took his own action. He explained to his coed classes that young women who dress provocatively were usually seeking attention and would not be taken seriously by boys. How you dress, he suggested, showed the world what you think of yourself. "So if a girl dresses like a tart or a boy like a bum, well . . . ," O'Reilly said. "After that only the hard-core kids continued to show up at games looking like *Baywatch* extras."

Chapter Three

The Wayward Pressman

In the summer of 1973, there was something big happening in journalism. In the wake of Watergate, the news business was dramatically transformed. Young people were inflamed. Overnight in the post-Watergate environment, journalism was no longer just a job, not even a profession, it was a calling.

Back in the mid-1970s, most journalism students were on a mission. All the best and brightest wanted to become the next Woodward and/or Bernstein. They wanted to right wrongs, clean up corruption, and safeguard democracy. They were filled with the noble desire to expose political chicanery, put the heat on wrongdoers, turn the spotlight on the political knaves, catch the thieves at the till who were robbing the American people blind, thwarting democratic process and the Constitution, trampling traditional American values. The new breed of journalism students were indignant, capable, and angry.

Into this cauldron of do-gooderism, while the pot was just coming to a boil, came an ex-jock from Long Island who had decided to give up teaching English and history in a south Florida high school to join the crusade. Bill O'Reilly was enrolling in the Boston University College of Communication, studying for a master's degree in journalism.

So he "bailed out," O'Reilly says tersely in his autobiography, about his hanging up his teacher's license in Opa-Locka and heading north.

Some might have thought he was having a midlife crisis at twenty-three, but O'Reilly had finally figured out what he wanted to do.

"I started to put things together," he told me. "I said, okay, I got this gift. But I never realized that I could market any of this until I got into the classroom when I saw the kids actually mesmerized by my ability to tell a story and drive a point home about history or English or a book or something like that. And I noticed that kids were flocking to get into my class."

The second thing in his taking stock was that he could write. He was a natural writer, he believed. "I never took a writing course. I just could do it. Let me start merchandising my talents. Let me go back to journalism school and get a master's degree. So I got into the University of Illinois/Champagne-Urbana and I got into Missouri and I got into Boston University. And since my father and mother had both gone to school in Boston and had known Boston, his father said, 'You've got to go there.' And I did."

What O'Reilly originally wanted to do with Rubino, after saying good-bye to his Mr. Chips career in Opa-Locka, was to start a counterculture arts and entertainment newspaper/magazine for Long Island, just like *The Village Voice* or *Rolling Stone*. Seeing themselves as the Batman and Robin of counterculture, the two buddies decided they needed degrees in journalism.

One of the planks in O'Reilly's later platform as a spokesman for blue-collar folks is that he worked his way through college by driving a cab. Both O'Reilly and Rubino drove cabs pursuing their degrees.

Jeff Cohen, a Levittown friend, drove a cab in New York City for a few years. Listening to Cohen tell his cab stories. O'Reilly said, "Hey, this is not a bad way to make money, but it's fun also." O'Reilly would return to Miami on his breaks at Boston University and drive a cab for Metro Transportation. He put himself through journalism school that way.

Somewhere along the way, O'Reilly, the ex-jock gonzo columnist cab driver, and his friend, realized they wanted to go into broadcast journalism as opposed to print journalism. Rubino went to Miami Lakes Technical Institute, which didn't give a degree but offered practical broadcasting experience. While O'Reilly was earning his master's at Boston University's College of Communication, Rubino changed careers completely. He took a management job with the same taxi company that he and O'Reilly drove for, Metro Transportation, then operating thirty-seven taxis from an old Miami gas station. "Next thing I knew I was a vice-president. The company had two hundred cars, three hundred cars, four hundred cars, eventually grew to be the largest transportation company in the country, Coach USA." He is now a consultant in the ground transportation field, advising companies that run busses, taxis, limos, anything that moves with wheels, as Rubino explained. "I don't do planes and trains."

O'Reilly's first triumph at Boston University was getting on the school paper, *The Daily Free Press*. "I just walked in and said I needed a column, you got to give me a column. I said let me knock out few. It was unheard of for a guy to just walk in and get a column."

The editor of *The Daily Free Press* at the time, and its leading columnist, was Bruce Feirstein, who was to go on to write *Real Men Don't Eat Quiche*. In addition, he wrote the screenplays for three James Bond movies, and is a columnist for *The New York Observer*.

"I first met Bill O'Reilly twenty-odd years ago," Feirstein wrote in the *Observer* in 2003. "I was a sophomore editing the daily newspaper. He was a graduate student returning after several years in the working world. One afternoon he strutted into our offices demanding a regular column. He's nine feet tall, and he starts telling me everything I am doing wrong.

"Even then he was referred to simply as O'Reilly," Feirstein wrote. "Even then he could be obnoxious, egotistical, and hilarious—the latter usually occurring when you call him out about being obnoxious or egotistical."

"You're ignoring graduate students," he lectured us. "And nobody's writing about the commuters—Massachusetts residents who can't afford to live on campus."

"O'Reilly was right," Feirstein wrote. "So we gave him the column."

Even back then, Feirstein later told me, O'Reilly's the guy who could strut sitting behind a desk. "And the thing I love about him, that I have always loved about him, was that you could puncture him, you could take the wind out of him, you could cut him down. You could actually look at him, and say, 'Okay, O'Reilly, I think the ego is just about crowding us out of the room right now.' It was always, 'So what network were you fired from now, Bill?' And to his credit he always took it with a grain of salt, always laughed."

"Very funny guy," O'Reilly says of Feirstein today. "We just created all kinds of terror and hell on the campus. That's when I really knew how power-ful the media is." He created terror and hell by just writing about the president of the college.

About the time O'Reilly arrived on campus, John R. Silber was starting his disputatious rule as president of the university. "[The] former philosophy pro-fessor from Texas," Fox Butterfield of *The New York Times* wrote in 1987, "has transformed . . . a mediocre streetcar college once beset by a tiny endowment, a growing deficit and shrinking student enrollment, trapped in the intellectual shadow of Harvard and the Massachusetts Institute of Technology across the Charles River, and made it a well-respected institution. But this progress has come with turbulence." The Boston University campus was a college journalist's dream. Every week there was a new Silber crisis: sit-ins, death threats, and ar-son; strikes by the faculty; a lawsuit by the Civil Liberties Union over a student's right to free expression, and a federal grand jury appearance about his possible tie to alleged corruption in the administration of former Boston mayor Kevin H. White, whom he hired to teach after the mayor quit politics. (Silber was never charged with any wrongdoing.) Ten of the university's fifteen deans and several hundred faculty members called for his resignation. An Immanuel Kant scholar, Silber eventually drove Boston University to become the fourth-largest private college in the nation. He saw no reason to apologize for his huge salary. "I'm not embarrassed to get one quarter of what a mindless anchorman on TV gets," he told the *Times*. President Silber gave O'Reilly a lot to write about.

"We had him," O'Reilly said of the issues that had made the college presi-dent a regular feature in his column. "And then there were the pinheads every-where, and they had plenty of those people on campus. It was unending. Plus, I had the whole city of Boston. Everything. It was just great." At the same time he was a reporter and columnist for the *Boston Phoenix,* the alternative news weekly, and working as an intern in the newsroom at WBZ-TV.

"The issues we were ignoring," Feirstein said, "commuters, Massachusetts, graduate students, we were ignoring. O'Reilly wanted to stand up and fight for them. Then he and I would have at each other in the paper occasionally. It wasn't left wing/right wing. We just argued. It was post-Watergate. So it was—I remember the phrase 'your liberal friends' coming up and 'the soft cushy Long Island kids.' Of course, I was not from Long Island, and he was."

According to Feirstein, O'Reilly's columns got a big reaction. "He was skew-ering a couple of raw things. At the time, if I remember correctly, he was on

Howard Zinn's case. Basically, here was this guy, a distinguished BU professor who was not teaching his course. Who was out protesting everything in the world, everything that America was doing wrong, who was basically teaching that the root cause of everything wrong was white corporate America, and O'Reilly went after him."

In 2003, Howard Zinn said he did not know O'Reilly had attended Boston University and did not recall the columns attacking him.

At the same time, O'Reilly supported bussing, the controversial moving of students from one neighborhood to another with better schools. "You can't pin this guy down in terms of being an ideologue," said Feirstein.

"Even then, you knew he was going somewhere. I saw something in him. When he turned up on TV a couple of years later, it was, well, that's the way it should be."

Zip Rzeppa was a classmate in graduate school, who went on to become a TV sports reporter and worked with O'Reilly at Boston TV stations. He recalls O'Reilly as a student: "He was just a tall, bright, observant, and outspoken guy in the class. But he was under control. He didn't try to take the class over the way he might do today."

O'Reilly wasn't the only student at Boston University who later distinguished himself. Howard Stern was there when he was.

"I knew who he was," O'Reilly answered my question about whether he knew Howard Stern at BU. "Because he and I were the tallest guys in the school, head and shoulders over everybody else. So when you walked down the hall, you'd know him. He was a big, gawky guy. He was floating around the dorms, you know, doing what he did. So there wasn't a lot of contact. But we were in the same school of communications. And I'd see him around. But I didn't have much to do with him. Because I was a grad student, he was undergrad. And I was on the paper. There wasn't any interaction."

Stern was the quietest guy in the class, O'Reilly told Rubino. "He would sit in the back of the room and say nothing."

He changed after graduation.

"So it took me exactly four weeks of grad school to realize I had made the right decision, that this was for me." O'Reilly was summing up his stay at Boston University. He was twenty-four years old at that point.

"Now, I wanted to work in print," the no longer boy wonder said. "But there were no jobs in the fall of 1974. But there were *beaucoup* jobs in the little markets in television."

This was before the invention of cable news networks. The traditional way for a neophyte TV journalist was to work for beans at small-market stations, which were eager to exploit the young journalists, a steady pool of the talented and untalented, all of whom thought they ought to be on TV. After hearing the call to journalism, it would have been logical for O'Reilly to go to one of the seven stations in the New York market and apply for a job as a reporter.

Aside from his communication studies at Boston University, he was qualified in many other ways. He could read. The TelePrompTer is not that easy. Some neophytes tend to follow it like a typewriter. You expect to hear a bell ring at the end of each line as they shift eyes to the left to start the next sentence. He could write. He was a good interviewer. He was articulate, aggressive, resourceful, not quick to take "no" for an answer. Physically, he looked good on camera, had good teeth, nice hair, a nice smile.

Most importantly, he was a native New Yorker. He knew the turf, knowing how to pronounce words like "Hauppauge." He had street smarts. He knew all about the LIRR, and other local jokes. He knew about the LIE. He knew about the joys and anguish of the New York Experience, the clogged arteries of transportation, bad train service, and the Mets and the Jets.

O'Reilly, a brash, pushy New York fellow did not walk into a New York TV station newsroom, and say, "I'm the answer to your ratings, which are sick. When do I start working?"

He had a major defect. His problem was that he was from New York. If you wanted to go on TV news in New York, you had to go out to the sticks first. Native New Yorkers had to work someplace else, perhaps many places out of town, before they would be considered suitable to work in their own hometown. This was one of the verities of TV news of the 1970s, just as people who wore glasses couldn't be on the news.

The mid-1970s were a time of transition in local TV news, especially in the New York market. The veteran New York reporters and anchors, whom

O'Reilly had grown up watching and who made local New York journalism the best in the nation, were being pushed off their thrones. It was also the start of "The Eyewitness News Revolution" at WABC/7, the period in which news was being downplayed in favor of happy talk. Instead of just reporting, newsmen were expected to joke around, trading quips about each other and laughing at their own jokes, few of which the audience was privy to. Ad libbing was a new investigative journalistic tool. Those who couldn't ad lib were in trouble.

Jim Jensen, one of the giants at WCBS/2 news, whom O'Reilly saw himself replacing as anchor someday, had difficulty with the new journalism. A producer once wrote a stage direction on the Channel 2 news TelePrompTer, and Jensen read it aloud: "Ad lib to sports here."

It was the era of the ordinary person as news god, the rise of mediocrity, the skimming off the cream, as management put the old respected names out to pasture. News executives were more comfortable with mediocrity than the superior journalists of the previous generation.

Viewers were supposed to be able to identify with the reporters, not look up to them. Rose Ann Scamardella of *The Eyewitness News*—the prototype for Gilda Radner's Roseanne Rosannadanna on *Saturday Night Live*—was everybody's cousin.

It was also the time of so-called ethnic hires. Sue Simmons met two minority quota obligations: being a woman and black. Race and sex may have been factors in her elevation in 1979–80 to coanchor of WNBC/4's *Live at Five* news hour. She added diversity in another way, as New York viewers would soon learn, she had trouble reading the news off the Prompter. It was as if English was her second language.

If O'Reilly was cocky entering his new profession, he had every right to be. He knew he was better, and he could say it with conviction. A cauliflower would have been better on camera than some of the successful TV news people in O'Reilly's formative years.

O'Reilly was ready to get his first broadcast job. Often the journey began with an internship. O'Reilly decided to serve his apprenticeship in Miami, which he had gotten to know as well as New York.

By the late fall of 1974, O'Reilly had resumed his life in the old apartment complex by the Miami International Airport, where Joe Rubino was still living.

A few days a week, O'Reilly drove a taxicab while he interned at Channel 10, WPLG-TV, the *Post-Newsweek* station, a subsidiary of *The Washington Post,* named after Katherine Graham's late husband, Philip L. Graham, covering the Miami-Fort Lauderdale area.

Even though he was very bright and wrote good stories for the Channel 10 TV news, it turned out to be a tough time for him. At Channel 10 he started receiving professional criticism.

The big criticism of O'Reilly, Rubino remembered, was his voice. "They used to say, 'Your voice is too thin. You'll never make it as a broadcaster with that voice.'" It was fashionable then to do the news as if reading from the bottom of the well or the top of a mount, that news broadcaster voice intoning a story about a two-car pileup on I-95 as if he had just come down with the tablets. Somebody at the station told him he didn't have that stentorian tone.

The station manager was tough on Bill, Rubino recalled. "A lot of the reporters were great to Bill and encouraging, but this guy running the news was telling him, blah, blah, blah, you're never going to make it, blah, blah, blah."

That was all O'Reilly had to hear. He's not a no-can-do kind of guy. Unintentionally, that news executive was probably the most inspirational of the many critics O'Reilly would encounter on the road up. O'Reilly would show him! And all the others, too.

It wasn't easy for O'Reilly to get that first real job in broadcasting. He sent forty-three demonstration tapes to stations all over the country. When he got the results, he was devastated. "I've never seen him so low," Rubino recalled. Of the forty-three tapes sent out, there were only two replies.

One station that would give him a look was in Fort Myers, Florida, the other was in Scranton/Wilkes-Barre, Pennsylvania.

"I don't know which one of these I should take," he told Rubino. "I like Florida. I don't really want to go to either Scranton or Wilkes-Barre." He was pacing the ramparts, mulling over the pros and cons. 'If I get in the north,' he said, 'it might be a little bit better, but I like the weather down here. And it's a growing market. . . .'"

"You know, what's bothering me, Rubino," he finally said. "The guy at Fort Myers who wants to hire me looks like Bud Abbott. I don't think I could work for a guy who looks like Bud Abbott," O'Reilly said. "A guy looks like Bud Abbott can't be serious."

Bill O'Reilly remembers that first crucial decision in his fledgling career differently:

"So I just looked in *Broadcasting Magazine.* There were two small stations, one in Fort Myers, Florida, and one in Scranton/Wilkes-Barre. They were looking for reporters with no experience. I actually went to Fort Myers because that's where I wanted to go. I said, 'Gee, Scranton, I don't want to go there.' But you had to shoot your own stuff in Fort Myers. You had to shoot as well as report, and I can't."

As a cost-saving device, news crews are being reduced all over the country today, but in 1975 Fort Myers was avant-garde, on the cusp of the next economy wave.

"I can't do anything technical," O'Reilly said, sadly. "I mean, I am the worst. It's pitiful how bad I am at that. So I said I can't shoot anything. So I went to Scranton and started my career."

Chapter Four

The Voice of Anthracite Country

I nternship over, the twenty-five-year-old Bill O'Reilly blew into Scranton/ Wilkes-Barre in January 1975 for the interview that would start the meter running on his new career.

The lucky station was WNEP 16, an ABC affiliate, which in 1975 was privately held by a small group of investors in the Scranton/Wilkes-Barre area, including Bill Scranton, former Pennsylvania governor and GOP presidential candidate. A smudge of coal dust on the broadcast map—Scranton/Wilkes-Barre is now fifty-third as a Designated Market Area (DMAs) tabulated by Nielsen Media Research—the station's offices and studios are located in Moosic, Pennsylvania, about halfway between Scranton and Wilkes-Barre.

"I got this call at home from this guy with a Long Island accent, a kid who wanted a job," said Tom Shelburne, then general manager of WNEP 16. "I said, 'I don't think anybody could understand you here. Why would you want to come here?'" O'Reilly told him, "I want to take over the world and be the best. I am going to come down and do a great job for you. You are going to be proud."

Usually, job applicants go through the news director, but O'Reilly had taken a more direct route, starting at the top. That's what impressed Shelburne.

Shelburne claims he gave O'Reilly bus fare to come for his interview. The way O'Reilly remembers his entry into the world of TV journalism is that he drove down from Boston for the Shelburne interview. He appeared in the general manager's office wearing his best powder blue sports jacket and double-knit slacks, midseventies hairstyle, a fashion victim who was only vaguely aware he was an eyesore. "All six foot four of me," he wrote a quarter century later, "looked like a barker at a strip club."

O'Reilly thought they hired him at WNEP because he worked cheap. "It was a shoo-in, because I agreed to work for a hundred fifty dollars a week. This was not smart. After taxes, my take-home pay was about four hundred seventy-five dollars a month. Because there was a rental housing shortage in Scranton at the time, my rent was two hundred fifty dollars a month. And I needed to get a new wardrobe to go before the camera and deliver the news with any hope of being taken seriously. Things were very tight."

He considered his time at "the tiny TV station in Scranton, Pennsylvania," good training, "but no guaranteed meal ticket." He was glad to get it.

"Brash. Cocky. Young kid. Someone determined to get what he wants" was Eldon Hale's first impression of O'Reilly. He didn't present a reel, recalled Hale, then news director at WNEP. A "reel" was the traditional job application, a visual résumé, a compilation of tapes of work on camera. O'Reilly did not have a reel yet, being fresh out of school. WNEP was a very small station and was just beginning to build a news department.

"I hired him primarily based on his attitude, on his aggressiveness," said Hale. "I personally like people who are very reckless, take charge, convinced they can handle it." He especially liked O'Reilly's passion. "There's not a lot of people like him with his passion for the business, with his dedication. I never worked with anybody who worked any harder than Bill at the job."

O'Reilly had a short learning curve in Scranton. "He was terrific," Shelburne said. "The stuff he had to say was good, interesting, and provocative. He had the accent and came on too strong, like a New Yorker . . . We needed these kinds of people to turn this TV station around. He was certainly good in that respect."

The WNEP newsroom had nine people at the time. O'Reilly was one of three general assignment reporters, or "a street reporter." He could go anywhere and report anything. At a network, a reporter turned in one or two stories a week. "He would turn in two or three stories a day," Hale said. "Everybody had to."

Management considered O'Reilly a very good reporter. He was tenacious, Hale remembered. "He came back with facts you could bank on. He did not exaggerate, he did not try to embellish. He came back with the story."

O'Reilly was a very fast writer. He was not what they call in the trade "a bleeder," somebody who takes forever to write a story. O'Reilly handled his own pieces from start to finish. "Because we didn't have anybody else," said Hale. "In those days, you did everything . . . edit film, put together a reel, and then hand it over to the director and then you would walk out onto the set, and that was it. You'd be producing as you went. Drop this story, because it was too long, or add something because it was too short. You did it. You made the decisions."

O'Reilly seemed to have all the basic skills. He was older than the average person out of college, and he was definitely more mature, Hale said. "What we worked on most was making sure that you could prove what you did other than the fact that 'I know it's true.' There were times when he wanted to say something, and I would say, 'You know it, and I know it, but where's the proof? We can't just say what we think. That's what young journalists do. They want to talk about what they think, what they think they know. And so we worked on getting facts to back up opinions."

O'Reilly had to work on that, Hale said, because sometimes he wanted to skip that crucial step.

O'Reilly came to be what local stations call their "action reporter." He was responsible for taking complaints from viewers and seeing what he could do to resolve the issues.

O'Reilly had gone into journalism to see justice done, to use the weight of media to improve society, even if it was only in a corner of northeastern Pennsylvania. He wanted to be a champion of the little people, "the folks," as he was to call them.

"He was very good as the action reporter," Hale said. "He liked the looking-out-for-the-little-guys stories, the consumer stories, the who-got-ripped-off stories. And let's nail them. Bill was definitely one who wanted to right wrongs."

"They loved me," O'Reilly said about his first job as a street reporter and a wise guy. "I was working for no money, and they really appreciated that I was there because the community was responding, and we were getting good ratings."

"We had a really powerful station doing different and real journalism!" said Tom Shelburne two decades later about WNEP 16. "There was no one else reporting from the viewers' point of view."

"That's what we did," said Eldon Hale, the WNEP news director. "We changed Scranton TV. We said we're not just going to go out and do a television story on a politician having a news conference. That's boring. A politician sitting there, speaking into the cameras telling us what he wanted to tell us. The politicians are not the story. The story belongs to the viewers. Tell me how it impacts Joe or Mary."

O'Reilly had an innate understanding of how to reach Joe and Mary Six-Pack. Perhaps, it was because he always thought he was one of them. He was later to have three words for reaching "the folks": emotion, emotion, emotion, a concept later refined at *Inside Edition* and Fox News.

One of O'Reilly's stories as the WNEP action reporter is still referred to as The Dog Lady Case. O'Reilly had interviewed a customer who had bought a sick German shepherd from a woman who was raising them in a kennel in the back of her house. An immigrant, she was alleged to be conducting a lively trade in sick shepherds. O'Reilly and station cameraman John Owens jumped in the company car and were off to confront, interview, and get some pictures of the kennel conditions to document this case of alleged animal abuse.

From Scranton, it took about two hours for O'Reilly and his cameraman to get to the breeder's house. "At the front door, Bill's mission was to try to get some information about how she was selling the dogs," said cameraman Owens. "While Bill was talking to her, I was shooting the pictures of the shepherds from the road."

"I'm not quite sure what went wrong," Eldon Hale said, "but all of a sudden the woman lost it and pulled a large knife out of a drawer, and started waving it at him, speaking in German . . . Because she was very upset at whatever it was Bill had done or said."

"The dogs were out in an open area in the back of the house next to a little gravel road," Owens said. "They started barking because they saw me shooting pictures from the road. She wondered why are her dogs barking? And then she came out and saw me. Waving the knife, she was on the porch, screaming in a thick Germanic accent, "Get off my property! Get off my property!"

O'Reilly and Owens jumped into the car, but the car wouldn't start.

"Bear in mind," Hale said, "we were a very small station. Small budget. The company car was a Toyota, then a box on wheels. Stick shift."

Still waving the knife, the breeder started to come down the steps. O'Reilly jumped out and pushed the Toyota, Owens popped the clutch, and off they went. "Drove all the way back to Scranton in time for the six o'clock news," Hale proudly recalled.

The Dog Lady story aired. According to Hale, O'Reilly didn't mention what happened to him in pursuing the story, "partly because it wasn't part of the story."

That wasn't the end of The Dog Lady Case. The station was contacted by the police. "I forget the charge," Hale said. "It wasn't trespassing. I know she filed a complaint against them with the sheriff's office. The sheriff's department called and wanted to serve O'Reilly, as I recall. Bill was gone. He had left the station, left the state, in fact. And every so often the sheriff would call back and say, 'I want to serve Mr. O'Reilly, tell us where he is, and when he'll get back.' Well, I tell you I don't think it was ever straightened out years after that."

WNEP encouraged enterprise reporting, newsmen coming up with their own ideas for stories. One of O'Reilly's bright ideas was for a Scranton TV newsman to go down to Florida with a cameraman to cover the Philadelphia Phillies spring training camp, interviewing all the star players at the time, like Mike Schmidt. To keep costs down for the station, O'Reilly decided to drive a sunbird's car north. He and Owens flew down, did their Phillies stories, then answered one of the "I need a car driven" ads. Picking up a car in Clearwater, they headed north. "Bill had sort of fooled the station on the fact that we could go down and do this," Owens said. "But also he would do a series on gun control, where he would contrast what Pennsylvania's laws were compared to other states."

They drove through the South, stopping to do stand-ups, pulling into various small towns, filming the gun stores, which were sometimes right off the road, supporting O'Reilly's thesis that it was easier to buy guns in the South.

In a small town in North Carolina, they pulled up in front of one small store with a huge sign out, GUNS FOR SALE. O'Reilly went in, and asked the owner about how difficult it would be for him to buy a gun? "This is without a camera, mind you," Owens said. "He came back out, and said, 'I want to do a stand-up here.' Because there was this huge sign. So we set up to do this stand-up. In the meantime, as I'm filming the outside, I noticed through the back of my eyepiece the guys are starting to come out of the gun shop. They ended up grabbing an empty boat trailer. Very strange, I thought, and I just kept rolling. As Bill is looking back, these guys come running across the street with this boat trailer in tow. Bill jumps out of the way, and the boat trailer sort of smashed into me, knocks me down. At the same time this was going on, a police car pulls up. I had visions of *In the Heat of the Night.*"

"You boys don't belong down here," the sheriff said.

O'Reilly and his cameraman were then escorted into the police station, where they had to explain who they were. The sheriff did not believe they were from a small Pennsylvania TV station. There was a problem, too, with the registration for the car. O'Reilly tried to explain that as an economy for the station, they were driving a senior citizen's car up to Philadelphia.

"I remember them calling Eldon Hale, saying, 'I've got some of your boys down here. They say they work for your television station. They're in jail right now . . .' "Well, we weren't really in jail. We were just at the police department. Eldon was probably trying to sort through this, figure out what we are doing."

"He was terrific," Shelburne remembered about that trip. "He went to jail for us by proving you easily could buy guns somewhere in Florida, or maybe it was North Carolina."

As the idealistic, crusading young reporter, O'Reilly especially liked to interview politicians. He wasn't one of the docile don't-rock-the-boat reporters who went to press conferences and accepted statements and press releases as the gospel truth. He threw hardballs at elected officials, who were used to softballs from TV news. His brash in-your-face New York style of communicating was unexpected.

"I never got complaints that I can recall," Hale said, "other than the dog lady. The photographers would talk about his style because they liked going with him to interviews for politicians. Bill asked them the questions he wanted to ask. He pushed until he got answers—or a stick-it-someplace indication that he was not going to get any."

He did hard-nosed, creative reporting. He was knocking on the doors of voting precincts, Tom Shelburne remembered, "And they closed the door on him because they knew he was coming in to prove that dead people were voting, that kind of thing. People were handing out candidate literature inside the polling area. He was pretty enterprising doing things like that."

His investigative reporting caused some problems for the station. "We were really strong about not interfering with news," Shelburne said. "There were about four stories we actually lost big dollars for his reporting on something. One of them was a repair shop that turned the speedometers back, and he caught them. I think probably Bill was responsible for us losing one of the major banks as a commercial time buyer for about a year for his investigating some of their practices."

. . .

To make ends meet in Scranton, O'Reilly roomed with Owens. Coming from Columbus, Ohio, the cameraman also was on his first job, having started six months earlier. Owens recalled that O'Reilly found a fully furnished, two-bedroom place with a color TV. "Pretty nice. Three hundred dollars a month— that was astronomical then. So he came up to me. Sure, why not? So we were roommates for a short period of time."

O'Reilly always traveled light. He kept his stuff in boxes, which he didn't unpack. He wasn't going to be long in Scranton or any other place on the way to the top. From the beginning, he was looking to move up in markets.

When asked what O'Reilly was really like on his first job in Scranton, Owens said, "He was no different then than he is now. He was opinionated, aggressive, confident. So he was really the exact same person back then."

And he was very ambitious. "I liked working with him because you could make extra money by stringing stories to the network. You could call them up, and say, 'Hey, would you like a story and film on this?' And they would maybe put it on their early news or *GMA [Good Morning America]*. Or they would put it on their feed to other ABC stations in the country. And you would get paid if they used your story. Right off the bat, Bill recognized that. He would make the call, and he would come back to me and say, 'Let's sell it to Eldon.' And we'd do a slight recut for the network, and we'd make . . . I don't know what it was at that time, but any extra money was great.

"Or maybe," Owens continued, "he was assigned something, and he tried to spin it so it might have national interest. He would make a contact with the network and do it that way. I remember we did Muhammad Ali. His training camp used to be in a small Pennsylvania town, Deer Lake, Pennsylvania, in the middle of nowhere. So we went there."

"We did other things we sold that Bill arranged to be shown on the network. He could put that on his reel."

"Occasionally, he would go out," said Owens. "He fancied himself as a ladies' man, but I wouldn't say that I saw a lot of evidence of it. At that time, he might go to a disco, a bar, whereas I would go somewhere to watch a rock-and-roll band. He would dress up and go to a disco lounge, wearing your traditional seventies-style clothes."

"Bill was not the most popular guy in Scranton," said Eldon Hale. "There were some really good people here who didn't get along with him. They used to complain about his abrasive style. He and I had a lot of long conversations about how on a small staff you can't do that, about how not everyone is going to be as direct as you are or think the way you do."

But he did not care. O'Reilly said, "Hey, I'm here to do a job and I'm doing my job, and if you don't like my way, too bad for them. Tough."

In Scranton, O'Reilly was one of those guys who didn't stick around at the office after the day's work was done. More like a blue-collar worker, he didn't appreciate that it might be good to hang around the newsroom and establish relationships. He didn't butter up fellow workers or figure out who could or would help him. He washed up and left the factory as soon as the whistle blew. His work was on the screen. He was developing the what-you-see-is-what-you-get pugnacious attitude that was to be O'Reilly all the way to the top.

O'Reilly's most noteworthy clash with management in Scranton was over money. As frugal as he was, O'Reilly was having a difficult time living on the same shoestring in Scranton as he had in Florida.

"I did a stupid thing," he confessed. He asked for a raise. "After less than two weeks on the job, I complained. I should have waited at least a month." He started with a low salary, Tom Shelburne recalled, and management tried to address his fiscal needs.

WNEP did a lot of "live" TV. Since he was articulate and quick on his feet, the station let O'Reilly do its "live" segment for *The Jerry Lewis Telethon*.

Writing gag lines for the station's Saturday evening monster movie program, *Uncle Ted's Ghoul School*, was Bill O'Reilly's personal telethon. "It brought in as much as an extra twenty bucks a week," O'Reilly said.

At Uncle Ted's, O'Reilly ran into another authority figure. "They hated each other," Shelburne said of Uncle Ted Raub and O'Reilly's working relationship.

Uncle Ted was a fixture on Scranton TV. He began hosting the *Ghoul School* late Saturday night horror show in 1974 and a variety of local live programs over decades. "The sixty-year-old Ted loved the sauce," O'Reilly said. "And I'm not talking Chef Boy-ar-dee here. Ted was usually half in the bag during the telecasts, which were live, and mangled some of my best one-liners."

Not unkindly, O'Reilly suggested to Uncle Ted that he lighten up on the Scotch and soda before airtime. "He came back with a creative suggestion of his own involving my committing an unnatural act on myself."

"I took action which might have been inappropriate," O'Reilly now confesses. When a movie called *Dracula's Daughter* was scheduled, he arranged with a local mortuary to send over a coffin in exchange for an on-the-air plug. O'Reilly suggested to the director that Uncle Ted, who looked like a vampire without using makeup, emerge from a coffin to open his segment.

Uncle Ted refused. It turned out he was claustrophobic.

O'Reilly called the station's general manager, who ordered Uncle Ted to go along with the skit. Infuriated, Uncle Ted climbed into the coffin. "And I locked it from the outside," O'Reilly recalled.

When Ted's live insert was cued during the commercial, he pushed with all his might. The lid stayed shut. The coffin rocked back and forth on live TV. The mike picked up Ted's muffled scream from inside.

O'Reilly stepped in as emcee, explaining to the amazed audience that Uncle Ted had accidentally been exposed to some garlic but would return the next week.

He did; O'Reilly didn't. After nine months at WNEP, an offer had come from a big station for a better job.

Chapter Five

On the Road

O'Reilly arrived in Dallas WFAA-TV early in 1976 even more confident, if that was possible. "I walk in there and I did the same thing as I did in Scranton as a kind of street reporter and wise guy, and they hated me. They hated me. The people watched me, but I was like the Howard Cosell of Dallas."

"The fearless crusader routine," as *Rolling Stone* writer John Colapinto dismissed O'Reilly's common man approach to journalism that had made him an "instant star in Scranton, and caught the eye of one of the country's best local TV stations," was not winning friends at WFAA in Dallas. What had worked in Scranton was annoying his new bosses.

O'Reilly was doing movie reviews on the weekends, and he remembered panning a Disney movie called *Castaway Cowboys*. "I go, 'This is the worst piece of garbage I've ever seen, it's just awful, and Disney ought to be ashamed of itself.' There were pickets the next day in front of the station. And, you know, the station manager didn't back me up. He says, 'What are you doing? Everybody loves Disney, everything Disney is good.' I said, 'No, it's a piece of garbage.' It was just a barrage of criticism."

WFAA-TV—the ABC affiliate in Dallas, owned by the Belo Corporation—was a powerhouse station. Everyone working at WFAA, it seemed, was ambitious, aggressive, battling each other for airtime. It was a faster league for the rookie newsman.

He had gone from a station that had been struggling, climbing, with very few people, to an established respected, fully staffed, nationally recognized news organization. If you were in TV news, you knew those call letters WFAA, and you knew Marty Haag, one of the top two or three most respected news executives in the country.

As far as O'Reilly was concerned, Haag had one major flaw: He hated O'Reilly. On the one hand, management hired him because he was O'Reilly. They wanted him to be himself. But then they discovered they really didn't like that self. A quarter of a century later, O'Reilly told me, "Haag really disliked me, and probably still does to this day, intensely. With some cause. I gave him some grief.

"I mean, I didn't like his style," O'Reilly continued. "You know, he hired some bimbo as an anchor. She had no experience. They threw her on as an anchor, and those of us who were toiling pretty hard would have liked the job."

O'Reilly said so in the middle of the newsroom. "What's this? What the hell is going on? It's outrageous." The room froze. "See, I thought it was not sound to bring aboard an untested anchor, just because she was supposedly running around with one of the station's big shots. Wrong. I found out that it happens all the time in the TV news industry. Bill didn't have that course."

O'Reilly had committed a cardinal sin. A rookie just didn't stand up and criticize a decision to hire a new anchor. Openly challenging an arrogant but successful news director is not the best way to get ahead. He also mouthed off to producers. "Dumb doesn't even begin to cover it," he wrote of the dangerous path he had chosen in Dallas.

O'Reilly's act of bravery regarding management's anchor hire was not appreciated. The rookie newsman was suspended for two weeks for insubordination.

O'Reilly was shocked again. "What insubordination? I had offered an honest and humble opinion, and I had offered it in the interest of giving the public a good newscast. Without freedom of speech, managers and owners of a TV station would not be making money. That's the foundation of broadcast journalism. So where does a station get off suspending me or anyone else for speaking freely?"

He had only been in Dallas for five months. "Haag suspends me," O'Reilly reminisced in an interview. "I'm out of the building. I'm home. I had to go home because: 'You're leaving the building, don't come back for two weeks, blah, blah, blah.'

"Well, I said, okay, fine, two weeks. I was making two hundred bucks a week. No Lava Lite and shag carpets on that budget. I get a call from a guy named Jim Simon, a legendary radio guy out of LA who had just moved to Dallas to start up WFAA-AM Radio, news talk radio. He goes, 'I heard you got suspended.' I said, 'Word travels fast.' Simon liked me. He goes, 'I want to hire you for radio. I'll double your salary.' I said, 'Okay, when do you want me in?'

"It was the same company, the radio's upstairs, television downstairs. He hires me for four hundred dollars a week for the two weeks that I was suspended. I walk back into the studio building, and there's Haag. I thought his blood vessels were going to break. And I just walked up the stairs, and what could he do? Because Simon ran the radio.

"I loved the guy," O'Reilly said. "He was one of journalism's true believers. He knew I had been sandbagged, and he didn't like it. Simon liked me because I was feisty, and I was me."

O'Reilly claims his work had been good in Dallas. "It had to be," he wrote. The powers that be got back at him "with lousy assignments, making Dallas the hell it was. But they had to put me on the air because I came through every time." He won a Dallas Press Club Award, Best Investigative Reporting, for his stories on George de Mohrenschildt, a CIA operative tied into Lee Harvey Oswald in the Kennedy assassination.

O'Reilly told a *Rolling Stone* reporter the level of intense dislike for him in the Dallas newsroom stemmed from his "excess of moxie and too strong impulse for honesty." He was "a straight shooter among spineless coworkers."

His WFAA coworkers saw it differently. "In a business, where there are a lot of reprehensible people," WFAA reporter Byron Harris told *Rolling Stone*, "he stood out as particularly dishonest, obnoxious, self-centered."

After his two-week suspension, O'Reilly was already seeing Dallas and Marty Haag in his rearview mirror.

O'Reilly took his boxes and moved on to KMGH-TV in Denver. He was at Number 32 in the nation's television markets for yet another tilt with authority.

"I didn't really have a confrontation when I started in Denver in nineteen seventy-seven," said O'Reilly. The highly respected news consultants McHugh & Hoffman had urged Paul Thompson, news director of KMGH in Denver, to hire O'Reilly. Thompson had come from KYW in Philadelphia. He was a very experienced news director, and McGraw-Hill hired him to run the CBS station in Denver. O'Reilly was his first hire.

"He is a smart guy. He brings me in and he wants young Turks causing trouble, getting that station attention, because he had two elderly anchorpeople who were going down the chute."

Thompson liked his brash style, paid him well, and allowed him free rein to roam all over Colorado in search of stories. O'Reilly's stories. This was O'Reilly's kind of job: developing stories in his style, in his way.

With a mandate to go out and cause trouble, O'Reilly did. "By causing trouble, I mean I broke stories and chased people around, and, you know, getting a lot of attention. And the ratings went up. And he encouraged that."

O'Reilly also was the weekend anchor at KMGH. He had no trouble at all with Thompson. According to O'Reilly's scorecard, being in Denver working for KMGH was the most fun he ever had in his life.

Unfortunately, Thompson left after a year for a better job. O'Reilly calls Thompson's replacement "Lucifer the Prince of Darkness."

"Are there nine circles of Hell?" O'Reilly writes. "I was sent down to level eight at least."

Divine intervention came in the form of winning his second major journalism award. In 1979, he won a local Emmy for the best breaking news coverage in the Rocky Mountain region, for his reporting of an airline skyjacking at Denver's Stapleton International Airport. The Emmy award became part of the station's advertising, burnishing the corporate image, and made him a hero. Or so he thought.

The Prince of Darkness was O'Reilly's curse. An Emmy on the coffee table is a fine thing, but the backbiting continued out of sight in the offices of upper management. "I still had not learned that you cannot challenge authority in the workplace without lining up some major forces to support you."

O'Reilly began to influence the agenda in the KMGH newsroom, another reason the Prince of Darkness was blowing smoke out of his ears over the New York troublemaker. "Bill was only twenty-nine or thirty," recalled a colleague Bob Cullinan, "but he pretty much ran that place." Cullinan was sometimes troubled by O'Reilly's journalism. "I helped him produce some stories," he says. "He would write the story before he did the interviews. Then he'd get the person to say what fit with his narrative."

Another pattern was discernible in O'Reilly's stay in Denver: his uncanny ability to divide a newsroom. Wherever he traveled, he was like Moses parting the Red Sea, those who hated him and those who loved him.

"One of the things that's never endeared him to people is how remarkably pushy he is," said one former KMGH coworker.

That was what the pro-O'Reilly faction liked about him. After about a year, O'Reilly accumulated a following as the station's news star. Younger reporters were especially awed by him, said Cullinan, then a twenty-three-year-old Nebraskan. The young Turks on the staff had admired O'Reilly's New York style. Cullinan said that O'Reilly cultivated these "disciples." Besides Cullinan, the inner group included Michael Scott and Joe Spencer, who was to become O'Reilly's best friend. The four musketeers would hit the local dance bars, led by Mr. Saturday Night Fever, O'Reilly.

Being on TV regularly since 1975 in Scranton was the greatest dating advantage a man could wish for, said O'Reilly. "There were just so many women floating around."

His social life escalated in Denver when he partied with Joe Spencer. A gregarious, adventurous person, Spencer was the perfect companion for O'Reilly because he loved to spend hours at the Denver bars, trying to pick up women. According to Jeff Cohen, he figured out if he asked a hundred women to go to bed, one of them eventually would.

O'Reilly always seemed to find somebody on their male-bonding adventure trips, Cohen recalled of the time he went to Club Med in Playa Blanc on the northwest coast of Mexico with the two newsmen. "He'd meet this one person, and that was the end. Joe Spencer's idea of sport was finding at least three or four different women. Bill was a lot more particular than Joe."

Every two years, O'Reilly organizes a group of about twenty kindred sprits to embark on adventure vacations. The trips began informally in 1978 with Spencer, Denny Shleifer, and other young Turks from the Denver station. As the years went by, he added sympatico producers, executives, and other broadcast rebels, expanded with friends from grammar school, college, and even a prominent veterinarian from the UK, known as the Birdman, whom O'Reilly had met at university in London. More formal O'Reilly trips began in 1990 with the O'Reilly crew white-water rafting in Hell's Canyon. What the eclectic group had in common was liking O'Reilly and being able to put up with with his ego and his controlling ways.

O'Reilly was the undisputed leader of the band of brothers. He decided where they would go every two years, playing pirates in the Caribbean, helicoptering in Hawaii, white-water rafting on the Snake River, taking mule rides down the Grand Canyon. In 2006, the O'Reilly crew of twenty-two chartered a boat for a snorkeling and scuba diving expedition to Eleuthera, San Salvador, and other islands in the Bahamas.

O'Reilly planned the trips, made the travel arrangements, managed every detail, kept the books, and handed each vacationer a pro rata bill at the end of the trip. He liked being the bookkeeper. His accounting sometimes led to contention within the ranks. On a white-water rafting trip on the Rogue River in Oregon in 1994, Cohen recalled, O'Reilly clashed with a Portland TV producer on the first night because too many bottles of wine had been ordered. "O'Reilly was going to have to pay for some of it," said Cohen. On a previous trip, Bob Cullinan questioned O'Reilly's split of the hotel bill. He thought he was being overcharged for parking. O'Reilly dressed him down in a crowded restaurant at the top of his lungs, Cullinan told a reporter, and they never spoke to each other again.

By O'Reilly fiat, wives and girlfriends were left at home to stew, which created domestic problems. If they couldn't handle it, in O'Reilly's opinion, they weren't worthwhile mates. Several members of O'Reilly's posse almost drowned on white-water trips. But it was fun, all agreed. "You get twelve or twenty guys together and you take over a Club Med and try not to get arrested," explained one member of an early O'Reilly expeditionary force.

In Denver, the Clint Eastwood side of O'Reilly's personality began to coalesce. "I admire the man and the actor," O'Reilly wrote in his autobiography. They had a lot in common. A self-made man who made it on his own, Eastwood had risen from his movie debut in *Revenge of the Creatures* to become the most successful movie star in the world in the late 1970s.

His hero had come to Denver to make what O'Reilly, the ex–movie critic in Dallas, called "one of those dopey monkey flicks" with his girlfriend at the time, Sandra Locke. Clint was making his 1978 comedy classic, *Every Which Way But Loose,* introducing the iconic truck driver/mechanic, Filo Beddo, who moonlights as a bare-knuckle fighter saddled with a loony mother, a dumb friend, and Clyde, the orangutan who steals the movie.

O'Reilly got the plum assignment to interview Eastwood from Lucifer. The Prince of Darkness knew it was an impossible "get." Eastwood was not doing interviews. They interrupted his daily grind of moviemaking. O'Reilly's boss was certain he would come back to the office with egg on his face.

Naturally, a regiment of bodyguards surrounded Eastwood, O'Reilly wrote. "But your young intrepid reporter, O'Reilly, was determined to get an interview. I found out where he was staying, bribed the doorman ten dollars for Clint's room number, and knocked on his hotel door without warning at nine thirty one morning, while my cameraman stood back in the shadows. A bleary-eyed Clint opened his door, wearing a bathrobe, pinned me with that patented squinty-eyed look. The camera was rolling, and I cheerfully welcomed him back to Denver."

In his famous raspy voice, Eastwood said, "Why don't you guys take a hike?"

"Shameless, I explained how an interview with me would be great for *his* career. Clint apparently found that amusing, and said, 'Okay, kid, gimme fifteen minutes, and I'll talk to you.'

"My colleagues were stunned by this coup," O'Reilly wrote. "Clint won greatest guy status in my eyes."

"I was in Denver for two years," O'Reilly said, That was enough in O'Reilly's opinion. "After Thompson left and went to California, they brought in this Lucifer, who O'Reilly said "destroyed the whole station. I said I ain't working for this guy." In 1979, O'Reilly left KMGH.

Before leaving Denver, O'Reilly acquired an agent. Joe Spencer's father was a radio guy, O'Reilly explained. He owned two stations in the Schenectady, New York, area. When Spencer and I got to the point where we needed representation, he recommended N.S. Bienstock. They took both of us." Carole Cooper became O'Reilly's rep. He kept her busy.

O'Reilly next landed in Hartford, where he finally had his first official full-time anchoring the news job, coanchor on the WFSB-TV news. By 1980, a magazine reported, he was let go because of what the station called "a conflict of chemistry."

Naturally, O'Reilly had a different spin on the situation.

"In Hartford, another unbelievable occurrence," O'Reilly was telling me. "This is why I believe God is looking out for me.

"I go into Hartford. There's a *Post-Newsweek* station. WFSB-TV. They hire me and this guy from Detroit named Don Lark. He's now in Syracuse anchoring the news. Anyway, I don't know this Lark from Adam, didn't know him, didn't really care." Carole Cooper always negotiated good contracts for him, he explained. "I mean, I get paid well, and everything is spelled out in the contract."

"And I went in and was coanchoring the six and eleven news with this Lark.

Both about the same age. I was thirty years old at the time, maybe he was thirty-three. Anyway, immediately, after like two weeks, I mean, I was blowing the guy off the desk. Because he was boring. And, you know, I'm me."

Lark knew he was being hit by a windstorm. He went in to Bill Ryan, the general manager who hired O'Reilly, and said, "I have to open every newscast. It has to be 'Hi, I'm Donald Lark,' and then he can say something. But I have to open." Up to that point, Lark was opening three and O'Reilly two. "I'm not a line counter like a lot of these guys are," O'Reilly said. "I don't care about that. If it's close to fair, I'll take it, all right."

O'Reilly was stunned when Ryan said, "Well, I'm going to give him what he wants. You have to pull back." I said, "No, you're not. You're not going to diminish my role because this guy's insecure. I kept asking Ryan, who is not a bad guy, 'Why did you hire me? I mean, you know what I did in Denver. You know what kind of very aggressive reporter and anchor I am, and now you're telling me not to be aggressive? Why? What's the point?'"

"Well, this is a conservative market," Ryan said.

"Why don't you hire another Don Lark?" O'Reilly suggested. "I mean, there's plenty of boring guys around, you know, they're legion."

O'Reilly told his agent, Carole Cooper, what was happening. "I thought she was going to have a stroke. Basically, I said, 'Carole, look, this isn't working out.' 'Wow,' she said, 'you've only been there like two minutes, what do you mean?' I said, 'This is not what you said it was.'"

Nine months and he was on the street again.

Chapter Six

New York, New York

Television news had brought O'Reilly's emerging vision of what is right and wrong in journalism to the people of Dallas, Denver, Scranton, not to mention Wilkes-Barre, and environs. The people O'Reilly wanted to reach were in the New York market.

New York was still the center of O'Reilly's universe. It was where he had to be the star, a center of attention, to be seen by the folks, starting with his father. Coming to New York would make it official that he was somebody. In 1980, "the unbelievable occurrence" after leaving Hartford happened. CBS offered him a job in New York City, the number-one market in the country, a huge step up the career ladder.

The job being offered wasn't on the local news, but on a local news magazine. At best, it figured to be a backdoor entrance to the big stage.

O'Reilly was lucky. Jeff Schiffman was the vice president of programming at WCBS/2, the CBS flagship station in New York, and loved O'Reilly's style. He offered him a job anchoring, interviewing, and doing commentary on a half-hour magazine program called *7:30 Magazine*. "I took the job," he said, "and that's what really put me into the big leagues."

Schiffman had known O'Reilly since his Boston University days. "He was my intern at WBZ-TV, Channel Four, in Boston."

Lincoln might have freed the slaves, but not if you worked as an intern at a local TV news show. O'Reilly was a very tall intern. "You could see his head everywhere in the newsroom," said Schiffman, who had been the news director. "But there was a quality to him, as I recollected even then. Aside from intensity, there was a real kind of doggedness about getting in there and doing as much as he could and taking advantage of any opportunity that was put his way and making himself useful. I don't remember him complaining then, which is something different from what I remember later."

Over the years, Schiffman would see and talk to his former intern about O'Reilly's adventures in broadcast journalism. "Usually I would hear how underappreciated and unhappy he was. He was never happy in Scranton, Dallas, Denver. He was never happy in terms of challenges or opportunity or acceptance." He was also not beloved, Schiffman said, ticking off O'Reilly's career problems. Schiffman felt he could trust O'Reilly to work his tail off. "On the other hand, there's no question that Bill has a somewhat sizeable ego. He is abrasive. In the somewhat political and collegial atmosphere of a typical television newsroom, he rubbed people the wrong way very often.

"What I remember from that time," said Schiffman about O'Reilly's work style, "was a kind of constant never-ending chatter from Bill about ideas, stories, what was good, what wasn't good, what we should do, where we should go, how we should do it. He never stopped, never. And then, when the decisions were made, he would never stop criticizing the decisions. He never shut up."

If you woke him at 4:00 A.M., Schiffman imagined, he would say, "I don't like this bed. They should make this bed with . . . Bill always wanted to be in a position where he would be able to deliver his criticisms and comments, and he would do it at meetings, do it behind closed doors and in front of closed doors, it didn't matter. He also had something of a survival instinct. I mean, he didn't want to always be out on the street. So if he ran into a really stiff authority figure he might, sure, he would listen. And then you were sure to hear about it later.

"If he didn't feel there was a deep enough appreciation for something he had done—and it was usually a nuance: 'Did you see my cutaway question in the middle of this boring story?' it would be even at that level—then he would say, 'Well, you know, of course, the idiot who is running the show didn't understand the massiveness of the contribution and the intelligence, the brilliance of the idea.'

"I think of Bill's memory as being like a real file cabinet," Schiffman continued. "I mean, he can dip back into that with absolute certainty. I mean, he will remember incidents, usually negative, about people, who he has long ago eclipsed and doesn't need to think about it or worry about it, and he will still have the same level of intense negative feeling about them, as he did four seconds after it happened.

"And he just never, doesn't give that stuff up. I believe that fuels him, has always fueled him. I'm not a psychiatrist, but I've always believed that the drive Bill had came somewhere from his feeling that he was underappreciated. If he had gotten a lot of affection and love and appreciation in his work early, I'm not sure where he would have ended up."

Of all the managers he worked with, Schiffman said, "I think Bill will tell you I was the only one he identified as a manager who somehow wasn't the total asshole in his life."

O'Reilly had stronger opinions about the Channel 2 station chief executive at the time, Ed Joyce. The first difference of opinion O'Reilly had with Joyce was over the cancelation of his show, *7:30 Magazine*. It was doing very well in the ratings, beating reruns of *Mork & Mindy* in the New York market. The inexplicable reason, according to O'Reilly: "Joyce didn't like Schiffman."

It was to turn out Joyce didn't like O'Reilly, either. On the upside, after canceling the magazine in 1980, Joyce did put O'Reilly in the newsroom at WCBS/2.

At last, he had made a New York TV news show. Not just any one, either. The Channel 2 News happened to be O'Reilly's favorite news show at home in Long Island.

CBS's heavily promoted local news hour on busses, subways, and billboards around town, was dubbed *The Channel 2 Newsbreakers,* anchored by the iron man of New York journalism, Jim Jensen. John Stossel, Steve Wilson, John Tesh, Tony Guida, Jerry Nachman were among the famed Newsbreakers O'Reilly would be joining. Famous athletes did the sports: Pat Summerall and Kyle Rote of the New York Giants.

For a long time the Deuce, as it was called in the news business, was the most prestigious of local news shows. WCBS was the flagship station of CBS considered "the Tiffany network," and the Channel 2 News was its Hope Diamond. The news still had the imprimatur of Edward R. Murrow before executives like Van Gordon Sauter and Ed Joyce turned CBS News into Filene's Basement.

O'Reilly did not get along well with Joyce, the general manager of the

Deuce. He felt he should be anchoring the Channel 2 News, which wasn't exactly how management saw it. They did let him anchor the weekends. Sometimes. Which only fueled his anger.

O'Reilly had arrived at the Channel 2 News in June 1980 during a state of transition, or what some called a state of chaos and confusion. Following the influence of Van Gordon Sauter, who had made a name for himself in Los Angeles at the local CBS affiliate, the news hour was expanded to two hours. In LA, there were four hours of local news, even though practically nothing ever happens there besides traffic on the freeways.

The game of musical anchor chairs to fill the added time slots was being played briskly. Jim Jensen, who had long been the station's marquee anchor, had been replaced as anchor in chief by the hot young newsperson Michele Marsh. She had come to New York from a small Maine station, with a brief stop in San Antonio. Six months before, she was doing the news in Bangor, Maine, where she had to run the TelePrompTer with her toe. Rarely had a woman in broadcasting come so far, so fast, with so little.

Marsh was a very good newsreader, a credit to Northwestern University, where she trained for journalism by being a theater major. Her major talent was a perky yet sultry voice. She also had the biggest pair of shoulders on TV since Clark Kent and Joan Crawford. There was a steamy quality to the way she delivered the news. The New York intelligentsia loved her. "If she is not the Walter Cronkite of her generation," said one of her fans, "at least you have to concede that she is prettier than Rolland Smith."

It was the Cinderella story of TV journalism story. She wore the glass slipper for a while but was soon replaced by Dave Marash, the respected, hard-edged former WNBC/TV newsman who had left Channel 4 two years earlier in 1978 to work for Roone Arledge, then launching Ted Koppel's *Nightline* at ABC News and was returning to the rival WCBS/2 in April 1981 to replace Marsh. News consultants said the Deuce was becoming soft-edged. After being thrown overboard, ex-anchorwoman Michele Marsh would be continuing at Channel 2 as an investigative reporter. Others on the reporting staff—once the most venerated in New York—laughed up their sleeves.

When Channel 2 had started the expanded two-hour news experiment, anchorpeople were being moved around like marbles on a Chinese checkers' board, Sir Rolland Smith, as the distinguished mustached newsreader was called, and Dave Marash began as coanchors. In January 1982, *The Newsbreak-*

ers had the first trianchor team in local TV history with Michele Marsh returning as a third anchor. Getting her second shot, the sultry Marsh had become
even steamier.

O'Reilly was overlooked on the bench while all of these wheels were turning. Working as an investigative reporter at the Deuce, he had won a local
Emmy for his exposé of the City Marshal's Office. "He was the guy who
evicted people in New York City," O'Reilly explained. A graybeard veteran
compared to Marsh in terms of actual experience, he waited for the call from
Coach Ed Joyce to go in there and save the game. The weekend anchor O'Reilly
was not even on the bench for the Big Game but in the Channel 2 parking lot.

Channel 2 had been the market's leading hard news program. The previous
year, something peculiar started to happen. Channel 2 became the main competition for the *National Enquirer* and *Midnight Globe*. All the famous Newsbreakers left, including Steve Wilson, John Stossel, John Tesh. They lost Jerry
Nachman twice, once as a reporter, once as an executive. They were playing the
theme from *Exodus* in the corridors of the Channel 2 News building on West
Fifty-seventh Street.

No one person could get the credit for the disintegration of the nation's best
local news show. It occurred most rapidly under the guidance of general manager Ed Joyce, who was soon promoted to a very important vice president's job
at CBS News under the new president Van Gordon Sauter. He later replaced
Sauter briefly as president of CBS News when Sauter fell or threw himself from
power at Black Rock in 1986.

The revolving door journalism at Channel 2 News under Ed Joyce was responsible for O'Reilly being at Channel 2 News, but he couldn't understand
why others were ahead of him in anchoring duties and general esteem. O'Reilly
watched all the machinations in disbelief.

Ed Joyce was a hard-nosed, hard-hearted enigma of a local station executive
when O'Reilly first made his acquaintance. Joyce had managed to rise through
the ranks of lowly station managers, going from one big CBS affiliate to another, to president of CBS News with, as it was said, no more soul than a shark.

Joyce had a unique management style. A bright, articulate man, he didn't
have a college degree but was extremely well-read and held his intellectual
ground with most in the CBS organization. He was aloof, unlike his boss, Van
Gordon Sauter. While Sauter roamed the halls pressing the flesh and dispensing
breezy salutations ("Hi, big fella"), Joyce kept to his office much of the time.

He didn't know how to get along with people, said Bob Chandler, vice president of administration for Sauter and Joyce. "He was shy, afraid, or, in compensation, he'd go the other way and suddenly get very tough, needlessly so, abrasively so."

His major function at CBS News was serving as Sauter's hatchet man, the designated bearer of bad news. Joyce was known as the "Velvet Shiv" bearing bad tidings—there was too much money being spent on this, no budget available for that—and it was Ed Joyce who did the firing and reassigning and demoting of people. "Joyce got all the shitty jobs," CBS Evening News executive producer Ed Fouhy said.

News star Bill Kurtis described the experience of working with Joyce as head of CBS News: "We don't see him for six months. Six months, doesn't pick up the phone. Doesn't walk down the hall. I thought he was mentally ill."

"He had a lot of charm about him," said Ned Schnurman, the late public TV producer, who had been a deskman at Channel 2 News in Joyce and O'Reilly's day. "Great sense of humor. But he was a real skunk. He had a way of complimenting people so they didn't know they were being fired."

The workplace at Channel 2 was not improved for O'Reilly by the addition of another executive on the news management team, Marty Haag. He was the famed news director who'd hired O'Reilly at WFAA in Dallas.

"That was another sneaky one," Schnurman recalled. "Whichever way the wind was blowing that was how Marty Haag was blowing. That was the way the whole team was. When he was there, you made sure you didn't turn your back. Even if you didn't, you were still in trouble. They were a perfect team. They could stab you in the back while they were standing in front of you. That's how good they were."

They both were "a pain in the ass to O'Reilly," Schnurman recounted. "He never got along with them. It was the one time I was ever on Bill O'Reilly's side."

Although Haag never missed a chance to bad-mouth O'Reilly, in O'Reilly's view it was Ed Joyce who gave him a hard time at CBS. "Joyce didn't have much use for me.

"I'm a rebel. A lot of these guys in TV are power-mad, and if you come in cocky, not afraid of them, not deferential to them, not kissing their butt, which I never do, they say, 'I'm going to take this guy down, I'm going to show this guy who's boss.' I saw it everywhere I've been. I usually would antagonize these people. To my own detriment many times."

O'Reilly-Joyce relations went south in the 1981 Governor Carey Incident. O'Reilly was the eleven o'clock reporter for Channel 2. He would come in and do the eleven o'clock shift, but usually they'd make him do a report for six as well. Governor Carey and his wife, Evangeline Gouletas, were to appear at Bloomingdale's for an Irish Night. That day *The New York Times* ran a poll on the front page. It said 60 percent of New Yorkers have an unfavorable view of Evangeline Gouletas and were holding it against Carey. Tony Guida, the political reporter, refused to ask Carey about the poll, citing how he didn't want Carey to get mad at him. He said, "If I ask, he's not going to talk to me again."

"Which is the way the game is played with these guys," O'Reilly said. "So Cohen [news director Steve Cohen] comes back to me, and says, 'Guida won't ask him. You have to ask him.' Because they knew I'd ask him, I don't care."

O'Reilly went to the Bloomingdale's event. There was a receiving line. The governor and his wife came down.

"Governor, Bill O'Reilly," he began the interview.

"I know who you are," the governor said.

"I don't want to be rude, I know your wife is here. But I have to ask you about the *New York Times* poll and 60 percent of the New Yorkers have an unfavorable view of your wife here, what do you think?"

Governor Carey let O'Reilly have it. "You are the rudest son of a bitch I have ever seen, and you're embarrassing my wife here, and, listen, I'll never talk to you again."

O'Reilly recalled, "He goes on for two minutes. 'Blah, blah, blah.'"

The Channel 2 cameras are rolling. O'Reilly rushes back to the newsroom, and they run the interview unedited. "Jensen was on. Boom. O'Reilly. Here is the confrontation. Two minutes of him in a tirade. Okay."

The next morning O'Reilly came into the station. He thinks he's going to be the biggest hero in the world. "Right away, I get a call. Come into Steve Cohen's office. I said (to myself), I'm going to get a raise. This is going to be tremendous. I'm going to be the next Arnold Diaz." Diaz, a star investigative reporter, still remained at the *Newsbreakers* after the Exodus.

"I go into Cohen's office. Cohen's looking at his shoes. He goes, 'We have to go down and see Ed Joyce.' I thought great, we are both going to get raises. This is tremendous. Everybody in the city is talking about it. It's going crazy. And Cohen goes, 'There may be a problem.'"

O'Reilly and Cohen went down to Ed Joyce's office. "Joyce is there with his little suspenders, his little Heinrich Himmler glasses," O'Reilly remembers. "He goes, 'You were rude to the governor. We can't have that here at Channel Two.'"

O'Reilly said, "What are you talking about? I just asked him a question that everybody wanted asked. I wasn't rude. If you look at the tape, I didn't say anything to him."

"Joyce says, 'You were rude, blah, blah, blah,'" O'Reilly recalls. "Cohen is still looking at his shoes, and he's not saying a word, not sticking up for me. So I knew there was something there."

O'Reilly didn't say anything. "I just absorbed this from Joyce for five minutes. It wasn't a tirade. He wasn't yelling. He was just saying this was rude and unacceptable and our reporters don't do this and all of that. And I don't know what he was talking about because I did exactly what I should have done."

O'Reilly walked out with Cohen and said, "What the hell was that all about?"

"I'll tell you later," Cohen said.

He never told O'Reilly, but another guy did. "I can't tell you his name," O'Reilly told me, "because he still works for CBS. He pulled me aside, and said, 'Bill Paley called Ed Joyce. Carey called Paley at home. Dead. Get rid of this O'Reilly, he's a son of a bitch.' Paley called Joyce and said you get this under control, blah, blah, and that's what Joyce did to me."

Another sign that he might have trouble getting ahead at the Deuce was his heart-to-heart talk with Morley Safer. It took place in the CBS cafeteria.

O'Reilly happened to be standing on the line one day when in walked Morley Safer, one of the stars of top-rated national show *60 Minutes*. Safer must have been in a hurry, O'Reilly theorized, "because he cuts into the line ahead of me and others. Nobody said anything, except for one solitary individual. Me. I looked Morley in the eye and let forth with, 'There's a line here, sir.'" Safer duly stepped aside and went to the back of the line, but he was not happy. "That's why I'm Mr. Popularity."

It was such a typically New York reaction by a New Yorker to an injustice. And it wouldn't have mattered to O'Reilly, either, if William Paley himself had cut in the line. Right is right in the O'Reilly code of justice. O'Reilly is the true democrat; we're all equal on a New York City line.

In March 1982, with the local Emmy for investigative reporting at the Deuce under his belt, CBS News, the network news division, offered him a job as a correspondent. CBS News president Sauter liked O'Reilly, even if Joyce didn't. This is what O'Reilly wanted. It had only taken him seven years to go from the anthracite mines of Scranton to Black Rock in the Big Apple.

It should have been his big break, but it wasn't.

"Why did people keep hiring me?" O'Reilly asks rhetorically in *The O'Reilly Factor: The Good, the Bad, and the Completely Ridiculous in American Life.* "I had worked at four different TV stations in five years. So, of course, I was experienced enough now to operate within a large bureaucracy.

"Yeah, and Al Sharpton cares for all Americans. I was about as perceptive as a telephone pole. Besides, I had no stomach for playing the corporate game. I enjoyed being a maverick. I relished my defiance of corrupt authority and my doomed crusades for justice in the newsroom. I insisted on being treated with fairness."

So O'Reilly marched down the halls of CBS News like his idol Clint Eastwood. "This was the same Dirty Harry attitude that had already gotten me in trouble in three different time zones. I was completely out of my mind. I became notorious."

Chapter Seven

Cry for Me, Argentina

———————

O'Reilly was sent to Argentina to cover the Falkland Island War of 1982. Fresh from El Salvador, where he had begun doing investigative reporting covering the dirty guerrilla war, much of which wasn't getting on the air since foreign news had a low priority on network news in the Van Sauter regime, O'Reilly arrived at the Buenos Aires Sheraton Hotel where CBS News had set up offices, eager to show his stuff. He was part of a large contingent of CBS News reporters, cameramen, and producers, the most famous of whom was Bob Schieffer, soon to be CBS News' chief Washington correspondent, anchor, and moderator of *Face the Nation* and anchor of "*The CBS Evening News Without Dan Rather.*"

The rookie CBS News correspondent O'Reilly and the veteran Schieffer had different attitudes about the war. In his autobiography, *This Just In: What I Couldn't Tell You on TV,* Schieffer called it "a ridiculous war over barren real estate which Darwin called one of the ugliest places on earth." What Schieffer remembered most about the experience of covering the war was the cuisine of Argentina. The specialty of his favorite Buenos Aires restaurant, La Mosca Blanca (The White Fly), Schieffer told about what he couldn't tell on TV, was a steak called *bif de lomo,* a huge cut of meat that filled a platter large enough to hold the average American family's Thanksgiving turkey. Atop the steak, Schieffer recalled, the cooks would add an enormous mound of fried potatoes. Atop the fries would be two over-easy eggs. Atop all of this—and by now the stack of food seemed about a foot high—would be strips of grilled peppers. "That was the main course," wrote Schieffer. "We usually ordered some kind of meat appetizer, barbecued ribs, perhaps, to start. La Mosca Blanca was not the place to cut back on cholesterol, and why the entire nation had not already died of heart attacks (they also smoked incessantly), I never understood. . . . In Argentina, we ate as if there were no tomorrow. After all, we told ourselves, there was a war going on, and we could all die. Actually none of us believed that. The food was just too delicious to resist."

For O'Reilly, the Falklands War was a testing ground, a chance to show his bosses back in New York how good he was. His being on the *Evening News* also would be validation for his father that he was a network foreign correspondent, that a major corporation was wise enough to have faith in him.

On this assignment, Schieffer would get plenty of "face time," on-air appearances on which a correspondent's ranking is dependent. "Over the next three months, I would file more than forty *Evening News* reports from Argentina, more than eighty pieces for the *Morning News,* and anchor several Saturday *Evening News* broadcasts from there, one from the balcony of the Casa Rosada, the Argentine presidential palace. Tom Fenton was covering London's side of the story, and our reports would often be placed back-to-back on the *Evening News.* For thirty straight nights, one or the other of us was the lead story and the other was second, a string I have not matched since."

All hell broke loose the day O'Reilly landed in Buenos Aires. The Argentines surrendered to the British. Thousands of Argentines took to the streets screaming for the head of President General Leopoldo Galtieri. The mob stormed the presidential palace, the Casa Rosada, and were met by the army. A riot broke out, and many were killed.

O'Reilly was ordered to get down to the Casa Rosada as fast as he could. He covered the mob pelting the government troops and police with rocks and coins. The crowd was chanting *Nunca La Derrota* ("Never surrender"), *hijos de putas* ("sons of bitches"). And O'Reilly was there when it all went down, engulfed by the mob, cameras rolling.

Without warning, the troops began firing. The mob panicked.

"I was right in the middle of it," O'Reilly recalled, "and nearly died of a heart attack when a soldier standing about ten feet away pointed his M-16 automatic weapon directly at my head. *Perodista por favor, no dispare!*" O'Reilly used the phrase that every Latin American correspondent was required to know:

"Journalist. Please don't shoot." "But, again, God was good," O'Reilly said. "The soldier didn't shoot and that indelible moment passed."

One of his cameramen was trampled. O'Reilly and his crew had to abandon an expensive camera. "All of us got banged up in the panic," he said. "Many, including me, were tear-gassed."

O'Reilly had it all on tape.

After several hours of pandemonium, he managed to make it back to the Sheraton with what he said was "the best news footage I have ever seen. This was major violence up close and personal, and it was an important international story." This time he knew he'd be leading Dan Rather's program.

"Tell New York I've got four tapes of riot footage," O'Reilly told a startled technician, bursting into the transmission room ten minutes before *The CBS Evening News with Dan Rather* was scheduled to go on the air. "Incredible stuff. No time to edit."

None of the other networks had any video from Buenos Aires until twenty minutes later. It was a stunning victory for CBS News. O'Reilly was elated. Now he would finally get the recognition he deserved.

The next day O'Reilly discovered that his footage had made the show, but he had disappeared. He was furious. "I was there when it all went down, who actually covered this thing, who almost got killed doing so. Doesn't that mean anything?

"Nope," he said. "In perhaps the most stunning thing that has ever happened to me, all the videotape was taken away from me and given to a big-name correspondent who was also slotted into *The CBS Evening News* to report the lead story." O'Reilly's exclusive footage wound up being incorporated into the nightly report from Bob Schieffer, which failed to mention O'Reilly's contribution.

That man had never even left the hotel to *see* the story, O'Reilly said. Yet the CBS producers made him the star. "In the parlance of network news, I had gotten 'big footed.' " "Big footing" is the high-tech procedure that allows a lowly foot soldier's reportage to be replaced by a star correspondent's pearly words.

O'Reilly had been voiced-over and vanished in Buenos Aires. Nobody was going to take his story away from him. He did it, therefore he deserved the credit. He was not going to be like his father taking crap from the system.

"To say I was angry is the understatement of the millennium," O'Reilly wrote. "I got the hell out of Argentina fast, landed in Miami and raised a major ruckus at the CBS offices there. The bureau chief, my direct boss, told me to pipe down. I told him to, well, 'rethink his tone.' A few days later I was called back to New York for consultations."

He returned to CBS headquarters on Fifty-seventh Street, marched into Dan Rather's office, and let loose. " 'What the heck was this?' I asked. 'What if a correspondent who wasn't even on the scene, Dan, stole your famous reporting during the Kennedy assassination? What would you have done? How can you abide by this?' "

Dan Rather was polite, O'Reilly recalled. "And I think I saw some sadness in his eyes. He said he'd look into it. I didn't believe him."

His highly principled stand turned out to be his one-way ticket to Siberia at CBS News. After questioning the system in a very public and assertive way, as O'Reilly explained, "I became a 'dead man walking' at CBS News."

The Buenos Aires riot coverage was another feather in Bob Schieffer's cap. Schieffer, incidentally, was rewarded for his work in Buenos Aires, replacing Marvin Kalb as the CBS News State Department correspondent, his biggest promotion since replacing Dan Rather at the post–Nixon administration White House.

Coincidentally, a character resembling Bob Schieffer appears in O'Reilly's first work of fiction—a 1998 suspense thriller titled *Those Who Trespass: A Novel of Murder and Television*," which the book jacket described as being a story about how "one by one high-level executives and correspondents are being murdered in the brutally competitive world of TV journalism." The Schieffer look-alike plays corpse #1. But I'm sure it's just a coincidence, as are the other five murders of those who made the story's anchorman angry.

Chapter Eight

The Boston Massacres

Ed Joyce, who had replaced Sauter as head of CBS News, didn't fire O'Reilly after Argentina. The Velvet Shiv just told him he should "start looking around." He decided to look around in Boston.

While most talent lives in fear of losing their jobs, for O'Reilly it was not the end of the world. His agent, Carole Cooper, could always find a small station that would be attracted by the very things the self-satisfied #1 station would not tolerate.

His entry-level job in Boston in October 1982 was at WNEV-TV, formerly WNAC-TV, a CBS affiliate, a troubled third-place station in a three-station market. At the suggestion of the station's general manager, Winthrop (Win) Baker, News Director Nick Lawler hired O'Reilly. They both remembered O'Reilly from Scranton/Wilkes-Barre, where he had been the voice of Anthracite Country. That was the voice they thought they wanted at Channel 7 in Beantown, too.

Lawler thought O'Reilly had an ability to communicate on television. "He had a charisma. A lot of television reporters don't have that charisma. They don't reach through on the tube. He knows how to talk to people on TV."

Not only did he have a great persona on TV, Lawler said he was struck by O'Reilly's teases. A tease is the line of print at the bottom of the screen telling you a big story is coming. It also can be spoken. Tease writing is probably the most difficult writing in television. Most of the time it gets done very poorly. "I remember watching and listening and just smiling at O'Reilly's teases, and, gee, I had no idea that I was really hiring such a craftsman," Lawler said. "He would write some of the best that I ever had heard." O'Reilly seemed to understand a basic premise of television that a lot of journalists don't: You reached the intellect through the emotions, whereas newspapers might reach the intellect. "He just had a way of zeroing in on the human element of the story in his teases and stories," said Lawler. "Like a laser, he would focus on issues that actually came across on TV."

Hired as weekend anchor and reporter during the week, O'Reilly quickly commandered the weekend broadcast. He was happy writing a good portion of the newscast. Then he knew it would be good. The copy was in his straightforward, breezy, New York style, blending hard-edged news, chat, and lots of fun, especially when he worked with the equally irreverent sportscaster, Zip Rzeppa. "All of a sudden it was the most interesting newscast on the dial," observed *The Boston Globe*.

"I first met the infamous Bill O'Reilly at BU, nineteen seventy-three–seventy-four," said Zip, whose name is Christopher. O'Reilly calls all of his friends by their last names. In Rzeppa's case, he was "the Big Z" on and off the air. At that time, Warner Wolf, the hot local sportscaster in New York at WABC/7, was called "the Big W." O'Reilly thought *Z* was sexier than *W*. "So we'll call him 'the Big Z,'" he said, "and make him a star."

O'Reilly had credentials as the weekend guy at Channel 2 in New York, and Rzeppa had made a name in Cincinnati as sports director of the NBC affiliate, doing off-the-wall things. Back in the seventies, when women journalists first went into men's locker rooms, there was a big stir. He went into the women's locker room in St. Louis to interview the University of Cincinnati women's basketball team, and they dumped a bucket of Gatorade over him, because they were so appalled that he would enter the women's locker room. "We had it all on tape, of course."

The most infamous, off-the-wall bit of the O'Reilly-Rzeppa years happened in 1983 and became a classic in the broadcast industry. A clip of the piece actually wound up at the University of Missouri Journalism School. A professor asked his students: What do you make of this, whether it was good or bad journalism?

On the eve of the Super Bowl in January 1983, Rzeppa went through a careful analysis of the Redskins against the Dolphins, concluding that the Miami Dolphins would defeat the Redskins the next day. When John Riggins ran roughshod over Miami in the fourth quarter of the Super Bowl, he was left in what he still refers to as "a pretty ignominious situation."

"We went on the air the next day, and Bill says, 'What happened to that prediction of yours? I thought you said Miami was going to win?' And I just looked at him, and I said, 'Bill, I admit it, boy, do I have egg on my face.' And I took a raw egg and smashed it on my forehead during the sportscast and let the egg drop down my face."

Susan Burke, the coanchor and a close friend of O'Reilly and Zip, started shrieking. The cameraman fell on the floor laughing. "No one knew I was going to do this. So I went to the highlights of Miami getting trounced. Bill threw me a towel, and said, 'Hey, that was pretty good, but what are you going to eat for breakfast?' "

The Boston Globe and the *Boston Herald* were not amused. "They just jumped on me the next day. They wrote columns about how unprofessional I was. And they just blasted me for this stunt." Forever afterward, whenever the *Globe* and the *Herald* referred to the Channel 7 sportscaster it wasn't Zip Rzeppa; it always was "Zip Rzeppa, the man who smashed an egg in his face."

Not everybody at the station responded to that kind of humor, either. "Zip was a very strange sort of fellow," coanchor Susan Burke recalled. "He would promote an interview, 'Larry Bird coming up at eleven.' And then, during the sports, he would literally have a yellow parakeet sitting on his shoulder, and he would attempt to interview him."

"Bill enjoyed me," the Big Z said. "He was always teasing my appearances, saying things like 'Coming back to the sports, the Big Z, the man Larry Bird likes to party with, Zip Rzeppa.' Well, I never partied with Larry Bird, but Bill would just make things up, you know. It was just a hilarious newscast, and we both had the times of our lives."

As was his way whenever he took a new job, O'Reilly never bothered to unpack his boxes in Boston. His rental space at Harbor Towers resembled an upmarket warehouse.

O'Reilly and Zip lived in the same condo building, double-dated, did the news together every Saturday and Sunday nights, went out and socialized afterward, looking for the night life and women. He had an eye for women, Zip said, "No question about that. We were both young and single, never been married. I was thirty; Bill was thirty-two at that time. Susan Burke always says when we would go out looking for women, Bill is looking for sultry; Zip is looking for genuine. Bill would be looking for the hot, hot chicks."

Saturday and Sunday nights in Boston are not exactly like New York. Especially when the two wild and crazy guys finished the news at eleven-thirty.

"We'd go to the Long Wharf Marriott on the harbor in Boston, and they had a disco," Zip said. "By the time we'd get there at midnight, it was kind of slim pickings. I think they closed at one. So it was kind of a struggle."

O'Reilly would never go home with anyone," the Big Z remembered. "He would take women's phone numbers if he found them attractive or interesting, whatever, and things might develop from there."

"The books tell you that the Roaring Twenties were pretty wild," O'Reilly said, "but I put my money on the Disco years." The 1970s and early 1980s, as far as O'Reilly was concerned, were the best dating years of all time, with the possible exception of the Roman Empire.

At thirty-two, he still abstained from drugs and avoided the women who took them. "My thing," he wrote of the Decadent Years in his autobiography, "was the music. I was a dancing machine. Sock it to me, Donna Summer! Let's shake this place, Gloria Gaynor! Get down!" The dancing got him dates. Since you couldn't hear any words in those places under the rotating mirror balls, he believed the dancing said, " 'Hey, let's have some fun and see what happens next.' Even Catholic girls had their inhibitions lowered by the howls of the Bee Gees or Sylvester. A few hours at clubs like Septembers or Shenanigans and most of my dates wanted to extend the evening at their place or mine."

When the dancing didn't work its magic, the young O'Reilly had another strategy. "By nineteen seventy-five I was regularly on TV and that was the greatest dating advantage a man could wish for. I was recognized instantly. Fame leads to dates, at least with some women. Is Puff Daddy one heck of a handsome devil or was Jennifer Lopez all over him because of his clout?"

During his TV gigs in Dallas, Denver, Boston and, later, Portland, Oregon, he confesses, he was absolutely shameless playing the power card. "Hi, my name's O'Reilly. Perhaps you've seen me making a fool of myself (heh, heh) on Channel Nine. Oh, you have? Can I buy you a drink or take you to Vegas?

"Yeah this was pretty shallow," he confessed, "but if you're listening to lyrics like 'We're doin' it, doin' it, doin' it' four nights a week, you might be pretty shallow, too."

The best part of his first look around in Boston was running into two news executives who were to become corpses in O'Reilly's novel about the anchorman who becomes a serial killer.

Despite O'Reilly making the WNEV-TV weekend news "the most interesting newscast on the dial," as the *Globe* called it, the ratings remained flat. In times of adversity local stations, like baseball teams, fire the manager. Nick Lawler, O'Reilly's fan, was thrown out in the winter of 1982, replaced by William (Bill) Applegate as vice president of news. Applegate looked around, and the first thing he didn't like was Bill O'Reilly.

"Bill was a can-do guy," said Susan Burke. "He liked controlling the people around him." His supporting cast, co-anchor Burke, sports guy the Big Z, Zip Rzeppa, the weatherman Shane Hollitt, were all his kind of people. The Nick Lawler administration may not have liked him being in control of their show, Burke said, "but they had to admit that he did a pretty good job."

Applegate and his minions were not impressed. The new vice president of news told O'Reilly that he was being forced to keep him because Win Baker, the general manager, wanted him. And that was okay with O'Reilly.

"I don't care. They were paying me a lot of money, and I liked Boston." So Applegate had what O'Reilly called "his little Nazi underlings" give him a hard time.

O'Reilly's contract, tailored by agent Carole Cooper to O'Reilly's lifestyle, provided that he had Thursday and Friday off. "Because I'm a bachelor, you know, and Thursday and Friday were okay days to get dates and run around, right? So he goes, 'Nay, I'm going to change it to Mondays and Tuesdays,' arbitrarily violating the contract. I said, 'No, you're not. I don't get Monday and Tuesday off. What am I going to do Mondays and Tuesdays in Boston? Nothing. There's nothing going on. So I'll work Monday and Tuesdays, as the contract says, and I'll take off Thursday and Fridays.' "

Applegate, according to O'Reilly, had three guys whose only job was to terrorize the newsroom. "So one of his little Nazis walks up to me and goes . . . I'm sitting at my desk doing some kind of work . . . I look up and he's standing over me. He goes, 'O'Reilly, I want you to come in here every morning with three stories ready to go.' And he's got his finger close, not touching me, but close.

"This is within earshot of everybody in the newsroom. It was a big wide-open space, and now the whole newsroom is looking at this, all right, because I'm the new guy on the block. I look at him, and I don't say anything now. I just look at him, and I look back at my work. And he goes, 'Did you hear me?' I don't look up. 'Yeah, I heard you.' He goes on the arm, 'You come in with three stories every day, okay?' The guy's name is Gleason. I look up and grab his tie. I pull his tie, like this down to my face. I said, 'You ever touch me again, Gleason, and I'm going to break your arm.' Now the guy's like just dangling, okay. I get up like this," O'Reilly says, standing up at his desk. "And the guy is like five-eight." I take him by his tie. I walk across the newsroom in front of everybody, okay. I'm dragging him like this. I go into the assistant news director's office, a guy named Jim Johnson, black guy, who was not a bad guy. I fling Gleason like this.

"I said, 'This guy ever comes near me, ever comes near me again, I'm not responsible for what happens to him," and I walk out.

"Johnson's door slams, boom, I never heard another word about it. But everybody was watching that whole thing.

"Now that guy Gleason, he was through in the newsroom, he's finished. He left four weeks, five weeks later, went to Omaha, Nebraska.

"And they couldn't do anything, because I had a two-year, no-cut deal, you know, and everything was spelled out in the contract of what I do and what I don't do. So they really couldn't do anything, because he had done that first, and everybody saw it. All right, it wasn't like I did anything to provoke it."

But that was the kind of behavior that didn't endear O'Reilly to people like Bill Applegate. "I mean they saw me as a threat to power, because I wouldn't take any crap. And people would see that in the newsroom. They would see how I treated this guy and humiliated him. And I did it on purpose. I humiliated him on purpose. I didn't like him, and nobody is ever going to do that to me anywhere, anytime."

There were maybe four or five incidents throughout his twenty-five-year career when he would confront somebody in a very menacing way, but the stories spread. "They go all over the country," said O'Reilly. "Not just in the Boston newsrooms, because people pick up the phone and tell their friends in Seattle. You should see what this crazy guy O'Reilly did to the assistant blah, blah, blah. Boom, boom, boom. So they're all over, you know, and my reputation preceded me everywhere. Everywhere I would go, they go, 'Oh, here he comes, trouble,' because that's very rare in TV news to have that kind of reputation."

. . .

Applegate was followed by Jeff Rosser. Of all the bosses who stood in the way of his achieving his goals, the worst in O'Reilly's book was Jeff Rosser. The new vice president of news at WNEV-TV, who replaced Bill Applegate in 1983, Rosser was even worse than Lucifer, the Prince of Darkness, in Denver. O'Reilly flatly named Rosser in a widely quoted *Boston Globe* profile as the Devil Himself.

Rosser—who was the worst of all the villains to die in the media bloodbath in horrific detail in O'Reilly's first novel—also had inherited O'Reilly. He still doesn't know what O'Reilly was so upset about. Having been in the business for so long, Rosser said, "There are probably one or two other people out there who are not big fans of mine." Rosser treated him like everybody else, badly, in O'Reilly's opinion.

"I don't recall a whole lot of contact with him at the time," Rosser says in self-defense. "To be perfectly honest, we had bigger issues and bigger challenges than our weekend newscast. But I'm sure I was among a handful or a very large number of people that just simply was not wowed by his presence, was not awed by his intelligence and talent, and had the audacity from time to time to ask a question that ran contrary to his purposes.

"I was moving from WBZ, which in those days was number one in Boston, competing tightly with WCVB. So I was moving from a very strong TV station to a station that had been built on an old Indian burial ground, supposedly, and was cursed. There were a lot of changes that I and others at the station felt were needed. So in that kind of environment with a fellow like Bill O'Reilly there, who believes that only his opinions count, and certainly no one else's, I can't know as much as him. Of course, everybody needed to do things differently. But how dare anyone suggest that he might do anything differently?"

Rosser didn't appreciate O'Reilly's brand of journalism. "His responsibility in the role and duty as a journalist was to communicate the news of the day in an objective, fair manner. All of our people were held to that kind of standard. I'm not sure he was very happy in that role, because I think he was in some constraint. Bill's passion is self-centered. It was then as it is now. I mean, it was just about Bill O'Reilly. My sense was that Bill O'Reilly was always trying to be the story. Bill O'Reilly wanting to be the center of attention. The role of news anchor was really just nothing more than a stage, to be the center of attention."

Rosser also thinks he was a social snob. "There were some station functions I recall being at with Bill. He would basically stand over in the corner rather than mixing and mingling. He would stand as an observer of what was going on, stand and wait for individuals to come to him so he could hold court, rather than his mixing and mingling." Rosser discounted O'Reilly's not drinking like everybody else at the party as a factor.

"My opinion of him then: He was terribly smug, that he felt he knew more than anybody else. Me, and everybody else. Anyone had the misfortune of supervising him, if that individual ever dared challenge or ask a question or to disagree, that person would be put on a rather long list of people that Bill just simply didn't care for and was not going to respond positively to. And I'm on that list."

Rosser fired O'Reilly the first opportunity he got, but in his mind he didn't fire him. "I don't recall asking him to make the move, encouraging him to make the move, or anything else," Rosser said about O'Reilly's departure in 1984. "I don't even recall how it happened. But he did leave the news department to go to work for our programming department at the station to anchor another program that was produced by programming, not by news."

Even if Rosser couldn't remember what he might have done to incur O'Reilly's homicidal tendencies, Zip Rzeppa had a better recollection of that turning point in their careers. "We were hired in one bloodbath where they fired just about everybody, the management, the anchors, and all kinds of people. And they brought in a new regime, a new News VP (Bill Applegate). The station was very, very low rated when we got there, and the ratings hadn't gone up appreciably, and that's why there was another bloodbath. Well, after nine months Applegate could see things hadn't turned around, and he left before they got him. Smart. And that left us all hanging out to dry. So the new guy— Jeff Rosser—came in, and said, 'Well, these guys aren't working obviously and ratings are not good enough and they're clowning around on weekends, let's get rid of them.'"

Rosser didn't like the tone of the weekend newscast, explained *The Boston Globe* about the latest bloodbath at the cursed Channel 7. He especially didn't care for Rzeppa's wild antics. O'Reilly was incensed when they fired the Big Z. Rosser announced he was going to bring in an entire new news team on the weekend. So not only was O'Reilly's favorite sportscaster fired, the weather-caster, Shane Hollitt, was fired, and Bill was "reassigned" to become the host of a new weekend afternoon show.

O'Reilly could have quit, as per his contract. He was hired as weekend anchor and reporter. But he didn't. It was a decision that would play a major role in the making of the Bill O'Reilly we know today.

Chapter Nine

O'Reilly Finds His Voice

Being reassigned, transferred, fired, whatever they called it, was the best thing that could have happened to O'Reilly in that phase of his career. He went to a magazine show where he learned how to interview in the long form, how to control flow and pacing, what worked and what didn't, skills that were to be the bedrock of his later success on *The O'Reilly Factor*.

Jeff Schiffman had been asked to come in and fix WNEV Channel 7's afternoon magazine show, then called *Look*. Schiffman was a one-man bomb-disposal unit in local television, having performed the same delicate mission on *7:30 Magazine* at WCBS/2 in New York.

The Boston bomb that was about to blow up had been a two-hour afternoon "live" show that went on after the soaps. The first thing he did to resuscitate the magazine, after changing its name to *New England Afternoon* and cutting it to an hour, was to call for O'Reilly, as he had done in trying to save *7:30 Magazine* in New York.

O'Reilly's crossing over to Channel 7's programming side to host *New England Afternoon* allowed the hard-news man to showcase another side of his personality. It wasn't enough to save the show. Reruns of *The Love Boat* clobbered it. *New England Afternoon* was history in six months.

"The corporate honchos, the suits, the station's big brainiacs made the decision to kill the show," said Schiffman. "O'Reilly's personality was not a contributing factor, Schiffman said. "I was under orders from the corporate people to drop all of the local productions, which were a sin in their eyes. Very expensive."

Schiffman was the first to buy *Wheel of Fortune* and *Jeopardy* in syndication. That's what replaced "New England Afternoon." He was able to buy them for pennies. "And it eventually is what drove me out of the business, too."

Fortunately, O'Reilly's boxes were not unpacked. O'Reilly landed in the tiny TV market of Portland, Oregon, in October 1984. "Not even he could have argued that his career was headed in the right direction," *The Boston Globe* wrote.

"I went there for a lot of money, more money than they ever ever paid anybody, and I only went there for one year," said O'Reilly of his new job as anchor of the six and eleven o'clock news at KATU-TV. "Because I didn't really want to go there. But I saw the worthiness of taking a station that was number three, and last, at eleven and moving it up. I said if I can do that in this small market, then I can get back into New York or a big market to anchor, all right?" That was the strategy.

It was a market that had never had any confrontation journalism on television. They were doing local news: Here's a parade, and here's a traffic accident, and here's a fire, and it's raining, see you, good night.

"That's what it was," said O'Reilly. "It's a nice sleepy little town. So I get there, and I go, well, look, let's start to take on some of the power in this state. And who's the most powerful guy? Mark Hatfield."

So O'Reilly put together a three-part series for the February sweeps, called *The Prince of Oregon,* on Hatfield. It was a balanced piece, the good and the bad, all the little deals he had made. "You know, he had some questionable run-ins with the cops that were unexplained. They didn't want to do it, but I got it on the air."

The station management was against airing the series, but O'Reilly had a supporter at that station, named Tom Dargan. "He's dead now. He was the overall guy in charge of this station. Old guy, in his sixties, married like eighty times, very flamboyant guy, and he hired me. He was the guy who brought me in because he knew about what I did in Boston, and he wanted to shake the market up. The guy was a real hero.

"All the other little guys at the station, I remember, were saying, 'We can't run this.' I'm going, "What do you mean, you can't run this? It's all true, we got it all documented, it's nothing but true. It doesn't slam Hatfield. It says, here's what's good about him, and here's what's bad about him, you know, like anybody, good and bad." So Dargan let us put it on.

"Now there was one thing. We found a guy who worked as a page in the Senate, and he had some unbelievably bad things to say about Hatfield. I mean, things that would have ruined him if they were true. I could not corroborate those things, independently of this guy, and he wouldn't come on to say them. Didn't use it, didn't use it, killed it.

"And so when they complained about this kind of stuff, I look at him [the news director], and I said, 'Look, you know what we have is true. We have other things that we don't know are true. We're not going to say anything about it.

"Now Hatfield knows somehow that I was on to this, you know, and confronted me with it. He got word that evidently this guy was talking to people, and said, 'Look, O'Reilly's got it.' He called me, and I told him the story. And I said, 'Listen, Senator, I'm not going to run it [that part of the story], because I don't know if it's true. I'm not going to give it to anybody. I'm not going to do anything with it right now, it's buried. But if it is true, I'm going to run it.'"

And what did he say?

"Nothing. He didn't say anything. And he was far and away the most powerful guy in Oregon, far and away. So I can imagine the heat that he brought on that station. But the piece ran. It got great ratings, and that was it. We got some, you know, provincial complaints, but it was a good, tough, fair piece on the most powerful guy in the state. What, you're not supposed to do this?

"I moved that station from last to first, from October to July, they knew it. I did a good job for those people."

As his pay scale increased, so did his frugality. In Portland, Betsy Rott, the producer when O'Reilly was anchoring the increasingly successful eleven o'clock news at KATU-TV, remembers the gang would go out for a drink after the show. "Being a wealthy anchorman," Rott said, "he would pay for the first round. 'But no coffee.' That meant Irish Coffee—with the whipped cream. A dollar extra more than beer, or the usual."

O'Reilly gathered his boxes and moved again after nine months in Portland. Mr. O'Reilly Sr. disapproved of his son's peregrinations. The son had an alarming—in Mr. O'Reilly's opinion—tendency to change jobs. O'Reilly's recklessness was the opposite of his father's Depression-milltown dread of being unemployed. You didn't quit a job just because you were unhappy.

Mr. O'Reilly cautioned Bill at first, Jan O'Reilly remembered, lecturing him about the dangers, urging him to mend his ways. But he stopped when he saw each time Bill left a job, he got another that paid more. Quitting jobs was a sign that young O'Reilly had broken away from the father's post-Depression mentality. Growing up in Levittown, he had been in orbit around the center of his universe, Mr. O'Reilly. It took maximum thrust energy to break away from a domineering father, and he did it through television's inexplicable—to an anxious Depression mind—economics.

If he had followed his father's advice, O'Reilly would still be working in the Scranton/Wilkes-Barre market today.

Mr. O'Reilly Sr. left Caltex for health reasons after twenty-three years with the company. He took early disability, Jan O'Reilly said, because he had ulcerative colitis. It hit him at forty-nine while he still worked for Caltex. "By fifty-two, he had to get out. It drove him crazy being housebound and in constant pain for almost eight years." In 1986, just after he turned sixty, and three months after being diagnosed with a melanoma, he died of cancer.

O'Reilly had driven cross-country in three days from Portland to spend the last week in Long Island, making peace with his father. Son and father had a lot to sort out. "Bill had a really tough dad," Joe Rubino said. He remembers O'Reilly crying several times after talking to his father, usually after some achievement. "It was like the movie *Fear Strikes Out*, the Jimmy Piersall story. Tony Perkins as Piersall would say, 'Dad, I went three for five.' Karl Malden as his father would say, 'What about the other two times?' "

No matter how well O'Reilly did on his way up the ladder, his father concentrated on what he didn't do.

Rubino recalled walking into their living room in Florida, and O'Reilly was sitting on the floor crying. "My goddamn father, he's the only one who can do this to me. He threw the backstop thing at me."

Mr. O'Reilly Sr. always reminded his son, "Don't worry, I'm the backstop. I'm here to bail you out the next time you screw up."

"Every time Bill called with good news, his father perceived a potential weakness," Rubino said, "and he gave it to him, rubbed his face in it. That's why Bill was so determined to succeed."

"Most of the time I didn't figure out where my father was coming from," said O'Reilly. "I was just afraid of him. Thank God, before he died, I began understanding how his mind worked and his concern for his family. Surviving his rigid, sometimes brutal regime, gave me discipline and motivation, the values that have been essential to my success."

After living with his father for seventeen years at home, O'Reilly was never frightened by anything again. His father had immunized him against fear.

On his last day, O'Reilly and his father watched a Washington Redskins football game on TV together in his hospital room. Mr. O was a lifelong Redskins fan.

Boston called again. By September 1985, he was working as a reporter and soon to be columnist-at-large for WCVB/5, the ABC affiliate in Boston. Doubling back on his tracks turned out to be a watershed in his career.

In the mideighties WCVB was considered by some the finest local TV station in America. "We had extraordinary local programming, a deep commitment to news," said Phil Balboni, the news director who hired O'Reilly. Balboni said he was interested in O'Reilly, because he had a strong persona. "He struck me as a person of not only vitality and intellect, but also somebody who had guts, wouldn't be pushed around." O'Reilly's reputation for being argumentative did not bother him. "I felt confident in my ability to manage diverse people," Balboni said. "I never had a problem with Bill. He was pretty intense, pretty ambitious. He was a good writer. Important particularly in doing commentary. I was his boss, and I liked him."

Having a boss who really liked him and, even more important, continued to like him, was a new experience for O'Reilly in Boston.

Emily Rooney, then assistant news director at the WCVB news, who was later to work at ABC News as Peter Jennings's producer, was president of the Bill O'Reilly Marching and Chowder Society. He walked like a cop, talked like a cop, Rooney recalled, and his suit sleeves were always too short. "He didn't spend every cent he made, which is what most of us do. He never spent a dime." In Rooney's opinion, "He hasn't changed a bit. If he walked in today, he'd be the same guy. What is it now—seventeen years ago? He's self-confident. I thought sometimes maybe a little self-conscious, a person who had a strong sense of himself and what was appropriate for him to be doing."

For the first time since leaving Scranton, O'Reilly was getting along with management. It was the rest of the staff that couldn't abide him. Producer Jeff Schiffman said that wherever O'Reilly went, "If he wasn't actively disliked—I mean people, didn't dive under their desks when he walked by—nonetheless, he wasn't that popular a guy." As usual, the newsroom in Boston was divided about O'Reilly, those who thought he was an egomaniac and those who saw his other qualities.

Balboni's recollection was that he and Emily Rooney were the two people, perhaps the only two people, who supported and liked O'Reilly. "He was a discordant note. I knew that when I hired him. That's what drew me to him. I was looking for somebody who was self-serving and confident, who projected a strong male image. As a result, he upset the newsroom. A newsroom has its own kind of carefully calibrated set of powers, and Bill kind of rippled those waters pretty heavily."

"He desperately annoyed people, including the anchorpeople," Emily Rooney said. "He was just unabashed about saying things like: 'I should really be the anchor here. No one's stronger than me.'"

At the time, Natalie Jacobson was the principal female anchor; Chet Curtis was the principal male anchor. Both disagreed with O'Reilly.

"I think some of the anchors, some of the powerful more established anchors, thought he was arrogant and self-satisfied," explained Balboni about the pettiness in the newsroom. "I don't think they thought Bill was right for Channel Five, and maybe they were right. He probably wasn't. But that was what I wanted. It was an experiment."

What really upset the old hands were O'Reilly's commentaries. Looking to spice up the eleven o'clock newscast, Balboni unfurled O'Reilly's commentaries designed to provoke. "This was a gambit on my part," said Balboni. "Periodically, the station did editorials, but not commentary." The commentaries, somewhere between a minute thirty to two minutes, would be attached to a related story or they might stand on their own. "He was the only one doing them in Boston at eleven. He was still a reporter, so this was tricky territory. It took more management input, more supervision than regular day-to-day reporting."

The commentary concept seems quaint in the context of the world of cable news today, where it's all-commentary all-night on prime-time cable news. It was controversial in the 1980s. Network news shows regularly had in-house commentators who were empowered to deal with complex issues in ninety seconds or less. Eric Sevareid had had that role on *The CBS Evening News* during the Vietnam War. Some called him Eric Severalsides. He would divide his time into equally balanced seconds on both sides of an issue. You decide! For a while, the commentator's slot in a network news show was used as a kind of an old-age home for senior anchorman. It's what happened to John Chancellor when the NBC suits decided it was time in 1982 to promote Tom Brokaw to "*The NBC Evening News* Without John Chancellor."

The commentaries O'Reilly was doing in Boston were different from the station "editorial" in which they might come out strongly against potholes. In turn, they would be forced to give equal time to propothole citizens for a rebuttal. Station editorials were usually delivered by underutilized station executives with all the charisma of a light pole, but worse were the people replying. "They were both awful," said Emily Rooney. The more cutting-edge progressive stations dropped editorials just to eliminate the replies.

O'Reilly had always worn journalism's central tenet of so-called objectivity as something of a hair shirt. Being able to speak out didn't trouble him. Videotapes of those commentaries now reveal just how much of today's O'Reilly was on display in Boston: the simple, smart, though occasionally manipulative way he framed arguments; his savvy in picking favorite targets and hammering way; the delight he took in reading mail from viewers demanding his decapitation. "I really don't think he's changed his persona," Balboni said. "He's no doubt refined it, but he's not changed it."

This was the true start of the man who wouldn't shut up. The eleven o'clock commentary allowed O'Reilly to continue what he did at the Boston University *Free Press*. He had a column of the air. Bussing. Corruption. The shenanigans of corrupt municipal politicians were O'Reilly's meat and potatoes.

From the campus of what he felt was the mostly middle-class school of Boston University, O'Reilly and his friends could look across the Charles River at MIT and Harvard, observing that more than a stretch of dirty water separated them. "Our degrees would not open as many doors as degrees earned over there. Our fathers did not have friends waiting to interview us for fast-track jobs as soon as we got our sheepskins."

In the summer of 1986, O'Reilly crossed the bridge. "In an effort to bring all sorts of people together in a creative mix," O'Reilly wrote, "Harvard's John Kennedy School of Government accepted me for postgraduate study in the middle of my broadcasting career." He began work on a master's in Public Administration.

"The Kennedy School was basically a look at the other side of life that I'd never seen in the United States before," he said to me one afternoon sixteen years after seeing the upper classes in London. "Fifty percent of the students at the Kennedy School are foreign students. Most of those students came from wealthy homes, prime ministers' sons and daughters, sheiks' sons you know, that type of thing. They get sent over to the Kennedy School to get trained for public service. I had never been exposed to that level of society in this country. And the students in the Mid-Career program were all accomplished profession-als, again, most of who [sic] were from wealthy families. I had glimpsed it but had never rubbed shoulders with them."

It was the first time he actually knew people who never had to think about money, he says about the first time he went to Harvard in 1986. "Their clothing was understated, but top quality, their cars were European and well tuned, and their rooms hinted of exotic vacations and sprawling family properties," O'Reilly further observed about what he imagined "the other folks" were like. "Winter skiing in Grindelwald? A must. I learned that a 'cottage' could be a twenty-two-room mansion on a Northeastern beach or a 'camp,' a forty-acre property on a lake in the Adirondacks with houses and outbuildings more than a century old."

O'Reilly had his own way of dividing people by class. Many of his new classmates at Harvard had three names. "And they expected to hear all three of them." He studied his Harvard classmates as intently as his policy courses at the Kennedy School. Generally speaking, his Harvard classmates remained out-wardly calm in all situations. Everything was under control. No one was flam-boyant, he perceived. No swearing or arm waving or bear hugs. Despite the class differences, O'Reilly managed not to embarrass himself at Harvard. Limiting the possibility of social gaffes, he kept to himself at the Kennedy School before dropping out in his first semester.

Chapter Ten

Spencer

"My best friend was Spencer, but he died." He was talking about Joe Spencer, whom O'Reilly met when they were reporters in Denver in 1978. People at the station called them Butch and the Kid, after Paul Newman and Robert Redford. Joe was the Kid. When O'Reilly moved on to Boston, Spencer went to Detroit, where he was a star reporter on the Channel Seven Action News at WXYZ. An ABC affiliate, in the 1980s it was the second most dominant TV station in the nation in local news viewer ratings.

Spencer was hired as an ABC News correspondent working out of the Chicago bureau. He was tapped to cover a meatpacker strike at the Geo. A. Hormel & Company plant in Austin in southeast Minnesota, a strike that brought out National Guardsman with billy clubs and riot gear. On the morning of January 22, 1986, Spencer covered the story for ABC's *Good Morning America*. After filing film in Minneapolis, Spencer and Mark McDonough, a producer, flew south in a helicopter to join their camera crew in Austin at the Hormel plant to cover late-breaking news for other ABC news shows, *World News Tonight* and *Nightline*.

Spencer and the producer boarded the Bell Jet Ranger helicopter. It was early morning. Low cloud ceiling of six hundred to two thousand feet and low visibility.

The chopper crashed into a cornfield about one hundred yards from Interstate 35, about eighty miles south of Ellendale, Minnesota, sometime during the morning. The discovery of the wreckage shortly before 1 P.M. was delayed by the heavy fog. There was no evidence of a collision with treetops or power lines. "It looks like they flew right into the ground," said Sheriff Donald Norlander of Freeborn County, the first one on the scene. "The way they dug out the ground for about two hundred feet when they hit indicates they hit it at a pretty good speed."

Joe Spencer, thirty-one, his producer, Mark McDonough, thirty, and Curtis Mark Haugen, thirty-three, the pilot, all died.

O'Reilly drove to Amsterdam, New York, Spencer's hometown, for the memorial service. St. Stanislaus Catholic Church was filled with ABC News brass paying homage to the correspondent who had died in the line of duty. Spencer's father, a radio executive, had asked O'Reilly to speak. It was a moving eulogy, which O'Reilly delivered without notes.

Roone Arledge, president of ABC News, was among the assemblage in the audience.

"Who is that man?" he asked his aides. "O'Reilly," Arledge was told. Arledge said, "Get him."

And they did.

In 1986, Arledge was the king of network news executives, wearing two hats as the president of sports and news. Arledge had been head of ABC Sports since 1964, creating *The Wide World of Sports* show that seemed to cover every sport ever played, including some that had yet to be, and *Monday Night Football*. He also allowed sportscasters such as Howard Cosell—one of the trinity of O'Reilly's TV heroes—to speak freely with a critical voice, a radical concept in the world of toadying sportscasters.

Hiring O'Reilly as a correspondent was not a major employment decision at ABC News that year. Arledge was preoccupied with raiding CBS News, stocking up for a major renovation he was doing on his premier news show, *World News Tonight*. By the time O'Reilly left Boston, a lot of the best journalists of the 1970s and 1980s were floating around the the halls of ABC News, the Sargasso Sea of journalism, a mothball fleet waiting for news emergencies to be pressed into service.

One of Arledge's earliest improvements as the head of ABC News in 1977, attempting to turn his third-place network around, was multiple anchors. He was the first to dream up triple anchorpeople. In 1978, his network evening news suddenly seemed to have more anchors than New York Harbor. *World News Tonight* whisked viewers around the world to see anchors standing on the streets in Paris, London, Moscow. It was the Wide World of News instead of sports.

One of the newsmen being moved around the world like a United Van Lines truck until he ultimately took over the store was Peter Jennings. Jennings was a major player in O'Reilly's fantasy life. His dream, even back in 1981 at WNEV/Channel 7 Boston, according to Susan Burke: "Bill always had his eyes on a job like Peter Jennings's."

Finally, at ABC News, he liked to believe, he would be on his way to becoming the next Peter Jennings.

Roone Arledge was O'Reilly's kind of boss. He was virtually invisible. Arledge was notoriously secretive, and days would pass without an Arledge exchange or sighting. Richard Wald, a vice president at ABC News, number two under Arledge during O'Reilly's period of employment, described Arledge's modus operandi:

"He stayed in his office and people came to see him. He was perfectly affable. He wasn't a total recluse or anything, but he didn't wander around the halls, you know, that form of management. He wasn't a watercooler kind of guy. But he always had someone who was. At ABC News, he had Joanna Bistany who was essentially the watercooler person. Roone relied on her to bring him the news and gossip of the division."

So the boss-hating O'Reilly had to deal with a different set of authority figures at ABC News, starting with Joanna Bistany, Arledge's prime minister without portfolio. "She was a distant figure in my life," he said. "I got to tell you, I stay away from all kinds of politics wherever I go. I was so busy running around doing my stories, I didn't have time to schmooze with Joanna Bistany, Roone Arledge, or any of the executives. I was kind of like a phantom. I mean, I knew who she was. But there was never conversation or anything like that. I was in the troops. The generals did not mingle with the troops."

At ABC News O'Reilly also ran into what he considered the worst human being he ever worked with in network news or anywhere. "I use the term 'weasel' a lot," O'Reilly explained in *Parade* magazine when talking about untrustworthy people you don't want as friends or associates. "Weasels are small carnivores that hunt alone at night and viciously kill their weaker prey. There are legions of human weasels in America today."

Even worse than a weasel in O'Reilly's opinion is a weasellete. "A true weasellete," as he described one of his colleagues at ABC News. "She has never covered a news story, never been in the field, never faced a deadline, and never got behind the desk and appeared in front of a camera. Doesn't matter. Her skills don't need to be learned; they are ancient. She has accumulated vast power over scores of working reporters by kissing ass and spying on her coworkers. She can damage a career with a well-placed diss or comment.

"This particular creature instinctively hated my guts," he writes in an abstract of the character in his autobiography. "Everybody knows who the woman is."

"Naturally, like most other people around the news, I should have smiled and stayed out of her way." Just as naturally, O'Reilly says, he played right into her hand by openly despising her right back. In fact, he made a point of showing his disdain at every opportunity. Jesus and Gandhi would have been kind to the weasellete, he says. O'Reilly wasn't.

The Weasellete of the Century's place in journalism history is enshrined by being the inspiration for Murder No. 2 on the hit list of the serial killer, TV anchorman Shannon Michaels in O'Reilly's first detective thriller, *Those Who Trespass*.

I asked Dick Wald, his nominal boss, if he remembered O'Reilly's work at ABC News. I mean, before he started writing novels?

"He wasn't exactly a shrinking violet. On the other hand, he was a good correspondent. He could write very well. And he was fast. He always went after the most extreme of stories. He loved the little guy fighting the system. He would forever be looking for that kind of story and trying to do them. And he always liked the emotional, emotive, the stuff that would get your gut. And you know there is nothing wrong with that, it's good television. Everybody has a hobbyhorse about what he wants to do, and that was his. It's the same hobbyhorse he is on now on his Fox News show, incidentally."

In covering breaking news for ABC News in the mid 1980s, the toughest battle was not doing good stories but getting them on the air. There were a hundred network correspondents and only enough airtime for less than half on the three major ABC news programs, *World News Tonight* with Peter Jennings, *Nightline* with Ted Koppel, and *Good Morning America.* "The competition for airtime ranged from ferocious to vicious," recalled O'Reilly. "This was Ego City big-time."

"For some unknown reason, Peter Jennings liked me and my work," O'Reilly said. "So I appeared on *World News Tonight* quite often. He liked my style. He liked my brashness. He liked my energy. He liked the working-class stories I put together, and he insisted on some occasions that they be put on his programs when those producers over there couldn't stand what I was do-ing. I had a pretty good success run at ABC. I got on more than a hundred times on *World News Tonight* in three years, and that's an enormous amount of time to get on for a general assignment reporter. And it was solely because of him."

What Jennings especially might have liked about O'Reilly's work was his willingness to do the sixty-second summaries of the big stories to come on that evening's *World News Tonight* that ran during the day's soap operas and local news shows. They were called "News Briefs."

"He'd call me at the last minute," O'Reilly said. "Peter can't do it or he doesn't want to do it, or he's hitting somebody and he's all covered with blood, or whatever. He admired me because I could go down with two or three min-utes' notice and knock it out, you know, and not stumble or anything. That's my local news training."

"Peter blew them off a lot," said Dave Tabacoff, an ABC News executive at the time. "And Bill was very happy to sit in for Jennings, who hated taking the time away from his other work. Bill embraced it with gusto. For someone like him, it was an opportunity to sit in and show his stuff in an anchor setting on the network."

As a general assignment reporter for *Good Morning America, World News, Weekend News,* and *Nightline,* O'Reilly would be sent out to cover breaking sto-ries. O'Reilly thought he was doing so well at ABC, he was telling friends he was in line for being the next Jennings. "He was always telling me that Jennings was grooming him," said Michael Rose, a cameraman who worked with O'Reilly in Boston.

A large obstacle in fulfilling his dream was Rick Kaplan, a six-foot-seven-inch news executive, then the *Nightline* producer at ABC. O'Reilly said, "He hated my guts. He despised me, and there's no reason for it. There's no history behind it. He just didn't like me. I took the job at ABC. I walked in, and he said, 'I'll never put you on the air.'"

And he didn't.

I asked Dick Wald, to whom they both reported, why they didn't get along. "Well, two very strong, acerbic characters who wanted to do things their own way," Wald said, laughing. "It's not at all unlikely that they wouldn't get along."

I asked superagent Richie Leibner, president of N.S. Bienstock, what the problem was between Rick and Bill. Leibner was Rick Kaplan's agent, as well as the husband of O'Reilly's agent, Carole Cooper. "Rick was intimidating," Leibner replied. "He was a big very tall grizzly bear, and here was this brash arriving kid, O'Reilly, coming down from local news in Boston. He had all these other established CBS people whom Rick preferred, because they have come over from CBS like he had, and they had bigger names. And Bill was a kid who thought he could do it better than some of the old farts. Bill was full of himself, and there were too many stars ahead of him."

"It's like putting these two scorpions in a bottle," said Phil Balboni, who knew both men. "I don't mean to suggest that either one is a scorpion. But you just have two people who are tall and forceful. It's not surprising they would dislike each other."

ABC's national news director at the time, Dave Tabacoff, said he didn't remember anything spectacular O'Reilly did in terms of assignment or performance. "He was a good solid guy, good reporter, good writer. What was always interesting about Bill is that he was very sure of himself. He had a vision of himself as quite different than a general assignment reporter, and that's a rough row to hoe. He wasn't going to be pigeonholed. As a general assignment reporter, you just sort of go out there and do what's assigned by the *World News* assignment desk, that kind of thing. You work in the New York bureau, maybe LA, and overseas for a couple of years, and wind up a general assignment reporter all your life. It's not an ideal fit for a guy like Bill."

When asked if O'Reilly had any major problems, Tabacoff responded, "I would look at it this way: Where he sees injustice, bad assignments, weird people doing weird things to him, he'll tell people. He speaks out loud. So I think that made an impact in terms of the way he was perceived. People want a get-along guy. You know, if we're going to send you to Mars for the week, you go to Mars for the week. So he was not like that kind of guy, but good at his job, and did it well. But he knew whom he thought worthy. People he didn't like, they knew it."

Late one chilly early afternoon in November 1986, there was a breaking story in Bridgeport, Connecticut. A parking garage had collapsed, trapping dozens of workers in the debris as night was falling. O'Reilly got a panicked call from the New York assignment desk. The ABC affiliate was preparing video coverage for the Jennings program, and O'Reilly had been tapped to do the voice-over for the breaking story. The problem was that the raw video coverage would not reach New York until about half an hour before national airtime. Could O'Reilly write and edit the story and tape the voice-over in time to lead off *World News Tonight?*

Of course! No problem. The adrenaline was pumping. The story had to be written while new information kept coming in. He had to choose the shots, put them in dramatic order, and make his words fit the footage. He had to explain a terrible disaster very clearly to viewers across the country—and also show respect for the victims and their families as the rescue efforts continued.

"In other words, I really could have blown it," O'Reilly writes. "But, thank God, I didn't. My story topped the program. Peter was happy with my piece but mostly with the fact that I'd made it possible for us to best both CBS and NBC. Neither one managed to air the story until much later in their newscasts."

Then *Nightline* asked him to go to the scene for a live report. "I hopped in my car and raced like Evel Knievel up to Bridgeport. I was on a roll. Here was my chance to change that producer's mind. I was on top of the story already. I had time to shape the *Nightline* segment in my head, and I was psyched about answering Ted Koppel's questions live on national television. As athletes say, I was in the zone."

There was chaos at the disaster site, but with the help of two ABC producers, O'Reilly immediately began shooting interviews and getting up-to-date information on tape. Freezing rains pelted them, but that didn't matter. *Nightline* mattered.

After about an hour of this feverish activity, one of the producers ran up to say that New York wanted O'Reilly to call the office immediately. This was before cell phones, so he used the phone in the satellite truck. "It takes a lot to leave me dumbstruck, but this phone call did it," O'Reilly recalls. "My blood rises when I think about it today. I was told I was being dumped from the story I had developed in favor of a reporter from WABC/7, the local ABC station in New York City. This *never* happens. When a network news correspondent is on the scene that correspondent is *always* used by a network news program. And since everyone in the business knows this, I could see the decision had been made for one reason and one reason only: to humiliate Bill O'Reilly."

There was nothing O'Reilly could do about the situation. The faces on the screen are not the power behind the cameras. He was one of the grunts from their point of view.

When word about this backstabbing got out, the producers of *Good Morning America,* who were decent human beings in O'Reilly's opinion, got in touch with him and assigned six live shots for the next morning. "Exhaustion took over, so I check into the Bridgeport Hilton to catch some sleep before my 4:00 A.M. wake up call. But the bedside phone startled me awake at 1:00 A.M. Shouting on the other end of the line was my powerful *Nightline* enemy himself. 'O'Reilly, get your ass back out to the building site; we might have to update the situation for the West Coast feed!'" Because of the three-hour time difference, *Nightline* can be changed when necessary for the folks on the West Coast.

O'Reilly was only half-awake but not brain-dead, as he put it. He had the sense to ask if Koppel was still in the studio. The producer exploded in obscenities. O'Reilly knew he had scored. If Koppel had already gone home, there was no way to update the program. Ted was already in bed. No West Coast update was actually planned. O'Reilly felt dirty games were being played at his expense. He turned on his cassette recorder to tape the producer's going ballistic. The tirade over, O'Reilly went peacefully back to sleep, content that he had caught the producer acting way out of line.

There were no problems in Bridgeport the next day. O'Reilly did the live shots from the site in the morning, filed a fresh report for Jennings, then drove home to New York. The story was over.

As it turned out the news story was over, but not the media story. The following morning an ABC vice president called O'Reilly into his office to accuse him of "refusing an assignment." This was no trivial matter; such a refusal is a firing offense.

"According to this network 'suit,' the *Nightline* producer filed a complaint that said I had directly refused to do a report for his program. In addition he accused me of laziness (and probably bestiality), but I'd stopped listening. Rising to my full height of six-four and looming over the veep's desk, I pulled out my recorder and hit the PLAY button. The man's mouth dropped open as he listened. I stopped the tape and explained that the whole thing was a setup. Koppel had gone home."

"You secretly taped an employee of ABC News?" the vice president gasped.

"Yeah, I sure did," O'Reilly concluded. "And it saved my ass. The incident was dropped."

O'Reilly hasn't identified the executive producer in any of his published work. It seems crystal clear to me, as a TV critic, it was Richard N. (Rick) Kaplan who gave him such a hard time in Bridgeport and made ABC News such a hostile environment for O'Reilly. Soon he wouldn't have O'Reilly to kick around anymore as both tall men moved on.

Kaplan went to CNN where as programming chief he was remembered for a number of fiascos, including the *Operation Tailwind* documentary, which got it wrong about the United States military using nerve gas to kill American defectors in Laos during the Vietnam War. CNN was forced to apologize and retract Kaplan's signature piece. Under his leadership from 1997 to 2000, CNN lost credibility and its ratings collapsed (down 23 percent during Kaplan's reign). After being fired at CNN, Kaplan soon took over perennial third-place MSNBC, where he advocated a programming strategy of "patience." He did little to improve MSNBC before being let go in June 2006.

Given Kaplan's track record of running out of gas in cable news, there may have been more to his mean-spirited treatment than the egocentric O'Reilly knew as he was about to take what some considered a wrong turn in his own career.

O'Reilly was talking to me about where he had been so far in his career, one day in his office with the sun setting over the Fox News Channel Tower on The Avenue of the Americas. It was minutes away from showtime.

"When we were growing up in Levittown, it was just straight talk. I mean there were no subtle passages or talking behind the back. You got punched in the mouth. Nobody hit you in the back. And I just adopted that in TV. So I was brought up in an atmosphere where there was never any subtext, never any nuance. It was: 'Here it is.' And even the dopiest kids understood, there it is. And I took this sensibility into the network news, and I got killed with it. Because there they really want you to not really say what you mean, kind of hint and be diplomatic. And I don't think journalists should be called to do that: be diplomats. I don't think that's our skill. If somebody's a charlatan, I'm going to go out and say that, in my opinion. But I'm going to back it up, too."

Chapter Eleven

Taking Out the Trash

———

Entertainment Tonight was a syndicated newsmagazine on the cutting edge of a news revolution that was taking place at the start of the 1980s. ET, as the news cognoscenti called it, premiered in September 1981 as a nightly half-hour journal of what was considered important news, covering every twitch in the entertainment world as if it mattered. Its syndicator, Paramount Television, made deals to facilitate getting guests exclusively. ET also was the first news show to allow PR agencies to decide what questions could be asked, giving the flacks the right to change answers. But ET was a paragon of high journalism ethics compared to its imitators. Extra, syndicated by Warner Brothers Entertainment, often seemed like a thirty-minute-long free commercial for Time Warner products, doing exclusive stories from People, In Style, Life, and Entertainment Weekly, as well as Warner Brothers' movies and TV shows.

The second part of the news revolution was the emergence of the new syndicated TV real newsmagazines, shows that combined entertainment and celebrity news with real news, namely, crime and human tragedy. It was a concept that became known as "Tabloid TV." A term coined by John Corey, a New York Times TV critic, Tabloid TV was the big "in" concept in print verbiage in those days, second only to "trash TV," made popular by print newsmagazines, which were saying it was the worst thing since the rise in fourth-class mailing fees. Network news journalists especially deplored Tabloid TV. It was a journalism form beneath contempt, for everybody except the public. In 1989, there were more than a dozen tabloid shows syndicators were preparing to drop on the news-hungry TV audience.

Whatever journalism snobs might say, Tabloid TV was nothing new. It focused on people, people with problems, concerns, and emotions, ordinary people to whom extraordinary things happen. The pieces were about crime, human tragedy, malfeasance, corruption, celebrities, and other sordid things. Of course, crime, human tragedy, malfeasance, corruption, and celebrities are also the formula for the most prestigious *60 Minutes* and its copycat *20/20*. One major difference among these network magazine shows and the Tabloid TV shows was they had famous correspondents like Mike Wallace narrating the stories.

The syndicated newsmagazine explosion began with *A Current Affair*, quickly followed by the journalistically inferior *Hard Copy*. Produced by an Australian journalist, Peter Brennan, and hosted by Maury Povich, *A Current Affair* pioneered in erasing the line between journalism and entertainment. They paid for stories, known disparagingly as "checkbook journalism," and used reenactments or re-creations, the act of staging news when parts of the news story are missing.

A Current Affair knew what the audience wanted: the mix of sex, violence, the truth, and half-truth. It scoured the papers and wires each morning and found the fresh story people would be talking about that day—be it Roseanne's face-lift, Johnny Carson's ex-wife, or Robert Chambers in a jail brawl. Get an exclusive interview. Buy up some photos. Attract viewers and keep them hooked.

Hard Copy was worse. The specialty of "Hard Sloppy," as I called it, was to run stories based on pseudofacts, near facts, or no facts. Syndicated by Paramount Television of *ET* renown, the show was the leader in the Michael Jackson School of Journalism. He was a story *Hard Copy* seemed to cover every night, just as the local news did the weather and sports. There was no restraint in turning up a pseudofact, near fact, or wild allegation, and saying to viewers: "Here it is, the story you've been dying to see."

A Current Affair became very popular.

In 1988, Roger King—one of the two King Brothers running King World—decided to copy *A Current Affair* but with a difference. A hybrid of news and entertainment reports, King World's *Inside Edition* would be aimed at a blue-collar audience, emphasizing emotional stories and sexy babes. The wrinkle: It would be a tabloid that wasn't a tabloid. They would also do serious journalism. Toward that goal, the King Brothers were out to poach the talent and the brain trust behind *A Current Affair*.

Peter Brennan was offered the chance to produce the clone. They were trying to get Maury Povich to host the new show, so it would sound like *A Current Affair*. Not every tabloid aficionado, going around the dial, would notice the difference. Instead of Maury, the Kings did manage to snare Bob Young and John Tomlin, the line producers who basically got *A Current Affair* on the air every day.

Inside Edition began so heavily laden with *A Current Affair* veterans, the show was known by insiders as "A Current Affair II." The people who were hired for *Inside Edition* weren't there to make journalism history. "They weren't hiring, you know, the crème de la crème of the network news," said tabloid historian Burt Kearns. "They were all castoffs and people whose careers just kind of hit a brick wall, people who really couldn't get hired anywhere else. Well, at the time your last stop was with tabloid."

The King Brothers, seeking to cash in on the tabloid trend with honor, were about to make an awesome casting decision. Trying to sanitize a genre that had image problems, they went upmarket, crowning Sir David Frost, the Concorde high-flying British television superstar, to serve in their anchor/host chair.

This wasn't just another washed-up talking head. This was David Frost, the man who had interviewed Richard Nixon in May 1977, the man who shook hands with such international celebrities as Julie Andrews and Lassie. In his earlier gig as host of the syndicated *The David Frost Show*, he set the Guinness World Record for saying, "Hello. Good evening. Super welcome to the show. Super to see you." He was also a leader in calling things "marvelous."

David Frost regarded the tabloid magazine show from a whole different point of view. In the debut of *Inside Edition* on January 9, 1989, he announced that this show would not be tabloid. "We're not going to show you those horrible things," he said, in effect, "like three-headed lesbians, and we're not going to be salacious, and we're not going after celebrities, and we're not going to show news that doesn't matter."

"The producers were standing near the camera with their mouths hanging open," recalled Burt Kearns, author of the history *Tabloid Baby*, about the premiere speech he considered Howard Beale doing trash TV. "What was he doing, killing the baby before it was born?"

Sir David also was on the soapbox fulminating against TV trash when he was interviewed by the press. *Inside Edition,* he told syndicated columnist Marilyn Beck, "won't follow the course of the garbage that was making a sewer of our airwaves. I was concerned when the King Brothers first approached me about hosting the show. But the assurances I received from them put my mind at rest. They share my views that broadcasters have a responsibility to the public."

By the third night on the high road, the suave, urbane Sir David, who promised he was only going to do responsible journalism, was on the air with traditionally hysterical the-sky-is-falling, irresponsible Tabloid TV. In one piece he warned viewers about "deadly dinner plates" imported from Southeastern Asia which if scrubbed for six weeks nonstop with steel wool pads the lead would come off.

The King Brothers had second thoughts. The ratings for *Inside Edition* were rapidly approaching the level of the test pattern on many of his stations. All the station managers were at the National Association of Television Program Executives (NATPE) convention the week King World premiered *Inside Edition.* It was a midseason replacement show. They all ganged up on Roger King, and said, "We love your show, but you have to get rid of that guy."

"Sir David and his accent was apparently just too much to handle," said tabloid historian Burt Kearns.

After three weeks, Sir David was sacked and given a ticket on the Concorde back to London. "It wasn't exactly his fault," O'Reilly wrote in his autobiography as he explained how he happened to get involved with the show. "What nut thought that this dapper, manicured Brit would appeal to the working-class target audience?"

The nuts in question were his new employers, Roger and Michael King. "We thought with the stories we were going to do," said original coproducer John Tomlin, "we could connect with the audience and then maybe his persona would sort of cushion the edge on those stories. Anchors were only on the air for two minutes a day. David Frost had some cachet. He could get us celebrities, so I thought, let's give it a shot."

Frost's departure was sudden. It happened so quickly, Tomlin said, there just wasn't time to find anyone else. "We needed a warm body to sit in that chair."

Warm body O'Reilly was ready.

. . .

O'Reilly had been lured away from ABC News in 1991 by Tomlin, because his career wasn't going anywhere. The plan still was to do tabloid, but they were going to be the *Newsday* of tabloid shows, not the *National Enquirer*. "And so that is sort of how we positioned it with O'Reilly," Tomlin said about the day he lunched with their potential hot new hire while he was still at ABC. And there were bound to be days when Sir David, given his commute back and forth to London on the Concorde, would be unavailable. O'Reilly would be the substitute anchor.

Tomlin thought O'Reilly would bring credibility to the show. "He has a good presence as an anchor. Trustworthy. You don't get a feeling that this is a sleazy guy. He's believable. And I think with an anchor on a show like that, that's really what you needed."

O'Reilly was hired as a correspondent, a job that normally included waiting outside Madonna's for her to come out and get a fresh shot for use on that night's show. But he wasn't the average correspondent. His title was Senior Reporter, Senior Correspondent/Anchor, which acknowledged his network credentials.

With the abrupt disappearance of Sir David, the face of the show overnight went from snooty British to a working-class guy. "O'Reilly felt like he should have been there all along," Tomlin recalled. "He rose to the occasion. He filled the chair immediately. It worked out great."

O'Reilly's spin on this turning point in trash TV, as he told me:

"The show was on the rocks, and it was going down. I got in there and basically said, 'I'll do it, but I gotta write it, including the promos.' I went in and changed the tone. We're not going to do any more topless shots, all right. The story has to have a reason to do it. The three of us [Tomlin, Young, and O'Reilly] revised the format to include aggressive investigative reporting—my strong suit—and also to sharpen up the entertainment stuff with a punchy point of view. King World basically kissed off the show. We stabilized it, and it turned into a monster success in syndication."

He had brought his "Long Island edge" to the failing show. It was O'Reilly's idea, he says, to level with the folks at home. "I said, 'Look we do fifty percent good stuff and fifty percent garbage. I'm gonna tell you what the good stuff is. And I'm going to tell you about the garbage.

"Well, the first three months the Kings couldn't believe it. They were yelling at me. If we're doing a stupid story, I'm going to tell the folks: 'Look, this isn't really important, but you might like it, because it's got some babes down there, or whatever.' " It was O'Reilly's homage to Maury Povich, winking at the audience as he introduced a bizarre piece of news.

The opposition was not threatened by the pinch-sitting rookie. "When O'Reilly was cast as the new host," said Kearns, at the time a producer at *A Current Affair*, "he was like a doofus, a hundred and eighty degrees from what he is today. He was polite. He was very, you know, sickening and polite. He would open the show—and this always got to us—by thanking the audience for being there. Thank you for doing what? Oh, thank you for not changing the channel?"

The King Brothers hired Av Westin from ABC News to add even more network news prestige to their tabloid organ. Westin had been executive producer of *World News Tonight* and *Nightline* at ABC News. Westin's other qualification is that he had worked with O'Reilly at ABC News. Trying to upgrade King World's intellectual stature, the new imported ex–network executive drew up "The Clean Air Act" for *Inside Edition*. His plan was to shape the show to be like a more with-it contemporary *60 Minutes.*

"So they started covering, you know, school buses with defective axles in Ohio," recalled Burt Kearns. "They were going up against—this was before Amy Fisher—the Preppy-Murder-type stories that we at *A Current Affair* were doing. It got to the point where I'd instruct my reporters and producers that every time there was an *Inside Edition* reporter/producer at the scene, whether it was Sammy Davis Jr.'s funeral, or any sort of big tabloid story, to go up to the *Inside Edition* guy and tell them they had no right to be there. They should be off doing a story on Russian wheat futures. *Inside Edition* was not a tabloid show."

Despite the sarcasm of its competitor journalists, all those early decisions to make the show inoffensive, very bland, and very much under the radar, worked. It still is on the air. Of all the shows that imitated *A Current Affair*, it's the only one that survived. Even *A Current Affair* eventually tanked.

O'Reilly did not see *Inside Edition* as a tabloid show, like the others. He saw it as guerrilla television that was out to catch the bad guys. As its voice, O'Reilly wanted his show to have a social conscience, but it also had to be entertaining.

Once again, O'Reilly reported stories on blue-collar issues, working-class problems. His most passionate pieces dealt with the abuse of children. He did a story on children in a poverty-stricken town in Mexico. The piece had the imagery of a Save the Children campaign: kids walking around in bare feet in disgusting filth, hanging out in a playground that was the garbage dump. "And he did a very compelling story," recalled Charlie Lachman, then the *Inside Edition* managing editor. After the story aired, O'Reilly organized a Christmas fund for the kids.

He did a memorable piece on homeless children in the streets of Rio de Janciro. Hired assassins, death squads roamed the streets of Rio. Four men opened fire on forty-five sleeping kids. Six kids, ages eight to fifteen, were killed by the thugs. Police suspected shopkeepers, because street kids had been a problem to merchants in the neighborhood, hanging out in the streets, sniffing glue, robbing stores.

O'Reilly asked one of the older boys, who had survived the attacks and had been left for dead, "Does anybody love you?"

The boy was stunned. "Couldn't come up with an answer," O'Reilly said. "Not the sort of thing you expected to see on trash TV."

In 1992, O'Reilly went to Guatemala to a town in which an American chemical company made glue. Banned in the U.S.A., the glue, addictive if inhaled, was being sold in third world countries. Central America was a major market. In Guatemala, homeless kids were living on the streets, sniffing glue. "They'd be sniffing a little baggie with some glue in it," cameraman Michael Rose recalled. O'Reilly exposed the American company making the glue the kids were hooked on, while doing a touching story about the homeless children living in the streets with hookers and filth, heartfelt stories about the human condition.

Another O'Reilly idea for a good story was anything involving travel abroad on the King Brothers' expense account. Especially when the stories took him to places he wanted to go to. Bean counters might call it "vacation" or even the euphemism "working vacation." O'Reilly called it "investigative journalism." It appealed to his thriftiness.

Michael Rose was his favorite cameraman. And with Rose, he would pick maybe five stories, and they would go off to Europe in the summer or South America in the winter. Rose especially remembers the carnival in Rio shoot. "It was just hysterical. We had Bill dancing the samba. He was in the procession surrounded by women who were fairly topless."

On another expense account trip, O'Reilly followed a priest from Queens who had gone with his parish to see the apparition of the Virgin Mary in Medjugorje, in the mountains of Yugoslavia. A tiny town in the middle of nowhere, as it seemed to cameraman Rose, Medjugorje had a huge cathedral and a lot of postcard shops and places that sold plates. "Basically, it's a large hill where the people go to where the Virgin was apparently seen. They climb up this huge very rocky hill. People who were infirm or got polio or whatever disease they may have. And they leave reminders of themselves, like photographs, wrapped in plastic, or parts of their clothing." At five o'clock, the woman who had seen the Virgin Mary makes an appearance and all the people try to touch her. "So they can be saved themselves. I mean, you can't go wrong with a story like that."

Producer Bob Young suggested they drive over to Turin, Italy, to do a piece on black masses and witchcraft. "We get to Turin and everything is supposed to be set up," Rose said. "And we ask all these people who are supposed to be our liaisons there. It's, like, what are you talking about black masses? Like witchcraft? There hasn't been stuff like that going on here for hundreds of years."

O'Reilly was upset. They just traveled over the Alps, and there was no story. He was irascible when things didn't go the way they were supposed to go because of incompetence or poor research. All the scholars set up to do interviews spoke Italian. The interpreter's Italian or English was less than fluent. "The people would say, like, forty-five words and our interpreter would give us three words."

From Turin, a disgruntled O'Reilly went to Munich, Germany, to do a story about the rise of the New Reich. He interviewed a very distinguished white-haired German gentleman, probably in his early eighties. Herr Schickelgruber, as Rose dubbed him, had been a former high-ranking Nazi who said in his interview with O'Reilly that the Allies were responsible for building the ovens, that the Germans had nothing to do with it.

"You're telling me you guys had nothing to do with this?" O'Reilly said, pointing his finger at the man. It was an O'Reilly moment. "He was in all his glory," Rose said, "because he had this guy nailed. He didn't even have to hammer him." With the cameras rolling, the German was deadly serious, saying, in effect, "*Ja*, we had nothing to do with it. It was not us. It was the Allies who just wanted to make us look bad. They came in after the war and put the ovens in."

Rose said, "We ended up going to Auschwitz, just outside of Munich, and getting footage of the Auschwitz that 'we' built."

O'Reilly didn't look like the classic foreign correspondent. He always looked as if he was going to a gym for the afternoon as he took off on a trip that might last three weeks. He'd have a large gym bag and his one casual suit in a plastic bag. A distinctive style note in O'Reilly's travel wardrobe was his jeans, which always had an ironed crease in them. And he always wore jeans with either flip-flops, thongs, or Stan Smith Addis sneakers."

He loved to sing as they traveled through Europe. Rose remembered O'Reilly would be surfing along the Autobahn in his Mercedes 300SE moon roof doing his version of "California Girls" and "Good Vibrations." His frugality didn't kick in on the King Brothers' expense tab when renting cars.

There were no previously owned Lamborghinis, Maseratis, or even Mercedes 350s in O'Reilly's driveway when he was paying. "Honest to goodness," Rose said, "even when working at Fox News in the late nineteen nineties, he was still driving this previously owned little blue Toyota Corolla, which he parked right on the street. It was the funniest thing, because it was probably about ten years old at the time, and he looked like Wilt Chamberlain getting into a Volkswagen. You know, he's like this towering guy coming out of this tiny little car.

"He always said to me, 'Rose, cars don't mean a thing to me. It's just nothing more than transportation.' He never understood why people would buy new cars."

At *Inside Edition* O'Reilly went from being a reporter/correspondent on a struggling tabloid show to being the successful anchorman, who was making more money than he ever thought he would. By 1996, he was earning a million dollars a year, but he still wasn't living like a millionaire.

For five years, while he anchored *Inside Edition*, O'Reilly lived in his late grandmother Drake's house in Teaneck, New Jersey. It was the first house built on Edgewood Street. O'Reilly's maternal grandparents had lived there since the 1920s. Grandmother Winifred was a supervisor with New York Telephone Company, a high position. She commuted every day to New York City. Grandfather Drake worked for the Erie Railroad, but O'Reilly and his sister didn't know what he actually did for the railroad.

The O'Reillys would take young Billy and Jan to "the country" in Teaneck from Long Island on weekends in their previously owned Nash Rambler. "We have pictures of Bill in the front digging in the dirt," said Jan. "Lots of trees, no homes. It was just beautiful. Like farmland at one time."

Sister Jan, who now lives in the house, was shocked at his living arrangement while he was at *Inside Edition* from 1991 to 1996. "You should have seen this house when he lived here. It was a shambles. It looked like something out of *The Addams Family*. It was very scary when I came to visit him from California. It was the original everything that my grandmother had when she died. Original curtains, the original shades. And all he did was go from the bathroom to his bedroom with a mattress on the floor upstairs and out the front door. He never really went to any of the other rooms. He had portable clothes racks with all his suits hung up on it in one room. The kitchen table was loaded with papers and a computer and books, and his clothes were in another bedroom. The kitchen was a disaster. I don't know how he survived. Thank God, he had money. He can get takeout or otherwise he'd be starving. He doesn't even know how to boil water."

Phil Tangle, a film editor who helped edit O'Reilly's pieces on *Inside Edition,* said, "I think he thinks he's fighting for the blue-collar guys. He was never this high-caliber anchor-type person who ended up, you know, bigger than the guys that were watching him on TV. Even with all the money he made, he was living in New Jersey with the doilies. There was a joke at the time that he didn't touch anything in the house. He still even had Grandma's doilies on the table."

He was so unbelievably cheap, another coworker at *Inside Edition* recalled, that he had a party at his house in New Jersey, and on the invitation to the staff, he wrote "CASH BAR." And nobody went.

In O'Reilly's opinion, his differences with management were always based on journalistic principles, and he was always on the right side of the arguments. There was the famous Av Westin–Bill O'Reilly debate about Barbara Walters.

O'Reilly and his favorite cameraman, Michael Rose, went to interview Barbara Walters one afternoon in 1991. An unauthorized biography had just been published that discussed her father. Lou Walters owned the Latin Quarter, a big New York City nightclub. It was a sensitive subject for the famous anchorwoman. "The book was really salacious, bizarre things that she didn't want printed," Rose recalled. "I'm not sure how true they were."

As the O'Reilly unit was going out the door, editorial consultant Av Westin told O'Reilly not to ask Barbara about the book, Rose remembered. "Bill knew he was going to ask Barbara about the book. You couldn't tell Bill what to do."

A formal portrait of O'Reilly at three as an angel. He is soon to enter St. Brigid/Our Lady of Hope Regional School, where he proudly recalls he was the second-worst student they ever had. He is holding a book, which he didn't have much time for while becoming what he calls "a hooligan and fiend" in the streets. *Bill O'Reilly*

This is the Levittown Bill O'Reilly first knew when the family moved to Long Island from New Jersey in 1951—a huge subdivision of identical, cheaply made houses sold en masse to veterans returning from World War II. Mr. O'Reilly Sr. bought one of the first of 17,472 eventually built in the William Levitt & Sons version of Utopia. Construction resembled the Ford assembly line, enabling the Levitts to finish a house every fifteen minutes. The wonderful thing about Levittown, O'Reilly's sister said, was "when kids were little, no matter what house you went into, you always knew where the bathroom was." As Bill grew up he saw teams of workers moving down the lanes, finishing the sidewalks, preparing for the landscapers, planting identical trees and bushes. *Levittown Public Library— Levittown History Collection*

Bill Jr., at four, in front of his house on Page Lane with his mother, before the Levitts did the landscaping. Ann O'Reilly was always somebody Bill could "whine to," as he put it. She was also "the facilitator" in his life, always available to drive Bill and his friends to ball games and skating at Old Westbury Pond. "All the guys came over to my house, and you got eight guys hanging out the windows of our car, and four or five hours later she came and picked us all up." *Bill O'Reilly*

Five-year old Bill Jr. and Bill Sr. in a quiet moment when Bill wasn't annoying his father. They are in the attic space, formerly used to dry laundry and converted by Mr. O'Reilly into a bedroom with the arrival of their second child. *Bill O'Reilly*

The spirit of the Bill O'Reilly we know today is captured at his First Communion at St. Brigid. *John Blasi*

The third grade at St. Brigid in January 1958. Bill is in the tall-boy row, standing to the left of Sister Lurana. One nun at the school called him "a bold, fresh piece of humanity" who was "on the fast track to Hell." Another later told him he wasn't going anywhere: "He would wind up in the State Penitentiary." *John Blasi*

In this enlarged photo of Bill, he is standing in front of the clothes closet, where for fun during recess he would tie classmates' coat sleeves together.

Fencing, anyone? O'Reilly was an active child, organizer of all the street games: stickball, baseball, football, roller hockey. Between seasons, he was ready for anything as long as it was competitive. Here he is about to duel with neighbor Gene Salomon. Bill is the one with the stick, a makeshift epee he has found in a construction site woodpile.
Bill O'Reilly

Saturday's Hero. Football is one of O'Reilly's three favorite
sports. At age six, Bill is suited up for the big game at Caddy
House Field, a few blocks from his home in Eisenhower Park,
where he was to become a sandlot gridiron immortal.
Bill O'Reilly

O'Reilly in his seventh-grade class at St. Brigid
in May 1962. He is still in the tall-boy row,
standing sixth from the right of Sister Thomas.
John Blasi

He does not look as happy as the
other students. He didn't get along
well with Sister Thomas.

O'Reilly at Chaminade, not the high school of his choice. His best friends had all gone to public school. Mr. O'Reilly Sr. thought the fancy prep school would keep him from turning into a thug. Bill is in the next-to-last row, third in from the right, flashing a sick smile in the 1964 group shot of his homeroom, IF Falcons. *Chaminade Crimson and Gold Year Book*

The official team portrait of the 1966 Chaminade Flyers hockey team. Playing hockey was O'Reilly's escape from the social put-downs he was getting from the snobs who looked down on his lower-class roots and manners. He is in the top row, far right. *Chaminade Crimson and Gold Year Book*

O'Reilly was the star goalie on the Chaminade hockey squad. In the opening game of the 1967 season, the Flyers defeated Bayville, 5–3, the school paper reporting, "Bill O'Reilly had a fine game in the nets." When not in the goal, he also played defense. Here he is (Chaminade 1, on the far right) sitting on the Flyers bench, waiting to take the ice in the game against Amityville at the Roosevelt Field ice rink. *Chaminade Crimson and Gold Year Book*

Chaminade graduation photo, Class of 1967. O'Reilly is off to the college of his father's choice, Marist, in Poughkeepsie, N.Y. *Chaminade Crimson and Gold Year Book*

O'Reilly and his motorcycle "gang," the Turtles, standing in front of a pub near the Opus Dei dormitory in London. Snapshot was organized by O'Reilly and friends as an example of his extracurricular activities at the University of London. The photo was sent home to freak out Brother Bellinger at Marist, who feared that O'Reilly would make trouble during his Third Year Abroad. O'Reilly is the tall one on the left, holding a bottle of soda pop, his substance of abuse. *Edgar Royce*

While on his Third Year Abroad, O'Reilly takes a detour in Spain to explore the sets where his hero, Clint Eastwood, shot spaghetti westerns. *Edgar Royce*

O'Reilly and college friends punting on the Cam while visiting a Marist student at Cambridge. O'Reilly is in the motorcyle jacket in the foreground. *Edgar Royce*

O'Reilly (left) and Edgar Royce, on their Honda 125s, plot their route through Portugal, Spain, Morocco, France, and Italy on an extended school holiday during Third Year Abroad. *Edgar Royce*

O'Reilly and his fellow "barbarians" at the Opus Dei dormitory, celebrating the end of Third Year Abroad. O'Reilly is in the first row, right. *Edgar Royce*

After graduation from Marist and two years as a high school teacher at Monsignor Pace High School in Opa-Locka, O'Reilly attends the wedding of Joe Rubino, his best college friend and roommate. O'Reilly, the best man at the wedding, is the tall one with sideburns in best Clint Eastwood cool mode, on the left. *Joe Rubino*

Promised a celebrity as a prize in a promotional contest for the Denver Broncos in 1978, the Denver TV station sent weekend coanchor and investigative reporter Bill O'Reilly. The disappointed Pony Express Bronco cheerleaders managed to smile, anyway. *Justin McDevitt*

The starting lineup for the Caddy House Favorites on a game day in the winter of 1985. O'Reilly (center) is the star quarterback, coach, general manager, and promoter of the games that are still played, snow or shine, in Eisenhower Park, on a field next to the golf course. *Justin McDevitt*

O'Reilly and his band of brothers on their first organized adventure vacation in 1990, a whitewater rafting trip down the Rogue River in Oregon. O'Reilly has the number two oar, front left. *John Blasi*

Four old neighborhood guys who grew up together in Levittown and remain the closest of friends. O'Reilly, the tallest, is with John Blasi, Jeff Cohen, and Lou Spoto (from left to right). This picture was taken on the Rogue River rafting trip in 1990. *John Blasi*

V. A. 269

MTGE 4212 PAGE 65

Parcel No. 4848

Bank No.

This Mortgage, made the 26th day of February, 1951 19

BETWEEN WILLIAM J. O'REILLY and WINIFRED ANGELA O'REILLY, his wife

residing at Lane,

, Levittown, New York, hereinafter referred to and designated as the Mortgagor, and **THE COUNTY TRUST COMPANY**, a banking corporation organized under the Laws of the State of New York, having its principal place of business at 235 Main Street, White Plains, New York, hereinafter referred to and designated herein as the Mortgagee;

The original bank mortgage paper from the County Trust Company, White Plains, N.Y., establishes that the O'Reilly home on Page Lane in 1951 was located in Levittown, as O'Reilly contends. *Bill O'Reilly*

In about twenty minutes, O'Reilly had gotten all his questions out of the way when he said, "So, Barbara, tell us about the book." She was sitting there like a potted plant, and her PR people were gasping. And O'Reilly and his cameraman were ushered quickly out of the building.

"We got back to the *Inside Edition* offices, and there was Av standing on the street corner with his arms crossed, looking just freaking ballistic. So Bill just looks at me, and says, 'Okay, Rose, this is going to be a good one.'"

O'Reilly was about a foot and half taller than Westin. The combatants screamed at each other from the sidewalk into the building. The security guards at the front of the building got out of the way. And O'Reilly finally was able to get Westin into his office. All over the building, people were gossiping about the fight going on. The fighting and the screaming in the office continued for a good five or ten minutes, Rose recalled. "I do remember Bill saying, 'I'm not your boy.'

"Av and he really never got along after that," Rose said. "Bill kind of thought Av Westin was more spin than reality. What a windbag. Not only a windbag but also a self-serving windbag. The great things he did at ABC, O'Reilly didn't really believe."

"Just a minor blip," O'Reilly says now of that clash. "It was not a big deal to me. I mean, when anybody comes in and tells me don't ask this, don't ask that, don't do that, I basically look him in the eye and don't do anything or tell him to get out of the office—depending on what the situation is. And I do exactly what I want. I've never in my life, under any circumstance in any job, you know, been told what I should or shouldn't ask. Ever.

"There is always yelling," O'Reilly added. "Yelling goes on all the time. It was a minor, minor thing. But, you know, it was another example of the suits trying to control—for whatever reason, I can't assign reasons—an interview, or something like that. I mean, I don't play the game, which is why I moved ten times in fifteen years. And why I couldn't cut it with the Rather people at CBS News on their terms. Because I don't play the game. You know, once you start to do that, you lose a portion of yourself. You can't just do it a little. It's like being in the Mafia. You can't just be in the Mafia a little, all right. You're either at the Bada Bing or you're not. You can't be a loan shark only on Tuesday. You're a loan shark or you're not. So I'm an honest guy or I'm not, and that's it. I've always looked at it that way. I'm not going to let somebody tell me what I'm supposed to ask or how I'm supposed to ask it or what demeanor or how to do it. It ain't going to happen. You hire me to do a job. I'm going to do the job, and if you don't like it, then fire me. I don't care. I've never been fired, all right, but I certainly have gotten mounds of garbage poured on my head for not going along with what the company wanted. Everybody who plays that game, everybody, you can see them erode. Their effectiveness erodes."

Not everybody was as happy as Michael Rose working with O'Reilly at *Inside Edition.* "He was universally hated," said a coworker at King World. "He was arrogant, mean-spirited. They used to say he had a charisma bypass. The nonsense he pulled on people. He was impossible. If you were on the set with him, he would signal you when he wanted you to be quiet. He would start pointing at you. Then he would start to scream at you to shut up."

"He was just so mean and abusive to people, and arrogant," another said. "He actually was the person you see on television today. He found a way to channel it, I don't know if for good, but he did find a way to channel it in a way that earns him money."

And not all of his coworkers were as impressed with his work as he was. "He was just the anchor, whatever that is," a source said, dismissively. "The meat puppet, as we call it. He never did the right thing. He was an awful guy, absolutely awful."

What did managing editor Charlie Lachman think of that assessment? "He'd be warm, kindhearted, generous, a terrific guy. He could also be difficult, ornery, and loud, and sometimes obnoxious. No question about it."

What caused the transformation? "I think when things didn't go quite well. He's a stickler for information and preparation. When things weren't done professionally. When he didn't have information he needed. When things weren't prepared. Every anchor has the same reaction: 'Jeez, what's going on here?' Did he have a temper? Absolutely. Was it legitimate, was it justified? Most times, absolutely. He is demanding. He is professional. He's all that."

Rose's take on the naysayers: "You know, he didn't really like a lot of the people who worked at *Inside Edition.* He didn't feel like they were up to par. Because he was really a cut above, as far as a writer, a reporter, a producer, as far as like most of the knuckleheads that were there. Bill's a salty guy. He likes things done in certain way, and he's got like a certain standard. You know, he's not difficult, he just expects a certain level of professionalism out of people. It was the first job for a lot of people who worked at *Inside Edition.* A lot of people just weren't cutting the mustard. You had to deal with a lot of people on a daily basis who weren't really pulling their own weight."

"I will tell you what he was like at *Inside Edition*," another former employee said. "He was a pain in the ass. But my feeling was that the real reason a lot of people didn't like him is that O'Reilly saw through people. He saw through so much phoniness. Saw through the bullshit. It didn't make him any less dour a character. It was like, 'Yeah, the guy is right about a lot of stuff, but we hate him anyway.'"

In the July 20, 1993, edition of *The National Enquirer*, the headline in Mike Walker's "Behind the Screens" column read: "Tabloid TV Anchorman & Crew Member in Slugfest."

"The end-of-season party on *Inside Edition* erupted in a wild BRAWL between anchor Bill O'Reilly and a production crewman. During the bash at a New York restaurant the crewman was told O'Reilly had blamed him for a 1½-hour delay in the last show's taping—and the furious guy walked up to O'Reilly and busted him in the chops. With 50 stunned people looking on, the two slugged it out toe to toe until peacemakers pulled them apart. To O'Reilly's credit, he apologized for the crack."

"His flip-outs were famous," one of his nonfans told me.

The flip-out that led to the fisticuffs that the *Enquirer* reported with partial accuracy—they spelled Bill O'Reilly's name right—was described by a more reliably informed source:

"Well, Bill had the fight with this guy, a producer. His name was Brian Walsh. Unfortunately, he passed away about a year and a half ago. Brian had a really funny, dry, sense of humor. Bill didn't like him because he was always trying to give Bill the needle. There was an argument on the set about the words at the end of the show, leading into a Sting song. And, apparently, Bill just lost his temper, totally, started flipping out and screaming at Brian on the set. I don't know where it came from, but he just went ballistic. It was a big shouting match between the two of them."

That was bad enough. Brian still found a way to pour oil on the fire. Another one of O'Reilly's coworkers somehow managed to tape the eruption. In terms of studio decorum, it was the equivalent of Mount Etna. Brian took the footage of Bill flipping out on the set, and he made a funny tape that everybody at *Inside Edition* saw—except O'Reilly.

Brian reversed O'Reilly's vocal pattern, and slo-moed it down, so it just sounded very Germanic. And he mixed it with old footage, like it was shot at the Nuremberg rally with thousands of people Sieg Heil-ing. And there's O'Reilly at the anchor desk throwing his arms up looking like he's Sieg Heil-ing also. And it was intercut with German ladies putting their hankies up to their eyes wiping away the tears of happiness.

"It was hysterical," my source said, "I mean, I was crying, because it was so funny. One of the funniest things I've ever seen."

O'Reilly got wind of the tape.

There was a party going on in one of the restaurants right around the corner from the *Inside Edition* studio. The place was packed with *Inside Edition* people. At five-eight and stocky, Brian Walsh was in the crowd facing the six-foot-four-inch and thin Bill O'Reilly. "I'm not sure who threw the first punch," the source said, remembering the confusion in what *The National Enquirer* said was "a brawl." "But it wasn't much of a brawl. Bill just attacked Brian. He punched him in the face. He knocked him to the ground with one punch." Almost everybody at the show had seen the tape at that point, and those that hadn't were eager to see it after the fight.

Chapter Twelve

Final Edition

To his agent's astonishment, O'Reilly announced he wanted to quit *Inside Edition* in July 1994. The threat to quit or jump from an established successful news show is a bargaining ploy. Over the years, it had worked for Rather, Brokaw, and Jennings, all the while each knew he was in it for the duration.

What was it with O'Reilly? He was the center of attention, the star of a nationally syndicated daily show. But something was wrong. O'Reilly was earning a million dollars a year, but he still didn't have complete control at *Inside Edition*. There were executive producers who would come up with the concepts, not to mention the King Brothers. There were many different forces affecting how the show was done. He had a good deal of power as the anchor, but not absolute power.

This was a problem for O'Reilly. "A magazine show is a producer's show," said Tomlin. "It's not like a talk show, it's not like O'Reilly does now. With a magazine show, it is all about the writing, the editing, and the story selection. And that's what a producer does. So he was not in the position to really produce the show. But he had opinions. We would talk about it. We would fight about it."

O'Reilly was always pushing to make the show more anchor-driven than story-driven. "There was no question that there was a professional tension," said Lachman. "And he tried to do point-of-view reporting and anchoring. And a natural resistance that producers would have is this really the show, does this really work, is this really appropriate for the show? I think you could accurately describe it as a continuing discussion about how much of the envelope can he push and what kind of point of view can he bring to a magazine show without going over the top?"

"So, okay, we are going to disagree about this and get pissed off about it," Tomlin said. "He would have an opinion about what story we are going to do and where it's going to go in the show, say, 'I don't think you should lead with that,' but he understood I was making the call."

Inside Edition coproducer Bob Young was different from Tomlin. O'Reilly saw them as Grant and Lee: They respected each other, but did a fair amount of fighting. Young was Australian. Michael Rose, the cameraman who worked with O'Reilly for almost five years on *Inside Edition*, said Young was much more boisterous and outspoken. "Tomlin's like a big teddy bear kind of a guy who's very quiet. So there were two opposing personalities."

A *New York Post* photo editor when Rupert Murdoch brought the Aussies and Brits in, Young was a member of the Fleet Street group who was known as "the poison dwarf" in the tabloid profession. "A punk," tabloid historian Burt Kearns characterized him, "a dork."

And then there were the King Brothers. O'Reilly always had a contentious relationship with King World and felt underappreciated by them. It was also the money. In O'Reilly's opinion, the misers at King World exploited him. "When I did *Inside Edition* that show was clearing like forty . . . fifty million net every year. I mean, I didn't have a piece of that show. They paid me well, but they didn't pay me anything near that. I mean, they were printing money on that show for six years when I was there. Now it's nothing, but it used to be a cannon." *Inside Edition* went from a seven rating to a two when Deborah Norville replaced him.

He also was unhappy about not being the kind of breakout star he thought he should have been, as Maury Povich was when he started *A Current Affair*. Before *A Current Affair*, nobody knew who Povich was. After it, everybody knew. And that never happened with O'Reilly on *Inside Edition*. "He felt it was because of the way he was promoted by King World, and to a certain extent that's true," said Tomlin. "They didn't put his picture in trade ads, and things like that. And I think there was some personality issue between Bill and some of the people—they didn't like each other."

Why do bosses exist? asked agent Richie Leibner. "Bosses exist to control people, that's their justification. Some people will accept so much control. It wasn't easy controlling Bill. Roger King wanted to run him, and nobody runs Bill."

"I don't think there was any love lost between them, but there was never a fight," Tomlin said. "I just think he thought if you promote me more and make me more of a star, the show will be bigger and more successful—and they had a different opinion. Besides, I think his goal early in his career was to be a network anchor, and I think he realized after his experience at CBS and ABC that, yes, he had the skills and probably the talent to do it, but he was not good at corporate politics that you had to play to get a job like that. I think he realized that and was looking for a different way to go."

O'Reilly told his agent Carole Cooper and her husband Richie Leibner in July 1994 "that I was done. Unless they changed the show the way I wanted it. And I wanted *The O'Reilly Factor*. And they didn't want to do that." He tried to get out of his contract in October, but the King Brothers said he had to stay until the next ratings period, the following March. O'Reilly said, " 'Look, you just hired Debbie Norville. Why don't you just throw her in there.' They didn't want to do that. They were scared."

By then O'Reilly wanted to leave not only *Inside Edition* but also television news. The locals came in with big money when the word got out that he was planning to walk.

"I could have signed with a local station for a million dollars, a station in LA," O'Reilly said. "But I didn't want to do local news anymore. So I just decided, hey, no more. So I told the Leibners—Richard and Carole—I said, 'Look, I'm going back to school.' I thought they were both going to have heart attacks."

" 'Maybe we ought to have a million-dollar deal on the table, Bill,' they said. 'Bill, we already have a million dollars on the table,' they said another time. I said, 'No, I'm going to pay thirty-three thousand dollars to go back to school.' But they knew . . . I mean, I've known them for twenty years. So they know I'm a little crazy."

Chapter Thirteen

Tall Man on Campus

In September 1995, Bill O'Reilly returned to the Kennedy School of Government at Harvard to complete his master's in Public Administration to add to his master's in Broadcast Journalism from Boston University and his bachelor's from Marist College.

Going to the Kennedy School had double cachet points. Even in conservative circles his having attended Harvard showed how open to new ideas he was, what an inquiring mind he had. The bottom line, in the public perception, is that you also must be smart to go Harvard.

Much to his surprise, he says that many of the faculty and students had seen him anchoring *Inside Edition,* which he described in his autobiography as "a nationally broadcast infotainment TV show that might delve into such politically significant subjects as Madonna's decision to have a baby." According to O'Reilly, his classmates at Harvard found it "*amusing.*"

"He probably was a little more outspoken than the average student," said Steven Singer, director of Communications and Public Affairs at the Kennedy School in 1995, who had been in classes with O'Reilly in 1986, and was then teaching one of O'Reilly's courses. "Say, if there were forty people in the class," Singer said of O'Reilly's class participation in 1995, "he took more than one-fortieth the share of the airtime. We were in a class on campaigns and elections and campaign management. You read a case. You're supposed to highlight a few key issues for discussion, and so the class depended heavily on an interactive discussion guided by the professor. He'd speak up a lot, and he was pretty opinionated, and a lot of people often disagreed with him. He was Bill. He was doing what he does everywhere."

Singer said as a teacher he didn't want to take O'Reilly's work as a student out of context and overstate it. "There were a lot of people with strong minds and strong opinions. It wasn't a place for wallflowers. He was probably more conservative than many. I think he had a bit of, a blue-collar sort of everyman's point of view, or presented it that way. If he thought somebody was being a little too academic and not really realistic about what people really thought out in the real world, he would point that out. He had a kind of posture, a combination of introducing a point of view that needed to be heard, and it was very much sort of pragmatic, less academic point of view. Sometimes people were feeling, okay, okay we got it, we got the point, let's go back to the point of view the professor wants to flesh out for a while."

Kennedy School students can register for courses in any of the Harvard colleges and at MIT. There are some three thousand course options for Mid-Career students. One that O'Reilly elected to take in his second time around at the college was with Marvin Kalb, the former network news correspondent and then head of the Shorenstein-Barone Center for Press, Politics and Public Policy at the Kennedy School. Kalb had spent so much time for CBS News at the State Department, he had been called the secretary of state-in-residence. Like O'Reilly, Kalb had jumped to another network (NBC News) before going up to Boston and the Kennedy School in 1987. Did the two former CBS News correspondents chew over their experiences at the Tiffany network?

"The answer is yes but no," Kalb said, ever the diplomat. "I mean yes, sort of, at the beginning when he was establishing himself with me. He talked about having worked here and having worked there. But I did not press him on any of those things. That was not my interest or responsibility. He was a student, a legitimate student."

O'Reilly came to Kalb's office and asked whether he could do a research and writing course with him. "I said I would be happy to do it. He always was bright, cheerful, self-confident, rigorously self-confident and certain of his opinions."

The proposed subject of his paper was *Time* magazine's coverage of an aspect of the Vietnam War. It was his idea. "I said, sure. We then talked about the ground rules for research. He agreed completely. I stressed that the research is essential because it is on the basis of the research that the student can draw a conclusion. It was always my belief from day one that Bill knew exactly what his conclusion was before he did any research.

"I was impressed by his writing style, which was good, the clarity of his presentation, which was good. But I always believed from day one that he was going to write that paper in that way whether he had done one hour of research. That is what he wanted to write. When I would challenge him and question him and push him, he played the game, and he played it very well. He gave me answers that a good student knows his professor wants, but in my soul, I repeat, I don't believe the research affected his judgment in any way.

"As a matter of fact, I'd go further. I think if he came upon research that contradicted his basic views, he would ignore it."

When I asked Kalb if the Kennedy School influenced O'Reilly's thinking in any way, he responded, "No. I think he thought the way he thought then and now thinks the way he thought. I don't think that Harvard had any intellectual substantive impact on him. I think he was at Harvard just to get a degree. I don't know why he wanted one. For all the obvious reasons, I guess. He did enough work to get his degree. He wanted a degree from Harvard, and he got it."

At Harvard, O'Reilly took eight courses with what he called "brilliant guys." One was "The Art of Persuasion," designed to help you persuade someone to see your point of view. He did a course on how the media subverts the government. He also took some foreign affairs course because he wanted to get the basic rhythm of the world and understand how United States foreign policy was developed, who was doing it, who was behind it. "Because the real power players are behind the scenes," he said. "They give you little glimpses into that."

On public television one night in 2002, Charlie Rose asked O'Reilly who was the smartest man he ever met. O'Reilly said the smartest man he knew was Frank Hartmann. Francis Xavier Hartmann is a former Catholic priest, a faculty member at the Kennedy School who works primarily in criminal justice.

I asked Hartmann if he remembered Bill O'Reilly. "Yes. He took my basic Criminal Justice Policies course, which is a survey course. And then I guess that worked well enough for him so that he asked to take a 'reading and research course.'"

The subject of the research paper was on Alabama's mandatory drug treatment for people in the prison system. "I don't remember if it was broad mandatory treatment for all drug offenders, using Alabama as an example, or specifically Alabama, but that was the general area he wanted to probe, and that was interesting enough."

There were usually twenty to twenty-two people in Hartmann's seminars, which were conducted at a long, narrow table. O'Reilly would always take the seat at the exact opposite of the table from Father Hartmann. He would always get there early enough, Father Hartmann remembered, sort of permanently claiming that seat. "So he was always directly opposite me. And what was funny it was like a tennis match. You could see the students who were alongside either side of the table look at me, look at O'Reilly, look at me, and look at O'Reilly. He wasn't a jerk. We didn't get people in class who were the jerks who would dominate the class with asinine things. But he was challenging."

In Hartmann's classes, he explained, roughly half were superbright young people, say, age twenty-six or twenty-eight. Incredibly high SATs. They've had one job, so they're smart, but they're not well versed in the world. And then the other half, roughly, would be people like O'Reilly. To the right of O'Reilly, Hartmann remembered, was a judge from Minnesota, a prosecutor from somewhere else, a police captain from New York. "It wasn't just O'Reilly and me. I mean, other people got engaged also, but O'Reilly probably brought something out in me that wouldn't have come out had he not been in the class."

He gave Hartmann a draft of the paper. "And I gave it back to him, and said, 'Bill, that's not strong, there's too much about assertions. Think about the audience you are trying to convince and whether or not that audience will be convinced by what you said—your evidence, and so forth. I'm not looking for a superacademic, forty-six-page, forty-six footnote paper, or something like that, but you've got to think if the audience will be convinced. It's not whether you convince yourself, but what evidence that audience wants that will basically convince them on their terms about the point you are trying to make.'

"And then he went back and did it all over again. And I think that it's possible I challenged him most because he had to do it over again. A lot of the students are as old as I am; it's not an issue of a power-seeker faculty and humble little student running around. We operate pretty much on a peer basis, where I can basically say, 'This wouldn't convince the audience you have in mind, what would? How do you think about that? How do you bolster the evidence, an honest forthright bolstering of the evidence of the point you are trying to make?' So maybe it may have been sort of that dynamic, or it might just have been the ongoing conversation in the class.

"He's so much better than any academic, or anybody around this policy arena at really simplifying. With any argument you're always at the margin of losing the essence, but it always takes us forty-three sentences to say something, and you know the person—the hearer—is lost by sentence thirteen. And Bill's very good at getting it down into three sentences and pretty much staying with the core. I think that's a particular gift that he has of cutting to the essence so the regular folk can hear it and can appreciate that argument. Obviously, he's always going to have a critic who says 'you simplified that so much that it is wrong' and that's the danger of that. On the other hand, the danger of saying things luminously is that nobody hears you, except those in the same arena, which is useless."

Hartmann is not sure that O'Reilly loved hearing the criticism. "No. No. He stood there and looked at me for a while. And he knows that I wasn't giving him a hard time for the sake of giving him a hard time, and I guess we had that relationship in the class. The class met twenty-five or twenty-six times in the semester, and it really engaged us."

Whenever Hartmann sees O'Reilly now, they kid each other. "He used a word in class once: 'carnage.' I said 'Bill, "carnage" is not a word that is generally used in a criminal justice conversation. You might use it on television, but "carnage" is not the right word.' So he'll laugh at his own use of the word 'carnage.' It was a relationship sort of between equals where you are really contesting what's going on, how do you think about it, what's the right evidence—and the whole class was that way."

O'Reilly's graduate thesis was titled: *Theory of Coerced Drug Rehabilitation*. It's on the problem of combating the drug problem. He actually sent the paper to President Bush. He paraphrased the thesis for me. Between four and eight million of the three hundred million Americans are drug addicts and involved in the culture. Approximately 70 percent of street crime is drug-related. That's an enormous amount of crime being committed by a very few people.

"My program would immediately drug-test every American arrested for any crime. It has already been proven in courts that you can do this. It's a public-safety issue. The courts have ruled that the police have a right to know the state of intoxication of anyone taken into custody, so they have a right to take a hair out of your head and administer a drug test, which might cost fifty cents. There's a machine you can use to do the test right at the police station. Persons found with drugs in their bloodstream in the commission of a crime then go before a judge and are given the opportunity to plead guilty to the crime and be sentenced to supervised mandatory drug rehabilitation that takes place in a prison setting. But it's not a regular prison setting. It's a combination residential drug treatment center and prison. But you can't leave and you have to follow the rules. On a first offense, you are sentenced for a year. During that year you are given psychological counseling, emotional help, and skills training—reading, job training, whatever you need. You are rehabbed for a year. But you must pay the state back once you get a job. It's not a free ride. Once you get out of there and start to be a productive member of society, you owe money to the state. It's like a loan.

"In Alabama—a state that uses this program—the recidivism rate of people who enter this program is thirty percent less than people who do not. So it is a successful program. They get thirty percent of people in these programs to stay off drugs rather than go straight back to prison. Most of those who go straight to prison come right back. For a second offense, you go in for two-and-a-half years."

O'Reilly went to Singapore researching his thesis. It's a lot harsher in Singapore than it would be in America, he explained. The person doesn't have to be committing a crime; all he has to do is be taking drugs, and they send him to mandatory drug rehab. "It's two years, and it's not nice," he said. "So there are no drug addicts in Singapore—none, and there's no street crime. But you cross a causeway into Malaysia—just a little bridge crossing—and you have chaos, because they don't have a strong antidrug program. Drug addicts are running around committing all kind of crimes. But come back to Singapore, and there is [*sic*] none."

Going back to school had not interrupted O'Reilly's social life. His extracurricular activities had been booming since coming back to New York to anchor *Inside Edition* in 1991. Off the air at the tabloid magazine, he enhanced his credentials as the dating lunatic. He even double-dated with Donald Trump.

Marla and Donald were going to one of those big events in which Marla and Donald walked around an arena for no apparent reason, and in the midst of the chaos they created, trailing behind were Bill O'Reilly and his date. She was Marla Mapes's friend, he told me, not his.

O'Reilly never was a going-steady kind of guy. "There wasn't a married track deal," he said. "Whatever town I was in, I had a girlfriend there or called up somebody."

And then the forty-two-year-old bachelor/man about television met Maureen McPhilmy in New York in 1992. The meeting wasn't dramatic, he explained. "I met her through a mutual friend. I knew this girl, and she introduced me to Maureen. That was it."

Maureen McPhilmy was in the television business at the time. She was vice president of DWJ, a public relations agency in Ridgewood, New Jersey. A PR service company, it did things for clients of PR agencies, producing and distributing video news releases and satellite media tours and public service announcements, called PSAs. McPhilmy also brought a lot of nonprofit socially active organizations business into the company.

Thirtysomething at the time of their undramatic meeting, from Syracuse, New York, she is a tall (five-nine) blue-eyed blonde, who some friends say is the sultry Irish version of Kim Basinger. A coworker described her as "full of social energy, very engaging." She was well liked and friendly with coworkers, unlike O'Reilly.

"I didn't know her before they got married," said Emily Rooney, his old friend from Boston. "In fact, we couldn't believe that he was marrying somebody so lovely and respectable. It was just, like, who would put up with all that, you know?"

O'Reilly always had a couple of women going, said Susan Burke Hollo, his coanchor in Boston, since married. "Bill's very methodical. He doesn't do anything not planned. He's funny and spontaneous in his humor, but in his life he's very methodical, very calculating."

Marriage had not been a priority. Moving around from market to market was very disruptive of a relationship. "And he didn't want to fail at anything," said sister Jan. "He knew how difficult it was. He needed the freedom to go. And I don't think he wanted the responsibility of a family at that time. And he knew it. So he didn't do it."

He dated a lot of women, and at some point he must have wanted to have kids, to have a more settled life.

"The best thing about marriage is the opportunity to make another person's life richer on a daily basis," O'Reilly has written. "And I also know that it's not easy. I agree with Robert Louis Stevenson: 'a certain sort of talent is indispensable for people who would spend years together and not bore themselves to death.' That's why you have to marry someone who complements you, not dominates you. Someone who complements you, not depends too heavily on you, dragging you down. The best partners are the ones who can live life on their own. Does that sound like a contradiction? It isn't."

Maureen McPhilmy obviously met these criteria for O'Reilly. They married four years later, when O'Reilly was forty-six. The wedding took place at St. Brigid's in Westbury on November 2, 1996.

O'Reilly said there were about one hundred people at the wedding, his mother, sister, relatives, and about forty of his best friends. One of them, Jeff Cohen, thought it was typical Bill. "He had total control of everything. I wondered about it. Aren't you supposed to go to see a priest before they get married? He didn't do any of that. He even brought his own priest."

Father Tom Jordan is a Carmelite priest, who works as a missionary based in Mexico City. The pastor at O'Reilly's grandmother's parish, St. Anastasias, in Teaneck, New Jersey, he had given O'Reilly spiritual guidance during his *Inside Edition* days. "I give him money for his work, and we're friends," O'Reilly said. He paid for Father Tom to fly up to officiate at the wedding in the parish where he had gone to grammar school. Friends Lou Spotto and Cohen walked O'Reilly's mother down the aisle.

Dennis Hartman was the best man. A high school teacher with O'Reilly at Monsignor Pace in Florida, who still teaches in a Miami Beach high school, Hartman was one of forty candidates for best man. O'Reilly said he didn't have an official best man. Hartman was the best man "simply because it was his turn, his turn to do something, you know. So I said, 'Hartman, you're being the best man, show up, just sit there, don't say anything.' That's what he did."

A reception followed at a club on the North Shore of Long Island. "He paid for this whole thing," Cohen recalled, still in disbelief. "Usually, the bride's family pays. He didn't want any of the traditional things associated with weddings. He didn't want to have any showers. He told all his friends if you want to give him anything, make a donation to Father Tom and just call it a day."

Maureen's friends, nevertheless, gave the couple gifts. After the ceremony, friends went to O'Reilly's house, which was in Manhasset at the time. "Maureen started opening some of the gifts, expensive things you may see in

Tiffany's," said Cohen. "O'Reilly doesn't get off on that stuff. He's right away sort of making fun of her. Typical Bill, I'm thinking, spoiling her big day. He just has to take control of everything."

Maureen was on the same page with him on the important things in O'Reilly's life, such as how they spend his money. "We don't skimp on our health," O'Reilly has written about values shared by wife Maureen. "I get the best pair of glasses I can find. What we don't buy is a list that's almost un-American, since we don't fall for the four-dollar frappucinos or the four-hundred-dollar cashmere scarves: no designer coffee, tobacco products, furs, jewelry, trendy cars, shirts with polo ponies on them, souvenirs of any kind from anywhere, expensive barbecue grill or tools, first-class airline tickets, silk or linen clothing, or any product at all labeled 'gourmet' or 'fat-free.' And you won't catch either of us wearing clothing with a logo; for advertising the man-ufacturer, we expect the clothing gratis."

There are occasional differences of opinion. Wives and girlfriends are now allowed, by O'Reilly fiat, to attend a day or two of the biannual O'Reilly men-only adventure trips before the men depart. Mike Dutko, a charter member of the band of brothers, tells the story about Maureen and Bill at the start of the guys' 2002 sailing expedition in the Caribbean.

"We had this deal at the Bluewater Hotel in Antigua where food and bever-ages were all-included. Alcohol was all-included. So you could go outside to this barbecue, eat your fill of ribs and chicken and hamburgers on the grill, and drink ten of those little drinks with the umbrellas in them. They didn't charge you anything extra. So we are out there loading up our plates with food and drinks and go to the table. Bill's across from me, and his wife is next to me. Maureen says to the waiter, who is walking by, picking up plates, "Would you please bring me a bottle of sparkling water?' So the waiter brings her a bottle of water, the only thing that is not covered in this all-you-can-eat-all-you-can-drink is water. They charge them, like, six dollars for this bottle of water. O'Reilly went crazy. He went crazy. 'Why did you have to order that? Why did you have to do that?' I thought, my God, only O'Reilly could find a way where it's all-you-can-eat-all-you-can-drink and have a problem with it."

Maureen just rolled her eyes, and looked at him, and said, "Don't."

"I think the conversation had occurred once or twice before," Dutko said. "Everybody knew what the *don't* meant."

O'Reilly was lucky, his sister Jan said. Of the hundreds of women he had dated, he had picked one who would not make the kind of waves that could upset domestic tranquillity. Another woman, for example, might want to go to the parties on the media aristocracy social circuit that O'Reilly qualified for. They really didn't get into that lifestyle, said Jan O'Reilly. "She's just a very down-to-earth person. She's not a demanding person. If he had a woman that was demanding or dependent on him, forget it."

Maureen was an independent woman. After the wedding, she continued doing PR work for charitable causes like homelessness. She also served as chair of the executive committee of Habitat for Humanity–New York.

Jan O'Reilly said of her sister-in-law, whom she finds very loving and caring of her brother, "I think she definitely understands him. He's not an easy guy to live with. I don't think I could live with him."

Part II

The Factor
Factor

Chapter Fourteen

Roger Discovers Gold

I n the summer of 1996, Roger Ailes was in the process of creating the Fox News Channel and gathering the dream team to man his twenty-four-hour cable news network.

Ailes needed personnel and was casing the pool of out-of-work TV anchormen whose paths had often been strewn with banana peels by news directors who had to blame someone for their own lack of ideas. Others realized they wanted to do something different, as was the case of Bill O'Reilly.

"Most television people are idiots," Ailes said. "O'Reilly is not an idiot. He is smart, smarter than people think. He had a take on the issues, was fearless in terms of his ability to express them. So when I came over here, he was winding up whatever it was he was doing—coming back from Harvard—and he made a pitch."

"I picked up on O'Reilly because I interviewed him on my show. Had I not done that interview, I probably wouldn't have hired him. There was nothing in his background that showed he could do what he's doing now. He was a field reporter. He had been a TelePrompTer reader. He was always in trouble with management. So it was sitting across the table on my show and watching O'Reilly and listening to him frame arguments that stuck in my mind. And then I said, I think I can create a television show with this guy. And, by the way, everybody advised me not to. Because he had been in the business twenty-five years, and he was never a star."

From time to time, Ailes took the night off from *Straight Forward,* his America's Talking network show. One night in early 1996, he invited the unemployed newsman O'Reilly to sit in for him. O'Reilly had selected Keith Hernandez to be his guest of the night.

Dave Brown, then *Straight Forward* producer and now *The O'Reilly Factor* senior producer, remembers the Keith Hernandez interview. "I didn't really know who O'Reilly was. I never really watched *Inside Edition,* and in walks this tall Irishman. Made a beeline right for where Roger's office was, and he goes and does his homework. Not all that talkative, just wants his information."

Keith Hernandez was the first baseman/outfielder in the 1990s with the New York Mets. He had been given immunity in a case against an alleged cocaine distributor. O'Reilly began by asking him about drugs in sports. "Hernandez did not want to talk about it," Brown said, "And I thought for sure—I am in the control room lighting the show with the director—Hernandez was ready to kill him. And I didn't know when we went to a commercial break, if Hernandez was going to leave, or if Hernandez was going to hit him. It was amazing television. I was sitting there, like 'Oh, my God' and it was great."

Hernandez finished the interview, but Brown remembered thinking, *He's going to slug him, he's going to slug him.* "I mean, it was really intense, and I was in awe. He didn't let up. And Bill held it together. He had to sit through uncomfortable silence for those two-to-three-minute commercial breaks. It was the same as what you see now on our air. I just didn't know who he was back then."

I asked O'Reilly if he remembered this turning point in his career. "Right. So Hernandez walks in. So what am I supposed to talk about, how he catches pop flies at first? You know, that's what he's expecting. So I go, well, wait a minute and what about this, how did this happen, tell me how this happened? How you made these mistakes? What you did to rectify the mistakes? How you got out of this crazy, self-destructive world? All legitimate line of questioning. . . . I'm not here to be Monty Hall. You want Monty, get him, he's in Toluca Lake.

"And I was a lot nicer to him then than I would be now. I didn't get a cogent answer. He mumbled something. Back then I went, 'Are you done answering the question?' Now I would have said, 'Hey, answer the question!' So I'm a much meaner guy."

· · ·

At Harvard, O'Reilly had a vision for the news show of the future, which he put down on what he called "a little memorandum." It would be a provocative hour, a personal journal, an opinion-driven news/analysis interview show with the slick packaging touches of a traditional newscast, with short segments to over-the-shoulder graphics. It would be heavy on print on the screen even when the anchor was delivering an opening commentary, what he would call the "Talking Points" memo, rather than end-of-the-show commentary not seen on network newscasts anyway since the 1970s. All capped by throwing the show open to the viewers, with letters and e-mails deliciously attacking the anchor or vigorously defending him, including his often-funny self-deprecating responses.

No speeches, he would tell the guests. Speak to the point. O'Reilly would let everybody know these are the facts, as he saw them, and this is what he thought about them. He viewed himself as an ombudsman for the viewers. "I would ask the questions that they would ask. My guests might not always be happy with me, but I'm not here to do public relations."

To make the show as entertaining as possible, though, he would use his tabloid skills. Stories with emotion. Combined with investigative reports about the news the establishment journalists were ignoring. His show would never be boring. People would either love or hate the show—and him.

O'Reilly had a version of how he got the job at Fox different from that of Ailes. The Fox people, he said, knew what he had done at *Inside Edition*. He had made it what he called a monster hit in six years. It made a tremendous amount of money. "These guys knew I could do that.

"And then when I came out of Harvard, I brought my idea for a new show to two places: Chris-Craft and Roger." He met in LA with Chris-Craft, the boat-building company that went into buying TV stations and became a coowner of UPN in 1995. "I didn't want eighteen meetings. I get my point across. I didn't need to meet any more. Yes or no? Chris-Craft wanted to meet a hundred times.

"One meeting with Roger, and he got it. And these guys [Fox] didn't have anything going for them, but that's okay. I said, 'Look, it's better, because then I could hone this, and I'm not going to be under this tremendous media spotlight right away. Only fifteen million subscribers. We're not in New York right away. We're not in LA right away.' So they gave me a little room to develop it to what I wanted it to be. It was great."

"It was ironical," O'Reilly mused the first time I began talking to him in 2001, "that I designed the program at Harvard, about as far away from blue-collar America as you can get. I decided I'm going to leave *Inside Edition,* and I'm going back into hard news. And I'm going to bring the same kind of blue-collar direct approach into that area, because I think it's going to work."

And then, luckily, he ran into Roger Ailes, who had the same kind of "no-bullshit sensibility. It was just perfect synergy," said O'Reilly.

Roger Ailes, the chairman, chief executive officer, and founding father of FNC, and O'Reilly had much in common. "I've always been a guy who just sort of says what I think and do what I want to do, and it kind of goes against the grain," Ailes said. "So I saw Bill as an outreach of that, because I believe news has to get more honest. And say, 'here's what's really going on.' "

Both are articulate, funny, outspoken, blunt, and have strongly held views on the same issues, expressed with passion based on their life experiences, not research. O'Reilly didn't believe in news consultants' "audience research," including surveys and focus groups, used for designing a show for the audience's preferences. "Whenever I hear the word [research], I cringe," O'Reilly said. "I just don't worry about 'research.'

"That's why all these other people fail on TV and in the movies, too. Because they rely on focus groups. If you're doing honest work that's not boring, that you're presenting well, you don't need a focus group. The only time you need a focus group is if you don't have any talent, and they're trying to mold you, like a Paula Zahn. All right. She needs a focus group because Paula has no talent. Paula's a robot.

"But you don't focus-group a Letterman. You know Letterman is going to go out there, and he's walking the rope, do what he does, because he's talented. Letterman is not about to care what some lady says. 'Yeah, thank you very much, this is very helpful, I appreciate it, Eloise. I owe you.'

"That's the difference, and most 'broadcast journalists' when they get in the anchor chair, they don't know how to anchor. They don't know what to do, and they have to be told what to do.

"Brokaw and Rather and Jennings have been grandfathered in," he said in 2003, "because they made their bones in a different era. And the comfort level with them is okay just because of their recognized ability. People accept them for who they are. It's a different world now. They couldn't make it now. You take Jennings, Brokaw, Rather, and say do an hour in prime time on CNN, go up against *The Factor*, we'd kill them."

Roger Ailes is not a major believer in research, either.

"I never did research," he said. "And I never did focus groups on any talent I put on the air. It was all done out of my gut. The marketing also was done out of my gut. I traveled around this country for thirty years. I know the American people pretty well, and they're basically kind, compassionate people. Even the conservatives. They just want the problems fixed. They're just tired of, you know, the deterioration of the institutions that made America great. The attacks on all the things that made America.

"We don't have any quantitative studies on audience or whether we ought to put a show there or here. I would never do that because I feel like I was relying on somebody who didn't know anything about the business to tell me what to do. If you don't have that kind of belief in what you do, then you shouldn't be in it.

"I think that's why we are winning," Ailes said.

Chapter Fifteen

A Star Is Reborn

Ailes was right. He could make O'Reilly a star. But it wasn't easy.

"He failed when he first started," Ailes said. "The first six months I had him at six o'clock, and the show wasn't working. People told me to fire him. You know, right now I give Bill full credit for the show, but I mean the truth is I managed that show very carefully when it was launched and helped develop it."

O'Reilly came to Fox with what Ailes called "his little outline of a show." It was the same show, basically, that is on the air now. "But the show wasn't totally focused yet," Ailes said. "We hadn't really defined the segments or what we wanted to be. Bill was still getting his sea legs, and my mistake was putting it in the wrong time period."

Ailes had some ideas for changes. He said to O'Reilly, "You can't be an angry white man for a full hour. You gotta lighten up a little bit in places. But I think the mistake is really mine. I have confidence in you. I have confidence in the concept, and I have confidence in the subject matter, and I think I screwed you up by putting it on the wrong time. So I'm going to gamble and put it on the best time in the lineup, prime time. Then we'll see if it works.

"Which was stunning to everybody," said Ailes, "because the show wasn't working, and everybody says, if the show's failing, you don't put it in the best time period. Usually, if a show fails for six weeks, everybody panics, pretends they have nothing to do with it. They jettison the show, and they blame it on somebody else.

"I did just the opposite," Ailes said. "I took what was not working and put it in the best time period on the network—at eight o'clock—and I was right. It needed that time. It needed more sets in use and a better time period, and it needed a better lead-in, and I was able to create that for it."

O'Reilly also decided to change the name of the show. At six o'clock, it was *The O'Reilly Report*. Everybody was *The Crier Report, The Schneider Report*. He wanted a flashier name. Explaining why he renamed his show, O'Reilly told me, "Nobody else was doing it. And I'm a factor in the show. It was just logical. I look for a clean, quick, boom, right-there name. And *The O'Reilly Factor* had a good ring to it."

O'Reilly might have heard the phrase back in the mid-1980s when his mates at the Denver station used it to describe small distortions and subtle shading that seemed to shape O'Reilly's reality. "We used to say back then that Bill would never lie, but he got more mileage out of the truth than anybody," said Bob Cullinan who worked with O'Reilly at KMGH. "So that became a catch-phrase for little O'Reilly stories: 'Oh, that was the O'Reilly factor.'"

There were a few other changes. "I think there was an evolutionary process," Ailes said, "where he got his little categories set up, the memo and the talking points and so on. He did letters at the end where he lightened up, and people said, 'Listen, you moron, you're an idiot.' And I think, basically, he got more comfortable with it. And, you know, people talk about it as if it's a talk show. The truth is Bill's a good newsman. He does pretty good research."

The show began to catch fire almost immediately in prime time. "But it was a hell of a gamble," Ailes said, "because once you make that change, if you then fail, then it's really a dead show. And maybe a dead career. And you look like a fool, because you've done something that is counterintuitive. Everyone would say, he took a failing show and put it in a better time frame and it failed again. The guy's an idiot. The show became the real tent pole in our prime-time lineup, getting the best ratings and holding the best ratings. So it was a gamble that paid off."

After twenty-five years, O'Reilly had a boss, Roger Ailes, who hired him for himself, and, more importantly, allowed him to be himself. It was the perfect job for a control freak. He was given carte blanche. He controlled everything, so he could finally do the news the way he wanted to, the way it had been in his head all of the years since Scranton.

"I got in here a month before the show went on the air. I'll never forget it. I walk in. We got seven people including Amy Sohnen [the original producer] sitting in a conference room, and I was to meet the staff for the first time. Basically I said, 'Here's the way it's going to be. We're going to be doing a program that's going to be very sharply focused, very un–politically correct, and it's going to have to be well researched. And you're going to have to do all kinds of things that you've never done before.' Because all of them came from America's Talking, that defunct network of Roger's. America's Talking was talk radio, where you don't have to do research. You don't have to do anything but spiel, nothing, no backup. I said, 'Everything that we do is going to be documented. So therefore you're going to have to apply a discipline.' "

Three of the people immediately quit. Ailes wasn't happy about it. O'Reilly said, "Look, Roger, this is like Marine boot camp here, okay? I know what I want. I've got to have a certain mentality to carry it out. I can't have namby-pamby people getting their feelings hurt about this bullshit, all right? They got to do exactly what I want to do because it's a complicated show, all right." Three more people were added to the staff. "I guess they had to drag them in to do it," O'Reilly said.

The second thing that happened was the establishment of the board. "I had ordered up a story—and I don't remember what the story was, but it was some kind of showbiz story. And it's up in a pink card, which means they're working on it. Anyway, I go home. The next day I come in the pink card is off the board. And I'm going, 'Amy, where is the pink card?' She goes, 'Well, Bill Shine told me we're not going to do this story.' "

Bill Shine was the executive producer of prime time, of all of Fox News Channel shows at this point. "I didn't even know who he was, never even met him, all right. I said, 'Amy, you never take anything off that board unless I tell you to take it off, never.' And I didn't say it in a nice way. I said it in a tough way."

Apparently, Amy got upset, and Ailes found out about it. "Then he calls me up," said O'Reilly. " 'Now your producer hates you.' I said, 'Look, Roger, let me make a deal with you. In a month if everybody hates me and everybody thinks I'm the devil, you can fire me. I'll walk right out of the building, okay? Give me a month and let me do this the way I need to, and if it doesn't work, you save a lot of money. I'll walk right out the door, all right. But you need to give me four weeks to get this damn thing right on the air."

For three weeks, it was hell for those people. "I mean, I'm kicking back packets [the fact file on stories staff compiled]. You know, I'm saying, 'Look, you got to answer this question, that question. You have a point of view, and you shouldn't [just be getting the facts]. You got to do this, that. At the end, a little light went on. I can see each one of them started to say to himself, 'Hey, we're really doing work that matters, number one.'"

I found Amy Sohnen, O'Reilly's first producer, in the basement of the Fox News Channel building where *The Factor* staff works. She recalls that O'Reilly actually had several typed pages of what the show would be. "So he comes in and he's an out-of-work newsman and he's got this concept of a show and he sells it to Roger and then he comes in to actually build this unusual concept. He handed out this memo, which outlined the show. And what he outlined is pretty much what you still see today."

In that first week, two weeks before launch, Sohnen said, they still didn't have working computers. They didn't have playback machines. They were launching the network and launching his show and putting in computers and building the newsroom all at the same time. "It was very challenging," Sohnen recalled. "I was probably the only person on the staff other than Bill who had news background. Most of them came from America's Talking. Good people, but not necessarily newspeople. Smart, creative. And young. There were a few people you could really count on, and there were a few people who didn't get it. At the time, I was the line producer and the copy editor. You know, you wore a lot of hats. And we just started making calls, and the bookers had a rough job. 'Hi, this is Joe Shmoe from the Fox News Channel. No, no, no, no, no, not Channel Five. Bill O'Reilly—you know him from *Inside Edition*. We had to explain who Bill was and we had to explain what the show was and we had to explain what the network was. We were coming out of nowhere."

O'Reilly did not do any test runs of the show during the month warm-up. "I don't rehearse. I don't do tests. In the business way too long. So no test shows. None of that bullshit. I sat down for a lighting-and-sound-track check. And then we went on the air."

Gen. Barry McCaffrey, President Clinton's drug czar, was the guest for the inaugural of *The O'Reilly Report* on October 7, 1996. "The reason we had him was because a friend of mine at Harvard was working for him. So he came in, and I destroyed him. I killed. I mean, I just cut him to pieces. Killed him. Killed him."

It was the first test of how the O'Reilly method would work in practice. He had pummeled the guest about the failure of the drug program, then lectured him on how he would solve the problem. "He had no clue how to fight the drug war, and I did my thesis at Harvard on it. And I'm going what about this . . . what about that . . . It's bang, bang, bang, bang. And I understand when he got off the air he started to yell at his guy, 'What did you book me on that show for?' You know, blah blah blah. That set the tone."

"So right away, everybody knows that it was different. This was different. This was confrontational. Matt Roush, who then worked for *USA Today*, picked it up the first day. I think he said something to the effect that it [cable news talk] was all the same except for this guy. And he got it. Boom."

The Factor's game plan was to connect all the dots of what was being reported, something establishment network news rarely attempted. O'Reilly gave me an example of his philosophy of going beyond the news when I interviewed him in May 2001. "One of the reasons we're in this gasoline mess is that you have all of these huge vehicles that get ten miles to the gallon. That's obvious. Everyone knows it. I go on the air one night with Gingrich. And I say, we don't have anybody with enough guts, including you, to say to the American public, you're part of the problem! You buy these big cars. You're sucking up that gasoline. You don't need that big vehicle. You don't need any of that. You don't need that big thing. If every car was mandated to have twenty-five miles to the gallon, we'd cut out consumption by forty percent, right? It's better economically. It's better for national security reasons and not depending on OPEC.

"Now Gingrich wouldn't admit it. He wouldn't concede that people didn't have a right, if there's a drought, and there's no water, the government can then say, no water, you can't water your lawn, and we're going to restrict the water to your house. It's a finite resource. The government has a right to do that, correct? Yeah, I said the same thing with oil. You don't have a right to get gas-guzzlers on the road. That's a privilege. If we have an abundance of oil, okay? But now we don't.

"You should have seen my mail! I mean, every SUV owner called me fascist, socialist. They called me every 'ist' they could get their hands on. And I'll take the heat. I'll take it.

"I think that's why people respect the show. Now I'll take a ratings hit. People will get pissed off, and they'll go away for a couple of nights, Aw, that O'Reilly!—but then they'll come back. And I'll do something they like. And it's kind of like that, but I don't care. I'm not going to calculate my show. I'm going to try to be a truth sayer at least from my point of view and let the chips fall where they may."

Chapter Sixteen

Cracking the O'Reilly Code

The hottest property on cable network news always had been the king, the old "suspendermeister," Larry King.

"When O'Reilly came on the scene," explained Roger Ailes, "Larry King was killing everybody. One and a half [millions], sometimes one point eight, one point seven, just crushing everybody. Nobody could ever get past those numbers, they all said. Bill's now basically doubled those numbers."

O'Reilly was the antithesis of the dean of cable network news, the man considered his chief rival. "Larry works," explained Ailes. "So does Bill. They're both originals. Copies don't work on TV. Whether you like Larry or not, you can go out on the street and find fifty guys who are better-looking, who won't do any homework, and you can put them in suspenders and put them on the air, and they'll fail. Larry doesn't fail because there's a nice-guy quality to him. He doesn't embarrass people he doesn't agree with. People who do his show know that he's never going to ask them a difficult question. He had O.J. He wouldn't bring up the recent unpleasantness about his wife. You ask him who his tailor is? You've got great clothes, you know? Talk about your golf swing, your two thousand yards at Buffalo. He wouldn't bring up the cocaine. He wouldn't bring up any of that stuff.

"O'Reilly would start off by saying, 'So, you murdered your wife, and you take cocaine. Now tell us why we should even talk to you?'"

O'Reilly began pushing the King from his throne the summer of 2001.

Summertime is normally the worst time of year for cable news shows. The summer of 2001 was particularly difficult. There was no real news. The hot story that summer was Chandra Levy and Representative Gary Condit. The air was filled with wild theories and mere speculation, laced with expert commentary and pundits' opinions about the missing Chandra and their suspicions about Representative Condit, demonstrating the principle that a man is guilty on cable news talk shows until proven innocent. The authorities, by contrast, never described Condit as a suspect or accused him of any wrongdoing.

Summer is also the time of the floater phenomenon. Cable news viewers float around the dial looking for specific stories. The floaters rule the cable airwaves.

During the summer of 2001, the cable news audience was composed of floaters only looking for Chandra news. O'Reilly didn't like to cover the Chandra story unless there was new "news." The floaters wanted all-Chandra-all-the-time. *The Factor* took a hit in the ratings the first week of August 2001. O'Reilly had stopped covering the story and paid for it. On Friday of that week, O'Reilly returned to Chandra Levy, and his ratings went up. "We lost 250,000 homes when we went away from it. Bam. A quarter of a million homes," he said, shaking his head.

For the first time that summer, *The O'Reilly Factor* ratings were sometimes better than the patriarchal *Larry King Live,* one week by a Nielsen count of seventeen thousand viewers, a significant number because Fox News was then available in only 64 million households compared to CNN's 81 million.

O'Reilly's eye was always on Larry. Having finally passed King in the ratings, he knew that summer of 2001 was the turning point. What followed was a fierce war between the two shows, a battle of wile and wits.

Twice a week, O'Reilly's troops assemble for a pitch meeting in which nine to twelve producers, talent bookers, researchers, and interns plan *The Factor*'s schedule. It's conducted in the Fox News Channel headquarters' basement, the engine room of the cable network's operation that's composed of bullpens or pods. O'Reilly walks past the Hannity & Colmes pod, the Greta Van Sustern pod, the Shepard Smith pod.

There is a sign on *The Factor* pod wall:

WARNING. RESTRICTED AREA. EXPLOSIVE AND/OR POLITICALLY IN-
CORRECT IDEAS AND/OR OPINIONS EXPRESSED BEYOND THIS POINT.
ALL PERSONNEL ENTERING THIS AREA CAN BE EXPOSED TO VERBAL
ATTACK AND/OR ABUSE FOR THEIR PERSONAL OPINIONS, BELIEFS,
AND/OR FEELINGS CONCERNING, BUT NOT LIMITED TO THE FOL-
LOWING: SEX, RACE, CREED, COLOR, POLITICS, ECOLOGY, MILITARY,
FINANCE, EDUCATIONAL, SOCIAL ISSUES, STATE, FEDERAL, GOVERN-
MENT POLICIES AND OTHER TOPICS. NO STUPID PEOPLE ALLOWED
BEYOND THIS POINT.

At two-fifteen, *The Factor* team had gathered to present their ideas for upcoming shows. The hour-long program is divided into five blocks, labeled A to
E. Pitches are made for possible subjects to fill the blocks—talking points,
crime of the week, most ridiculous, and so forth. Producers, bookers, researchers, and interns sat on the edge of their chairs as the boss sauntered in.

Chewing a wad of gum like a baseball pitcher in the old tobacco chaw days,
O'Reilly took his seat next to the board, a big cork bulletin board covered with
yellow, blue, and pink index cards, indicating works in progress.

"Okay," O'Reilly said. "Couple of notes . . . Larry King has now decided to go
tabloid, which is, you know, going to spike him up a little bit. So they did Loretta
Young's blood child last week and Rock Hudson's gardener, or whatever. Well, we
can't really count on that, but if you do find Lon Chaney's blood child . . . But
that's what they're going to do. They're going to go strictly tabloid across the
board, which is going to help, there's no question about it. Especially this summer
when there are older people watching. The political stuff isn't working for anybody, so just keep your eye on that when you're making pitches. These guys just
aren't pulling in the ratings. Political stuff has gotta to be very poignant."

O'Reilly thinks he has something like a radar beam that guides him in the
selection process for stories. It's not ideology, so much as what he calls "emotional content." He is interested in a topic that will keep an audience's attention
while allowing him to get something off his chest or stomach before they turn
that dial. The cable news audience has the fastest fingers in the west or east or
central, O'Reilly explained. "There should be an Olympic event for remote control users. Americans would win easily. If what they are viewing is not their subject, they are out of there."

The staff has been going over the day's news with a vacuum cleaner, looking for stories from local markets that do not usually get a national spotlight, that raise compelling or challenging issues, O'Reilly's kind of stories. They had arrived for the pitch session, armed with clips from the wires, the Internet, newspapers, and magazines. Arranged in a horseshoe around him, the staff nervously waits while O'Reilly, frowning, studies the board indicating what the staff is already working on.

"Okay, whatdaya got?" he finally asks. He listens with a sour expression on his face as the staff throw new story ideas at him.

"In Tennessee," a production assistant pitched that afternoon, "eight people brought a complaint, a lawsuit against the foster care there, and won, and the judge agreed that the state had mismanaged the welfare system. The state agreed to settle the lawsuit and spend millions . . ."

O'Reilly starts to snore.

"Wait, wait, they put a nine-year-old in a homeless shelter for one year as part of his foster care."

"Next?"

"A First Amendment attorney has come out against obscenity laws," an associate producer begins. "He says obscenity laws actually hurt little children."

"Why?"

"Because it doesn't give them the critical thinking skills to live in our society."

"Okay, I'll take it. E-Block."

"Hugh Downs has a new Web site starting today in Arizona," a booker says.

"Really? How old is he— a hundred and twelve?"

"Going to be interviewing people on human values, including Hugh Hefner."

O'Reilly raises his eyebrows. "Hef on American values? All right, Back of the Book [segment]. How come he has Hef? Ask him . . . but be careful. I don't want to give him a heart attack."

"I just have one thing," an associate producer says. "Fox News on Friday will release the results of a poll they did on Monica Lewinsky's blue dress. It hasn't been given back to her, and people want to know why. Because she would probably like to sell it."

"What are we going to do with that?"

"I thought you could have a debate."

"About what?"

"Does she deserve to get the dress back or not? And why are they holding it up?"

"Give that to Larry."

"America's greatest thinker has been picked," an intern says. "Some woman in Cape Cod."

"Yeah, but we've done that a million times. What else do you got?"

"A *U.S. News & World Report* writer did an op-ed regarding Canada, where he says that—no, wait, just wait—they are our biggest terrorist threat."

"I know I'm frightened to death of those Canadians myself. What else?"

"I know you wanted Bill Murray on a long time ago," a talent booker says.

"He's a crazy guy. He's not going to come on."

"He's got a new barbecue joint opening. Do you have anything you want to talk to him about, politics?"

"We'll talk about his barbecue place, if you can get him. And his movie career. Tell him I thought he was brilliant in *Charlie's Angels.*"

"One more. There is a woman in the middle of Utah who says her neighbor has a topless maid. She was wearing a thong bikini to do her gardening. We have video."

"All right, we'll do it. It's ridiculous enough. My *Inside Edition* past is flashing before me."

"Erin Brockovich," a booker says. "She is now going to be with the people in upstate New York, the homeowners whose homes have been contaminated by . . ."

"I only want Erin Brockovich if she had an affair with Condit."

And so it goes. Managing the news is his idea of fun. "It's a good story," he sagely tells the production assistant who keeps pitching as O'Reilly stands up and starts to go, "but we won't get a good number on that." He leaves the pod, throwing out suggestions about upcoming stories: "Tell Lieberman we'll use him, but he should lighten up. Ask Reich what he wants to talk about. He's a socialist. Maybe we can rile him up about some subject."

Talent bookers and producers start working the phones. It's not easy getting guests on *The O'Reilly Factor.*

Roger Ailes understands why. "Do you want to be lectured by some eight-foot guy telling you you're an idiot, and you don't give a shit about the country, and he gives you the last word, then he interrupts and goes to commercial? I don't know, I wouldn't."

O'Reilly has a simple way of dividing the world: those who will appear on his show to answer his questions, take his abuse, and otherwise be what he calls "accountable," and those who won't. They are dismissed as, among the kinder things he thinks of them, cowards.

"He punishes those who don't want to answer the call," Ailes said. "But, you know, it's also what makes him so good and the number one guy. In other words, he's so focused on that show that you don't want to take any of that drive and passion out of it. You know, it's a lot better than a star saying 'Nobody wants to do my show.' What the hell, given the two choices, I'd rather have Bill."

In his first seven years on the show senior producer Dave Brown said he knows of forty to fifty times that Hillary Clinton's office had turned down his, producers Nate Fredman and Rob Monaco's invitations. O'Reilly has gotten a lot of mileage out of Senator Clinton's continuing failure to appear.

"Bill would be more than happy to give Jesse Jackson a half hour for a conversation," Brown said.

Most members of Congress will come on the show. "Every time he asks me, I go," said Congressman Barney Frank of Massachusetts. "I consider it an obligation." Members of the Bush administration think twice or three times.

Celebrity gatekeepers often consider *The Factor* a risky venue for their clients. George Clooney, Alec Baldwin, Barbra Streisand, Martin Sheen, Rob Reiner, Harry Belafonte, and Sean Penn boycott the show.

Staying away from *The Factor* is not the best way to deal with O'Reilly. Those individuals and institutions whose stories he is examining may feel they are giving validity to his attacks by answering them. The ostrich approach doesn't work with him. He keeps digging and coming back to the subject, as Jesse Jackson discovered in O'Reilly's sixty-eight stories on his finances in *The Factor*'s first four years on the air. Not answering the call in O'Reilly's universe is tantamount to being guilty.

The best defense against O'Reilly, as his boss Roger Ailes explained: "First of all, don't do whatever he is accusing you of. Second, correct the error of your ways. Third, come on the show and face him. If you've done something that O'Reilly thinks is wrong, come on, say you're full of baloney and here is why."

He tends to treat those who bite the bullet and come on *The Factor* with respect that sometimes verges on fawning. He admires their courage. It sometimes shuts him up. Trying to ignore him is a red flag in the bull's eye.

. . .

At four o'clock that afternoon, a production assistant handed O'Reilly "the numbers." O'Reilly is like a tuning fork that starts to hit high C when he studies the Nielsen overnights. He devours them. He would drop a phone call from the Oval Office to look at ratings, although he can do both as a major multitasker.

He tracks numbers the way the National Hurricane Center follows weather patterns. Nielsen ratings are taken every fifteen minutes. "So we can see every fifteen minutes the audience flow. We know what the audience is doing."

King's numbers were going up, as O'Reilly had predicted about the new tabloid slant. "He is not as dead as he had been for a while. I was at *Inside Edition.* I know what tabloid can do. You have to stop them."

"Not only are we up against the other cable networks," he told me, "King. Geraldo, Williams. We also have to look at *Survivor, Weakest Link,* whatever else they got on at eight. The cable audience cruises, and you gotta get them involved fast as they go around the dial. They have no idea what they are watching, it's hypnosis now. But they do know if they're bored. My world basically is figuring out what night it is and how to engage the audience at the top so they'll stay for the first four or five minutes, and then tease something they want to see. It's a psychological warfare game."

By November 2001 *The O'Reilly Factor* was beating *Larry King Live* regularly by half a rating point or more. It was the largest margin a King opponent ever had at the time. By 2003, a ratings loss for *The O'Reilly Factor* against *Larry King Live* in the previous two years was so rare it was considered newsworthy. "I just murdered him," O'Reilly was telling me. "And since that time, it's grown, it's grown. And Larry himself is having a nervous breakdown. He's physically going crazy. And he still gets the big-name guests. Today they had Colin Powell on. I had Lenny from Astoria, okay, okay. That's who I led with. He didn't get his check from the United Way. Lenny kicked Colin Powell's ass, okay? Now they thought they were going to get enormous numbers with Colin Powell over at CNN. They got shocked when they came in and tanked. And the reason they tanked was everyone knew that Larry was going to go, 'ah huu, ah huu, ah huu,' and Powell was going to do his talking points. They weren't going to get any information from him. You were going to get the same stuff he said a thousand other times. Lenny was pissed. They wanted to hear why Lenny, you know, his poor wife was dead [in the World Trade Center], he got kids screaming at him, you know. So Lenny beats Colin Powell. Because of, you know, people's sense that Lenny is honest, that's real.

"And that's why the networks are crumbling. It's not a real situation over there. And now people they've seen it; they've seen what aggressive journalism can be. It's hard to go back to what they're giving you at CNN."

In the spring of 2002, O'Reilly had started his syndicated daily two-hour radio show, known as *The Radio Factor*. It launched on May 8, with 215 affiliates. "It was off the charts," O'Reilly said. "It had the largest rollout in radio history. I think we had the most successful first year, made more money than any freshman radio show in history." He now has over four hundred radio affiliates.

O'Reilly had a contract to do a syndicated late-night TV show in 2002, Roger Ailes told me. "He wisely said, 'I'd rather do radio. I'm going to come in at ten-thirty in the morning anyway.' He figured he could squeeze in the radio show from twelve to two. It would be a warm-up for his TV show, and he could get out of here at seven or eight."

To make the double-header smoother, syndicator Westwood One built a special studio for O'Reilly in the Fox building. "I'll try to get one guest into the studio for each hour," O'Reilly said of the M.O. for *The Radio Factor,* and keep them on. I drive the discussion for the first half hour, and then callers pick up for the second half hour."

The radio show gave him a chance to get more of his opinions and sermons out there. He can be saying one minute, "If President Bush doesn't believe in global warming, he is nuts. To deny that is crazy." And then he will jump to media abuse, cultural trends, injustices in the legal system, mixing in advice on everything from dating to thrift to parental relationships, religion, how to dress to be a success. He won't cover some stories that other radio people do day after day after day. "We did Iraq a little bit today," said Dave Tabacoff, executive producer of both the TV and radio *Factor*s, "but then we had what he calls an 'all-skate.' Which is anything. Because he gets bored. In fairness, there's only so much he can say, whether it's Iraq or the Condi Rice story. He wants to tell that story, then he wants to move on. I think that's good for the listener and him." His favorite subject is terrorism. "It's a very lively show," said Tabacoff. "There is nothing like calling somebody un-American to fill up the phone lines."

On radio, he also has a platform during the day to be in touch with the folks as the news is happening, instead of depending on the eyes of his staff. "What say you?" his signature going to the phones, is his direct line to the folks.

O'Reilly is different on radio than TV, aside from length, which is twice as long. On radio, he has more time to develop arguments. "I'm a lawyer," said Lis Wiehl, the radio show's cohost, a liberal whom O'Reilly sometimes describes as being from the planet of Oz. "Bill takes you point by point in a logical progression down to the conclusion of his argument. So many other radio talk-show hosts argue by jumping right in at the conclusion. O'Reilly would make a great trial lawyer."

He can be a funny guy, which is harder to appreciate on TV. He has a sense of humor, and he can mock himself and mock others. He had a guest one day who wanted to put a tax on fast foods. "So that the morons who ate there would help defray the cost of their medical benefits," O'Reilly said in support of the proposal. "Guy goes through the drive-in window: 'Give me two artery-cloggers, please.'" On radio, he can do his imitation of Howard Cosell, while reminiscing about having done the last interview with his idol before he died. The bumpers between commercials are opportunities for wry commentary. On a bad day in Iraq, O'Reilly suggested that "Drew Carey should be in charge. The Iraqi people need a laugh." And on the radio he gets a chance to play snippets of his beloved seventies music.

You can hear a lot more of O'Reilly's personality on radio. It's more conversation than debating. "He has much more to offer," said Dave Tabacoff. "He is interested in a lot of things, social issues, political, economic, and cultural. He is not a political hack who just goes down a certain line."

Liberal callers attack him regularly. "Same thing on the right," O'Reilly said. "You get these crazy nuts on the right. I mean, you got a guy who will say, all homosexuals are disqualified from any kind of public position because they're all going to hell. And it says so in Deuteronomy. What do you do? What do you say? They can't be Boy Scout leaders because they're all going to hell because Deuteronomy says they are? I mean, if you're coming at it from that point of view, your mind is chained, and you're never going to see what it really is."

As a reality check, every day O'Reilly has an intern listening to Rush Limbaugh and jotting down what he talks about. "Because we compete against him and we want to see what he's doing. It's the same thing every day. Democrats are bad. You figured maybe once they'd be okay. Out of three hundred sixty-five days, maybe they'd luck into one good position. The planets are aligned, so like one thing they say is good? No, nothing ever. And I'm just saying to myself, you know how can you listen to this day in and day out, when no matter what the Democrats say or do, it's going to be bad. I just have no patience for this. But, listen, he's made gazillions of dollars. He has a huge following. I'm not trying to be petty. I'm just saying the way I look at the world is not that way."

The extra money, of course, was another reason for doing a radio show. "Once you get the franchise running," explained O'Reilly, "it's extremely lucrative, and it fits right in with the TV programs as synergy." While still trailing number-one radio talk show host Rush Limbaugh in the number of affiliates—625 to 420 in 2004—O'Reilly was seen as more of a menace because he has two pulpits. Limbaugh was a failure on TV in 1992. "And that makes us extremely powerful," O'Reilly said, "which is why *The New York Times* is just scared to death of the show and me."

By September 2004, Mike Wallace on *60 Minutes* was saying "more than twenty million people a week watch the O'Reilly TV show, but there are millions more who hear him on the Radio."

His books have sold more than four million copies. *The O'Reilly Factor: The Good, the Bad, and the Completely Ridiculous in American Life*, his first book, was published in 2000 and was on the *New York Times* Best Seller List for thirty-two weeks. A classic of short-attention-span literature, the 150 pages was a print version of his TV show, a series of opinions, enriched with facts, factoids, homilies, and sermons taken from his life and show, in which, as the *Wall Street Journal* critic summarized, "Mr. O'Reilly unburdens himself on everything from what made him a good date in his bachelor days to the table manners that will tip off your prole origins."

O'Reilly's second book, a best seller published in 2001, *The No Spin Zone: Confrontations with the Powerful and Famous in America*, was a compendium of his favorite interviews, including sessions with the noted philosopher Sean "Puff Daddy" Combs, James Carville, Dr. Laura Schlessinger, Al Sharpton, and Dan Rather. It was on the *Times* Best Seller List for twenty weeks, eight weeks at No. 1.

The premise of his third nonfiction book, *Who's Looking Out for You?* is that common folks need somebody to protect them. Filled with useful tips, the book is by a Bill O'Reilly "who is mad as hell—and he's not going to let you take it anymore," as the book jacket suggests.

His first work of fiction, *Those Who Trespass*—the murder thriller in which the author managed to assassinate some of the real-life characters that plagued him in his professional real life—was published in 1998 and sold 80,000 copies. "The publisher was incompetent," O'Reilly explained. A 2003 paperback version sold 110,000 copies. Mel Gibson had optioned it for the movies. "Gibson is a big *Factor* fan," O'Reilly told me.

In his downtime, he also was writing a syndicated weekly newspaper column that was appearing in over three hundred papers from the *Ketchikan Daily News* in Ketchikan, Alaska, to the *New York Post*. And there is always a magazine like *Parade* that wanted to know more about his thoughts on friendship and going down the Grand Canyon by mule and other adventures with O'Reilly and his band of brothers.

O'Reilly is also an accomplished stump orator, flying around the country in a private jet delivering his body and golden words to adoring multitudes. By July 2004, with his TV and radio schedule, he was only doing one or two speeches a month. "I hear that he speaks at Ku Klux Klan meetings," joked veteran newsman Doug Johnson, who worked with O'Reilly at ABC News. "They couldn't get Hitler, so they got O'Reilly," added columnist and lecturer John Leo of *U.S. News & World Report*. The bodies hearing the sermons from the O'Reilly mount actually included an economics club in Michigan, a group of orthodontists, an association of national roofing contractors, the Automotive Service Association, and the Jewish Federation of Los Angeles. Generally speaking, he discussed current events, his thoughts and views. It's *The O'Reilly Factor* where the flesh can be pressed, said his lecture agent, Don Walker of the Harry Walker Agency.

"To give you an idea of the demand, when he started doing this in 2000, he was getting $10,000 per speech," Walker said. "By June 2006, Bill received $80,000, plus a private jet, per speech. But the price keeps going up." By comparison, Tim Russert was getting $50,000 a speech at the time.

O'Reilly is also a merchant prince with a flourishing self-marketing empire that seems to sell everything on his Web site except O'Reilly Kleenex—as yet.

On billoreilly.com, the master merchandiser offers, besides his books and audiotapes of the books, accessories every Spinhead would want, many of whom buy: "Spin Stops Here" doormats, "Spin Stops Here" beach towels, license plate frames, coffee mugs and "The Rain Stops Here" umbrellas ($37.50). "The Buck Stops Here," the Web site proudly announces in a testimonial to free enterprise and the making-it-while-you-can spirit that made

America strong. Some of the proceeds, as O'Reilly regularly explains on *The Factor,* go to "Bill's Charities."

There is also a premium Web site for advanced Spinheads. They get to "enjoy *The Radio Factor* on demand at 9 P.M. (EST) each day," as well as listening to previous shows in the show's library anytime. "Get Bill's opening monologue every day."

He ended one night's news show by reminding viewers that a full line of Bill O'Reilly products can be found on ShopNet Daily. "Purchase a copy of Bill O'Reilly's *The No Spin Zone* and receive a free *No Spin Zone* bumper sticker and a free three-month trial offer to *Whistleblower* magazine." The end of his program, with its plethora of *tchotchkas,* sounds like a public TV show during pledge time begathons.

"He sells too much crap on the show," Roger Ailes said. "But he also gets the highest ratings in the history of cable news."

O'Reilly doesn't like to talk about how much money he makes. His father told him not to, and he still doesn't. But he will say that in terms of salary he is one of the top five broadcast journalists in the nation. Other sources claim that a six-year contract with Fox News he had signed in 1999 would earn him $24 to $30 million. He has since signed a new six-year deal, ending in 2009. With bonus and escalation clauses, it's probably in the neighborhood of $50 million from the Fox deal alone. He is cheap at the price. One-tenth of all FNC revenue comes from *The Factor,* a business magazine estimated. O'Reilly thinks that "one-tenth" is too conservative.

In a profession where offices tend to have a direct correlation with ratings, O'Reilly works in a hole in the wall located in a corner on the seventeenth floor, high atop Fox News Channel headquarters. Furnished with office furniture that seems to be on loan from a thrift shop, his office space seems more a foxhole than the center of the O'Reilly moneymaking empire. It has the feel of a temporary abode of somebody who doesn't unpack his boxes, a habit developed in O'Reilly's twenty-five years of moving around the country until he reached the seventeenth floor. As much as it is possible for a man who is on TV and radio fifteen hours a week, Bill O'Reilly keeps a low profile.

There is room in the office for a two-seater couch, two chairs, and a laptop. The office couch is fully occupied by post office containers overflowing with mail and packages from "the folks," adoring fans and enemies. No matter how many times I came to the office during the two years of interviews, I was amazed by what a mess his work quarters were. The medium-size desk is piled high with paper and books, the raw materials for all the writing he grinds out daily.

You don't realize how tall O'Reilly is watching him on television. Fortunately, guests like the former secretary of labor Robert Reich (four foot ten and one half inches) are always sitting down. Off camera, O'Reilly looks puffier, his hair thinner. His face is a splotchy pale white, not the healthy robust orange of pancake as seen on TV. Every night the wan look is miraculously transformed. Dressed in his pale blue shirt and bland sober tie, he could easily pass for an accountant like his father, someone who can't wait for five o'clock and the train back to the suburbs.

He is sitting at his desk with his feet planted firmly on a "Hillary" doormat. The walls in his foxhole are festooned with career and academic achievements. There are his diplomas from Marist and Harvard, framed advertisements from trade publications, depicting such high spots in his work history as *Inside Edition*'s ratings breakthrough year, and a montage of snapshot photos of his family and the top twenty or thirty closest friends. His Marist College football jersey Number 12 is under glass on the wall. At the far end of the office, he has mounted a newspaper front page from September 15, 1901, the day after President McKinley died from an assassin's bullet. Few TV news stars think about McKinley anymore. The flag on the wall is from the United States embassy in Saigon, given to him by a Marine who had taken it down right before they began pushing the helicopters off the aircraft carriers during the fall of South Vietnam.

O'Reilly's day begins in a North Shore Long Island town where he lives with his wife, Maureen, and their two children. "She's as old as Jesse Jackson's," he explains about his daughter, Madeline, born in 2000. "But she's legitimate." The O'Reillys' son, Spencer, named after O'Reilly's best friend, newsman Joe Spencer, who died in a helicopter crash, was born in 2004. "Ten pounds sixteen ounces," O'Reilly said. "Big boy. His middle name is William. I saddled him with that."

In 1980, O'Reilly had purchased a town house in Harmon Cove, a condominium community located in the Meadowlands of northern New Jersey near the stadium where the Jets and Giants play. "I made a lot of money on that place," he explained about his first home. "I bought it in the beginning, you know, when they were building them, and I sold it in nineteen eighty-two at the top of the market. But I was never there. It was just basically a place where I used to put my stuff, my boxes, because I was working so much."

Rather than build a palatial manor like other media millionaires, O'Reilly buys old, needs-work homes. He enjoys the experience of expanding a smaller house. Fixer-uppers are also cheaper.

"I know Long Island as well as anybody knows Long Island," O'Reilly said. "There are a couple of places I figured when I got some money I would like to live there. I didn't want to live in Old Westbury, the estate area, or any of that. I wanted a neighborhood. So I moved to Manhasset nine years ago [1995] and bought a nice house." Small backyard, a living room, dining room, kitchen, "not opulent," according to his agent, Carole Cooper.

"This was before I was married," O'Reilly said. "It was a wreck. But I had my guys come in and fix it up. Guys I know who are carpenters and painters, who I know aren't going steal from me. I bring them in, and they just fixed it up, beautiful. So I lived there, and then I got married and needed more space."

Roger Ailes had been worried about the living arrangements his hot new star had made for himself in a nice open neighborhood as the show gained momentum and became such a hit. "Bill, now you're out there pissing off half the world, I think you ought to think about moving to a little more secure situation."

"I had my eye on this house," O'Reilly said when he started looking around for a little more space. He had a real estate agent who showed him a million homes, but there was one location he wanted. "It was up on a little hill, a beautiful view of the Manhasset Bay, and it's an ancient New England Colonial, a style which I like." After three years, the house finally came up for sale. "And I had the means to buy it."

The real estate agent sealed the deal by telling O'Reilly his dream house had "a little history." Groucho Marx once lived there.

"I said, 'Wow.' So I did a little research, and it was a very interesting story.

"In the twenties, Groucho and Chico and Harpo were here on Broadway doing vaudeville. Fatty Arbuckle had just been tried for that terrible thing, and his career was shit. Apparently, Chico was running around with thirteen-, twelve-year-old girls, and the manager of the Marx Brothers got really scared. So he moved the guys out to the only house in a section of Manhasset. This house they hated, because after the show the car would take them there, and they were looking at trees. Nothing to do."

The Marx brothers were in residence several months, then went back to the West Coast, but they kept the house as their East Coast home. They sold it in the thirties, and it's only had three other owners.

"We feel like it has a lot of laughter in this house," Maureen says of the Marx Brothers connection. But there was nothing funny about it when they moved in.

O'Reilly bought the house without his wife's advice and consent, just as his father had done. "The people I bought it from had run it down really bad, and whereas the outside was still nice, the inside was a wreck." O'Reilly's wife was appalled. Don't worry, he assured her, he would fix things.

The original house on a half-acre site was built in 1906 and had been re-modeled often in its first century. But nothing like what O'Reilly did to it. "I just gutted the whole thing, added about four or five rooms, and restored it. We had to change every room except one tiny bathroom. The living room was red."

"All red," said Maureen, laughing. "The ceiling, the trim, window frames, ceiling to floor. It was like an open vein.

"So I came in and said, 'We'll just do it all over again.' I wanted to add two wings to the house and a new master bedroom. There was a detached guest-house, a monster that we knocked down. I made it all happen."

He's the one who designed the house, Maureen said. It now has five bed-rooms, four baths, an office, living room, dining room, kitchen, and family room. "I just decorated it. And furnished it. We have different talents."

"I can't hammer a nail," said O'Reilly, "but I can visualize, you know, in my mind what I want the thing to look like. So it came out exactly the way I wanted it to."

"I'm a nail hammerer," Maureen said. "I'm the handy one. I fix everything in the house and build things." In her spare time, Maureen volunteers for Habitat for Humanity. She helped build houses before Madeline was born. "So I learned a lot of skills. Like plumbing. The plumber was wondering, no offence, why I was asking what size pipes he was using. How did I know the difference?"

Painted white with black shutters, the O'Reilly place doesn't stand out among the neighbors' Colonials. Black-eyed Susans edge the modest lawn. Up the asphalt driveway to the side of a two-door garage is an outdoor basketball hoop. Across the street by the water's edge is a swimming pool left by the previous owners. It is the only one in the town, which bans pools. It was built by Groucho Marx surreptitiously, in retaliation against the local restricted country club, which barred him from membership because he was Jewish. "My wife is Christian," he argued, "so couldn't my son wade in your pool up to his waist?" Marx built the pool, disguised as a wing to the house until the scaffolding came down. O'Reilly hates the pool, but his daughter loves it.

"I have to tell this story," volunteered old friend Emily Rooney, who had been invited to visit. "I got such a kick walking into his house on Long Island. First of all, it was a lot about what he paid for it and what a good investment it was. Every painting or whatever you want to call it, every piece of work on the wall, is something about him, you know, his degrees, his this and that, his awards, his historical letters collection, and they're all posted too high. You know, they're like his eye level. You know how you're supposed to have everything one-third down the wall, no matter how tall anybody is? Everything is his height. It's hilarious. So obviously Maureen had nothing to do with hanging the artwork. I couldn't believe it."

After talking for two hours on *The Radio Factor* one afternoon O'Reilly described for me how he managed his workload. "I'll give you my schedule. This is how it goes down."

He gets up around six-thirty and plays with his kids whenever they wake up, between seven-thirty and eight. They sing songs watching TV together, Barney and Elmo. "I like Elmo. He's a good guy." He had taught Madeline three Beach Boys songs, "Surfer Girl," "In My Room," and "Fun, Fun, Fun." "I'm the whitest guy on the planet," he says, even though he is great admirer of Motown.

He'll stay for a little bit in Madeline's room because he doesn't get to spend much time with her at night. When O'Reilly comes home, Maureen said, "Even if I think she's asleep, the door will open, and I'll hear her going, 'Daddy, Daddy, Daddy.' She's awake and waiting. And he'll go up and tell her stories and read with her and talk about her day."

Mommy reads stories and Daddy makes up stories. "She's already in bed, and it's dark in there. So by making up stories, he doesn't have to turn on the light to read and she can stay in a state of half sleep. She tells me about those stories. He tells stories that have a nice moral. He's teaching her lessons, which is very nice. It teaches her to use her imagination, which she reminds me all the time. She'll be playing something, and I'll say, 'What are you doing?' She says, 'Mommy, I'm just using imagination.'"

O'Reilly told me about his theory of child-raising, which is different from his father's. "I'm basically grooming them for public service, like the Kennedy kids. My role at home is basically to provide them with some serenity, so the house isn't chaotic. I take care of any danger or anything that could have impact. What my kids get from me is a sense of security. My little daughter is afraid of bees. And I said, 'Well, no bees will ever come around when Daddy's here. Bees are afraid of Daddy.' She loves it, she loves it. Her birthday was three weeks ago, and she said, 'Daddy, you can't come to the party unless you're friendly to the kids.'

"This is the kind of stuff she comes out with.

"I'm letting my wife micromanage them because I'm not there all day, I just want them to be kids. That's my big thing. I want them to live in a fantasy world, play, have fun and no stress. If they want to be on a soccer team, they can be, but I'm not going to be at every game. I want them to build a little self-reliance. I also want them to know that Daddy is not going to micromanage their life for them, and neither is Mommy. Sometimes I have to pull Mommy back and say, 'Look, just let her play.'"

Young Spencer is already expressing his independence at three. He told O'Reilly one weekend in 2006, "Daddy, go away."

O'Reilly's attitude toward little boys of a certain age, like three, is that they are monsters. He talks about Spencer in terms of what disasters he has been involved in: Spencer is currently climbing up the linen closet, Spencer is munching on the drapes. He is in his tough-guy Clint Eastwood mode, talking about his little fiend.

"I wasn't an insecure kid. I mean, I knew my father was going to come home with the rent money and the food was going to be on the table. There was going to be a structure. Sunday we're going to church. We'll go out for breakfast every Sunday at Thomas Ham and Eggery on Old Country Road. We'll go to the beach on Saturday. It wasn't chaotic. But there was always a sense in the house, on my mother's part, my sister's part, and my part, that anything could happen. There isn't that in my house. I mean, nothing is going to happen in my house unless I want it to happen. See, my father couldn't control himself at certain times. I always control myself."

O'Reilly comes down from Madeline's room by about eight or eight-thirty. And then he starts reading the morning paper, watching the TV news, checking the radio. "Checking everything out," Maureen says.

The O'Reillys only get the *Times* at home, but he says he reads about a dozen a day. They are stacked up at the office waiting for him: *The Wall Street Journal*, the two New York tabs—the *Post* and the *Daily News*—*The Washington Post*, the *Chicago Tribune*, *The Boston Globe*, and *USA Today* among them. "He reads the paper much faster than I do," said Maureen, "because I'm kind of a cover-to-cover-type person, and I think he kind of skims first. He reads the important things."

The most important thing he is looking for is evidence of bias in the *Times*' pages. It's a rare day when he doesn't find it.

Before *The Radio Factor* began, O'Reilly would go out for breakfast at a village coffee shop. He'd set up his A.M. headquarters at Louie's Restaurant on Manhasset's main street. It proved, in his mind, that he was still "a regular guy." "I'd have a little breakfast there. Sometimes I have eggs, sometimes I have fruit, it doesn't matter."

Bill O'Reilly's not like Long Island's other media luminary, Howard Stern, who has insulated himself from the community. "He wanted to be a rock star," O'Reilly says. "I didn't want to be a rock star. I don't mind people coming up and saying hello to me. Nobody bothers me. I zip around. I take a book and go to the beach. I don't need to have bells and whistles going twenty-four hours a day."

What he liked about his morning headquarters in the coffee shop is that it had cops, firemen, construction guys. "They just filter in, and I just say, 'Hey, what's going on, what do you think,' and they like this, they don't like that. I get a lot of good stuff there. People know I go. They come in, and I find out what they think and what they're interested in. It's a good barometer of what they're talking about."

Then he goes home, and into the shower, throws clothes on, jumps into the car about nine-thirty.

Until recently, he drove into the city in a regular, previously owned sedan. "Nothing fancy." Then he gets stuck on the LIE like a regular guy. Driving a car from Nassau County through the borough of Queens is the root canal of automotive experience. "The Expressway," he explains, "has been under construction since the Revolutionary War. They build roads better in Zambia than they do out here, and they use coconuts."

Sometimes he also took the LIRR. "It's good because I get to talk to people, the conductors, all telling me what they like and don't like."

One of the bad things about his increased work schedule with the radio show is that he is now driven into the city in a black car. "I always liked driving. Just because I can, you know, play around with the radio and stuff. I just don't like the black car concept, but now I have to do it." He never takes a stretch, the vehicle of choice for stars of his magnitude. "All I need is Mike Kinsley seeing me riding around in a stretch. I don't even feel comfortable in a limo. I never know what to do with my legs. I keep slipping off the seat."

At ten o'clock, while in the car, O'Reilly does his radio conference call, during which the producers map out what they are going to do for the radio show, which is laid out in four half-hour grids.

That conference call lasts about fifteen minutes. Then at ten-thirty, the television show calls to set the lineup for the day with the producers. "I'm still in the car, because it's the LI Expressway. I may have gone a half mile, you never know. And then we lay out the TV program."

About eleven, O'Reilly arrives at the Fox News Channel building. "And they try to give me research for the radio. I get e-mails and things like that. I try to grab something to eat."

At noon, he is in the Westwood One radio studio. He talks for two hours, opining on the day's news, throwing the mikes open to listeners with his "What say you?" He reads the papers and eats a grilled cheese sandwich during commercial breaks. "And then at two I'll come up to the office here and maybe take a ten- or fifteen-minute break.

"There isn't a lot of action during the day, other than me just doing administrative work," he says. "Writing the show, calling people up, that kind of thing, answering inquiries. Writing my column. Writing the next book. And then I have to go down and start work on the TV show."

On Mondays and Thursdays, he gets a haircut, then goes into the *Factor* pitch meeting in the Fox News basement. There is always an air of suspense as the *Factor* production team, mostly twentysomethings, wonder what kind of mood the boss is in today. They throw story ideas at him. To a producer who suggests a segment on a book about charity, he responds, "While you were saying that I was thinking of the Mets game." Dyspeptically, he looks around the circle of chairs. "Give me something I can put on the air, please." He rarely pauses more than five seconds on a topic.

On his way out of the pitch meeting, he has been handed "editorial packets," what they call the factual material for that night's show. The packets are like term papers. "But they have to be short," explained producer Amy Sohnen, who helped originate the method. Every day each of the *Factor* producers become an expert on something. "You have to have a lot of information, but it has to be shaped so that it's not too much for him to absorb. He can absorb a lot, but we're doing six segments a day so it has to be laid out in a visually and editorially appealing way. You have the topic, a few paragraphs about what the subject is, the most important information in the packet in a cogent way, you have the guest, the location of the guest, the title, political affiliation. And you can't leave any of this stuff off the template, because it's all really important. And then you have the guest's point of view, and you have to put in that packet the opposing point of view. You have to give Bill enough ammunition to be able to challenge the guest. Now, thankfully, Bill is one of the smartest people I have ever worked with, and he knows what he's looking for. And, trust me, if that information isn't in the packet, you hear about it."

Between two and three, O'Reilly devours the editorial packets, Sohnen said. "Really absorbs it, reads it, questions it."

At three o'clock, it's time to write the show. Few network news superstars write their own material. He closes the door of his office and writes it all—from the Talking Points Memo at the head of the show to the segues for the segments, from the A to E Blocks, to the responses to viewer snail and e-mail. The mail sorters had picked out the good, the bad, and the completely ridiculous. The ones he especially dotes on are those saying he is the biggest idiot alive. He loves tangling with "the folks," letting them take their best shot at him, a technique he learned in Boston local news. At the end of each night's program, he runs the best of the unflattering e-mails. As is his way, O'Reilly gives himself the last word. His editorial response—in Block E—often pokes fun at himself, some say, a charming way to embrace his severest critics. He even writes the promos, teases, and sales pitches for *The O'Reilly Factor* merchandise.

It takes him less than two hours to bang it out, as he puts it, like an old newspaperman. What is written sounds like O'Reilly talking. And it is. He finishes at four-thirty, takes and makes a few personal phone calls, reads a personal letter or two, fields intercom calls from fact-checkers, producers on stories in progress, and talks to his wife Maureen about their children and what's for dinner.

And then it's showtime. Slipping into his designer-supplied suit jacket—he has gone from Arnold Brandt to Joseph Aboud in recent years—he finishes dressing for the show, picking one of the nondescript bluish ties, which look like leftover Father's Day gifts. He puts in his contact lenses, goes to the bathroom to brush his teeth, comes back to the office, slides the packets under his arm, and saunters to the elevator and a first-floor studio, a space that seems like a closet. They waste no expense on fancy studios at Fox News.

As O'Reilly gets ready for the six o'clock taping, the action really starts. "You got the video stuff flowing in, the last-minute teleconferencing call hookup details with guests around the country, and doing the show. That takes us to seven. So a full day."

O'Reilly does not socialize or stay in town after leaving *The Zone*, as he also calls the show, except when he is booked to appear on an early morning news show, like *Imus*. He is not a regular at East Side cocktail parties. He doesn't go to Le Cirque for dinner with other media celebrities and agents or spend quality time at 21 pressing the flesh with the faithful. He and his wife Maureen don't attend openings.

His idea of fun after the taping is going home and taking his family out to Nathan's Famous on Old Country Road in Westbury. "Last night I had a root beer and a corned beef sandwich. A lot of screaming kids in Nathan's, though. When I walk in there, people are, like, stunned. 'What's he doing in Nathan's?' I like Nathan's. It's like you should be in the Hamptons with the rest of the media superstars. I hate the Hamptons. Haven't been out there once this summer.

"I mean, I used to be a water safety instructor for the Town of Babylon, okay? So I still got a pass to go to those beaches for the rest of my life. It's beautiful. Why do I have to go down to the Hamptons for three hours in traffic and pay eighteen dollars for a hot dog?"

The Hamptons to O'Reilly is a place to go clam digging. "My father took us out there. My uncle, my father, and a guy named Joe Russo, who was my next-door neighbor. I was only six. We'd go out and get the boat, drive to the clams, the back route. Three or four buckets of clams. My father would take the cherrystones, chop them up. Big dinner. And nobody was out there in those days. When you went to the Hamptons there was no traffic jam. We could whip out there in an hour. It was amazing. If I had just known, I would have bought up as much property as I could have gotten."

O'Reilly enjoys going to baseball games. At Yankee Stadium, he sits in George Steinbrenner's box, but he has never been a Yankee fan. The Mets are still his passion. People recognize him at the ballpark. "He just loves it," Maureen says. "It gives him a chance to talk to people. He gets so busy that he doesn't really see many people, because he's always rushing from place to place. He likes to talk to them. They'll come over and tell him what they like, don't like. At baseball games, in the church, restaurants. It never bothers him when they come over. Most people are very nice, very accommodating. They'll say hello, chat with him, and he's very grateful, very appreciative of anyone who comes over and says, 'I watch your show . . . I love your program . . . Thank you . . . thank you.' He's very cognizant where his popularity comes from."

Maureen enjoys going to an occasional baseball game. What she doesn't like is watching games on television. "Every time we have to sit and watch baseball on television I think it's dreadful. He's a big sports fan, any game. The only reason we got the big TV is so he can watch games on a big TV. I tease him. 'I don't understand why you have to watch the pregame,' I say, 'then you watch the game, and then you watch the highlights of the game. Why do you watch the highlights? You just watched the game. It doesn't make sense to me.' He says, 'One day you'll grasp it.'"

O'Reilly says he doesn't have time to watch TV like "the folks" at home. "I try to get engaged by it, but it's very difficult, because I kind of know what's going to happen all the time." When I asked him about West Wing, he responded, "No, I tried and tried to get into it. Maybe because I just deal with that every day. I talk to these pinheads. I talk to Rob Lowe every day. I don't need to see him for an hour at night." He doesn't have political discussions at home after his show, either. "He doesn't talk much at home," sister Jan O'Reilly says. "That's another side of him a lot of people really don't know. He's very, very quiet, you know. He usually eats, and then he goes off on his own. There's not a lot of interaction. I guess he's too exhausted to talk."

He reads. "I've got four books going right now. I'm a history major, so I like history. People don't realize I can never leave this job. That's the downside. You're always thinking: What are you going to do tomorrow, next week? And you always gotta be looking for different and building up your frame of references, so you don't look like an idiot. But my wife drives me crazy, because she keeps asking me to turn off the light."

Maureen watches The Factor sometimes, not regularly like real Spinheads.

"It's always on, but she's giving Madeline a bath, and a lot of stuff is going on. So just in and out. If I weren't on it, she would probably not watch the show. She's not a political junkie."

Maureen will react to individual stories. O'Reilly watches her reaction to stories. She will say, "I hate that guy." Or comment to O'Reilly: "You're an idiot." Or "You're an idiot with him."

"That kind of thing. I like the feedback, because it's coming from somebody who knows the business a little bit. But she's not looking at it with any agenda. She's just reacting emotionally to what's she's seen on the screen."

When she says he's an idiot, it doesn't provoke an argument. "I don't debate it. I mean, I just take it in. Sometimes, I'll go, 'Oh, why do you think I did what you didn't like?' I mean, she's a focus group, and I don't believe in focus groups. Look, Maureen's style is not my style. The way she handles things is not the way I handle things. And she's coming at it like most people from their own style."

O'Reilly's favorite way to spend his money is to collect autographs and letters of historical importance, especially presidents, which are framed and hung very high everywhere on his walls. Few TV anchormen prize a genuine Millard Fillmore. He has correspondence signed by every American president, including George Washington. James Garfield in one letter is explaining he wasn't drunk, as reported in the press. Even John Hancock's famous signature is on O'Reilly's crowded wall-to-wall of fame.

Another wall in a hall leading to his study has his collection of Clint Eastwood movie posters, and other cultural influences.

He still has his boxes with all his stuff. "I tried to empty some of them when we moved here," Maureen said. "There are just too many."

"I think I'll do it when I retire," O'Reilly said.

O'Reilly was in control of his life now. The only thing he couldn't control was his health. In October 2002, O'Reilly's kidney stones were acting up. He was terrified when he went into the hospital, said his sister Jan, the nurse. O'Reilly had had the kidney stone condition for two years, and hadn't sought medical help. He is absolutely fearless, Jan said, except for seeing doctors. "He doesn't like doctors. He doesn't want to go to one, consult one, unless he absolutely has to."

"He was lying there on a stretcher like a zombie," she recalled of the day he finally went into the hospital for surgery.

"Oh, boy, was that brutal," O'Reilly said. "You got to play through the pain, you know. I can't take a lot of time off. So I got it surgically taken out of me, and four hours later I did the show." Nobody knew, he said proudly. "The doctor said he never saw anything like it. Basically, I just Zen it out. They knocked me out for the procedure. Afterward, it was a lot of blood and stuff. It was intense, but what are you going to do? God is punishing me for being too tough on some of my guests, I guess."

O'Reilly suffers from Wally Pipp Syndrome, the fear of being replaced by a Lou Gehrig who took over for Pipp, the Yankees' first baseman, one day and subsequently played 2,130 consecutive games. It wasn't until years later that Roger Ailes was able to convince O'Reilly to take Fridays off. "He doesn't come to work anytime he's not supposed to now," Ailes said.

O'Reilly fears leaving his destiny in somebody else's hands. "God forbid if he gets any major illness," sister Jan said. "He has to have that control because it makes him feel safe."

After his kidney stone operation, Bill said to me, "I'm one of these guys that doesn't even fear death. I mean, if I die I'd say to myself, listen, I've done just about everything I ever wanted to do, accomplished much more than I thought I was going to."

One of O'Reilly's favorite forms of relaxation is reading his viewer mail, another measure of his success in the television business. "We get three thousand letters a week," he said in 2002. "Nobody believes me. This is just surface mail, not the e-mail. This is just people putting a stamp on a goddamn envelope." He opens a Jiffy Bag. "It may be a snake," he says. "I got a watch yesterday. I had to send it back." This one turned out to be a framed poem, singing his praises.

By 2006, more than fifteen hundred e-mails a day were arriving in *The Zone*. They come from all over the world, people sounding off about every subject and thing you can think of, he explained. "And one of the most popular topics is me."

"How could such a shy guy generate so much, uh, feeling," he asks. "I can't figure it out."

Millions, by his own count, saw him as rude. O'Reilly is the first to admit he's a loudmouthed, conceited lout. As he told a viewer named Norman—

O'Reilly often withholds last names on the air, a witness protection program for his correspondents—who called him on it:

"I have to admit I'm not a humble guy. But that's not my fault, as all my ancestors were conceited louts. I need your sympathy, Norman, not your scorn. I need a government program to save me."

O'Reilly invites a vast array of ideological adversaries on his program whom he usually decimates, using a variety of debating tactics and strategies often misunderstood by viewers, the most noticeable being the loudness factor.

O'Reilly men are all very loud, said sister Jan. Grandfather O'Reilly established the family tone. He was a New York City street cop who was very loud, a tough guy who carried a billy club on the beat, which he gave to his grandson. O'Reilly mentioned the keepsake on *The O'Reilly Factor* one night. Grandfather O'Reilly never used it, but it's one of O'Reilly's treasures stored away in his basement in his father's Navy trunk, along with Japanese swords, flags, and similar booty brought home from World War II occupation duty.

O'Reilly's interview technique was the butt of jokes on TV satire shows, *Mad TV* and *Saturday Night Live*. The sketches show the guest not being able to get a word in edgewise. Even *The Factor* senior producer Dave Brown admitted, "It's very funny to watch him being spoofed." If the boss hadn't seen the latest takeoff, Brown said, "We show it to him."

There are three reasons for his seeming to interrupt, according to O'Reilly's spin. He doesn't want to waste viewers' time. "Far too many interviewers allow their guests to blather on about nothing," he says. "I want them to be pithy. I want them to tell the truth or what they think is the truth. I don't want bloviating, equivocating, or weaseling of any kind. I'm a simple guy. I ask simple questions. If they can't answer a simple question, they're going to get cut off."

If a guest denies the facts, which O'Reilly explains he has in hand, "verbal confrontation immediately ensues. I don't mean to be rude to these people, or anyone, but we have staked out a no-spin rule on my program. I expect facts and reasonable arguments."

And then there is the time factor. Television is now run by computers. Each interview segment lasts five minutes before the so-called hard commercial break automatically throws a spot on the screen. "You have to be finished at that moment," said executive producer Dave Tabacoff about the way the machines have taken over. "He's not cutting off the person because he doesn't want them to talk. I think there's a balancing act. He has to let people talk enough to make a point, but people don't realize that if you have five minutes, they're full minutes. And Bill is going to provide half the commentary in that time."

O'Reilly also believes he inherited his taste for brevity from his late father, "who would walk out of the room if you couldn't make your point in sixty seconds."

E. Jean Carroll, advice columnist of *Elle* magazine, analyzed his personality one night on *The Factor*. "You're sometimes extremely volatile with guests."

"Yes," he said. "When they lie."

O'Reilly keeps a mental notebook of those who have failed his polygraph test. "We have researched the subject very well, and if somebody starts to deny something that we know is true, like this Zoë Lofgren, a congresswoman from California." In 1997, he found it necessary to take apart the six-term Democrat representing the Sixteenth Congressional District. "I said, 'Look, you're not telling the truth, Congresswoman, you're not telling the truth, and the audience should know that.' You should have seen her face."

O'Reilly is egocentric. "He is so self-centered," Congressman Barney Frank said. "I remember I was on one show, and he expressed surprise that I wasn't aware of a position he expressed a year earlier. He says, 'You didn't know?' I said, 'Gee, no. I didn't know that was your view also of John Ashcroft.' "

O'Reilly is also an egomaniac. And he has an explanation for that, too. "Anyone—and I mean anyone—who delivers a strong opinion in America is going to be labeled an egomaniac. That's just how it is. In many parts of this country it is considered extremely ill-mannered to voice a dissenting opinion. You'll ruin Thanksgiving dinner. You'll start a fight in a bar. You'll *offend* somebody. Dating Rosie O'Donnell or falling into a pit of vipers is not the number one fear among Americans, public speaking is. The country founded on freedom of speech is populated by human beings who are often deathly afraid of speaking up in front of a crowd."

O'Reilly is not one of them. A Type A argumentative personality, O'Reilly finds it easy to turn hyper every night in *The Zone*. Certain subjects make him especially explosive.

"Drug dealers," Jan O'Reilly was saying about his reaction to what happened to a woman who went to the police and complained about pushers on her street in Baltimore. The woman and her five children burned to death when the dealers burned her house down. You could see O'Reilly's emotion that night on TV. "Oh, my God, he just loathes them. It was as if he had that pusher by the throat. I think he could kill him. He just can't fathom anybody selling drugs and doing it for a living and corrupting young people's minds. He can't understand that at all."

Crime stories, in which justice is not being served in his opinion, set him off. *The O'Reilly Factor* strikes some observers as not a news show so much as a cop show. "O'Reilly: Special Victims Unit," Nicholas Lemann suggested in *The New Yorker*. Sex offenders and child molester cases not in the mainstream television news are covered more extensively by *The Factor*. In 2006, for example, O'Reilly was on the case of Shawn Strawser of Florida, a twenty-year-old who induced four preteen girls to perform oral sex on him. O'Reilly was waging take-no-prisoners journalism against Vermont judge Edward Cashman who originally sentenced a convicted molester of a six-year-old girl to sixty days in jail. After O'Reilly's series of reports, in O'Reilly's opinion, the sentence was increased to a minimum of three years. O'Reilly also took on the case of Matt Dubay, another story not on everybody's lips. A twenty-five-year-old would-be deadbeat from Michigan, Dubay was in O'Reilly's scope for suing to avoid paying his former girlfriend child support because he didn't want the child that he fathered.

O'Reilly sometimes ignores the activity of others in handing out awards for good deeds done by O'Reilly. In the case against Judge Cashman, for example, the governor of Vermont played an active role. So did such programs as the late, great Dan Abrams show *The Abrams Report* on MSNBC, which had a pack of legal beagles on the story.

The Factor starts off with those magical words: "Caution, you are about to enter a no-spin zone." A brilliant Orwellian conceit—black is white; peace is war; entertainment is news—since it is actually all spin. Watching the show is like being in a Laundromat with all the machines on spin cycle. The difference is it's all O'Reilly's spin.

The basic spin is picking the subject he wants to talk about, the topic for a segment. He defines the parameters of discussion, which facts are "the true facts." He determines who is spinning and who is not, who is telling the truth or dissembling, prevaricating, and pettifogging.

"O'Reilly is pretending he's calling a spade a spade," said *Harper's* publisher Rick MacArthur, who has been a guest on *The Factor*. "At least, he is entertaining in sort of a crude sideshow way. It's fun to see the obscure bearded professor from some state college being eaten alive. It's sick, but its fun."

The humiliation factor was the secret of Reality TV's success. I asked O'Reilly if he thought people tune in to watch him humiliate guests. "No, they tune in for the joust. They tune in to see who's going to have the better point. Look, morons are not going to watch this show. If I wanted *The Bachelor*'s audience, I'd do the show in a hot tub, all right? Those people don't watch public affairs."

He is a rough interviewer, who sometimes can ask tough, useful questions. "I think most people on the air don't ask the right questions," Roger Ailes said. "They don't know what to ask. They don't know how to ask them. I sit there and think, 'Oh, please, ask this question. Now is the right time to ask and they don't.'

"Bill does that to a certain degree. He knows why the guy's there. He knows what he wants to get out of it. Sometimes he forces it a little too hard because of the time. But he doesn't ask him how tall he is. I mean, he kind of stays on point. A lot of people don't do that on television. So you have to wade through a lot of crap to get real value. You spend your life going through television crap trying to find a real moment."

"I just returned from a trip to Vietnam," Sen. John McCain was saying in a blurb for O'Reilly's first book, "and one of the reasons I went was to prepare myself for being back on *The O'Reilly Factor*. Because Bill O'Reilly uses some of their old interrogation techniques."

O'Reilly sees his debating style as a boxer, punching and jabbing, looking for openings. But he is not totally merciless. When somebody is down, he doesn't kick him in the kidneys. He will go to a neutral corner.

"Most people I'll save when I feel them going down. I'll pull back. I don't want to humiliate anybody." He has made exceptions. James Wolcott of *Vanity Fair* and Mike Kinsley, then with *Slate*, were two early victims he enjoyed humiliating. He felt both had written "some low blows" about his family.

O'Reilly has never lost a debate, he told me. Strictly speaking, that is not true. He remembered losing one. "I let Barney Frank roll over me in the mistaken notion that I should do that once. It was an experiment on my part that failed miserably. I said, look this guy's so vitriolic and he hates me so much that

I'm just going to let him go. The audience will see what he's made out of. Because he'll just rant and rave, and it'll make no sense. I'll sit there in a classy way and just let him do it, let Barney expose himself. And Barney just went after me like crazy.

"Well, the audience got mad at me. You wimp, you didn't stand up against him. And that was the last time that ever happened."

No more Mr. Nice Guy, O'Reilly decided. He continues to invite Frank, the gay liberal congressman from Massachusetts. "We'll call him for some left-wing thing that's out there. I think he enjoys coming on. He likes the joust. I beat him, you know. I don't break a sweat."

Barney Frank, O'Reilly says, is the best debater he's come up against. "He's got a very nimble mind. He's quick but also vicious. If he's losing, he'll attack you. He'll go right to your jugular. He'll try to pettifog the issue. Losing the debate, he'll say, 'Ah, you right-wing fascist,' or you this or you that, trying to throw you off your game. He knows all the tricks. A guy like that is used to just steamrolling over everybody. And he also filibusters. When you try to stop him, he goes, you always interrupt, I can't get my point across. He tries to paint you as this ideologue guy who doesn't hear his point of view. I'm sure he thinks he wins every time."

Barney Frank's first battle with O'Reilly was in November 2000, during the re-counting crisis in Florida. O'Reilly was trying to argue that the Democrats had manipulated certain things in counties they had controlled. "I had fortunately read some stuff beforehand," Frank said, "and I found his technique was the use of selective information. His facts were wrong. I mentioned that, and he was taken aback," Frank recalled. "He just generally overargues wildly. In the Florida vote debate, it was basically a case of sort of getting inside the wild swing and playing out things that he said that were just wrong.

"And then he got very upset, because for like a week afterward on the air he was complaining about how rude I'd been and that his viewers were complaining. He said he thought it was best to show the world what I was doing. He even got a telegram from Charlton Heston, congratulating him on his restraint in the face of my rudeness. I assumed Heston meant he didn't shoot at me.

"If somebody is interrupting, you have two choices. Do you interrupt back and look as rude as he is? Or do you sit there and get overwhelmed? Occasionally, you get to the point when you have no choice. That's the problem with him.

"I did a couple of sessions," Frank added. "He was preparing to attack something I was doing in Congress involving immigrants, and after I explained it, he says, 'Oh well, that's not so bad,' and then he changed the subject on me."

O'Reilly is a master of the rhetorical sidestep. Another device O'Reilly has found effective in turning a debate around is when he seems to be losing an argument, after the bell has rung, ending the round, he says, "Well, that's your opinion, thanks for coming on." As if he wasn't presenting his opinions.

"Do I like it that he disagrees with me?" asks David Corn, Washington editor of *The Nation* magazine and a Fox News regular contributor, frequently in the ring with O'Reilly. "Or that he says you're crazy or nuts or stupid or wrong? Of course not. But I always find that I do at least get a shot at what I want to say, which is different from when you go on *Hannity & Colmes.*"

Of the some fourteen thousand debates, confrontations, inquisitions, interviews, whatever you call them, on *The Factor* in its first ten years (1996–2006), O'Reilly says his best was against George W. Bush during the 2000 presidential primaries.

It was Super Tuesday eve, Bush was in play in California. *The Factor* has a large audience in California. So the Bush people made a decision, O'Reilly said. "All right, we'll go in with this animal O'Reilly. We'll talk, but we think we can control him."

The Bush team strategy that night was to expound on "fuzzy math," "compassionate conservatism," and "reformer with results," as he had been doing in every interview and speech on the campaign trail. Bush came in with his usual ten talking points. "But my job is to blast him out of it as fast as I can." O'Reilly asked him an opening question, which he had thought about for two or three hours. O'Reilly believed it to be the hardest Bush had ever been asked. "Governor, during the debates you said Jesus Christ was your personal philosophy and model. Whether you believe he's God or not, certainly his philosophy has been incorporated into Western civilization for two thousand years.

"Now he's loving it, and I said, 'But if he's your philosopher model, what do you think Jesus would think of you executing all those people in Texas?'

"You could see all the rehearsed answers go out his ear. Shoooom! Because he's on the record, and since Jesus was a victim of capital punishment, I thought he'd have a pretty good point of view on it. So you know he danced around. But I wouldn't let him go, and finally he said, 'I really don't know what he would think. The New Testament doesn't really address it.' And I said, 'Well, I don't know, I think Jesus might disagree on this one.'"

It was the best interview he'd ever done, O'Reilly said, "Because he forgot everything he was supposed to say, and then we just talked. He's not stupid. His syntax was perfect, because he wasn't parroting everything he was supposed to say."

That's what O'Reilly was trying to bring to *The Factor*, unpredictability. "Don't let them control the interview. You control the interview."

There is no doubt that O'Reilly can be an overwhelming debating figure. "We had a lot of guys sitting out there," Roger Ailes said about the strife in the executive suites at Fox when he was considering giving O'Reilly his dream job, "and saying he'll beat the shit out of a person, and he does. I don't feel sorry for them one bit. If you're not up to the fight, don't do it. You know, he's like the big Irishman in bars. He's willing to fight but you don't have to."

Part III

The
Meltdown

Chapter Seventeen

Are They Out
to Get Him?

B y 2002, O'Reilly had come a long way. At Fox, where newsman and boss at last were on the same page, he was speaking out on the issues he considered important. He took the Red Cross and the United Way to task for alleged mishandling of the 9/11 charity funds. O'Reilly was the first to call for government oversight. His continuing coverage was at least partially responsible for making sure money went where it was intended to go. During an interview with the head of the United Way, the man first claimed that "one hundred percent" of the money was going to the families. But after aggressive questioning by O'Reilly, he finally admitted sheepishly that in fact the subcharities were using the funds to cover administrative costs. Twenty-four hours after O'Reilly's interview aired, and the subsequent media attention to O'Reilly's relentless riding the story, the United Way announced that it would start making payments to the victims' families.

"When was the last time you heard anyone talking about something they saw on *World News Tonight*? O'Reilly asked a reporter in 2002. His stories were getting action. When he railed about the outrage of Pepsi hiring rapper Ludacris, famous for his thuggish lyrics, to be its pitchman for commercials aimed at kids, he rallied "the folks" at home to barrage PepsiCo with phone calls and e-mails. They rose up. Pepsi, according to O'Reilly, fired Ludacris the next day.

In the wake of Katrina, and rising gas prices, he called for a gas boycott ("Buy no gas on Sundays") and attacked oil companies for price gouging.

O'Reilly told an industry apologist one night in 2005, "Gas is not a luxury item. People need gas." As a capitalist, he believes in making money. "But this was obscene. Corporations have obligations to the public in a capitalist society. Oil companies are capitalist trash. Call me Fidel O'Reilly, Ho Chi O'Reilly," he said, but he was demanding that oil companies immediately cut their prices by 20 percent. "They'd still be swimming in money if they cut prices twenty percent," he was still saying in April 2006, urging oil companies to roll back prices to 2005 levels "for the good of the country."

"We've changed the country," O'Reilly was telling me that summer. "We influence policy. What I say is heard by people in power. Look at Jessica's Law. Forty states are going to pass that law. I started the campaign with one. In politics every politician knows that they have to come through here now. We've got a lot of stuff done. We say, this is bad. This is what we have to do, this is what we should do. Sometimes it happens, sometimes it doesn't. I'm not on some kind of crazy jihad thing. Bad guys get it. They'll pay the price for doing bad things."

He listed the judges the program has gone after for what O'Reilly considered dereliction of duty: in Pennsylvania, Vermont, Ohio, Florida. Judge Harry Rapkin in Sarasota, he was saying, "He let this guy out, could have incarcerated him, and two days later he killed this little girl. We nailed him. Walked off the bench. Quit. Nobody ever outed as many guys as we've outed. And that's never been done on TV before. Ever. We serve a watchdog role no other television program serves at this point."

Although he was so far ahead in the ratings race, he hadn't lost the fire in his belly. "We can't just win," he told one reporter. "We have to crush."

The goal of cable news since 2001 had been to stop Fox News, and the way to do it, tacticians in the rival cable news network war rooms concluded, was to stop O'Reilly. All they needed was the right superstar, the right format, the right sets, the right news music. Toward that end, CNN and MSNBC have spent millions.

Since 1996, *The O'Reilly Factor* has had to face ten different opponents on CNN alone. Here are the shows that ran against O'Reilly at 8:00 P.M.:

- *The World Today* (nightly, January 29, 1998 to December 29, 2000)
- *Newsstand/CNN & Time* (Mondays, May 3 to September 6, 1999)

- *Wolf Blitzer Reports* (nightly, December 18, 2000, to September 21, 2001)
- *The Point with Greta Van Susteren* (nightly, December 18, 2000, to January 4, 2002)
- *Live from Afghanistan* (nightly, November 21, 2001, to January 31, 2002)
- *The Point* (nightly, January 7 to April 8, 2002)
- *Live From . . .* (nightly, January 16 to June 21, 2002)
- *Connie Chung Tonight* (nightly, June 24, 2002, to March 19, 2003)
- *Live from the Headlines* (nightly, April 16 to September 5, 2003)
- *Paula Zahn Now* (nightly, from September 8, 2003).

At the same time MSNBC was firing thirteen deadly missiles at *The O'Reilly Factor*:

- *The Big Show,* anchored by Keith Olbermann (nightly, October 1997 to December 4, 1998)
- *Hockenberry* (nightly, December 7, 1998, to January 22, 1999)
- *McLaughlin Special Report* (Monday–Thursday, January 25 to March 4, 1999)
- *Equal Time* (nightly, February 1 to July 1, 1999)
- *Time & Again* (nightly, February 19 to March 19, June 1 to August 19, and November 5, 1999)
- *Special Edition* (nightly, July 8, 1999, to July 18, 2000)
- *Weekend Magazine* (Thursdays and Fridays, February 11 to October 13, 2000)
- *Crime Files* (Mondays, Wednesdays, Thursdays, Fridays, March 6 to October 23, 2000)
- *Decision 2000* (nightly, October 11 to December 29, 2000)
- *MSNBC Investigates* (nightly, August 22, 2000, to July 6, 2001, plus ten specials airing in 2003)
- *The News with Brian Williams* (nightly, July 9, 2001, to July 12, 2002)
- *Donahue* (nightly, July 15, 2002 to February 28, 2003)
- *Countdown w/ Keith Olbermann* (nightly, March 31, 2003).

Not included are news specials and major event TV, like election and war coverage.

And O'Reilly has cut through the opposition, big and small. "Here's how bad we beat them," O'Reilly was telling me by the summer of 2006. "You can add up our four competitors: CNN, CNN Headline News, MSNBC, and CNBC. I beat all four combined—with two hundred fifty thousand homes left over. With that kind of dominance, I'm costing them millions of dollars."

At home and at work, he was a contented man, but there was a gathering storm. His success made O'Reilly a lightning rod for resentment within and without the communications world. He was such an inviting target. Self-reverential, self-important, pompous. O'Reilly was waiting to be punctured like a hot-air balloon.

O'Reilly is deeply concerned about the press and its shortcomings. He sees himself as a watchdog perpetually on guard against the miscreants who abuse free speech. His observations on the practice of journalism are sometimes shrewd but not without self-interest.

"The checks and balances deal," growled O'Reilly one week in his syndicated column, "worked pretty well for us here in America. We have a process whereby other powerful people can hold most powerful people in the public sector accountable for their actions. 'Hi, there, Richard Nixon.' But there is no oversight on the press, which is a private enterprise. We get a free pass, and now that's beginning to hurt the nation. When it comes to the news media there is no FCC to fine us when we do something unsavory, like intentionally mislead the public."

According to the polls, O'Reilly wrote, "Most American know the press is not looking out for them, since journalists are ranked near the bottom of all admired professions, right between lawyers and car sales people. The reason that we wretches are under so much suspicion is that we are perceived as being arrogant. That charge is tossed my way often."

Ten years ago, most of the media policed itself, at least somewhat, O'Reilly argued. Today that's rare. "What's changed," says O'Reilly, "is that many press outlets are now run by ideologues on a mission. The gloves of fairness are off. These editors have set the journalistic rules on fire, and there is no one to put out the flames."

O'Reilly's fire watch includes anything ever written about him, in any organ, no matter how small. Two kinds of stories upset O'Reilly: those that cover him and those that don't. Every time *The New York Times* or any publication wrote any article about the cable news revolution, cable news, or even television, it pained O'Reilly not to be mentioned. On a good day, he took it as an affront, on a bad day as a personal attack on him.

He tends to view the media through a simple prism: It's either for or against him. This is typical of his egocentric view of the world. A perfectionist about his work, he exercises the same high standards toward stories about him, all of which he goes over carefully.

O'Reilly is attacked from all angles. He has even become a metaphor for everything critics hate about cable TV news. It's his brash, brassy, in-your-face quality. It's his voice. It's his attitude, his thinking that he is always right. His politics. His opinions. And don't even mention that evil, mean-spirited, unfair, and unbalanced network he is on.

"For seven years, the former *Inside Edition* anchor has brought a brand of dyspeptic discourse to the airwaves, lording over a talk show that is as much about his bully tactics as it is about the issues of the day," NPR writer Bruce Kluger summed up O'Reilly's early contributions to journalism in the pages of *USA Today* and the *Los Angeles Times*.

It had not been easy for O'Reilly to reach this point as an inviting target. "You know, when I came in here," recalled Rob Zimmerman, then a top Fox News PR executive, "for three years it was Bill O'Reilly? Bill O'Reilly? Who's that? Wasn't that the guy who did *A Current Affair*?"

O'Reilly is the Mt. Everest of cable TV anchormen now. Who bothers attacking Keith Olbermann? Or Wolf Blitzer? Or Anderson Cooper? Or Paula Zahn? "It took a lot of work," Zimmerman said. "You push the boulder up the mountain. And then, finally, when you get to the top, everyone's, like, 'Now I know who this guy is.' And they jump on the boulder coming down the hill."

O'Reilly was puzzled by his bad reviews in the beginning. "You figure that the critics are so tired of walking through the dopey predictable garbage that when something new comes on that's interesting they would like it. But it's almost a knee-jerk reaction, if you're outspoken or if you take risks, that they're not going to like you."

Monica Collins of the *Boston Herald* was an old archenemy of O'Reilly from his local Boston TV days. He decided to do an interview with her in 2003 promoting his new book, *Who's Looking Out For You?* "Which was a mistake.

But I said to her up front, I said 'Monica, you've given me a hard time my whole life.' Can you just be fair here? So her opening question was, 'Well, how come the show is so successful?' So I told her. I said, 'Well, this is why I think it's so successful.' Then her lead paragraph is: 'O'Reilly, who doesn't lack for self-esteem, says his show is a hit because . . .' You asked me! You say it was a hit. I didn't come out there and start bragging about the show."

The press had not been kind to O'Reilly in the early years of *The Factor*'s success. "Gasbag," *GQ* called him. "A loudmouthed cable news talker with an ego bigger than his audience," *Brill's Content* raved. "Worthless," Tom Shales of *The Washington Post* wrote. "The unspeakable O'Reilly," said Reuven Frank in *The New Leader*.

O'Reilly believes he is reviled in many media quarters and in Hollywood because he goes after the corporate assault on our culture on his TV and radio shows. "So they try to label me. They've got to have some kind of adjective to throw in: cocky guy, conceited guy. Usually I send them a list, and then they can just check it off. Tell me what adjective you're going to use here. It can't just be 'the journalist' for a while. No, I can't have that."

The adjectives are normally used after the writer confers the label "conservative" on him. That also gets his goat. "Why? Because in the world of the elite media a conservative is someone who can airily be dismissed as a narrow-minded, predictable thinker. There are certain code words in the elite media's lexicon and 'conservative' leads the list. In reality, I am a conservative on some issues, liberal on others, and sane on most. But because I go after issues and certain people with passion, I am a definite threat to many in the media. Put it another way, I am not playing by the clubhouse rules."

O'Reilly will take on a story he claims the print press doesn't want to report. "Many American newspapers are in big trouble," he wrote in a syndicated column. "Earnings at the New York Times Company are down more than fifty percent this quarter." There are many reasons for the depressing situation, but the one O'Reilly singles out is the collapse of journalistic standards causing readers to turn against newspapers. According to O'Reilly, "In thirty days following Hurricane Katrina, *The New York Times* ran fifty-three columns criticizing President Bush on its editorial pages. Even Barbra Streisand might consider that overkill." His presumption is that people buy or do not buy papers because of its editorial page. The 99.8 percent of America's TV viewers, many of whom are now lip readers, might disagree.

Fueling O'Reilly's vigilance of the Gray Lady is his personal storehouse of *New York Times* slights against him. Somehow he is unfit to print, he senses. He has a computer chip in his brain indexing all the times they did not do him right, if not actively wrong. O'Reilly cited a grievance from the dossier at our first meeting. He was in Washington attending the correspondents' dinner. "You know, all the commentators go down there and annoy each other," said O'Reilly. "So this guy, the keynote speaker, makes a joke about me, and now I'm the center of attention.

"After the thing is over, Fox has a big suite, and all the big shots come in and schmooze around. Madeleine Albright comes up to me, and says, 'I loved your book. Can you help me? I have a book, and I need some help on how to market the book, the way you did it.' I said, 'Ms. Secretary, I'd be happy to help you, here's my card. When you get ready, call me, and I'll tell you what to do, which venues sell books and which don't.' And I don't know her very much, but I'm willing to help anybody. She seemed like a nice woman.

"The *New York Times* reporter overhears this conversation between Albright and me, because it's right out in the middle of the floor. 'Can I write about it?' asks Jim Rutenberg, the media reporter. 'You have to ask her, but it's okay with me.' She said, sure. So he comes over and he interviews me on this and that. He goes, 'I want to make it a big piece on this. It's very interesting.' I said fine.

"He got spiked. They spiked the story. Because they see me as this humongous threat. They're going, no more, no more, he's had enough [publicity]. And I know that is going on. I absolutely know it's going on."

O'Reilly sees his differences with *The New York Times* as a continuing major news event. His opening commentary the night of September 9, 2003, declared, "Well, the culture war is heating up. Over the Labor Day weekend, a *New York Times* book reviewer named Janet Maslin attacked me. What else is new? But Maslin's gleeful libel demonstrates the viciousness that has enveloped *The New York Times* . . . The *Times* is a troubled institution. The Jayson Blair scandal badly damaged the paper. And as *The Factor* demonstrated, the *Times* inaccurately reported the battlefield situation in the opening days of the Iraq war.

"Now I knew that once I took on *The New York Times*, the paper's character assassins would take dead aim on me. That's why few public people will ever criticize the *Times*. They know the paper comes after them in a very personal way . . ."

214 The Man Who Would Not Shut Up

"Well, this kind of stuff is journalistic terrorism designed to punish people who had opposing points of view. And I'm not alone here. *The New York Times* actually called Mel Gibson a 'Jew baiter' for daring to film a movie based on a passion of Jesus. The *Times* knows that the courts will allow this kind of libel, because in this country famous people deserve no protection.

"Now I know most of you could not care less about *The New York Times*," O'Reilly added, "but here's what you don't know. The network TV news takes much of its point of view from the pages of the *Times*. And your local newspaper may very well reprint the *Times* articles. The paper is extremely powerful in shaping public opinion. And God help those who go up against it. But that kind of power must be challenged when it becomes abusive. The Fox News Channel is one of the few media outlets that currently watches what the *Times* does. And that is why *The New York Times* attacks us so frequently.

"This is a high-stakes power game that influences decision making in America . . . the culture war is getting bloodier. It will be interesting to see who ultimately will prevail. And that's the memo."

"During the past year," writer Nathaniel Popper of *The Jewish Daily Forward* calculated in March 2004, "O'Reilly has been mentioned in almost a quarter of Rich's weekly column." Few of the mentions by Frank Rich, the former chief drama critic turned socio-politico-cultural affairs ombudsman at *The New York Times,* went unnoticed by O'Reilly. The two had disrespectfully disagreed on most of the weighty cultural political issues of the past year, from William Bennett's gambling habit to gay marriage to Janet Jackson's infamous peep show moment at the Super Bowl.

O'Reilly frequently critiqued "the liberal permissiveness" of Rich, whose zeitgeist was summarized by *The Factor* host: "Let's tolerate anything, except people with whom we disagree." For his part, Rich has shown more than a little disdain for O'Reilly's insistence that he is in touch with the true voice of the people. "It's the unwritten rule of our culture that the public is always right," Rich wrote in a Sunday column. " 'The folks,' as Bill O'Reilly is fond of condescending to them, are always innocent victims of the big bad cultural villains."

Each has accused the other of taking their dispute too far. "If you go up against the elite media, it's not going to be pretty," O'Reilly said one night on his show. "You'll be branded a bigot, racist, anti-Semite, homophobe." On the other hand, as the *Forward* observed in its report on the Rich–O'Reilly War, Rich has said that O'Reilly's constant references to "the left media elite" are a veiled "code word" for Jews. "Whenever he attacks me (as a member of the elite media), it sets off a flood of anti-Semitic e-mails and voice messages," Rich told the *Forward*.

Both are members of "the media elite," whether they like it or not. It's an honor automatically conferred on Rich because of his employer, *The New York Times*. O'Reilly refuses to recognize his elite status, despite his presence on TV, radio, newspaper, and the Internet. O'Reilly, in fact, would seem to be super media elite compared to Rich.

Nevertheless, with limited access, Rich has gotten under O'Reilly's skin. In responding to an e-mail writer he found distasteful, on a completely separate topic, O'Reilly said, "You ought to have dinner with Frank Rich."

Frank Rich had attacked him again in September 2003. O'Reilly had interviewed Mel Gibson about his movie, an excerpt of which ran on *The Factor*. It was one of those quid pro quo situations, Rich implied, because Gibson had optioned O'Reilly's first mystery, *Those Who Trespass*, for the movies.

"Yeah, I'm on the pad now. I've been bribed, according to Frank Rich."

O'Reilly actually had interviewed Gibson several times about the movie, surely a newsworthy subject given the controversy and what was to be its astounding box office performance, but Rich claimed there was something devious about the coverage. They are in business together, he was saying.

The public brawling over the Gibson movie was the most heated round yet, lasting for six months, beguiling media fight fans. O'Reilly believed Gibson was being attacked because America has become a secular society, even though it was not founded that way. One of O'Reilly's passions is history, and he has done what he calls heavy research on the separation of church and state issue. The founding fathers were almost all deists, he argues. In God, they trusted. They did not mean freedom from religion but freedom of religion.

O'Reilly's defense of Gibson's virtue later ran into a rough patch in the summer of 2006 when the actor uncorked a stream of anti-Semitic statements while being arrested on a drunk driving charge in Malibu.

On *The Factor* of August 2, 2006, in a discussion with Fox News correspondent Geraldo Rivera, O'Reilly called Mel Gibson's anti-Semitic remarks following his July 28 arrest "inexcusable. Nobody can make an excuse for what he did . . . No excuse made. That point is on the record . . . I'm not letting him slide . . . I was very tough on him [in a previous show, when the story broke]. I want to get this clear. Nobody will be allowed to apologize for Mel Gibson, except Mel Gibson, on this program . . . Okay, that won't happen." But O'Reilly thought Gibson's travail illustrated a larger point that needed discussion. "There comes a point where the media and individual Americans start to enjoy the suffering of rich and powerful people. They wallow in it. They can't get enough of it. They've got blood all over their mouths, these vampires, okay? These media people: this is what they live for . . . it's morally wrong. It's maybe not as bad as what Gibson did, but it's approaching that. Because there comes a point where every human being does stuff wrong. Everyone. We all do wrong things."

"Look, to me the deal about Bill O'Reilly," Frank Rich said, when I asked him what he really thought of O'Reilly, "is that he is first and foremost an entertainer, and I don't say that in a pejorative way at all. He's not a journalist. He runs basically a talk show and basically the idea of Fox is to provide that kind of entertainment with a particular political slant that he has. To me, he's in the tradition of Rush Limbaugh, Joe Pyne, people like that who are on the right, but also people you'd say were more or less on the left, like David Susskind, way back when. It's not reporting, it's just gab in the same way Charlie Rose is gab. You know, he just has a different slant."

Paul Krugman, the *Times* op-ed columnist, had furious debates with O'Reilly in print and on Tim Russert's MSNBC cable show in 2004. O'Reilly also was feuding with *Times* columnist Nicholas D. Kristoff, who on December 11, 2005, took exception to O'Reilly's many reports and commentaries on the alleged campaign to take the "Christmas" out of Christmas. Two days later, O'Reilly added Kristoff to his cast of evil characters on *The Factor*, dismissing Kristoff as one of the usual "committed left-wing ideologues." A week later, Kristoff fired another round, further irritating O'Reilly by calling him one of those "demagogic table-thumpers who exploit public religiosity as a cynical ploy to gain attention and money." Then he went on to label O'Reilly "a self-righteous bully in the style of Father Coughlin or Joe McCarthy." Kristoff challenged O'Reilly to use his media power to stand up to genocide in Darfur. "If you really want to defend traditional values, then come with me on a trip to Darfur . . . travel to a real war against Christmas values." O'Reilly said he couldn't take time off from his many commitments, parrying Kristoff by accusing the *Times* of "continuing to ignore the child predator situation here in the U.S.A." Kristoff launched a reader pledge drive to raise money to send O'Reilly on a reporting trip to Darfur.

Ideology-driven media on both sides are frightened by O'Reilly, in O'Reilly's opinion, and they have not been slow in responding. In one week, he was attacked by a far-right editorialist in *The Wall Street Journal* and what he calls a "loony left writer" in the *Los Angeles Times*. "I'm somewhat flattered that in the history of the *L.A. Times* nobody was ever personally attacked worse than I was," O'Reilly said. "Collectively, these guys describe me as some kind of out-of-control sociopath. I mean, these attacks were personal; they went far beyond professional disapproval. The bottom line is that these guys are going to try to destroy me. I know it, and I got to live with it.

"Here's the problem," O'Reilly told me another day. "When you reach this level—and this is with Mel Gibson, Schwarzenegger, Bill O'Reilly, or whoever is in the public eye—when you reach this level in this country, where you have power, and you can say and do things far beyond what other people can say or do, there is an element of society that will try to destroy you. This has happened ever since the founding fathers were in. It has to do with power. It has to do with jealousy. It has to do with ideology. It has to do with money. The more power I get, the more lawyers I have to deal with, the more insanity I have to deal with."

Chapter Eighteen

O'Reilly Goes to War

By the summer of 2002, magazines like *New York* and *The New Republic* were spending what O'Reilly termed "an inordinate amount of time trying to convince their readers that your humble correspondent is, in varying degrees a nitwit, poseur, or worse."

Examining the life of Bill O'Reilly as a form of journalism had begun at *The Nation* in the spring of 2000 and exploded on the Internet. Soon there were hundreds of Web sites devoted to O'Reilly and his foibles, for example, oreilly-sucks.com. A phalanx of bloggers, journalists, media professors, and university research teams were conducting LexisNexis searches for O'Reilly inconsistencies, misstatements of fact, or what they called lies. Beginning in the summer of 2004, the liberal Web site, Media Matters for America, had assigned a full-time monitor to O'Reilly's radio and TV shows to alert critics. They were even counting the number of times he called somebody an "idiot" or used the words "shut up."

The Oh Really? Factor: Unspinning Fox News Channel's Bill O'Reilly by Peter Hart was an example of the intense study O'Reilly was warranting. A media analyst at FAIR (Fairness & Accuracy in Media), Hart had been covering O'Reilly regularly for *Extra!*, FAIR's bimonthly journalism review. Leader of the stats geeks who specialized in counting the times leftists and rightists appear on *The Factor*, Hart collected statistical evidence for lengthy analytical pieces proving O'Reilly is as conservative as J. P. Morgan.

Hart's ambitious *Oh Really?* fascinated me, because it purports to be a complete list of every misstatement and mistake O'Reilly ever made. It gives the impression every word that O'Reilly has said since he arrived at Fox has been scrutinized. And he said quite a few of them on TV, radio, in newspapers, magazines, and speeches.

The deconstruction of O'Reilly starts with doubting his claims to blue-collar status. The basic thrust is to prove that his regular guy act is a fake. His bona fides as a working-class Irish-Catholic growing up in suburban Levittown is suspect. The common-man stuff is bunk.

"It's part of his persona," said Peter Hart, the O'Reilly scholar in residence at FAIR. "He plays a character for Fox, and the character is working-class tough guy, champion of the little man. It makes more sense for him to flaunt his working-class credentials, a blue-collar Catholic, who claims to be on the side of the underdog. It's a marketing bull's-eye, a trifecta. He gets three unrepresented classes on TV news. The whole lower-class shtick is a little trick he does that makes it perfectly clear that he is one of the folks." Reality complicates his life story, Hart says. "So many of his tales are all about the importance of class in America, and the way he had been snubbed by people who looked down on Irish Americans."

His enemies argue he can't be a working-class guy. He went to private schools, Chaminade, a Catholic college-preparatory school on Long Island. The subtext is that all its students must be well-heeled. "My father broke his back working in order to send me to Chaminade," explained O'Reilly.

And not only that, he went to Harvard! "Yes, that's right," O'Reilly said. "At forty-two. I barely got into Marist College at eighteen. I had to paint houses," he said, about how he worked his way through college. "Levitt houses."

Furthermore, his enemies say, his father, William O'Reilly Sr., was an "accountant," the idea being that we might think of him as an audit partner in one of the Big Four. In reality, Mr. O'Reilly was an anonymous numbers cruncher in the currency department for Caltex before it was swallowed in a merger between Chevron and Texaco. He was more of a white-collar slave, a drudge, one of the faceless guys toiling away in the back rooms. A respected naval officer during the war, a man made to command, he wound up working as a glorified bookkeeper.

Mr. O'Reilly Sr. went to a small Catholic college, St. Francis, with its asphalt-paved campus on Butler Street in downtown Brooklyn. He was earning $35,000 a year after twenty-four years in the same job, which he hated, and only quit because of his ulcerative colitis. Having to stop working at fifty-two, the start of his possible moneymaking years, added to the frustration of the job itself.

O'Reilly still doesn't understand what the problem is when asked how can he represent working Americans or have the blue-collar sensibility if he makes a lot of money. "I say to myself," he explains, "look, you can be who you want to be in America. Money does not define who you are. It's how you behave, how and what you do with the money, and how you live your life.' There are forces of evil who say, 'Oh, no, since he gets a big contract, and makes a lot of money, he can't possibly sympathize with people in Levittown anymore. He's not one of them anymore.' And it's just so insulting. And I'm saying number one: You don't know me, and, two, how can you make that ridiculous broad assumption that I sold out because they pay me a lot of money? Money doesn't mean anything to me, you know. If it comes, I use it as a freedom lever. But am I riding around in a brand-new Ferrari? No. I don't care about material things. They're traps. So that kind of stupidity, I hear it all the time."

Peter Jennings in the spring of 2003 discussed his protégé O'Reilly's feeling of class differences. "Does the phrase [sic] 'tweener' mean anything to you?" Jennings asked. "I never heard the phrase [sic] before meeting Bill when he was here. I once assigned him to do a story on what it was to be a tweener, one foot in the middle class, one foot in the working class. But I think that strikes me as a fairly accurate description of Bill."

Jennings added, "He's tone deaf these days. Because he's trying too hard to tell the middle class all the time that they have to understand the working class. There's that intensity about him, always wishing to remind you that he is somehow grounded differently, and his behavior must somehow reflect it."

Even more galling to O'Reilly was the controversy stirred up about where he grew up. In Levittown, he always says. In Westbury, say the hornets swarming around what they call another O'Reilly "lie."

Al Franken was among those claiming O'Reilly got it wrong about where he was from. As he wrote in his "He Ain't From Levittown" section of his "Bill O'Reilly: Lying, Splotchy Bully" chapter in his exposé *Lies and the Lying Liars Who Tell Them.*

"So I asked Bill where he grew up? Was it Westbury or Levittown? Seemingly a hard question to spin. Backed into a corner, he replied with a crazy lie, saying that he had grown up 'in the Westbury section of Levittown.'

"There is no Westbury section of Levittown. They are two separate villages several miles apart. It was like saying he had grown up in Brooklyn—the Manhattan section of Brooklyn."

Levittown is commonly considered to be of a lower economic status, Franken seemed to be arguing, whereas a place like Westbury means "swanky." "Westbury" might mean that O'Reilly, deep down at his roots, must be a ritzy guy.

The theory is wrong. It depends on which part of Westbury you are from. "Westbury is a very varied area," explained Stanley Cembalist, a Nassau County social-status scholar. "Some of it is horse country; some of it isn't. So it's hard to put one label on Westbury. It's like trying to describe Manhattan. Park Avenue in the Seventies and Eighties is different than Park Avenue above Ninety-sixth Street."

Westbury is such a big place, in fact, it has six zip codes, compared to Levittown's one. O'Reilly's family home on Page Lane, where his mother still lives and where he grew up, is technically in Westbury. Zip code 11590.

After World War II, Bill Levitt bought up all the potato fields, miles and miles of potato fields, O'Reilly says. "He made little box houses. There were so many of them that the post office said, 'Hey, we can't deliver the mail to all these little box houses in Levittown, you gotta divide it into four towns besides Levittown,' which they did: Hicksville, Wantagh, East Meadow, Westbury, each with its own zip code."

Those are the four post offices that took over the original Levittown. The USPS confirmed this sequence of events in the 1950s. The O'Reilly house ended up by a block or two into Westbury. "But it's all Levittown," O'Reilly said. "Because it's all Levitt houses. Same little box house. Same exact yard. Same dimensions. Same little snotty kids running around. Same Nash Rambler in the driveway. Same everything, that's how it all came out.

"The reason I wrote that I was from Levittown," O'Reilly said, "is because nobody knows what a 'Westbury' is but everybody knows a 'Levittown.' It's kind of shorthand.

"Over Easter," O'Reilly wrote in his syndicated column when the Levittown/Westbury controversy burst into flame again in 2004, "I was rummaging through the attic of my mother's home. There I found the house deed from February 26, 1951. It was sent to my parents by the County Trust Company of

White Plains, New York. The address of the house on the deed is: '——— Page Lane, Levittown, New York.' "

Another charge against O'Reilly credibility came up during the BookExpo America Convention at the Los Angeles Convention Center on May 30, 2003. BookExpo is an annual sales event at which publishers and authors hawk their fall books. O'Reilly, Franken, and Molly Ivins were launching new books in the same season. Seven hundred booksellers sat waiting for what promised to be a civilized exchange of contrasting views.

Franken was the author of *Lies and the Lying Liars Who Tell Them: A Fair and Balanced Look at the Right.* His previous contribution to political discourse had been *Rush Limbaugh Is a Big Fat Idiot and Other Observations* (1996), which inspired the 325-pound radio talk-show host to go on various diets. By 1999, Limbaugh told Tim Russert on CNBC he was down to 215 pounds.

O'Reilly's new book was *Who's Looking Out For You?* the third in a series of autobiographical works.

Molly Ivins, the columnist who claims her greatest honor was a Minnesota police force naming its mascot pig after her, had a new book, cowritten with Lou Dubose, entitled *Shrub: The Short But Happy Political Life of George W. Bush.*

Acting as the moderator, former Colorado senator, Pat Schroeder, was about to be an innocent bystander. The event was being televised on C-SPAN2's *Book TV*, live, for two hours, ending at four-thirty in the afternoon, and was to be followed by live interviews and call-ins from five to five-thirty.

Franken, fifty-two at the time, had emerged by the spring of 2003 as the champion of liberal Democrats. O'Reilly, now fifty-three, was described by *USA Today* "as the conservative talk show host." He looked relaxed and calm, having delivered the final manuscript to his publisher, Broadway Books, the day before he caught the red-eye to LA.

His appearance was a lot different from his picture on the display of books serving as a visual backdrop to the panelists. Behind the panel was a giant foam core Franken book cover, featuring pictures of President Bush, Vice President Cheney, Ann Coulter, and O'Reilly. Especially unflattering was that in the picture O'Reilly looked splotchy and ill-tempered. As Franken was to describe the BookExpo artwork, "Blown up ten times, he looked ten times splotchy." It occurred to Franken that O'Reilly's having to walk past the giant foam core book cover calling him a liar on his way to his seat might light what Franken called "O'Reilly's notoriously short fuse."

In his opening remarks, O'Reilly decried political commentators who "call people names." Then he called Al Franken—"the liberal humorist," as he was described by *USA Today*—"an idiot." Molly Ivins gave a funny summary of the presidency of George W. Bush. "If at the end of this short book, you find W. Bush's political résumé a little light, don't blame us. There's really not much there. We have been looking for six years." Then it was Franken's turn.

He began by holding up his book. "My book," he explained, "is called *Lies and the Lying Liars Who Tell Them*." And on the cover were pictures of Bill O'Reilly, President Bush, Vice President Cheney and Ann Coulter, each on an individual TV screen. "Now, Bill," he said, "this is a just a rough of the cover. If you don't like the picture, you can pick a better picture."

O'Reilly was not laughing. He was not overjoyed to find his face among the lying liars on Franken's book jacket. Apparently, it was the first time O'Reilly was seeing the cover, according to copanelist Molly Ivins, who told reporters afterward in her folksy down-home Texas way, he was "teed off to the max."

Then Franken said to the audience, "Let me tell you why his picture is on the cover." He tells the story of O'Reilly and the Peabody Awards. As Franken saw it, O'Reilly, as host of *Inside Edition*, was accused of running a tabloid show. And O'Reilly said on *The O'Reilly Factor* of August 30, 1999, as Franken paraphrased the exchange with a guest, "How can you accuse my show of being a tabloid show? We won a Peabody. Journalism's most prestigious award."

Franken claimed that in a later interview, O'Reilly said, "We won two Peabodys." Three months later, he was interviewed by somebody else, and again said, "We won Peabodys."

So, Franken says, "I went and looked up the Peabody Awards. And I called the Peabody people, and asked, did O'Reilly win a Peabody? Did his show win a Peabody?"

"No," they said.

"So I called O'Reilly and asked him about it. And he said, 'I'll get back to you.'

"Five minutes later, he called back, and said, 'We won a Polk Award. We didn't win a Peabody. It was a Polk.' He called it the most prestigious award in journalism.

"But you called the Peabody the most prestigious award in journalism?"

" 'So,' " O'Reilly said, according to Franken, 'well, the Polk Award is the most prestigious award.' "

Franken says he said, " 'But how can there be two most prestigious awards?' The point is he said it three times, then when he corrected it, he exaggerated the thing again."

O'Reilly said he had corrected the mistake. Molly Ivins politely told Franken that since O'Reilly had corrected the mistake, "Let's move on."

Franken continued anyway, asking him, "Bill, don't you think it's strange that you got it wrong about a journalism award?"

It appeared to luncheon guests and to viewers watching on C-SPAN2 that O'Reilly didn't know the name of the award he claimed he had supposedly won, and he never bothered checking. He seemed to be guilty of puffing up his credentials.

Al Franken was in Bill O'Reilly's face and exposing him as somebody who exaggerates. At the time, it was a startling event.

C-SPAN2 is the network of intellectuals and book readers. Its audiences are not normally people who watch *The O'Reilly Factor* or the Fox News Channel, but they still know who Bill O'Reilly is. And what he stands for. The audience enjoyed watching *The O'Reilly Factor* anchor finally get what some thought was coming to him. Franken appeared to be engaging in some good old-fashioned public humiliation of a pompous conservative pundit.

For cable news addicts, especially, this was a great moment, the stumbling on a major news event, the reward for endless hours of floating from channel to channel. For O'Reilly to appear to be losing a debate, or even to be behind in points, was so rare.

At the start of his rebuttal, O'Reilly said to the moderator, Pat Schroeder, "We're each given fifteen minutes, and you let Franken talk for thirty-five minutes. And what's he got? After six and a half years of research? Forget it. So I mixed up the Peabody and Polk. Big deal."

Franken is saying from his corner, "No, that's not what I said. I said you lied about it. And then you were called on it."

"This guy accuses me of being a liar, ladies and gentleman, on national television," O'Reilly said. By now, as they say, his Irish is up. "He's vicious—and that's with a capital V," O'Reilly added in respect to the literary credentials of the audience—"a person who's blinded by ideology. All he got in six and a half years is that I misspoke, that I labeled a Polk award a Peabody!"

When Franken tried to interrupt, O'Reilly "went ballistic," according to the *New York Post.* In what Molly Ivins later called in her column "the high point of the debate, he cleverly riposted Franken's account of his lies by screaming, 'Hey, shut up, you had your thirty-five minutes, shut up.' "

Franken took umbrage at being told to shut up.

"This isn't your show, Bill," he shot back. "We're not on Fox News."

Franken again questioned O'Reilly's veracity and O'Reilly called him "a propagandist," a moderate pejorative in O'Reilly's verbal artillery arsenal. He usually called those with whom he disagrees "pinheads" and "idiots."

Franken said, "It's time for liberals to stop taking it and to call conservatives on their lack of civility."

That set off O'Reilly, according to *USA Today.* "You wrote a book called *Liar, Liar,* and you talk about incivility? Unbelievable!" O'Reilly, in a calmer moment, later told me he was trying to elevate the discourse about politics. "I don't call anyone a liar or fat."

Pat Schroeder, the moderator of the panel discussion, was being a nonmoderating moderator. It wasn't that she was letting them have at each other, to enliven a panel, as some moderators do. She didn't seem to know what to do. At that point Franken said to her, "Aren't you going to keep order here?" She then cut the microphones of both. The hour of hand-to-hand in-your-face-to-face combat was over.

O'Reilly stalked off the platform, a cloud of radioactive steam over his head. He was hot under the collar, but not nearly as ready to pop a blood vessel as James Carville regularly on a *Crossfire* discussion when he is saying "hello."

Roger Ailes was still fuming days later. "When somebody calls you a liar to your face, you know, sooner or later, you either say 'shut up,' pop him, or leave. I mean, there's not much more you can do. You can't sit there and listen to that crap. I think Bill was restrained. I wouldn't have given a shit. In the old days I would have popped him one."

Who had won was the next debate.

By and large, the media saw O'Reilly's performance as an embarrassing public meltdown, topped only by Dr. Dean's screaming concession speech at the Iowa Caucus the following year.

There was no doubt in the mind of Frank Rich of *The New York Times*. "For . . . [liberals], it was a rare red-letter day when Al Franken . . . landed a rhetorical uppercut to the jaw of Liberal Nemesis No. 1, Bill O'Reilly, and left him even more senseless than usual."

Much of the postdebate discussion by the experts focused on O'Reilly's use of the phrase "shut up." Apparently, it wasn't that unusual for O'Reilly to tell somebody to shut up. Jack Shafer, the editor-at-large at *Slate*, did a Nexis search, counting how many times the phrase "shut up" was heard on *The O'Reilly Factor*: fifty-two times in its first half decade.

The real winner might have been Molly Ivins, who came out of the debate as the voice of reason, something conservatives don't usually consider a person who has called George W. Bush "a shrub." Whoever had won in TV politico-journalismo-machismo terms, the book luncheon guests loved it.

The live debate was repeated in its entirety later that night and the following Sunday on C-SPAN2. By 2004, it seemingly was being rerun as often as *M*A*S*H* on cable.

The media hoopla after the debate was equally fascinating. It could be argued that O'Reilly is that rare breed of journalist, a newsman who is the news whatever he does. Still, it was startling the way newshounds at competing cable news networks pounced on the story. O'Reilly losing his cool exchange was treated as a major news story. CNN ran the shut up clip every hour the next day. MSNBC played highlights on a loop reel. MSNBC's talk shows had pundits debating whether Franken was right on the lying and other media bias issues.

Al Franken had won a place for himself as a victim in O'Reilly's next murder mystery, but a Fox publicist questioned O'Reilly's motivation for tangling with him in the first place. "Bill's ego gets away with him, you know," Rob Zimmerman explained. "He gets carried away thinking, 'I can handle it, I can handle it, I can handle it.'

'Bill, you know what,' I said to him when he told me he was going out to LA, 'you should pass on this one. It's a book convention, who cares? People are going to buy your book anyway. Don't you think the bookstores are going to sell your book, Bill? I mean, you've been a two-time number one best seller on the *New York Times* lists, and your paperback was number one. They're going to carry your book. You don't need to have to sit there and pander to a bunch of booksellers. You're just going to give Franken more ammunition. It's exactly what Franken wants.' So the bottom line is he made a mistake."

. . .

But that was nothing, said the Fox publicist who had heavy duty shoveling up the media mess after the Peabody/Polk imbroglio. "His biggest mistake was saying he wasn't a Republican when he was."

"O'Reilly, who warns guests they're in a no-spin zone, refuses to be pinned down by political labels, claiming he's neither liberal nor conservative," reported the New York *Daily News* in December 2000. Since 1996, he had always been saying he wasn't a Republican. "A search of voter registration rolls in Nassau County, where he lives, shows he has been a registered Republican since 1994, something he insists he was not aware of until the *News* asked."

I asked O'Reilly one afternoon, "Are you now, or have you ever been, a card-carrying member of the Republican Party?"

He pushed himself away from the computer where he was finishing the night's script and offered to explain the embarrassment of how he happened to be registered a Republican. After the *Daily News* story ran, he explained, "I called up Nassau County. I said, 'Hold it. When I moved here in 1993, you gave me a form to fill out so I could register to vote, and there was no "Independent" on it. So I didn't put anything in there. What am I doing as a registered Republican?'

"'Well, you know why you're a registered Republican,' they said. 'Because when you handed in the ballot, and because the Republicans controlled Nassau County votes, they just put you in that category.' I said, 'What the hell is that?' And, you know, they're hemming and hawing, but I saw the game. I said, 'Now send me my new credentials.' Okay, so now I'm a registered Independent."

The kissing cousin to being a Republican was the charge that he is a dyed-in-the-wool conservative.

"They say Bill is conservative," says Roger Ailes, his boss at Fox News Channel. "He beats up Jeb Bush for a month. He beats up John Ashcroft every night, and you can hardly call that conservative. Well, he is probably conservative in the blue-collar sense, and somewhat culturally conservative. But he doesn't fit into any pigeonhole."

For example, O'Reilly is against capital punishment. "On the grounds that it is not cruel or unusual enough," Ailes said. "It's a different take." O'Reilly favors ongoing hard labor in a remote location with zero amenities. "This means no cable TV," O'Reilly argues. "Is it enough to have them sit there watching cable TV, lifting weights, and having sex with their cellmates? I mean, that doesn't sound like big punishment to me."

"I would argue that in many ways Bill is closer to an old blue-collar Democrat than even a Republican," said Ailes. "Because Republicans tend to be more impressed with power than Bill is. Bill really sort of takes on all authorities. He says things to challenge people, sometimes pisses people off, and that's useful."

He regularly attacks Hillary and Bill, Jesse Jackson, gangsta rappers, the ACLU, the INS, the FBI, and "the constitutional terrorist," Attorney General John Ashcroft. O'Reilly's stance on Secretary of Defense Donald Rumsfeld, Ailes said, "loses some of the far-right Kool-Aid drinkers." Even before Abu Gharib hit the fan, O'Reilly devoted much of early April 2004 excoriating Rumsfeld for his "giant screwups" in Iraq. He is not a windup robot doll like Limbaugh. You'd never catch O'Reilly, for instance, trying to brush the Abu Gharib scandal under the rug the way Limbaugh did when he said that the action of the soldiers looked like frat-house hazing and that they merely wanted to "blow some steam off." O'Reilly voiced genuine outrage over the photos, and although he stopped short of blaming the prison abuses on the Bush White House, he at least had on guests who voiced that opinion. He wasn't an unabashed cheerleader for the Republican Party, like his Fox News colleague, Sean Hannity. In November 2005, O'Reilly wrote in his column, "The forecast for the Republican Party was dark. Six months later, bats are now hanging from the White House ceiling."

It isn't easy playing the ideologue card with O'Reilly. Guests often call him "a conservative." His eyebrows furrow. "Tell me two conservative positions," he shoots back. "Why, everybody knows you're a conservative," the argument often goes. "Okay, test me, go through my beliefs and come up with the appropriate 'isms,'" he challenges.

- He is against SUVs. He would "suggest" automakers develop cars and trucks that would be far more fuel-efficient than they are today. "If they don't, the government ought to slap a huge tax on them."
- He is for gun control.
- He is against special interests and for campaign reform. "Why can't we see that government is corrupted by special interest money?"

- In conjunction with strict border enforcement, O'Reilly argues the U.S. should set up a "guest worker" program. "If the Mexican government would cooperate, U.S. companies and individuals that need labor would be able to participate in the programs. But it would be administered in an orderly manner and taxes would be paid."

- People are stunned when O'Reilly says, "I would rather have gay adoptions than have these kids in foster homes." Where is this coming from, they ask?

- He also believes homosexuals should have equal protection under the law. He takes thunder from the right on this issue. "I happen to believe all Americans have a right to make a living and have a lifestyle free from religious judgment. As long as gays or any other group do not intrude on you, they should be left alone. Let God sort the private stuff out. He is smart enough to do it right."

- He is against waste in the government, especially in entitlements. The war on poverty, he says, didn't end poverty. On the other hand, he is not ready to take away everybody's welfare check. Still, he doesn't like the idea that the biggest day in the 'hood is when welfare checks arrive.

- He supports Sex Ed in the schools. As he was telling Jocelyn Elder, former Surgeon General of the United States, "The repercussions of irresponsible sex, that's what must be taught. The links between irresponsible sex and poverty, divorce, violence, and disease should be drummed into every American kid from age ten onward. I mean, pedal to the metal."

- He is for government regulation of violence in video and computer games. It's the source of violence in schools and elsewhere in the young, many suggest. He puts rap music in the same category. The way to regulate it is basically put a rating system on music and video games the way they do on movies. "I would say, 'Look, if we find out you're marketing this to children, and children are participating, and you're being irresponsible in policing it, we're going to fine you.' The government is always screaming they don't have enough money. They're raising taxes all over the place. You can raise an enormous amount of money just by enforcing the law."

- He is in favor of ordering the Department of Energy to monitor strictly any kind of price collusion or gouging—and impose massive fines on any company found guilty of these crimes.

- He is in favor of the federal government negotiating discounted drug prices with pharmaceutical companies so that there would be an affordable Medicare drug benefit. "These manufacturers should be pressured to be 'generous' in their pricing and rewarded with tax incentives for complying."

"What do these beliefs make me?" O'Reilly asks. "To what party or ideology do I belong? Tell me—I'd like to know."

Clearly, he is not a laissez-faire purist who believes that government governs best when it governs least.

O'Reilly answers all these attempts to pin the tail on the elephant with this declaration of independence. "I am an independent. I vote for the most honest and most effective problem solver in the running. The politician in my lifetime I most admire is Bobby Kennedy, a Democrat. The politician I least respect is Bill Clinton, a Democrat."

Chapter Nineteen

Suits Pressed
While You Wait

When people read the chapter about him in Franken's book, I told O'Reilly one afternoon in 2003, Franken's charges have a cumulative effect.

"That's right," O'Reilly said, "that's why you have to challenge it. If you let it go, it becomes part of your résumé. Now everybody knows that I am refuting this guy, calling him a smear merchant. Now you can choose what you want to believe, that's America. You want to believe I'm a liar, go right ahead and believe it. But, thank God, I had the power to get my word out. A lot of people don't have the power to do that, and they're the people who wind up smeared."

O'Reilly remembered what happened in the election of 2000 when Al Gore's enemies demonized him as being "this liar who said he invented the Internet." Al Gore didn't reply to the claim. He let it take on a life of its own. "I told Fox you cannot allow this stuff to go unchallenged. Because it gets into the Internet, and it will surface in every story that's ever written about you hence. 'O'Reilly who lied about where he grew up.' Yeah, I'm going to see that now until the year 2050. But now they can't do that without saying, 'O'Reilly, who denies . . .' It's a very difficult position to be in, but this day it's absolutely essential that you challenge this stuff.

"Very early on I said to Fox, 'Look, this guy is coming after us. He's going to use every defamation tactic he can. He's going to lie, he's going to get on all the shows, you can't let it go unchallenged. This is a well-organized campaign to smear the Fox News Channel and me—because I'm the big gun—any way they can do it.'

"Franken is being run by powerful forces in this country," O'Reilly said. "He's the Donald Segretti of the New Millennium. He's doing exactly what Donald Segretti did for Richard Nixon. Donald Segretti was in charge of smear campaigns against anybody Nixon thought was a danger. They're using him. No fingerprints. And he delights in this kind of thing. He's done this before. He made money off calling Limbaugh a big fat idiot. This is what he does, you know, he calls people names.

"Now I know I sound conspiratorial here. I understand that, but what I'm telling you is the God's honest truth. I know people in the DNC. I know people at *The New York Times*. I know what Frank Rich is doing. I know what Janet Maslin is doing. I know what they're all doing. They see me and Fox as a huge threat because we hold them accountable. They're using Franken as the point man, all right.

"I answer it by saying that's a bunch of garbage, and he's a character assassin, that's what he does. I answer it the way I always answer it. And then you believe what you want to believe. This guy is really bad. Franken is a worm. And not only that, he's not funny anymore. Too much an ideologue."

Fox and O'Reilly decided to squash the worm by suing Franken and his publisher. "You know, he's got my picture on his book with the word 'liar' next to it," O'Reilly told me cheerfully the day the suit was filed. "That's libel per se. Defamation. I want my face off that book cover. I don't want any damages, just take my face off the book cover."

The suit was ground zero in what was to turn into a major disaster area for O'Reilly and the Fox News Channel. The Fox lawyers at Hogan & Hartson LLP were unable to make a case for removing O'Reilly's face from the cover of Franken's book. As described earlier, the cover also had President Bush, Vice President Cheney, and Ann Coulter on the TV monitors. The other alleged liars did not wish to join in a class action suit or even sue as individuals. Fox's lawyers apparently concluded the case would be difficult to win because O'Reilly is a public figure. His face, even blotched with what looked like a skin condition, is in the public domain.

Before filing the suit, Dianne Brandi, Fox News' vice president for Legal and Business Affairs, sent a letter to Penguin Group (USA)'s lawyers, Cahill Gordon

& Reindel, on behalf of Fox and O'Reilly. The letter opened by making a libel claim. It said, in effect, how dare you put his picture on a cover with the word "lie" on his face. You seem to be saying he's a liar. Floyd Abrams, the partner who was handling the case for Cahill Gordon & Reindel, wrote back on behalf of Penguin, that they were, indeed, calling him a liar. If sued, Penguin would defend on grounds of truth.

O'Reilly and Fox filed the suit anyway on August 15, 2003, choosing to go down another legal road. Fox News Channel's lawyers decided to go after the fact that Franken was using the Fox motto "fair and balanced" in the title of the book. Their lawyers felt it was a legitimate trademark infringement case. Fox's lawyers accused Franken's publisher, Penguin Group (USA), of parodying the Fox News logo.

In copyright infringement suits involving parody or satire, the plaintiff always says, "They stole our thing," and the defendant says, "Yeah, of course, we used your thing because we are satirizing it." Parodying is not a crime in a democracy. The Supreme Court ruled in favor of parodists in *New York Times Co. v. Sullivan* (1964). The court said that protection of an individual's reputation had to yield to the promotion of uninhibited, robust, and wide-open debate. Satire, it also ruled, is a legitimate form of criticism, which is protected by the First Amendment of the Constitution. So it's always the First Amendment versus copyright. That is standard.

What was unique about *Fox News Network LLC, Plaintiff v. Penguin Group (USA) Inc. and Alan S. Franken, Defendants* (03 Civ 6162), is that the plaintiff took the liberty of not just saying "you stole our thing" but also "your guy isn't funny." Fox escalated their problems by using strong language in describing the defendant as "a bizarre person," calling him "a parasite, shrill and unstable," "a C-level commentator," and, worse, "not funny." "It was one of the most extraordinarily abrasive affidavits I've ever read," said Penguin lead counsel, Floyd Abrams.

The strategy evolved into a public relations debacle for Fox. For Franken, the suit was a dream situation, a writer's wildest fantasy come true. To be targeted by the Evil Empire, the conservative Press Lord Rupert Murdoch and his people, was to be taken seriously. "You can hardly imagine anything better for the book," said Larry Arnstein, the ex–*Saturday Night Live* writer. "It almost seemed like he hypnotized them. 'You will sue me . . . and you will use the words "shrill" and "unstable." When I snap my fingers you will not remember. . . .' "

. . .

Fox had its day in court on Monday, August 25, 2003, the next working day after briefs were filed. The United States District Court Southern District of New
York, the Hon. Denny Chin presiding, was packed with newspaper and cable
network news reporters.

The day lasted an hour and ten minutes. It began at three-thirty in the afternoon. In opening, Fox's lawyers objected to the use of the picture of Bill
O'Reilly, claiming "it could be mistaken as an endorsement of the book."

Judge Chin asked, "Do you think that the reasonable consumer seeing the
word 'lies' over Mr. O'Reilly's face would believe Mr. O'Reilly is endorsing the
book?"

Lead attorney for the plaintiff, Dori Ann Hanswirth, so believed. (Laughter
in the court.)

In response to the argument that the title would lead to making such mistakes, by including the Fox "fair and balanced" trademark, Judge Chin said,
"My question is, do you really think it is likely that someone who walks into
Borders and picks up Mr. Franken's book, would believe that this book has
been sponsored in some way or endorsed in some way by Fox?"

Counselor Hanswirth said she did. (More laughter.) The trouble was, Ms.
Hanswirth said, "the way the title is set up it's too ambiguous. It does not say
parody or satire."

Judge Chin said, "If the defendants put on the cover 'This is a satire,' would
that somehow salvage it?"

Ms. Hanswirth assented. "That's all we want, Your Honor." (More laughter.)

A half hour of arguments and counterarguments later, in which the judge
asked, "Is Fox really claiming that it has a monopoly on the phrase 'fair and balanced'?" Fox reiterated its copyright infringement claim. "All right, I understand the points. Let's take a five-minute recess, and I'm going to come back out
and rule."

There are hard cases and there are easy cases, Judge Chin said after the recess. "This is an easy case. For, in my view, the case is wholly without merit,
both factually and legally."

"Factually," His Honor continued, "there is no likelihood of confusion to
the origin and sponsorship of the book." Along the way of reaching that decision, Judge Chin observed, "A person would have to be completely dense not to
realize the cover was a joke."

The Court said further, "I can't accept that that phrase ["fair and balanced"] can be plucked out of the marketplace of ideas and slogans. Even assuming for the moment that it is a valid mark, however, and even assuming there is some danger of confusion, here the First Amendment trumps. Parody is a form of artistic expression protected by the First Amendment. The keystone to parody is imitation. Here whether you agreed with him or not, whether you like what he says or not, in using their mark, Mr. Franken clearly is mocking Fox."

After more legalistic discussion about the parameters of satire—what is and what isn't—and about the definition of "parody," Judge Chin decided that Mr. Franken's work was of "artistic value" and "fair criticism."

"Of course," Judge Chin observed in closing, "it is ironic that a media company that should be seeking to protect the First Amendment is seeking to undermine it by claiming a monopoly on the phrase 'fair and balanced.'"

"The motion for a preliminary injunction is denied. We are adjourned."

After hearing the Court's opinion, in dropping the suit on day one, Fox spokeswoman Irena Steen said Fox had decided "it's time to return Al Franken to the obscurity that he's normally accustomed to."

Penguin's lawyers said the ruling was a victory for the First Amendment.

Franken said, "The ruling was a victory for satirists everywhere, even the bad ones."

The charges by his detractors were still driving O'Reilly crazy. "I went on a show the other day," O'Reilly said, "where they started raising the same points, and I said, 'Look, number one, I'm not going to answer these charges anymore because I answered them a thousand times.

"Levittown. It's like saying that because you have a Jackson Heights post office, you don't live in Queens. Because you have a West Hollywood post office, you don't live in LA. That's insane. That's the game he's playing. All right, I couldn't go to Westbury High School. I wasn't in the school district. If I lived in Westbury, I certainly would have gone to Westbury High School. So when you hit them with that, and I mean I told the *New York Times* editors, there's no reply, there's never an attempt to right the record."

Months after the LA debate, the charges still followed him. It left him in a fighting mood. The chips on his shoulder were now the size of redwoods. Often he would find himself on programs following Franken appearances to give a semblance of fairness and balance. The math did not add up for O'Reilly.

Franken usually received the royal treatment and looked as happy about the situation as he was at the LA BookExpo. The end of O'Reilly's benign tolerance for what he felt was unfair and unbalanced treatment of his book came on public radio.

O'Reilly had agreed to appear on Terry Gross's *Fresh Air* program on October 9, 2003. He had regularly attacked National Public Radio as a biased, leftist waste of taxpayers' money. To those who claimed the media leaned to the right, O'Reilly always gave as the counterbalance NPR.

The tone was intense from the start of the taping on the previous day. Gross began by asking O'Reilly to respond to accusations made against him by Franken, O'Reilly's principal ideological antagonist and competitor on the best seller lists. O'Reilly bristled. For the first fifty minutes, Gross was focused on discussing the common perception of what a bad person O'Reilly was, not his book. O'Reilly told Gross he found her line of questioning "objectionable and hostile." He accused the host of conducting the interview "in attack mode" and "full of typical NPR liberal bias." "You should be ashamed." When she began reading a quote from a critical *People* magazine review for his reaction, O'Reilly ended the interview by walking out of the studio. Not without suggesting that she find "another line of work."

A firestorm of controversy followed, fed by the usual extensive press attention and e-mail correspondence awarded any O'Reilly controversy, possibly heightened by O'Reilly's warning his viewers about the outrage that would be taking place on NPR the next day when *Fresh Air* ran the interview. O'Reilly explained to his listeners that he had to break off the discussion because National Public Radio, which receives a subsidy from the federal government, "is an extreme leftist outfit. This interview is unfair and meant to trap me."

Reviewing the controversy a week later, NPR ombudsman Jeffrey A. Dvorkin found the Gross-O'Reilly interview was "quite unlike . . . [most] interviews on NPR where the tone is civil but often unchallenging of the guest." He found Gross guilty of baiting O'Reilly, "using critical quotes from the Franken book and a *New York Times* book review. That put O'Reilly at his most prickly and defensive mode, and Gross was . . . [unable] to get him back . . . in an effective way . . . [She came] . . . across as a pro-Franken partisan rather than a neutral and curious journalist. . . . By the time the interview was halfway through, . . . [she] was 'carrying . . . Franken's water.' It was not about O'Reilly's ideas, or his attitudes or even his book. It was about O'Reilly as [a] political phenomenon."

A particularly disturbing aspect of the interview for the NPR ombudsman was that Gross continued to read the *People* review after O'Reilly walked out of the studio. "That was wrong," ruled Ombudsman Dvorkin. "O'Reilly was not there to respond. It's known in broadcasting as the 'empty chair' interview, and is considered an unethical technique." The NPR ombudsman concluded that the interview was not fair to O'Reilly. "I believe the listeners were not well served . . . Unfortunately, the interview only served to confirm the belief, held by some, in NPR's liberal media bias."

O'Reilly was vindicated. There was a downside to being on the defensive all the time in terms of public relations.

"O'Reilly has to be more careful what he says, watch his words, be less sweeping in his statements," said Rob Zimmerman, the Fox PR man who had spearheaded the media effort to get rid of O'Reilly's earlier sleazy tabloid *Inside Edition* image. "The big danger is that he may start to come across as a whiner, somebody who is always complaining about being misquoted, misunderstood, mishandled."

Glenn Collins, a reporter for *The New York Times,* had an interesting theory about O'Reilly's problem. "What he may consider just a good honest analysis of what he perceives as the way it is on any issue," Collins said, "there is a tendency for others to take as a voice of God. When he opines, to the dedicated, it is not only O'Reilly opining, but also a higher power. Every thought, every political opinion no matter how silly, is thus taken as words from the Gospel, according to Saint Bill."

Franken and the other critics were not only impugning his integrity, his basic honesty, but the authority of his voice.

There were other signs of the coming meltdown in the confrontation between O'Reilly and Jeremy Glick on *The Factor* the night of February 4, 2003. The son of a 9/11 victim, who had worked for the Port Authority at the World Trade Center, Glick had coedited a book titled *Another World Is Possible* and had signed an antiwar ad. In the "Personal Stories" segment, Glick tried to explain that he rejected the clichés of the absolute Good and absolute Evil and saw in the United States violent and narrow-minded foreign politics, a factor that led to the death of his father.

Outraged, O'Reilly interrupted his guest. "You are mouthing the position of the totally marginal extreme left in our society, and it's your right to do it," O'Reilly explained.

Glick wanted to talk about the recent past and the still-warm links between the "terrorists" and the United States government. "Six months before the Soviet invasion of Afghanistan, during the Carter administration, and even more during the administration of Bush's father as head of CIA, we recruited ten thousand radical mujahaddin to fight against the Turaki government in Afghanistan."

O'Reilly: "I don't want to discuss world politics with you."

Glick: "Why not? It's all about world politics. Just let me finish. You are using September eleventh to justify everything from the looting of public finances to international imperialist aggression. You talk about compassion for the victims of September eleventh . . ."

O'Reilly: "That's a bunch of crap. I've done more for the 9/11 families than you ever hope to do. And even they recognized it."

Glick: "Okay."

O'Reilly: "So you keep your mouth shut when you sit here exploiting these people."

. . .

O'Reilly: "I hope your mother is not watching this because you—that's it. I'm not going to say anymore."

Glick: "Okay."

O'Reilly: "In respect for your father . . ."

Glick: "On September fourteenth, do you want to know what I'm doing?"

O'Reilly: "Shut up. Shut up."

Glick: "Oh, please don't tell me to shut up."

O'Reilly: ". . . In respect for your father, who was a Port Authority worker, a fine American, who got killed unecessarily by barbarians . . ."

Glick: "By radical extremists who were trained by this government . . ."

O'Reilly: "Out of respect for him . . ."

Glick: "Not the people of America . . ."

O'Reilly: "I'm not going to . . ."

Glick: "The people of the ruling class, the small minority . . ."

O'Reilly: "Cut his mic. I'm not going to dress you down anymore, out of respect for your father. We will be back in a moment with more of *The Factor.*"

Glick: "That means we're done?"

O'Reilly: "We're done."

Former news talk host Charles Grodin analyzed O'Reilly's anger problem. "I can't look at Bill O'Reilly's smug, self-righteous face on his show," he wrote in his memoir about working in television, "but I did watch him for about a minute as he was being interviewed by Tim Russert on his weekend cable show after 9/11. Predictably, he wore his rage over September eleventh as a badge of honor. Obviously, we're all enraged, but O'Reilly needs to be the most enraged. This would all resonate a little better if he hadn't been enraged for years . . . I don't doubt Mr. O'Reilly's rage over September eleventh. I also believe he has a general problem with rage."

O'Reilly loves fights. Combat seems as essential as oxygen to him. "He lives and breathes attention and combat," said Martin Kaplan, an associate dean of the Annenberg School at the University of Southern California.

The most exciting thing is that you never know when the explosion will take place. He can be taking on an individual, an institution, or a whole country—and, suddenly, it's another O'Reilly Moment.

Where O'Reilly's fights in the early years seemed to be on substantive issues, in the meltdown period, which began in 2003, they seemed to grow increasingly personal and often bizarre. It was as if media attention seemed to be the driving force. Sometimes the fights made him look absurd, as in the case of his war against San Francisco.

In November 2005, O'Reilly made banner headline news in the *San Francisco Chronicle* when he blasted some "completely ridiculous laws," as he put it, that were passed by the San Francisco municipal government against the Iraq War. O'Reilly was saying it was now okay for Al Qaeda to attack San Francisco and that the United States should not protect it, or some such nonsense. Got a lot of attention, but it was embarrassing.

By the second half of his show's ten-year dominance as the most watched on cable news, his favorite opponents more and more seemed to be people and institutions in the media, especially when they attack him first, giving him the pretext for treating the attack as legitimate news and requiring further coverage. In any week, he has a number of feuds going, like branding irons in the fire.

The O'Reilly-Stewart War broke out the night of September 17, 2004. Jon Stewart, anchorman of Comedy Central's *The Daily Show with Jon Stewart*, was appearing on *The Factor*, pushing his new book, *The Daily Show with Jon Stewart Presents America (the Book): A Citizen's Guide to Democracy Inaction*. While analyzing the audience for Stewart's popular eleven o'clock news/analysis show, O'Reilly was saying, "You know what's really frightening?"

"You've been reading my diary," Stewart said.

"You actually have an influence on this presidential election. That is scary."

"If that were so," Stewart responded, "that would be quite frightening."

"But it's true," O'Reilly said. "It's true. I mean, you've got stoned slackers watching your show every night. Okay, and they can vote."

"What am I," Stewart protested, "a Cheech and Chong movie?"

"Come on, you do the research. You know the research on your program. Eighty-seven percent intoxicated when they watch it. You didn't see that?"

Stewart laughed off the collective insult. "I took it as a piece of humor," Stewart said on his show the night of September 30, 2004. "Unfortunately, Comedy Central took it seriously. They released a study saying that our viewers actually are better educated than O'Reilly viewers. The University of Pennsylvania actually had a study saying that *Daily Show* viewers are better versed in current events than people who only watch news channels. . . . What's up, nerds?"

Stewart threw oil on the fire the night of October 18, 2005, having O'Reilly as a guest on the nation's "most trusted fake news show." There was buzz about the coming battle of the titans of cable news analysis. Stewart teased the widely anticipated interview by saying he would be swapping recipes with O'Reilly. O'Reilly was there to plug his newest book, the paperback version of *The O'Reilly Factor for Kids*.

After summarizing O'Reilly's achievements in TV, radio, and best sellers, Stewart said, "Life is so good. You still seem so grumpy. Why so angry?"

"Lot of things wrong in society," O'Reilly said. "It's the right thing to take on the bad people."

Stewart says, "And when are you going to start doing that? [Cheers from the audience]. I don't know if you know this, but they haven't found the weapons of mass destruction. [Cheers.] Who do you pick on? Cindy Sheehan. Why not the Neocons running the country?" [Cheers.]

"Every night you have to bring a sense of outrage to the table." O'Reilly explained his editorial philosophy. "Not like you. We're not playing for giggles. Let's make fun of Katrina."

"I will say we add insult to injury," Stewart said in his version of O'Reilly's last word. "But you add injury to injury." [Cheers.]

Keith Olbermann has been at war with O'Reilly since March 31, 2003, when his *Countdown* show debuted on MSNBC in the time slot opposite *The Factor*. A regular feature is O'Reilly winning Olbermann's weekly "Worst Person in the World" award. At least fifteen times, when I stopped counting. One week, O'Reilly was named worst person in the top three places. The award is Olbermann's way of criticizing what he considers O'Reilly's bad behavior and is widely reported in the press.

Olbermann made media headlines again by opening his session at the Television Critics Association annual meeting in July 2006 by whipping out a mask of O'Reilly and giving a Nazi salute. Fox News Channel chairman and CEO Roger Ailes called it "over the line."

But O'Reilly is above the battle. Unusually for him, he never mentions Olbermann by name on *The Factor*, preferring "a notorious smear merchant."

"He'll be fired by the time your book comes out," O'Reilly assured me. "His ratings are awful. He's been last in his time slot for three years. When CNN's *Headline News* is beating you its pretty bad."

Olbermann appeared to be gaining some traction, despite O'Reilly's downbeat projections. "Clearly, he has no viewers except when he attacks Fox News and Bill," Ailes said of his commitment to continue the war.

O'Reilly's one-man war against Canada, a classic O'Reilly controversy that spilled over into the papers, began with his taking umbrage at one person in the media and soon spread to the whole nation. It was a debate about Canadian press censorship.

The New York Times suggested that O'Reilly's involvement "threatened Canadian-American relations."

In the spring of 2004, the Canadian cable industry filed an application with the Canadian Radio-television and Telecommunications Commission to begin including the Fox News Channel among its offerings. Previously, Canada had been a country where they had legalized same-sex marriages, teased their neighbors south of the border for burning down their own White House in the War of 1812, and was dedicated to keeping Canada a Fox-free zone. Alone among his colleagues in the cable news network fraternity, O'Reilly was incensed that Fox News had been banned in Canada for all its eight years at the time. Nothing can set off his love for the First Amendment more than an attempt to silence him.

John Doyle, the television critic for the *Toronto Globe and Mail*, Canada's most influential newspaper, fired the first shot by poking fun at Fox News and O'Reilly: "Bring it on, I say. We're all in need of a good laugh. The barking-mad Fox News Channel is something that most Canadians have only heard about. It's time we saw it for ourselves and made up our own minds about the phenomenon. We'll find out if this Bill O'Reilly fella is as stupendously pompous and preening as he appears to be in the rare clips we see of Fox News."

In a second column, he described the Fox News Channel as "a kind of live theatre of the airwaves with right wing pundits playing journalists in an ongoing soap opera. In this soap opera there are good guys and bad guys. The bad guys are the Democratic Party and a dark force that is sometimes known as the Liberal Media Elite and sometimes known as the Looney Left.

"No wonder the channel is so popular in the United States," he added. "It is superbly entertaining in an old-fashioned, operatic way. It's camp, it's dramatic and as a viewer you are in a constant state of bless-my-soul excitement, because you're wondering just how angry the people playing journalists on Fox are going to get."

In "The Most Ridiculous Item of the Day" segment on *The Factor*, O'Reilly responded mildly to Doyle's media critique, finding a weakness in the argument coming from a columnist he described as being on "the far left" *Toronto Globe and Mail*. In "The Most Ridiculous Item" two days later, O'Reilly again chided Doyle and his anti-Fox rantings as a product of a newspaper on "the far left."

Calling the *Globe and Mail* far left, Doyle rejoined, "only proves my point that the Fox News Channel is the most hilarious thing on American TV since *Seinfeld*."

Ten days later, the war with Canada broke out again. On April 29, 2004, O'Reilly told his viewers the *Globe and Mail* had struck another low blow by suggesting that O'Reilly and Fox appealed to the lunatic fringe. "This is about the *Globe and Mail*'s eighty-fifth attack on me and the Fox News Channel." He called it "pathetic rambling."

The nasty stuff about *O'Reilly v. Canada* took place on the Internet.

"The people who support Fox News must be the most uncivil and foul-mouthed creatures on the planet," Doyle wrote the next day about the e-mails that had flooded his mailbox in response to O'Reilly's comments on air. "This is an informed opinion. They'd give English soccer hooligans a run for their money."

The Bill O'Reilly Brigade is ready to take up arms and pens and computer mice on any issue. A word from Bill—and they overreact.

O'Reilly's foreign relations with Canada had been frosty since 9/11. It was O'Reilly's belief that Canada was not supportive enough in the war against terrorism. The story of the two U.S. Army soldiers who had sought asylum in Canada that spring combined his two major issues. As he explained to the Spinhead Nation: "Now all of this week we've been telling you that organizations like the *Toronto Globe and Mail* continually put the U.S.A. in a bad light. And we believe that glorifying army deserters is over the top."

The next night he resumed his jeremiad. In "The Most Ridiculous Item of the Day" segment, O'Reilly explained, "The media dishonesty continues. Now as you might have expected the Canadian media, some of who [*sic*] have glorified deserters, are not happy about my criticism. Today the Canadian Press, a newswire service like AP, ran an article, which said the following: that many consider me, your humble correspondent, an ultraconservative shark."

Why the hostility toward the United States and the Fox News Channel? O'Reilly asked columnist Peter Worthington of the rival *Toronto Sun,* who was not so hostile, launching a long discussion of Canadian journalism and its unfair and unbalanced coverage of O'Reilly. "The media is really out of control," O'Reilly told Worthington. "Last topic: You got two army deserters up there, and I've read some of the coverage. It's like these people are heroes." These two men are interesting, O'Reilly went on, "Because they're supposedly conscientious deserters [not objectors?] and joined the army, which is an oddity, anyway. I think if you look at it objectively, they're cowards."

Then came the bombshell.

"Now if you don't send them back," he threatened the Canadian nation, through Worthington, "we're going to institute a boycott against Canada. You have got to get this message across to those guys [Canadian media and government]," he told Worthington. "They may be pandering to the left, but when millions of people stop buying Canadian goods and stop going there, it's going to hurt. We don't want to do that. But we can't have this undermining of our military by our neighbor in the north."

This was the use of the editorial "we." By "we" O'Reilly always means "me" and the rest of "the folks." His "we" is, if not a country, a force.

It wasn't an idle threat. The possible boycott action was first announced on May 1, 2004. He asked for economic sanctions while summarizing the sad state of affairs. "Canada may grant safe harbor to two American army deserters," he told the folks, "thereby undermining our war on terror there. We can't have that."

Then he called for a vote. In one of his famous polls, described on the "Personal Story" segment and posted on billoreilly.com, it asked:

"Will you boycott Canadian goods and services if that country does not return two American deserters who are glorified by some of the Canadian media? Yes . . . or no . . ."

The O'Reilly audience, at least that faction that likes polls and is computer literate, pays attention to *The Factor*'s calls for community involvement. Spin-heads feel an obligation to exercise the franchise and vote.

Conceding it was "an entertainment poll, not scientific," O'Reilly announced the results of his call to arms on May 3, 2004. "The responses poured in," he reported of what he considered a strong turnout. "About forty thousand of you came in. Eighty-six percent say they will boycott; fourteen percent say they will not. Not good news for Canada. We'll let you know what happens."

O'Reilly had gone to economic war against countries before. Noticeably France. After the Chirac government's "craven conduct" in the UN, not supporting the war in Iraq, O'Reilly threatened, then dropped *The Factor*'s ultimate weapon, the B-bomb (for boycott).

"France is feeling the sting," he warned *Toronto Globe and Mail* columnist Heather Mallick, who had dared to call the two deserters "fine American men." After verbally abusing Mallick as anti-American, calling her "a socialist," and someone who writes "stuff that is not true," O'Reilly really got testy.

"I don't think your French boycott has done too well," she interrupted.

"They've lost billions of dollars in France, according to the *Paris Business Review*," he thundered, ending the debate.

As a matter of fact, there had been a breakdown in *The Factor*'s research process. The billions France apparently lost might have been caused by the 2001 recession, and there is no such magazine as the *Paris Business Review*. These were two of the facts lost in the melee that broke out in The Zone, according to *Rolling Stone*.

The mother of all O'Reilly's media wars might yet be the acrimonious exchanges with David Letterman in 2006. O'Reilly told me a few years earlier that he liked Dave. They always had a good show every time O'Reilly appeared in the past, but he couldn't understand why he hadn't been invited the last few years to promote his books. He finally got his chance to sit down with the cranky *Late Show* host on January 3, 2006.

It started innocently enough, with Letterman stirring his pencil in O'Reilly's glass of water before he came onstage. They then engaged in heated discussions about his crusade against taking the so-called Christmas out of Christmas, over Cindy Sheehan, over the war in Iraq, over the Bush administration liking him.

O'Reilly contested that charge. "They are not kicking down the door to come on my show."

The largely hostile anti-O'Reilly audience cheered Letterman's content analysis of *The Factor*. "I'm not smart enough to debate you," said Letterman, "but I have the feeling about sixty percent of what you say is crap." He then admitted he didn't know that for a fact since he didn't watch the show.

It could also be argued that 60 percent of his jokes were crap, O'Reilly could have rebutted. How did Dave know without watching? The last time Letterman seemed so intellectually embarrassed was when the terminally inane Drew Barrymore jumped up on his desk and started exposing her breasts.

Letterman seemed to have shanghaied O'Reilly's style, putting him on the defensive, clobbering him as O'Reilly does his guests, rarely giving O'Reilly the chance to get a few words in edgewise.

It was great television. Also on the upside, after twenty-five years Dave was finally taking a stand on something substantive. It was shocking. Normally, his position is to the left of Paul Shaffer onstage. This was O'Reilly's major contribution to public discourse in 2006, along with saving Christmas.

O'Reilly logged many minutes on his TV and radio shows talking about what he called his "shoot-out" with Letterman, posting a video clip on his Web site. Clips also ran on MSNBC and Fox. He gave a telephone interview to *The View* on ABC, saying he didn't feel ambushed. "I had no problem with the interview. I enjoyed it."

The confrontation was widely discussed on Fox, especially on *The Factor*. The next night Fox News analyst Juan Williams likened the segment to a knife fight. "In some sense," he told O'Reilly, "it's like inviting you into their house and you find out you've been invited by John Wayne Gacy."

Chapter Twenty

What Was He Thinking?

The enemies who were out to get him in the fall of 2004 discovered they had a new ally: O'Reilly himself.

On October 13, 2004, Andrea Mackris, an associate producer on *The O'Reilly Factor*, filed a lawsuit against her boss, Bill O'Reilly, and his bosses at Fox News Channel. She complained that O'Reilly had bombarded her with unwanted sex chatter and graphic language in person and by phone since 2002 and continued to do so until she left the Fox News network in September 2004. O'Reilly, she alleged in the brief, forced her to have phone sex with him on three occasions, that he made repeated sexual advances, and that he warned her in advance that he would destroy any woman who dared expose his conduct.

"The details of Ms. Mackris's complaint are grisly," explained *The New York Observer,* "and involve late-night dinners, dirty conversations and an electronic apparatus that no boss should ever recommend to an employee as office equipment."

To support her contention, her lawsuit, filed in the Supreme Court of the State of New York, County of New York, contained "steamy soliloquies," as thesmokinggun.com summarized what it called "an incredible page-turner that quotes O'Reilly on all sorts of lewd matters." In its instructions to legal scholars regarding the twenty-two-page brief, thesmokinggun said, "While we suggest reading the entire document, TSG will point you to interesting sections on his

Caribbean shower fantasies with a loofah, a Thailand sex show, Al Franken, the climax of one August 2004 phone conversation."

O'Reilly's alleged lewd and vile behavior began in May 2002, Mackris charged in her complaint, after she had broken up with her fiancé at a time when she was struggling financially. O'Reilly took her to dinner, offered her a raise, and gave her sexually inappropriate relationship advice. During the course of their dinner, she charged, "His demeanor abruptly changed. His eyes became glazed . . . suddenly without provocation or warning, he proceeded to inform the Plaintiff that he had advised another woman to purchase a vibrator and taught that woman how to masturbate while telling her sexual stories over the telephone . . . The woman had her first orgasm via masturbation as he spoke to her on the telephone." Mackris claimed she was shocked and embarrassed.

After dinner, he didn't ask her up to his hotel room, where he was staying because of an appearance the next morning on a network early news show.

In May 2003, she had dinner with him again, this time with a college friend. Again he talked dirty, but she was powerless to object, she said, because he was her boss.

In September 2003, the twice-shocked and embarrassed employee went to dinner again, where she said he talked dirty again.

In December 2003, she dined with O'Reilly again. Same crude behavior.

Seeking higher pay, Mackris left Fox in January 2004 for a similar position at CNN without complaining to anyone at Fox about his unwanted behavior.

In March 2004, O'Reilly called and said, according to Mackris, "If anything bad happens to you at CNN, I'll get you a job."

In April 2004, she again dined with the alleged perpetrator. She claimed his previous inappropriate behavior was a source of conversation that night. Nevertheless, she agreed to go back to his hotel room. They watched TV, a presidential press conference.

O'Reilly didn't touch her that night or at any other time. But he did offer her the chance to return to Fox. Unhappy with the conditions at CNN, where she worked on *The Paula Zahn Show,* Mackris took O'Reilly up on his offer. He agreed to rehire her at her former starting salary of $73,000. When Mackris balked at the amount, O'Reilly offered to match her salary at CNN, the difference coming out of the budget of his syndicated radio show.

In July, she returned to Fox. By the end of that month, she said, he was up to his old tricks of talking dirty on the phone. A call on August 2 was especially graphic, according to her, describing things that he imagined they might enjoy doing together, the most notorious of which was the shower scenario. Nevertheless, three weeks later on August 24, she had dinner again with O'Reilly.

On September 1 at 11:06 P.M., she claims he even called her for phone sex in the midst of the Republican convention.

Mackris was seeking $60 million in damages for his allegedly saying crude things to her on the phone and over dinner.

A native of Missouri, Andrea Mackris, thirty-three, graduated from Westminster Christian Academy in St. Louis in 1989, earned a B.A. in English at the University of Missouri in 1993, and attended Columbia University School of Journalism. Her prior work experience included a stint as a White House intern under George W. Bush before being hired at *The O'Reilly Factor* in April 2000. As a talent booker on *The Factor* production team, she was highly regarded for her aggressive style in getting the tougher interviews. She loved her job—it was a challenge and involved her in the kind of work for which she had studied and prepared. Single, she lived on Manhattan's Upper West Side. With raises, she eventually earned $93,200 a year at Fox. She always felt underpaid and deserving of a preferential promotion because of her Columbia Journalism School background, of which she often reminded her fellow employees.

Her complaint raised some very awkward talking points for the outspoken newsman.

O'Reilly responded to the charges with self-righteous hauteur, slapping his accuser with a countersuit charging extortion. He was the first to go public, denying the still-to-come allegations by several hours.

In his countersuit—filed in the Supreme Court of the State of New York, County of Nassau, where he lives—O'Reilly and his attorneys, Epstein Becker & Green, accused his employee of "a multimillion dollar shakedown attempt." O'Reilly's claim against Mackris and her attorney, Benedict P. Morelli and his firm, Benedict P. Morelli & Associates, said that Morelli demanded $60 million in "hush money in return for not going public with a scandalous and scurrilous claim on alleged inappropriate comments" made to Mackris by O'Reilly. "Defendant's outrageous demands cannot be justified by any alleged harm that Mackris claims to have suffered."

Mackris originally wanted $600 million, a participant in the negotiations said. Her attorneys told her that figure was ridiculous. They talked her into a lower figure. Sixty million was more reasonable, reducing the suffering and anguish by ten times.

"Mackris must have figured that O'Reilly was worth $600 million a year to Fox," one legal observer calculated about how she had come up with the original number in presuit discussions with O'Reilly's lawyers. "Out of the goodness of their hearts, her legal team would be willing to settle this matter for ten cents on the dollar. If he acted right now, O'Reilly could get away with the bargain-basement price of sixty million dollars."

"Defendant's demands," the O'Reilly suit papers explained, "are based on the threat to sully the reputation of a successful cable news network and nationally renowned television and radio host, columnist, and author. Their demand is blackmail, pure and simple."

The story titillated millions, especially the media, who diligently reported the key elements of the alleged harassment: the values of a loofah for a working gal, how O'Reilly expressed his support of threesomes, had regaled the plaintiff and a college friend she brought along to dinner with stories of the loss of his virginity in a car at JFK, the two really wild and crazy Scandinavian airline stewardesses, and a girl at a sex show in Thailand who had shown him things in a back room that "blew my mind."

The story had hit the Internet faster than a Paris Hilton video. Thesmokinggun .com, the *Drudge Report*, and dozens of wannabes set cyberspace sizzling as armchair legal scholars studied the juicy lurid details, weighing the case. For a few days in mid-October 2004, the story knocked the Laci Peterson trial off the front pages, especially the New York tabloids. The election campaign became the "B" story. Forget the Bosox, the latest Osama tape. The war in Iraq was in a far-off country.

O'Reilly's predicament started a new cottage industry in O'Reilly jokes. Andy Borowitz, "winner of the first ever National Press Club Award for Humor," as his blog site acclaims, reported authoritatively in "the breaking news" section of *The Borowitz Report*:

"Elsewhere, a $600 million class action suit was filed today on behalf of Americans who claim they have been permanently traumatized by the fear of receiving a phone sex call from Fox News personality, Bill O'Reilly."

The intense Web response was engendered and reinforced by cable network news' relentless overcoverage.

All of this was coming at a particularly embarrassing and untimely moment for O'Reilly. Out that week was a self-help book for children, *The O'Reilly Factor for Kids: A Survival Guide for American Families*, a collection of O'Reilly sermons on sex, money, drugs, alcohol, and friends. Published on September 28, 2004, the book was number six on the *New York Times* Best Seller List with 225,000 copies in print. O'Reilly canceled his promotional book tour. Appearances were scrubbed on ABC's *The View*, HBO's *Real Time with Bill Maher*, and CBS's *The Early Show*. His chapter on sex was widely quoted on the Web.

"I repeat my mantra," O'Reilly wrote, "sex is best when you combine sensible behavior with sincere affection. That's the ideal and it is smart to wait for it . . . it's also smart to recognize that there is no area more potentially dishonest than the sexual arena. Girls, some guys will tell you anything to get that sex thing going. Then, after it's done, they will brutally drop you. Don't let that happen. Make your boyfriend prove (himself) over time, and don't ever allow yourself to get drunk or stoned to have sex. That's how most girls get pregnant. And, guys, if you exploit a girl, it will come back to get you. That's called 'karma.' "

True or not, whether it happened or didn't, the situation was bad for O'Reilly.

"The problem with asserting moral authority nightly on live TV," asserted *Time* magazine's Rebecca Winters, "is that inevitably someone will one day challenge it. For Fox News anchor Bill O'Reilly, that time is now." O'Reilly had called the Mackris suit "the single most evil thing I have ever experienced."

"Well, we guess," *Time* explained, "that means Michael Moore is off the hook."

There is nothing many Americans like more than to see moralists brought down from their pulpits. Who can forget the tearful televised confession and apology by the Reverend Jimmy Swaggart? Or learning that America's self-appointed morality guru, William Bennett, had a gambling problem? Then there was the Reverend Jim Bakker's combination of sexual peccadilloes and a financial scam that bilked thousands of his faithful Christian audience out of their life savings? Or Newt Gingrich and other GOP moralists forced to resign from political office because of one scandal or another.

While his enemies were dancing around the grave, O'Reilly went on the offensive in his ultimate career crisis. First, he had sued, then he went public. On the night of October 13, O'Reilly began a commentary, titled "Enough is enough."

"Hi, I'm Bill O'Reilly . . . thanks for watching us tonight . . . we are living in treacherous times. That's the subject of this evening's Talking Points Memo.

"Just about every famous person I know has been threatened and worked over by somebody. Fame makes you a target. It is something that has to be taken seriously. As I've mentioned before, I have received many threats over the years . . . everything from death letters to some guy running around the country offering people twenty-five thousand dollars to sign affidavits accusing me of whatever.

"The lawyers here at Fox News have been great in dealing with these situations . . . but there comes a time when enough is enough . . . and so this morning I had to file a lawsuit against some people who are demanding sixty million dollars or they will 'punish' me and Fox News . . . sixty million. I really can't say anything else. I don't want to waste your time with this. The justice system has the case. We'll see what happens. But in the end, this is all about hurting me and the Fox News Channel. And that's the memo."

O'Reilly did not stand down, as some might have hoped. Just a few weeks earlier Gov. Jim McGreevey of New Jersey, when faced with a sensational embarrassing sex problem, abdicated. O'Reilly had not delivered a farewell address.

He was about to enter a No Talking Spin Zone, refusing to discuss further the dueling suits on the air. On *The Radio Factor* the afternoon of October 19, 2004, he broke his silence once. Responding to one listener, he said, "I had to protect my family. This is my fault. I was stupid, and I'm not a victim. But I can't allow certain things to happen. And I appreciate your support. We get thousands of letters. I'm not—I am stupid. I am a stupid guy, and every guy listening knows how that is. That we are very stupid at times.

"But there comes a time in life where you got to stand and fight. And I knew these people were going to do this. I knew they were going to do everything they could to try to destroy me and the channel. And I just made a decision that I'm going to ride it out, and I'm going to fight them."

Not only did he not crash and burn as his enemies hoped, but his ratings went up.

"Bill O'Reilly may be in personal torment over the phone sex flapola," wrote Doug Vasquez, who follows cable for medialifemagazine.com, "but his career as Fox News's host-in-chief is . . . thriving." On the day after Mackris filed her charges, Thursday, October 14, 2004, O'Reilly saw dramatic increases in every key demographic, including adults 18–34, 18–49, 25–54, households, and total viewers, versus his show's averages for the previous year's third quarter.

"Yeah, that scared me," Roger Ailes said, looking back. "I thought he might go out and do it again. If he did it. You know, look, a lot of people were waiting for a train wreck, waiting for him to melt down. But I think it made him more interesting to the public also as a person."

There had been speculation about how well the numbers would hold once the Train Wreck Factor ended. Would O'Reilly viewers from the religious right drop the show in indignation over Mackris's charges.

"The folks" had been waiting to hear what he had to say. Much to the disappointment of his detractors, the expected turnoff factor did not kick in. *The O'Reilly Factor* continued to be 30 percent above the pre–Mackris suit numbers. The morbid-curiosity crowd had stuck around.

O'Reilly considered it a mandate from the people.

There were puzzling aspects about the Mackris story.

Her complaint was remarkably specific for a case like this, a lawyer told me. The transcripts of O'Reilly's alleged phone calls, which were part of the lawsuit, have a lot of "ah," pauses, "umms" in it. You had to be a very fast note-taker, have a remarkable memory, be a clever fantasist to come up with that. Or you had to use a tape recorder.

The specificity of detail in her complaint suggests she taped O'Reilly's calls. If there was a smoking tape, would the whole tape show the plaintiff was being provocative and setting up a boob defendant? The suit papers do not reveal her side of the conversation, what she might have been saying in between the alleged heavy breathing. The alleged inappropriate words could have been taken out of context. Without seeing a full transcript, no one can know for sure.

How can you have phone sex against your wishes? Why didn't she just hang up if she found it so offensive?

Returning to Fox was another problem. If O'Reilly bothered Mackris, why would she work with him again? Why didn't she report him to Fox management? The news channel has procedures in place for dealing with sex harassment cases. It certainly would have bolstered her case, made her out to be less of an opportunist.

Matthew Paratore, who owns an Upper West Side bar, reported that Mackris boasted she had written a book "to take him [O'Reilly] down" (as O'Reilly's lawyers phrased it)—months before she went back to work for him at Fox. Mackris was also an acquaintance and political admirer of O'Reilly's archnemesis, Al Franken, Paratore claimed. She had spoken to a publisher earlier in the year, according to O'Reilly's lawyer, Ronald Green. She was told her book had to have more impact, she had to do more to make the book more interesting and exciting, Green said.

"What we thought we had here was somebody trying to hit us up for a lot of money," said O'Reilly's lawyer, Ronald Green. "Now we know it's much more than that." Mackris's lawyer called talk of a book project "ridiculous" and "garbage."

On the other hand, in judging O'Reilly's side of the argument, *what* was he thinking? O'Reilly was not saying. He refused to discuss the case. Others' lips were not sealed. Sources at Fox and *The Factor* spoke to me with a request for anonymity.

First of all, there are no angels here. Sexual banter goes on in TV newsrooms all the time. Joking about sex is a commonplace occurrence. At Fox, Mackris was in the middle of all of it, giving as well as taking, the Fox source said.

O'Reilly was foolish to continue that line of inappropriate conversation outside the newsroom with her. What he was doing was, as they used to call it, kidding around. You can't do that anymore in the workplace.

His biggest mistake was considering her not just an employee but a friend. In his mind he was dispensing friendly advice about how to deal with a personal problem she was having, the sources said. His well-documented propensity not to keep his mouth shut could have led him to saying those crude things.

It had been his practice to help many young people on his staff, male and female, taking them under his wing. He fought for raises for people, male and females. He befriended, counseled, and sometimes dined with them. "There was a little bit of the benevolent dictator in O'Reilly," a former Fox executive said. "He's very tough on them. He yells at them. Everybody knows he wasn't Saint Bill. He has a caustic attitude, uses rough language, and is insensitive to feelings. The reason the show got such high ratings, he felt, is because he ran it like the Green Berets. He had more of a personal relationship with his staff, unlike

Paula Zahn, who could never name her staff members. She'd go down to the pod and talk to them, and had no idea who they were."

O'Reilly staff people were angry with Mackris. Her coworkers felt betrayed because it disrupted the collegial team atmosphere. They were also shocked. O'Reilly had always been so careful and smart about maintaining his aloof persona. She was smart to use O'Reilly's paragon-of-virtue image against him.

Mackris had left Fox because she was unhappy that another woman on *The Factor* staff had been promoted to producer, a job she had wanted. She had been joking around with Bill, thought she was Bill's favorite, and in the end, the job went to another woman on the staff, the Fox sources said.

O'Reilly's lawyer told the New York *Daily News* that Mackris had a crush on her boss. Talking that way to her, she hoped it might bloom into a more meaningful relationship. But it was all talk.

She also had money problems. Her previous boyfriend had been a successful Wall Street guy, and she had gotten into the habit of buying expensive things. She had $99,000 in credit card debt and student loans, Drudge reported.

She was shopping for a condo in the million-dollar range before the incident. A close girlfriend of hers brought a successful lucrative sexual harassment suit against an executive at CNN, and it gave her ideas, one source claimed.

"If you hate the way he talked, why didn't you get out of Dodge?" one source wondered. "And why are you coming back? She obviously had her sights on a big payday," another coworker said.

She begged to come back to Fox, executives say. She was good at her job, good at identifying what worked for *The Factor*, but the show could have gone on without her. Nevertheless, O'Reilly hired her back.

She went to O'Reilly's secretary, Makeda, and asked three times if she could find a night that Bill was staying in town so she could take him to dinner to thank him for bringing her back. O'Reilly is zealous in not paying for dinners. Even with childhood friends in his inner circle, they still split the checks despite his financial status.

She may have led him on, but he let her lead him.

As suits and countersuit excerpts were flying through the air on the Internet and in newspapers, rumors started hitting the blogs and print that settlement discussions were under way.

O'Reilly's first instinct was to go out there and fight it in the courts and the press, said Fox publicist Rob Zimmerman. "Make it a big public issue and go crazy. But then he actually learned something from the Franken thing. 'I'm going to sit this one out,' he instructed the Fox PR people. 'Don't bring the press in here. Don't let me make stupid comments, don't push the issue.' Because, look, he lost to Franken in the press, and that burns him to this day."

Many lawyers believe that O'Reilly would have won at trial. Sexual harassment isn't harassment unless the advances are unwelcome, and it appears that his alleged advances were not enough to keep her away from the dinner table. "The jury would almost certainly conclude that the conduct and language wasn't [sic] unwanted harassment," one lawyer said. "Given she apparently suffered no career consequences, made no complaints to Fox's management, returned to work for Mr. O'Reilly after her stint at CNN, voluntarily accompanied him to dinner on many occasions, didn't hang up on the phone calls, and so forth," it could be argued that she set him up, the lawyer believed.

Settlements always make the settler appear guilty, even when the charges are refuted. O'Reilly thinks he would have won in court. Yet he quickly settled. "In dealing with O'Reilly," said Roger Ailes, "nothing ever surprises me."

Every lawyer involved told O'Reilly he would win, but it would take two years at least. Crack reporters would be investigating his private life, interviewing his early girlfriends, subpoenaing phone records. He didn't want to put his wife, mother, and family through the ordeal. He would win the legal battle eventually, but it would be a pyrrhic victory. Two years down the road, everything would be destroyed. "Whatever happens, you're ruined," said Roger Ailes. "I don't blame anybody for settling and getting past it."

He settled because he knew public memory lasts as long as an MTV video. Ironically, he was able to use the news cycles that cable TV news had created: maximum exposure on a story, followed by its immediate disappearance. A speedy settlement, and the story would be like a rock falling in a lake, except on Air America where months later they were doing promos promising an hour-long documentary on *The O'Reilly Sex Tapes*, as if they were the missing eighteen and one-half minutes on Nixon's Watergate tapes.

In O'Reilly's favor, whatever dirt was due to come out that was damaging—the only kind that would be reported—had already hit the headlines, thanks to thesmokinggun.com and other bloggers. No other recipients of unwanted phone calls came forward.

There was an election that fall of 2004, which meant lots of news besides O'Reilly and his adult conversations. Get over it fast and before the election, the theory at Fox was. After the election, it would blow over. And they were right.

This was a one-hundred-thousand-dollar go-away-nuisance case, someone familiar with the settlement said. "Mackris's guys refused to move from sixty million. They said 60 million or we're going to the press at eight tomorrow morning. Never moved off that number. Wouldn't even come down to fifty-nine." O'Reilly's camp and his countersuit repeatedly characterized this alleged failure to negotiate as "extortion."

"And Bill never even touched her. Even she said that. This is a maximum one hundred thousand, okay, she got her feelings hurt," the source said.

I don't know how much the settlement was. A Fox executive claimed that the only certainty is that Fox didn't pay a dime of it, since it happened after hours.

What I do know about O'Reilly having to put his money where his mouth was, given his frugal nature, is that if it didn't break the bank financially, it broke his heart. Two million? Two hundred thousand? "Twenty dollars would have kept him awake at night," a friend said.

Andrea Mackris has her settlement, whatever it was. She has disappeared from the printed page and won't appear again until she returns as a corpse in O'Reilly's next murder mystery.

"I was ready for an influx of 'We'll never watch you again' e-mails," said Roger Ailes. "A few said, 'Oh, you phony, you scumbag . . .' but I'd say over half said, 'You got set up, this is bullshit . . .'"

The scandal didn't affect O'Reilly's broadcasting. He told the public what he was doing, and they let it rest.

"He was as tough as anybody I had ever seen," Ailes said, right after it happened. "I've seen strong guys dissolve in these kinds of situations. He didn't. You had to respect the fact that he'd go out there every night and do his job, never affecting his performance. Bill is a truly tough guy. Some guys could not have done what he did. They would have taken three weeks off. He sucked it up every night and went up there and did it."

Not only didn't he implode, but the Mackris suit energized O'Reilly. Rather than being personally crushed, he seemed to rise to new levels, becoming even more popular with "the folks." By the week of October 24, 2005, *The Factor* still led all cable network news shows with 3.3 million viewers, almost three times as many as *Larry King Live* on CNN (1.2 million).

After it was all over, he was dejected off camera. "I'd never seen him at such a low point," said former Fox publicist Rob Zimmerman. "You know, he's always got this complex that everyone is out to get him. This time he said, 'That's it. I'm not doing any more press. No more interviews. I have my audience,' he said. 'My audience believes in me. No more trying to convert the heathens.' Before he was trying to proselytize. He has gone into a shell."

The case also changed his style at work. He was not making as many phone calls. He was not having dinner with too many employees. There were now always two or three other people around when he talked to anybody. But it hasn't affected his personality. He is just as hostile, belligerent, and outspoken as before, still doing smash-mouth interviews, still taking on tough subjects. He hasn't become diffident in any way.

He is just as difficult as he always was. "About a week after we were in the middle of it," said Roger Ailes, "and I sent word down to the executive producer, 'How's Bill doing?' And he said the staff just says, 'It must be going well, because he's back to being a prick.'"

Part IV

The Last Hurrah

Chapter Twenty-one

The Future Lies Ahead

It's amazing that *The O'Reilly Factor* is still around. No television program lasts forever. There is a cycle, usually short, then shows are gone like a soap bubble in the air.

Conceivably there will be a day when viewers lose interest in finding out what he is upset about. *The O'Reilly Factor* sometimes seems as if it has become a show that is about Bill as much as about the news. The folks could grow tired of his paint-stripping interviews or grow bored watching the nightly morality dramas.

He is only as good as his last night's numbers. O'Reilly could fall into the Sixth Dimension and disappear, if people were not tuning in to *The Factor*. Such a "no" vote eventually would make O'Reilly lose favor in the eyes of his bosses at Fox News Channel.

Is the end near? How long will he last? Will he burn out?

"What I worry about is that he will implode someday," his good friend Peter Jennings said in 2003. "Because it's quite a high-wire act he does. I worry because I do genuinely like him. While I think he has a very good internal core—I think he believes in family, believes in his wife, believes in children, believes in the basic values of bringing up children well, etc., etc.—somehow he has an internal governor regulate all of this, but one of the strings is rusty."

"I want to be the top-rated show," O'Reilly told the *Daily News* in 2000. "When we started, there were ten in front of us."

The late-blooming O'Reilly had long since reached that goal. He had attained levels of achievement in his career enough to satisfy even a megalomaniac. His books were all best sellers; his newspaper column seen, if not read, by millions; on radio, the folks were jamming the lines to answer his "What say you?" On TV, he had received the highest honor of all, astronomical Nielsen numbers.

"In the past you walked away from jobs," I asked him. "Is there any chance at some point you will do that again at Fox?"

"Sure," he said. "If I don't like what I'm doing, I'm not going to stay and do it. But why would I do that now? I've had forty thousand interviews, and I'm just warming up."

But that was in 2004.

"When I first came here ten years ago," he told me in the summer of 2006, "I had no idea the show would become an icon. I had no idea people would be quoting the phrases we used—the No-Spin Zone, keep it pithy. No idea we'd be such a cultural phenomenon. Four years in, it started to catch fire. We began to see the influence it was having. I didn't take the show as seriously in the beginning as I should have. We kind of swaggered around. I just thought it was fun. Okay, let's go out and have a great show, and have a lot of laughs after. Not anymore. It's not a lark anymore. When people started attacking me and my family, that has put a damper on the fun side of the program. Now it's a serious business. It's not a talk-radio thing. It's a serious show."

By 2005, he was confessing that he was growing tired of everybody being out there to get him. "Now it's so bad that I spend an enormous amount of money protecting myself against evil." There are death threats. He had to hire bodyguards. "I got to watch every move I make. Everything is monitored by Makeda. I can't socialize with strangers anymore." He now has to have a third person listening in when he talks to anybody on the phone. There are people on the street with cell phones, instant paparazzi. They snap a picture one minute, and post it on the Web the next.

"I never felt sorry for people like Lindsay Lohan in my life. I thought they are dopey little movie stars. Now I feel sorry for those people. That poor little girl is nineteen and can't leave the house without some idiot doing something."

When O'Reilly was asked about his future after his current contract at Fox News Channel runs out in the winter of 2009, he blurted out the "R" word: retirement. "I might, I might," he told a newsman in the winter of 2005.

He doesn't have to do the show anymore. "I can quit anytime," he says. He's as famous as he needs to be. He doesn't like being so famous. He can't take his family and stay in a hotel. So what good is it? "Anyone can accuse me of anything, and then it's on a Web site," he said. "You have to worry who's looking at you. Are they taking your picture? Did you curse at this guy? If you nudge somebody's bumper, are they going to sue you for eighty million? Who wants to live like that?"

How long he does *The O'Reilly Factor* depends on his health, he told me. "I work enormous hours, am under a lot of stress. You gotta figure that sooner or later it's going to get to you. If I'm not feeling well, I'm not going to do it. It's as simple as that."

There is no other job he wants at Fox or in television. That's what he says, but whatever he says for now is just talk.

The ultimate O'Reilly Moment is reading the Nielsen numbers at 4:01 every day. As soon as the earliest drop is recorded, he will be computing its significance. Corrections in course—story selection, guest lists, crusades launched or ended, going tabloid—will take place, and if those don't work, O'Reilly will get the message. He won't have to read in the papers that his show is "in trouble" or "on the bubble." O'Reilly will know when the jig is up. He'll be long gone before they hand him the pink slip. And there will be none of the usual whining of the vanquished. He will have had a good run, far exceeding any of his other jobs.

If he does retire, what will he do? There are those who think he will go into politics, an interest fueled by the faculty at the Kennedy School. "All the guys at Harvard," O'Reilly said, "not only teach but work as consultants on political campaigns." He actually took a course in how to run for Congress, how to make a budget for the campaign, and how to win.

In 1996, he was considering running for Congress in Massachusetts, said his friend from Boston University, Bruce Feirstein. He also mentioned it to Michael Rose while they were working in Boston. Feirstein and O'Reilly even batted around issues. What are you going to do about abortion? Feirstein asked. "And he had a very interesting nuanced position, which may have changed since then. It was, 'Look, what we really need to do is get into a position where there is enough education [which obviously meant sex ed] that the goal should be to have fewer young women in a position where they need an abortion.' That would seem to go against his Catholic upbringing. You can't put this guy in a box, ideologically."

Running for office would fit his Bobby Kennedy role model, but he soon got over it. "The political climate in the U.S.A. has changed in favor of crooks and incompetents. How can you guarantee yourself a future in public service? Be willing to sell out for campaign money. And if you're an especially talented liar, you can go very far. Both major parties would be happy to have you join in the hustle. After watching the Clintonites operate, after listening to the likes of Newt Gingrich and Ross Perot pander and babble and weasel, and after analyzing the continuing stream of vile and dishonest propaganda from both parties, I've seen too much. I'm suffering from political post-traumatic stress disorder."

Still, the political bug could bite him again. There is precedent for politicians to come from a TV base. Ronald Reagan's campaign started with *The GE Theater*. Pat Buchanan, the CNN commentator, has managed to become the Harold Stassen of the Republican Party, by running for the presidency every fourth year. The only thing that could get O'Reilly into politics would be a duty to stop what he considers a major threat to the nation: Hillary Clinton.

His contract at Fox News is up in 2009. He might be amenable to heading a Bipartisan Citizens Committee to Stop Hillary for President movement in 2008.

"She'll run for president in 2008," Ailes predicted in 2003 about what might get O'Reilly to throw his hat in the ring. "I think she stashed other files back there at the White House that haven't been found yet, and she wants to go back to get them before they find them. That's my theory.

"I don't think O'Reilly's running is out of the question, although I think Rudy Giuliani is thinking the same thing. I think a lot of people are. I don't think it's as easy as Bill thinks it is. But Jesse Ventura and Arnold Shwarzenegger ran and won. So we live in a world where even you or I could run, and we might be serious candidates, depending on who we're up against. I think the world's changed in that the public is open to anything. Bill will certainly be a well-known name with strong opinions. Could he run? Sure he could."

The only problem with this scenario is that O'Reilly denies he's a candidate. "I won't run for office until they change the campaign finance stuff," he told a *Daily News* reporter in 2001. "And then what party would I run in? I'm against the death penalty. Are the Republicans going to go for that? I want a big government watching over environmental issues. I want gun control. There are just so many issues I come down on against both parties that it would be hard for either one to embrace me."

Denying you're a candidate in American political tradition, of course, is tantamount to throwing your hat in the ring, a way of saying you're available at least for an honest draft, and if that is not forthcoming, an engineered one.

"I will be surprised if he ever runs for any office," Peter Jennings told me in December 2002. He was having too much fun, in Jennings's opinion, and there is too much money in TV. "Because I do believe that Bill wants a good life for his family. He prefers the stratosphere to the subterranean, and television provides him with that. I mean, he doesn't wish to live as the working-class guy, and no working-class guy really does if he can get the ladder out. But more than that, and I'm guessing here a little bit, Bill thinks that politics ultimately on that level is not safe. It's dangerous. It's tricky. You can lose. And Bill has never really lost. He will tell you he's lost, but I don't think he believes he's ever lost. His curve has always been upwards. The thing about politics is that it's utterly unpredictable. That's why it's attractive to some people, but I think Bill likes safe."

This is the age of the rich man in politics, which is the most compelling reason why he would not run. Millionaire candidates today often spend their own money, especially in the early days of a campaign when they are denying they are candidates. The Bloomberg-Corzine model of today's megabucks candidate wouldn't play well with noncandidate O'Reilly. Based on his reputation for penury, he wouldn't spend a quarter of his own money.

What will become of O'Reilly? As he ages, we might see another side of O'Reilly. He could soften his manner and manners and come across more like Ed Murrow.

He could return to university life. "I could teach a couple of journalism courses," he said. "I get lots of job offers. Columbia, Harvard. Get up there with all the radical leftists."

He could wind up narrating PBS documentaries, like many old network hands, even do commercials. John Cameron Swayze was more remembered for his Timex commercials than his work at NBC News. Or infomercials. David Brinkley ended up as spokesperson for Archer Daniels, tainting his image and legacy.

Will he ever have enough of what he's doing? I asked Roger Ailes. He has a record of leaving every job after a certain point, the media version of the seven-year itch. "Yeah, I know," Ailes said. "He's a hard guy to read. I would suspect that as long as he makes big bucks, he'll stay at this. The day he doesn't [make big bucks], he's out of here. I don't think Bill has the same emotional need for it as some performers do. Bill could find fulfilment doing other things. He's as happy beating the crap out of an anonymous single person as an entire audience and guest. I mean, he can joust his paperboy, and he'll feel fulfilled.

"So you know he could run for office. He could retire and write. He'll always do guest appearances. He'll always be Bill O'Reilly. But I don't see quite the fear of not being on television that most celebrities have. Most celebrities, if not on that day, feel there is somebody standing on their air hose. Bill doesn't have that."

Part V

What Say You?

Chapter Twenty-two

The New Journalism

Of the many bad things that have been said about O'Reilly what bothered him most was that some people thought negatively of him as an angry guy. I remember him telling me the first time we talked how upset he was about a *Primetime* interview on ABC. "Chris Cuomo must have asked me twenty times: angry guy angry guy angry guy. At one point I just said, 'Cuomo, you know, you're either going to get it or you're not. If you sign on to be a journalist, part of the deal, written in stone, is you've got to have an edge, you got to be skeptical. You got to resent the fact that powerful people take advantage of the folks. You got to go after these people, that's part of the job. You want to do *Entertainment Tonight*, go ahead and do it, but if you want to be a good journalist, every single good journalist in the history of the world has had that one attribute. They were antiauthority, skeptical of power. Period.

"There is a basic energy that traditionally came out of journalism that is pretty much lacking in American journalism today," he continued. "Whether you agree with me or not, whether you like my style or not, you can't deny that what we're trying to do here is not only report the truth, but hold people accountable for their behavior."

O'Reilly's goal in his ten years at *The O'Reilly Factor* has been to hold people accountable. "What I've seen is that society can never get better, can never improve itself until the people know who's looking out for them and who isn't. Who the people are in power who are trying to change things for the better, who the people in power who are not. And that's my sole purpose: to shed light on those people.

"That's why I was on John Ashcroft's case so much. Because Ashcroft was in a position where he could be a prime player to right wrongs, and he sat back and on Christmas Eve announced he's not going to indict Gary Winnick [CEO of Global Crossing, once known as 'the richest man in LA' before the international fiber optics company filed for bankruptcy in 2002]. Well, why does he announce it on Christmas Eve?"

Next to rhetorical questions, O'Reilly's favorite form of communication I had learned early, is rhetorical answers. "Because he doesn't want you to know it, all right. Why doesn't he want you to know it? Because he knows that his position is indefensible." Winnick had been investigated for possible accounting fraud. He earned more than $600,000 from sales of his stock in a company that later went bankrupt. "But John Ashcroft did not have enough guts to come out, hold a press conference, and explain why he won't indict the man. Instead he releases his decision on Christmas Eve and hides in his office. No, there is nobody in the press that I know of who's going to expose that but me. Because I'm genuinely disturbed. I'm angry about it. But if you go down to the others over at ABC, NBC, CBS, CNN and yeah, yeah, right, business as usual. 'Let's have lunch.' They don't care.

"Now why don't they care? I don't know. I don't know whether it's that they're so self-absorbed, they can't see the pain that this man caused everybody, while he lives in his Bel Air hundred-million-dollar home. So there's something within me that's always been there that says, 'I'm not going to let these bastards get away with it. I'm going to humiliate them. I'm going to pound them. I'm going to kick the TV set in. And if my ratings suffer, they suffer. I'm going to do what I think is right. But first I'm going to do it in a way that you can't dispute it. You know I'm going to tell you what it is, tell you what the facts are. I'm just not going to go with a blunderbuss, just shooting wildly. It's all very well researched, methodically presented."

What was missing from the news all those years when the network news went into decline was anger at the way things were going. In the old days you could watch the news and yell at Walter Cronkite. But what was the point? Walter Cronkite couldn't hear you. But O'Reilly, in the minds of his folks, is listening, expressing their anger.

A lot of people are angry, very frustrated. People don't know if they are going to have a job. The workingman is threatened by Mexico, India, China. "Wait a minute," some are saying, "Why are we helping these guys in other countries if they are shipping all my jobs out?"

The nonunion workers who think they were underpaid all their lives because union workers had all the good jobs are angry. Disgruntled union guys who have the good jobs are angry. They are angry at losing benefits. They are angry about paying taxes. They're saying, "Holy shit, they're taking fifty percent of my money and nothing ever gets fixed." Everybody is angry at oil companies and their high gas prices.

O'Reilly's anger came from two sources. If the world is not going your way, then you yell about it. For years the world didn't get his way of doing things. Therefore, he was mad about it. "I also think he never got over being the cub TV reporter who was being dirt bagged all the time," said veteran publicist Ted Faraone. "The way they treated him at CBS News and ABC struck so deep into his core was not something he could laugh off."

Secondly, there is a lot to be angry about in the world.

Since 1996, O'Reilly has been fighting on five or six segments a night on television. But his anger clock starts earlier in the day with the two hour *Radio Factor*, where he is both the power listener and power talker. He is also blazing away in his newspaper column and on his Web site, leaving a trail of enemies, wherever he goes.

O'Reilly's anger dimmed for a day or two after the Mackris flap in 2004, but the fire never went out. His rage burns like the escaping gas at oil refineries. He is perpetually upset. Every night he brings passion to the tube. The need not to "let those bastards get away with it" is an eternal flame, a nuclear pile of anger continually recharging itself.

Those are the things that won me over. I liked O'Reilly's anger. He goes after the dragon, what Fred Friendly, Ed Murrow's producer at CBS News, used to say was the true function of news. O'Reilly has the fire of a reformer, a man who got angry at social injustice, as he saw it. I liked the way he spoke up about the news that would just vanish in the information overload. I liked the way he didn't pretend to be unaffected. He wasn't afraid to get involved. He wasn't just complaining about some alleged wrong or wrongdoing over drinks at the bars where journalists gather to drown their frustrations at not being able to tell it the way it really is. In his way, he wanted to be part of the process of positive social change by telling the audience what he thought was really happening, and why they also should be angry.

Sometimes he is off the wall. I don't agree, for example, that the newspapers are out to get him in an organized way, that the Cultural Terrorists are plotting to bring him down as if he were the Twin Towers of journalism. They are only expressing their opinion, under the First Amendment, the same amendment that allows O'Reilly to be O'Reilly.

The Iraq War buildup was not his shining hour, even though he later admitted the government duped him. He can be a little sloppy in his choice of words, examples of which are dredged up continuously by his opponents. Air America nominated him for inclusion in the "Top Fifty Lies of 2005" documentary on its *Morning Sedition* show of December 19, 2005. He was accused of lying twice: that he was "in the service" and "in combat," which the documentary judges interpreted as meaning he was trying to say he was in the army in battle. Actually, he was in high school and college for the Vietnam War, but he was under fire often as a CBS News correspondent covering the guerrilla wars in El Salvador and during the Buenos Aires riots in the Falklands War. He is not perfect.

I think it's probably a better world having people like him on the TV news.

It makes O'Reilly angry to be dismissed as an entertainer. "I'm tired of getting cheap-shotted by journalism professors around the country who just cannot abide the fact that there's a news/analysis program on the air in prime time that they disagree with. And I just think that it's awful that they can't at least explain to their students that television news is evolving now."

O'Reilly spent twenty-five years learning how to get the news, synthesize it, and deliver it. He is not one of those network newspeople who need PR people to call his attention to what they consider a news story that invariably puts their client in a favorable light. He also has mastered the art of communicating on television. As Roger Ailes reveals the magic formula: "Just look at me and tell me what's going on, using the same language that you use over the dinner table. Tell them the truth, and things will work out."

.   .   .

Some people disapprove of O'Reilly's journalism, because it isn't objective.

Everybody is in favor of objectivity. The only thing is, it's impossible to achieve.

There is no such thing as objectivity. It's not real. It doesn't happen. It's never happened. Even-handedness is a delusion, a trick, a sham. The illusion of objectivity, nevertheless, gave rise to the conventions of balance or narrative neutrality that commercial TV network news hides behind.

Molly Ivins disposed of the objectivity question for all time when she observed in 1993, "The fact is that I am a forty-nine-year-old [sic] white female, college-educated Texan. All that affects the way I see the world. There is no way in hell that I'm going to see anything the same way that a fifteen-year-old black high-school dropout does. We all see the world from where we stand. Anybody who's ever interviewed five eyewitnesses to an automobile accident knows there's is no such thing as objectivity."

O'Reilly is a serious journalist who doesn't play by the rules of objectivity. He is not alone in considering news/analysis valid journalism. Actually, he is a throwback to the way it was in the old days when CBS News was the paragon, the model for all TV news.

Before Walter Cronkite became the archetypal newsman, delivering so-called pure journalism, there was Ed Murrow. An ex–foundation official from a logging community in Washington state, led into journalism by a speech teacher in a small state college, drafted by William S. Paley to give CBS Radio an identity in the late 1930s, Murrow began the tradition of reporting the news and analyzing it, giving his opinion of what it all meant.

O'Reilly as a proponent of subjectivity and activism in the news is more in the channel of Ed Murrow than Walter Cronkite and his successors. Few remember today that Murrow's legend is built on the opinionated positions he took in his news reports.

The classic example of news/analysis was delivered by Murrow in his reporting on Joseph McCarthy. His courageous crusades against the tobacco industry—Murrow was the first to report on the link between cancer and smoking, even though cigarette companies were heavy TV advertisers, and he was a heavy smoker—and his fights with agribusiness and other corporations exploiting the workers behind the "Harvest of Shame" are well-known. My friends are stunned when I tell them of the other unsung, unpopular positions Murrow regularly took on *The CBS Evening News*.

After giving the headlines with correspondents' reports from abroad and at home, he would do an end piece, a closing essay, which had the newsman weighing in on the hot issues, continually treading in dangerous waters, as far as his boss, William Paley and CBS sponsors, were concerned. Murrow was against segregation at home, apartheid abroad, J. Edgar Hoover, the atomic bomb, and stockpiling of weapons of mass destruction. He was prounion and antibusiness. He was a dissident on United States foreign policy at the end of World War II, speaking out against the Truman Doctrine, which had us supporting fascist dictatorships in Greece and elsewhere, because they were anti-communist. He was against supporting Chiang Kai-shek and his Nationalist army, which John Foster Dulles told us would retake the Mainland someday, if they didn't die of old age first. He was hard on Douglas MacArthur, the crossing of the Thirty-eighth Parallel (the Yalu), the Pentagon snafus in Korea that were getting our troops killed. He was critical of our French Indo-China policy (pre-Vietnam), how the Eisenhower administration was supporting the puppet Saigon government led by a Riviera playboy, Bao Dai. He was against Red Channels and blacklisting and the House Committee on Un-American Activities, which had us thinking there might be a Communist under every bed. He was even attacking television itself, which he warned had the capacity to "distract, amuse, and delude."

Murrow was a heretic, with heretical ideas, continually taking sides. "I don't think you can be neutral, being on both sides," he said. There weren't two equal sides of an argument, a concept the anti-Murrowians at Black Rock championed. The only fair thing, the right thing to do, the balanced thing to do, they argued, was to give time or space to both sides, no matter that sometimes there are more than two sides and sometimes fewer.

Ironically, it was Murrow and the news analysis practiced by his team of correspondents, quickly copied by the other network news departments, that led to the creation of the objectivity fiction still stunting TV journalism's growth today. Objectivity is an oxbow created when the networks needed a defense mechanism against Congress in the 1960s.

At the time, the networks were frightened by the threat of government intervention because of journalism like Murrow's. The networks were primarily interested in the freedom to expand, to increase the number of stations they could own. It also was an age of fear. There was a fear of being called names, especially "communist." It was a time when one communicator, hauled before a congressional committee, said, "I'm an anticommunist."

"I don't care what kind of a communist you are," one of our lawmakers reprimanded.

All these years since William S. Paley made Ed Murrow and CBS News shut up—by closing down his shows—commercial network news has been in deep denial. In the dark ages after Murrow, the most powerful commentary on network news was the raised eyebrow of David Brinkley after reading a piece of news on NBC. Subjectivity and activism became the no-man's-land of TV journalism. A generation of telegenic and totally uninvolved journalists evolved.

I'm not saying O'Reilly is the new Edward R. Murrow. Aside from being opinionated, Murrow was an urbane, restrained voice of reason. Nobody faulted Murrow for cutting people off or pointing his finger in a face. Murrow never lost his aplomb or his aversion to first-person-pronoun journalism. He agonized using "this engine of power," as he thought of TV as an information tool. There was only one Ed Murrow.

As unlikely as it may seem, O'Reilly may be the prototype for the new journalism based on the Murrow model. The seed O'Reilly planted ten years ago is starting to grow. In the post-Murrow period, newsmen were afraid to be human on the pseudo-objective commercial network newscasts. If they felt emotion, they wouldn't show it. Brian Williams did that after Katrina.

Instead of just standing around outside, bending like a palm tree in the Hurricane Dan Rather style of weather reporting, where they don't even dare criticize Mother Nature, Williams on *The NBC Evening News* went inside and began reporting on the human side of Katrina. He was in the Superdome giving us the tales of agony and misery that thousands of Katrina victims endured and still endured weeks after the storm. His coverage was scathing, angry, appalled at the bungled relief effort. "Don't you guys watch television?" he had chewed out FEMA officials. "Don't you listen to the radio?"

Equally astonishing was the coverage of the scandal of Katrina by Anderson Cooper of CNN, host of *Anderson Cooper 360*. Once perceived as a lightweight, vapid, Gap-style model newsman, Cooper kept Katrina on the air as a personal badge of honor with a nightly feature on *360* called "Keeping Them Honest," highlighting the latest disgrace in the recovery effort with stinging attacks on the incompetent bureaucrats. He was not only giving the news, he was reacting to it. And his career was pumped.

The year 2005 had been an amazing period in TV journalism history seeing the transformation of these two generic newsmen. They had thrown off the straitjackets of objectivity. They had stopped being the sphinx of news that scanned the horizon and saw nothing worth telling us. And now they were speaking like honest people. They were angry at what they saw and told us so.

And it was good. "When at summer's end," Reuven Frank, a former president of NBC News, wrote in *The New Leader*, "the present network anchors appeared in the hurricane soaked streets of the Gulf Coast—no press officers, no embedding—they debated, contradicted, and shamed the public officials they interviewed. They told America about dehumanization, ineptitude, and failure. For a fleeting moment, TV journalism regained the trust of its audience."

The way to deal with an O'Reilly is not to shut him down, as my friends would have it, but to get more people like O'Reilly on the air.

Well, not exactly like O'Reilly.

I want other idiosyncratic newspeople, qualified journalists. What we need is more of O'Reillyismo, reporters who know how to find the stories others are unaware of or ignoring, and the courage to speak up, risking the calumny of enemies and embraces of friends, which as I. F. Stone used to say, could be deadlier.

I want my newsmen to be serious journalists who aren't afraid to step out from behind the desk, people who are smart, able to deal intellectually with the spin doctors, news-warpers and -weavers, dream merchants, think-tank turret gunners who make the rounds of news shows, spinning, their yarns. I want newsmen who will not be taken in as journalists were during the buildup to the Iraq War, and having swallowed the fairy tales, come down with war-makers' remorse.

In short, I want people even better than O'Reilly.

We need to encourage the development of other forums like *The Factor* with other voices, other points of view. There are other folks out there who also need their views expressed and are not getting it from existing widely accessible news sources. Murrow, for example, in the golden age of opinionated news/analysis, was one voice. The folks also had Fulton Lewis Jr. and Walter Winchell.

Is the future of TV journalism in the old traditional style of so-called objective journalism with its safety shield of unattainable balance? In passing the torch to the next generation will the commercial broadcast networks be burned further, continuing to lose the audience still looking for something different? Is O'Reilly, as the champion of Subjective Journalism, a Foxic blight on landscape of news? Will O'Reillyismo be the future of TV news or will it wither away?

Like it or not, we are now in the age of the New Journalism. Bill O'Reilly is the future—and past—of TV news.

And that's the memo from this "No-Spin Zone."

ACKNOWLEDGMENTS

I want to thank Roger Ailes, without whom O'Reilly as we know him today would not have been possible. Even worse, this book wouldn't have been possible.

I want to thank Peter Block, the editor of *Penthouse,* who first asked me to write a profile of O'Reilly. I wrote so much on the subject, apparently, that Peter asked, "What are you writing, a book?" It was a good idea.

I want to thank my wife, Carol Kitman, who suffered through five years of my search for the real Bill O'Reilly. "Warning," O'Reilly begins his nightly TV show. "You are about to enter the no-spin zone." "No, I'm not," was Carol's first reaction. "The man has a problem, and I don't want to find out what it is." She went from walking out on him to acknowledging, after reading nine or fifteen versions of the manuscript, that I wasn't totally insane finding him worth study.

I want to thank Diane Reverand, my editor at St. Martin's Press, who commissioned the book and is responsible for the final version. I appreciated her reminding me that O'Reilly is as yet not in the category worthy of the four-volume *LBJ* by Robert Caro, my role model as a biographer. I was amazed and delighted by her line-by-line editing. Along the way, she taught me something about narrative in biography.

I want to thank my agent, Jonathan Dolger, who had to build a wing on his East Side apartment house to hold the accumulating sometimes six hundred-page manuscript drafts, which eventually rivaled the weight of many *National Geographic* collections.

I want to thank my former assistant, Noelle Daidone, who was a one-woman search machine assembling the many words of Bill O'Reilly on television, radio, and print. The collected O'Reilly transcripts are making my basement sink below sea level in the Meadowlands of New Jersey. She also kept me up on what I was missing at my day job at *Newsday*, covering the real world of television. The *Newsday* library staff is to be complimented for helping retrieve from the archives my old columns and other dusty materials. David Cassidy and Iris Quigley and all the researchers went the extra mile for me.

Kathy Simunovic heard more than she ever wanted to know about O'Reilly by transcribing most of the twenty-nine interviews. Edwards Grimes-Carrion, my vice president for new technology, dealt admirably with a computer-impaired writer.

I want to thank my son, Jamie Lincoln Kitman, for feeding me ideas, and my daughters, Suzy Kitman and AJ Knight, for their continuing encouragement and not asking, as others were, "When are you going to finish that damn book?"

I want to thank members of the O'Reilly family who contributed material, among them, his sister, Janet O'Reilly; his wife, Maureen; Aunt Trudy (Gertrude Collins), and Dr. Ray Ripp, a close friend of William O'Reilly Sr. and the family dentist.

I want to thank O'Reilly's friends, who told me many things about O'Reilly that he didn't mention in our interviews. Joe Rubino, Justin McDevitt, Jeff Cohen, John Blasi, Edgar Royce, Mike Dutko, Ed Fogarty, Gerry Tyne, and Michael Rose were especially helpful. Ed McCarrick, publisher of *Time* magazine, who was the second-worst student in the history of St. Brigid's, and Mike Vickery, a star on the Caddy House Favorites and now an officer with the Rockville Centre P.D., also contributed valuable insights, although their words wound up on the cutting room floor.

I want to thank the seventy-three other people who graciously gave their time to talk with me about a subject which, for some, was painful.

There were the members of the academic world who had to put up with O'Reilly in his formative years. Brother Richard Hartz told me all about O'Reilly at Chaminade High School. At Marist College, I was aided by Dr. Peter O'Keefe, O'Reilly's history teacher and mentor. Coach Ron LeVine recounted O'Reilly's years as the man who would be Joe Namath. Brother Bellinger gave me his side of the story about O'Reilly's watershed year in London and on the Continent. Shaileen Kopec of the Marist administration put his college days in perspective.

I want to thank the faculty at the Kennedy School of Government at Harvard, which saw O'Reilly twice, ten years apart. Frank Hartmann, Richard Parker, Marty Linsky, Steve Singer, Sue Williamson, Alex Jones, and Marvin Kalb were all important sources.

I want to thank all of O'Reilly's colleagues at the Fox News Channel for their help, especially Dave Tabacoff, Amy Sohnen, Dave Brown, Nate Fredman, Dangerous Dan Cohen, Rob Zimmerman, and Lis Wiehl.

His friends and enemies in journalism spoke to me candidly. Many of their words are cited in the text. Of those not cited, or insufficiently cited, I especially am grateful to Tom Snyder, Reese Schonfeld, Mike Wallace, Walter Cronkite, Brian Lamb, Larry King, Don Hewitt, Dave Laventhol, Ted Faraone, Rick MacArthur, Taya Kitman, Sandy Socolow, Gene Shalit, Martin Garbus, Eric Alterman, George Minkoff, Morley Safer, Gabe Sanders, Stephen Chao, Van Gordon Sauter, Dr. Martin Abend, Stacy Hochheiser, Mark Schubin, Bob Shanks, Howard Schuman, John Cleese, Joan Konner, Geraldo Rivera, Jeff Erdel, Nancy Glass, Larry Josephson, Stuart Sucherman, Dan Green, Tony Gentile, Betsy Rott, Art Lovell, Henry Schleiff, Merv Block, Ellen Bollinger, David Corn, Ed Joyce, Marty Haag, Rory O'Connor, Mike Kandel, Sim Kantin, Mike Kolatch, Larry Josephson, Sam Vaughn, Andy Hiller, Av Westin, Debbie Norville, Andy McGowan, Doug Johnson, John Leo, and Harry Shearer.

Peter Jennings, Neil Postman, Ned Schnurman, Al Levin, and Lou Meyers, all of whom helped me, are great losses to journalism. They will be missed.

Sidney Offit, curator of the Polk Awards, was especially helpful in sorting out the Peabody-Polk controversy, in which I learned the Polks, awarded only to journalists, are actually more prestigious than Peabodys, whose recipients over the years include Lassie.

Paul Manton of the Levittown Historical Society was my go-to man in straightening out the Levittown/Westbury confusion. Amy Patalano, librarian of the Levittown Public Library, dug out the archival Levittown pictures.

Keith Olbermann was especially magnanimous in providing a rigorous analysis of O'Reilly's achievements as a punter and pitcher, even though it was not in his self-interest. He could have done a whole segment on O'Reilly's Tom Seaver story alone, he told me before the book was published.

I was lucky to have some friends who not only had open minds but were ready to help me when I faltered. They included Christopher Lehmann-Haupt, Natalie Robins, Victor and Annie Navasky, Glenn and Sarah Collins, Richard Bernstein, Richard Lingeman, Alida and Steve Scheuer, Larry Arnstein, Abe and Helen Chutorian, Joe Muzio, Robin and John Brancato, David Freman, Howard Ginsberg, Ayal and Beth Gabay, Ed and Arlene Friedman, Alan Alda,

Nick Taylor, Dennis Ainsworth, Jim Weikart, Sid Jacobson, Evelyn Berezin, Herb and Ryna Meyers, Arthur Aranda, Jim Bouton, Dr. Frank Mellana, Burt Dorfman, Trevor Howtham, Harold Holzer, Mickey Perloff, Dr. Robin Motz, Mike and Gloria Levitas, Gene Bourg, Dr. Greg Lutz, Charlie Ferguson, Al and Wendy Fiering, Doc O'Shea, Bill and Pam Blank, Mary Schilling, Jane Masi, Tony Gentile, Dr. Joseph Tenenbaum, Michael and Maria Osheowitz, Brian Attridge, Glenn Schmid, Giles Bucher, Mitchell Kriegman, Jeffrey Orling, Michael Winship, Joe Spieler, and Dr. Erika Freeman.

I want to thank Makeda Wubneh, O'Reilly's longtime assistant, who amidst deadline crises was diligent in arranging interviews and coordinating our schedules, fact-checking, and contributing rare photographs of the early O'Reilly.

And, of course, I want to thank Bill O'Reilly for giving me the twenty-nine interviews that form the backbone of the book. I am expecting no thanks for what I have written, but if he is so inclined to show his gratitude, he might consider suing me as he did Al Franken, which could be a boon to sales.

NOTES & SOURCES

FOREWORD

"6.5 million hits instantly." As of October, 2005. *Newsday*, October 25, 2005.

PROLOGUE

1   Jennings lung cancer. *USA Today*, July 14, 2005.

2   Age fifty-seven . . . as of 2006.

4   Matthews's past career. Howard Kurtz, *Hot Air* (1996), p. 315. Some journalists thought Matthews was remaining a bit too cozy with the pols when Tip O'Neill, Bob Dole, and twenty-seven other members of Congress hosted a book party for him in the Capitol. "I think we're all friends after 6:00 P.M.," Matthews told Kurtz, "and I don't see the problem." I do.

5   "hummed Hail to the Chief." Interview, Roger Ailes.

5   Chapter also based on interviews with Bob Shanks, Howard Schuman, Victor Navasky.

5   "#1 for 226 weeks." Advertisement, *New York Post*, March 1, 2006.

5   O'Reilly's opinion why "so far ahead" in ratings. Interview, Bill O'Reilly.

6   Why O'Reilly successful in opinion of his agent's husband. Interview, Richard Leibner.

6   "Look at the stand-up reporters." Interview, Stephen Chao.

6   O'Reilly's "more simple answer." Interview, Bill O'Reilly.

6   Why O'Reilly so successful: authenticity. Interview, Roger Ailes.

PART I: THE MAKING OF AN O'REILLY
CHAPTER ONE: In the Beginning

11   Opa-Locka derivation. City of Opa-Locka official Web site.

11   Graf Zeppelin base. Alicia Momsen Miller, *From Rio to Akron, Aboard the Graf Zeppelin* (1933).

13   "Took the crap." Interview, Bill O'Reilly.

13   Original Levitt "ranch" price: Lynne Matarrese, Levittown Historical Society's History of Levittown, Levittown Historical Society Web site.

13   "His wife didn't even see the house." Interview, Jan O'Reilly.

13   "My father was an autocrat." Bill O'Reilly, *The O'Reilly Factor: The Good, the Bad, and the Completely Ridiculous in American Life* (2000), p. 111.

14   "father is always a Republican." Ibid., p. 92.

14   "smashing pumpkins." Interview, Justin McDevitt.

14   "One more time." Interview, Bill O'Reilly.

14   "O'Reilly admits he was a pain." Ibid.

15   Not *Ozzie & Harriet*. Ibid.

15   The O'Reilly family origin. Ibid.

15   "one hundred percent Irish." Ibid.

16   "A working class [*sic*] family . . . for a hundred years." Niall O'Dowd, Q&A, *Irish America* magazine (April/May 2001).

16   "Play it safe." Ibid.

16   "It was tuna." Interview, Bill O'Reilly.

16   "You'll eat the spaghetti and shut up." Ibid.

17   "respect for the dollar was extreme." Ibid. "He was a thrifty kind of guy," childhood friend Jeff Cohen said. "He never bought a new car, always looking for coupons for two-for-one deals to go out to dinner."

17   Working at Carvel. Interview, Jan O'Reilly.

17   High cost of breaking bats. Interview, Bill O'Reilly.

17   House painting. Interview, Jeff Cohen.

17   "Mr. O . . . ecstatic." Bill O'Reilly, *The O'Reilly Factor, op. cit.,* p. 70.

17   "He didn't care about money growing up." Interview, Bill O'Reilly. He didn't do too badly in the present department, in the eyes of younger sister, Jan. "We got a lot of presents. I mean, not a whole lot, but it was very simple back then. So my brother had trains, and he had lots of guns and holsters. He had an outfit for every activity, an Indian, or he was a policeman, or he was a cowboy. He had the whole garb, lots of hats, police hats, cowboy hats, Indian feathers. He had all of that." Interview, Jan O'Reilly.

18   "His guys were basically up for anything." Interviews Bill O'Reilly, Jan O'Reilly.

18   Justin McDevitt describes Saturday matinee fun. Interview, Justin McDevitt.

18   "open up the exit doors." Interview, Jeff Cohen.

19   *The Longest Day* with Mr. O. Ibid. O'Reilly's friends thought Mr. O was a funny guy. He always poked fun at his son's friends' foibles. Jeff Cohen was always hungry, and would look into the O'Reilly fridge and help himself. For a Cohen visit, Mr. O would put price tags on the leftovers: "apple pie slice . . . 25 cents."

19   Stevie Wonder at Westbury Music Fair. Interview, Justin McDevitt.

20   "those who liked him and those who didn't." Interview, John Blasi.

20   "Mostly it was shouting matches." Interview, Justin McDevitt.

21   "If you were ranked out." Interview, Bill O'Reilly.

21   Mr. Oberwager. Interview, Justin McDevitt.

21   "match should be seen by everybody." Ibid.

22   "tall one in the class of sixty." Bill O'Reilly, article, "Chronicle: Growing Up
        Together" (St. Brigid's class twenty-fifth reunion), *The Newsday Magazine*
        (August 21, 1988).

23   "not the worst student." Clement Simonetti was the worst student. Clement
        was O'Reilly's best friend at St. Brigid's. Aided and abetted by Eddie McCar-
        rick, now the publisher of *Time,* they were coconspirators in a plot to drive
        the good sisters of St. Brigid's crazy.

23   "Mrs. Boyle . . . actually liked him." Interview, Jan O'Reilly.

23   Sacrament of Penance. *The Newsday Magazine,* op. cit.

23   "Billy would always try to go to confession . . . after . . . Clement." His other
        sins included getting O'Reilly to join in the successful plot to kidnap the sec-
        ond lead in the major class play, a production of *Rip Van Winkle,* causing
        pandemonium in the auditorium.

23   "Sin was a major subject." *The Newsday Magazine,* op. cit.

24   "Billy's basic . . . sin." *The Newsday Magazine,* op. cit.

24   "when you wanted to answer." Interview, John Blasi.

24   "By the third grade, the faculty was beginning to understand Billy." *The
        Newsday Magazine,* op. cit.

25   state penitentiary. Interview, Jan O'Reilly.

25   "What O'Reilly couldn't figure out." Interview, Bill O'Reilly.

25   "waiting on the street corner." Interview, Jeff Cohen.

26   "didn't have the grades or the jack." Interview, Bill O'Reilly.

26   "*beaucoup* trouble." Ibid.

26   "hours of homework." Interview, Jan O'Reilly.

26   "no clue to what was going on." Interview, Bill O'Reilly.

27   "At Chaminade, a jacket and a tie were required." Ibid.

28   "O'Reilly adjusted to it." Ibid.

28   "Sing Sing": Bill O'Reilly syndicated column, in *New York Post,* April 8,
        2006.

29   Father didn't go to games. Interview, Bill O'Reilly.

29   "O'Reilly went home after the Babe Ruth snub." Ibid.

30   "will never forget what his mother had done." Ibid.

31   "Football coach wouldn't let me go out for team." Ibid.

31   O'Reilly was an immortal in the annals of sandlot football, as played at
        Caddy House Field. Located next to the public golf course in Salisbury Park,

renamed Eisenhower Park in a burst of "We Like Ike" patriotism in the 1960s, it is called Caddy House Field because the caddies would wait there for the summons from the adjoining golf course. O'Reilly himself put up goalposts, as he was the team's star punter and extra point kicker. Usually the Caddy House Favorites played two-hand touch football. "Bill preferred touch football," Justin McDevitt said. "He really didn't want to get his uniform dirty." They also played tackling without equipment, the Long Island version of rugby. O'Reilly still doesn't play golf.

32	"at that point I was playing hockey." Interview, Bill O'Reilly.
32	"Hockey was a big sport." Ibid.
33	"I would do anything just to not let that puck go in." Ibid.
34	"Mr. O'Reilly Sr. didn't want his son getting a swelled head." Ibid.
34	"His friend would always brag about his Nordic good looks." Interview, Joe Rubino.
34	"Okay they are going to hate me." Interview, Gerry Tyne.
34–35	"Marist had a good club football team." Interview, Ron LeVine.
35	"a ball-breaker." Interview, Gerry Tyne. It didn't help his popularity with the Chaminade jocks that O'Reilly had challenged the varsity to a game against his Caddy House Favorites and whipped them badly.
35	"They made life miserable." Interview, Gerry Tyne.
36	Why he was called Flash. Interviews, Gerry Tyne, John Blasi.
37	"Slap on a little Brut." Bill O'Reilly, *The O'Reilly Factor*," p. 99.
37	The Sharon Patterson crush. Interviews, Bill O'Reilly, Sharon Patterson.
37	O'Reilly discovers girls. *The O'Reilly Factor,* p. 99–100.
38	O'Reilly dates a cheerleader. Interview, Ed Fogarty.
38	O'Reilly and not drinking. Interviews, Bill O'Reilly, Jan O'Reilly, Ed Fogarty.
38–39	O'Reilly smokes first and last cigarette. Interview, Bill O'Reilly.
39	"a little pot in the room." Interview, Joe Rubino.
39	The Doors and Motown. Bill O'Reilly, *The No Spin Zone: Confrontations with the Powerful and Famous in America* (2001), p. 35.
40	In person . . . totally out of sync." Interview, Joe Rubino.
41	Rubino would tell him: " 'Pith,' as in 'that statement has a lot of pith. Pithy is the verb.' " O'Reilly would question every word he didn't know. "Perspicacious? You're making this shit up." Then it would show up in his vocabulary and, eventually, on *The O'Reilly Factor. Ibid.*
41–42	The exposé of Nate column is described in *The O'Reilly Factor,* p. 159.
42	"not many people . . . got O'Reilly." Interview, Joe Rubino.
43	"Because I was a hooligan." Interview, Bill O'Reilly.
43–48	Description of O'Reilly's Third Year Abroad in London based on interviews with O'Reilly and Edgar Royce.
45	Opus Dei dormitory. Interview, Brother Bellinger, director of Third Year Abroad at Marist College.

48–51   The Ed McMahon Coup of 1971. Interview, Joe Rubino.

51–53   O'Reilly and the Monarchs and Mets. Interview, Bill O'Reilly.

CHAPTER TWO: Man About Miami

54   "aspirations . . . to be a *somebody* in sports." Interviews, Ed Fogarty, John Blasi.

55   "His father encouraged him to get a middle-class job." Interview, Bill O'Reilly.

55–56   O'Reilly discovers public speaking at St. Brigid's. Ibid.

56   His favorite heroes. Proust Questionnaire, "Bill O'Reilly," *Vanity Fair*, March, 2003, Interview, Bill O'Reilly.

56–57   Why Monsignore Pace? Ibid.

57–58   Rubino spin: girls, girls. Interview, Joe Rubino.

58   How they survived: pineapples and bananas. Interview, Jan O'Reilly.

58–59   Press credentials and the Miami Dolphins. Interviews, Joe Rubino.

59   "no shortage of women." Ibid.

61   "O'Reilly was tough on the kids": Interview, Mike Dutko.

62   Four students reminisce about O'Reilly as a teacher on the twenty-fifth anniversary of graduation from Monsignore Pace High School. Letters, Alicia Gonzalez Grugget, Jennifer King Carnes, Gloria Garcia, Ana Ortiz Cooper (courtesy of Bill O'Reilly).

63   O'Reilly plays football with students. Interviews, Mike Dutko, Joe Rubino.

63   O'Reilly as a high school football coach. Interview, Mike Dutko.

63–64   On the town with O'Reilly as a drinking buddy. Ibid.

64   Football anyone? The "Kennedy thing." Ibid.

65   How O'Reilly got air-conditioning in Florida. Interview, Joe Rubino.

65   Fighting the school administration. *The O'Reilly Factor*, p. 71.

65   Talking about sex with students. Interview, Bill O'Reilly.

66   How to dress for a football game. Ibid.

CHAPTER THREE: The Wayward Pressman

67   Taking stock. Interview, Bill O'Reilly.

68–69   Driving a cab in Miami. Interview, Joe Rubino.

68–71   O'Reilly gets a column at Boston University in *The Daily Free Press*. Interview, Bruce Feirstein. Column, *New York Observer* (2003). Interview, Bill O'Reilly, Bruce Feirstein.

71   Howard Zinn doesn't remember O'Reilly. Interview conducted by Noelle Daidone.

71   The other tall guy at BU is Howard Stern. Interview, Bill O'Reilly.

72   Why O'Reilly couldn't have gotten a job at a local New York news show is

based on analysis of the New York media in a series of "Marvin Kitman Show" columns, *Newsday* (1979–84).

73   "Jim Jensen . . . had difficulty with the new journalism. Producers allegedly were supplying his questions for interviews, like 'How old are you?' It was said Ted Baxter on *The Mary Tyler Moore Show* was based on Jensen, although others said Ted was actually the sitcom version of LA local news anchor, Jerry Dunphy. "Marvin Kitman Show," *Newsday*.

74   Ft. Myers or Scranton/Wilkes-Barre? Interviews, Joe Rubino, Bill O'Reilly.

CHAPTER FOUR: The Voice of Anthracite Country

76   "I got this call." Interview, Tom Shelburne.

76   "Fifty-third as a Designated Market Area," ranked by the number of television households. Scranton-Wilkes-Barre had 552,060 TV households, as of September 2002. (*Broadcasting & Cable Yearbook*, 2003–4, p. B-223). That's a lot better than number seventy, Fort Myers-Naples, with 401,330 TV households. It was in the major leagues compared to number 209, North Platte (15,670 households) and number 210, Glendive (4,960). Interview, Mark Schubin.

77   "They hired him at WNEP because he worked cheap." *The O'Reilly Factor*, p. 71.

77   "Brash, cocky." Interview, Eldon Hale.

77   First job analysis. Interviews, Tom Shelburne, Eldon Hale.

78   "very fast writer." As the sports columnist Red Smith once said, "Writing is easy. All you have to do is sit down and open a vein."

78   O'Reilly the "action reporter." Interviews, Eldon Hale, Tom Shelburne, Bill O'Reilly.

79   "The Dog Lady Case." Interviews, Eldon Hale, John Owens, Bill O'Reilly.

80   Covering spring training in Florida. Interview, John Owens.

80   "GUNS FOR SALE." Interviews, John Owens, Eldon Hale, Tom Shelburne, Bill O'Reilly.

81   Grilling politicians and "hard-nosed, creative reporting." Interviews, Eldon Hale, Tom Shelburne.

82   "To make ends meet." O'Reilly's life in Scranton. Interview, John Owens.

82   "not the most popular guy in Scranton." Interview, Eldon Hale.

83–84   *Uncle Ted's Ghoul School.* Interviews, Bill O'Reilly, Tom Shelburne. "Who cares?" O'Reilly said when people tended to deprecate his concern that Uncle Ted was not delivering his one-liners with the proper respect. "Well, let me tell you, you can get caught up in those shows. Who was watching moronic monster movies in Scranton late on a Saturday night? Voters for the Emmy awards."

CHAPTER FIVE: ON THE ROAD

85   "Howard Cosell of Dallas." Interview, Bill O'Reilly.

85   "fearless crusader routine" not working. Article, "Mad Dog: Shut Up," *Rolling Stone.* August 11, 2004.

85   "doing movie reviews." Interview, Bill O'Reilly.

86   O'Reilly clashes with Marty Haag over anchorperson hire. Interview, Bill O'Reilly. I later asked Marty Haag about the incident. He said, "I don't remember that at all." No surprise to author.

86–87   Jim Simon hires him for radio. Interview, Bill O'Reilly.

87   Wins Dallas Press Club Award. Ibid.

88   O'Reilly happy in Denver with mandate to do stories in his way. Wins award for reporting. But then the Prince of Darkness takes over. Interviews, Bill O'Reilly.

88   O'Reilly influences the newsroom, where they love him or hate him. *Rolling Stone, op. cit.* Interviews, Bill O'Reilly.

89   "social life escalated." Interviews, Jeff Cohen, Bill O'Reilly. Refined, cultured girls weren't his type, but working classes seemed to like him. According to O'Reilly, "He had a car, a sense of humor, and plenty of packs of gum." *The O'Reilly Factor,* op cit., p. 101.

89   "undisputed leader of the band of brothers." Adventure trips. Interviews, Jeff Cohen, Mike Dutko, Bill O'Reilly, *Rolling Stone,* op. cit., *Cigar* magazine.

90   Clint Eastwood comes to Denver. "The cameraman," O'Reilly told author, "looked closely to see whether Dirty Clint was armed."

91   O'Reilly lands in Hartford. Leaves quickly. "Conflict of chemistry." *Rolling Stone,* op. cit.

92   What really happened. O'Reilly spin. Interview, Bill O'Reilly.

CHAPTER SIX: New York, New York

93   Return to New York. Schiffman gives him TV magazine host job at WCBS. Interview, Jeff Schiffman.

95   Ed Joyce cancels *7:30 Magazine* but hires him for Channel 2 News. Interviews, Jeff Schiffman, Bill O'Reilly.

95–96   State of local TV news and musical anchor chairs at Channel 2 News. Columns, "Marvin Kitman Show," *Newsday* (1978–1983).

97   "Joyce had a unique management style." "Marvin Kitman Show," op. cit. Interviews, Ned Schnurman, Jeff Erdel, Ted Faraone, Ed Joyce, Bob Chandler, Ed Fouhy, Bill Kurtis, quoted in Peter J. Boyer, *Who Killed CBS? The Undoing of America's Number One News Network* (1989).

98   Marty Haag comes to WCBS/2 News. Interview, Ned Schnurman, Jeff Erdel, Bill O'Reilly. After his stint at Channel 2, Haag returned to Dallas,

where his station's news won many awards. I found him still at WFAA in 2003. I asked him what he thought of O'Reilly. Haag was surprisingly vague about O'Reilly. "Marty tries to be vague about everything he can't control," said ex-employee Ned Schnurman.

99   "Governor Carey Incident." Interview, Bill O'Reilly.

100   Morley Safer breaks in the line. Ibid. Later I asked Morley Safer about that memorable, if brief, confrontation with O'Reilly, the clashing of titans in the CBS cafeteria that O'Reilly always makes a big thing of in his autobiographies. A decade had gone by, so I gave him a short summary of the details to refresh his memory. By telephone from his studio in the Connecticut woods, Morley Safer said, "I have no memory of it. This is news to me. I've never met Bill O'Reilly. I didn't even know he worked at CBS." Another example of O'Reilly's egocentric total recall of grievances. He is the center of the universe. But perhaps Safer regularly broke in the line. So why should he remember it?

100–1   CBS News hires O'Reilly as a foreign correspondent. He had worked at four jobs in five years. Had he learned anything? *The O'Reilly Factor,* op. cit., p. 75.

CHAPTER SEVEN: Cry for Me, Argentina

102   Schieffer in Falklands War based on his autobiography, Schieffer, Bob, *This Just In: What I Couldn't Tell You on TV,* G. P. Putnam's Sons (2003), pp. 280–1, 285.

103–5   What O'Reilly did during the war is described in his books, including *The No Spin Zone,* pp. 134–5, *Those Who Trespass,* pp. 21–2, and in interviews. The big footed by Schieffer experience is also reported by Nicholas Lemann, *The New Yorker,* March 27, 2006.

105   O'Reilly's first novel was loosely called "a mystery." Totally ignored, dismissed by critics in 1998 as a potboiler, it is actually a prequel to his later autobiographies. In its way, it tells more about O'Reilly, who plays anchorman Shannon Michaels, than his tell-all nonfiction. As a novelist, he disguised the real-life identity of his characters by combining characteristics of several individuals who had done him wrong. In the case of Ron Costello, the network star correspondent covering the war in Buenos Aires, he used every artifice except giving Bob Schieffer's social security number. For inspiration, O'Reilly the novelist apologizes, he had to choose "just a few examples out of hundreds in order to keep the story on track. Not that anyone in my novel really resembles anyone in real life." *The O'Reilly Factor,* p. 43.

CHAPTER EIGHT: The Boston Massacres

106   Nick Lawler hires O'Reilly for his entry-level job in Boston. Interview, Nick Lawler.

107   "All of a sudden . . . most interesting": Article, "The Meanest Man on Television," Neil Swidney, *Boston Globe Magazine,* December 1, 2002.

107   Adventures of the Big Z as O'Reilly's favorite sportscaster. Interview, Zip Rzeppa.

108   O'Reilly's eye for women. Interviews, Zip Rzeppa, Susan Burke Hollo.

109   "I was a dancing machine." *The O'Reilly Factor,* pp. 101–2.

110–12 Applegate. Interviews, Bill Applegate, Bill O'Reilly.

112   "worst of all villains to die." *Those Who Trespass* is a work of fiction, of course. And any relationship to persons living or dead is purely coincidental, of course. But the coincidences in O'Reilly's fiction are startling, even hair-raising, for anybody who might be giving Bill O'Reilly agita these days. How these accidental coincidences occur in the creative process is always a thing of wonderment. In this case, Zip Rzeppa offers a clue: "When he was writing the book, O'Reilly would gloat to me. He says, 'Well, I killed off Rosser today, Big Z.' He says, 'You'll recognize the character. It was easy: All I had to do was take out my diary and copy it all down.'" Interview, Zip Rzeppa.

112–14 Rossergate. Interviews, Jeff Rosser, Bill O'Reilly. A typical difference of opinion in the war between O'Reilly and his boss, Rosser, was the case of the missing typewriter. Apparently, O'Reilly took his typewriter with him when Rosser moved O'Reilly out of the news department, and Rosser was furious, demanding its return, which made O'Reilly furious.

     "If it happened the way he describes it," Rosser told me, "it's an example of questioning something he (Rosser) had done. You move to a different floor of the building, you move to a different department, and you took one of the news department typewriters that needs to be given to whoever is replacing you in the news department. So where's the typewriter?" Interview, Jeff Rosser.

CHAPTER NINE: O'Reilly Finds His Voice

116   O'Reilly landing in tiny TV market of Portland, Oregon. *Boston Globe Magazine,* op. cit.

116–17 Senator Mark Hatfield series. Interview, Bill O'Reilly.

117   Mr. O'Reilly Sr. cautions son about changing jobs. Interview, Jan O'Reilly.

118   Father's health problems. Ibid.

118   Last days at bedside. Interview, Bill O'Reilly, Jan O'Reilly.

118   Father makes O'Reilly cry. Immunizing him against fear. Interviews, Joe Rubino, Bill O'Reilly.

119   "Boston called again." Interviews, Phil Balboni, Emily Rooney, Bill O'Reilly.

119–20 Rooney got a kick out of O'Reilly. When she sent him a memo outlining a new vacation policy, O'Reilly shot back a note of his own: "Very nicely written memo." Rooney said, "It was like he was grading me." Interview, Emily Rooney.

121 The promotion to commentator was an excuse, covering the pushing of the anchor into the water without a splash. Having the opportunity to speak his mind, the pushee would usually declare, as he threw himself from power at one of the three most important jobs in the nation, this is what he always wanted to do. Or so it was said. Paraphrased from "Marvin Kitman Show," *Newsday*.

122 O'Reilly goes to Harvard. *The O'Reilly Factor*, op.cit. Interview, Bill O'Reilly.

CHAPTER TEN: Spencer

123–24 "Butch and the Kid." *The O'Reilly Factor*, op. cit., p. 178. Spencer death. From news reports and O'Reilly interview. Spencer apparently had a blotter on his desk, O'Reilly told me, where he noted times he appeared on ABC newscasts:

- 7:32 Tornado story, *GMA* . . .
- 10:32 Flood story. *Nightline* . . .

The last story made the air. *World News Tonight* led the broadcast that evening with Spencer's meatpackers on strike story. It was the last signing off: "Joe Spencer, ABC News."

124 Spencer Eulogy. Interview, Bill O'Reilly.

124 "Who is that man?" Ibid.

124 Roone Arledge contributions to TV journalism from "Marvin Kitman Show," *Newsday*. circa 1970–80s.

124 By the second wave of talent poaching, Arledge wrote in his memoir, "At CBS a sign was posted in their Washington bureau: 'will the last person leaving for ABC, please turn out the lights,'" Arledge, Roone, *Roone: A Memoir* (2003), p. 249. Things were equally in flux at ABC News when they hired O'Reilly. "If it hadn't been for ABC dropouts," Arledge wrote, "how would Ted Turner ever have staffed his new CNN?" *op. cit.*, p. 248.

124 Arledge work style and office politics. Interview, Richard Wald.

126 O'Reilly on weasels and weaselettes. Interviews, Bill O'Reilly, Richard Wald, Richard Leibner. Article, "It's About People You Can Trust," excerpt from *Who's Looking Out for You?* in *Parade Magazine*, September 21, 2002.

127 "Peter Jennings liked me and my work." Interview, Bill O'Reilly.

127 "grooming him." Interview, Michael Rose.

127 Jennings appreciation, O'Reilly wrote, "was equalled by the loathing of the senior *Nightline* producer (unnamed) who banned me from ever appearing on that fine program. What had I done to this man?" I called the unnamed producer to deny or confirm the story in whole or part. Rick Kaplan, whom I have known for years, declined to comment, through his representatives. Not

once, but fourteen times over a twenty-three-month period. Attempts were made by myself and my assistant Noelle Daidone.

127–28   O'Reilly's work as general assignment reporter at ABC News and writing news briefs. Interview, Dave Tabacoff.

129–31   "Breaking story in Bridgeport." Humiliation for the network correspondent. Interview, Bill O'Reilly. *The O'Reilly Factor,* op.cit., pp. 44–6.

131   "straight talk." Interview, Bill O'Reilly.

CHAPTER ELEVEN: Taking Out the Trash

133–34   Development of Tabloid TV, traced in "Marvin Kitman Show," *Newsday,* January 6, 1989. "Tabloid TV" and its synonym "Trash TV," as often seen on the cover of *Newsweek* was a nice pejorative, though not as good as "Poison TV" ("Watch it—and you will die") was the theme of print news magazine coverage. Interviews, Jeff Erdel, Ted Faraone.

134   *A Current Affair* history. Burt Kearns, *Tabloid Baby* (1999). "Marvin Kitman Show," *Newsday* multiple columns. Interviews, Bert Kearns, Ted Faraone, Jeff Erdel. Reenactments were a staple on *A Current Affair.* They didn't merely report the Jessica Savitch story, for example, they reenacted the NBC News correspondent's drowning death, holding some production assistant underwater, videotaping her struggle for breath. There was no story too sleazy for *A Current Affair.* "It was journalism run amuck," explained Burt Kearns, an early *A Current Affair* producer. "They were turning their backs on the networks and their pretentious notions of TV news, dropping their pants, giving them the mooning they deserved." Burt Kearns, *Tabloid Baby,* xviii.

134   "Hard Sloppy." Unique journalistic style of *Hard Copy.* "Marvin Kitman Show," *Newsday,* December 13, 1993. Interviews, Jeff Erdel, Ted Faraone.

134–35   *Inside Edition* invented, 1988. "Marvin Kitman Show," *Newsday.* Interviews, Burt Kearns, Ted Faraone, Jeff Erdel. A tabloid without being a tabloid. Interview, John Tomlin.

135   David Frost debut. Interviews, Burt Kearns, John Tomlin, Ted Faraone, Jeff Erdel.

136   "After three weeks, Sir David was sacked." Sir David's game plan had been marvelous. He planned to fly back and forth every week to do his TV chores in America for the King Brothers without interfering with his social obligations in the UK as a permanent member of the British TV aristocracy. He would fly home on the Concorde Thursday, returning on the Concorde Monday morning. His brief run on *Inside Edition* turned out to be not so marvelous. The decline and demise of the Concorde, one theory goes, can be traced directly to loss of income in the wake of Sir David's premature dismissal at *Inside Edition.*

136   "The nuts in question." The King Brothers are famous for being loquacious. They love to talk. But apparently not on the subject of who deserved the credit for picking Sir David. They declined to comment for this book, according to their representative. Attempts by Noelle Daidone.

137–38 How O'Reilly planned to save *Inside Edition*. Interview, Bill O'Reilly.

138   O'Reilly perceived as "a doofus." Interview, Burt Kearns.

138   Av Westin's " 'Clean Air Act' for *Inside Edition*." Interviews, Av Westin, Burt Kearns, Ted Faraone, Jeff Erdel, Ned Schnurman.

138   "guerrilla television" on *Inside Edition*. Interviews, Bill O'Reilly, Michael Rose, Charlie Lackman, John Tomlin, Phil Tangle.

139–40 Expense account trips. Interviews, Michael Rose, Bill O'Reilly, John Tomlin.

141   "O'Reilly didn't look like the classic foreign correspondent." Interview, Michael Rose. "Where's your clothes?" Rose would ask him. "Where's your bag?" Rose was laden down with what he said was like one hundred pounds of gear at the start of a trip, just clothing. "Rose, you got to pace yourself," O'Reilly would say. "Wait until you're my age."

        "It was funny," Rose recalled, "to see a guy as tall and as thin wearing creased blue jeans. Like they had an ironed pleat in them, like sometimes you'd see it on a woman."

141–42 Life in Grandmother's house in Teaneck, New Jersey. Interviews, Jan O'Reilly, Bill O'Reilly, Phil Tangle. "You couldn't even look out the window," said Jan O'Reilly about her visit to her brother at their grandmother's house. "It was all foggy."

142   "the famous Av Westin–Bill O'Reilly Debate about [the] Barbara Walters [book]." Interviews, Michael Rose, Bill O'Reilly, Av Westin. In June 2003, I asked Westin about that O'Reilly interview with his friend, Barbara Walters, and the aftermath. Westin said he didn't recall it. But he did tell me what he considered wrong with television news—basically that he was no longer employed in a top management position.

144   "He was universally hated." Interviews, Charlie Lackman, Michael Rose, Ted Faraone.

145   O'Reilly flips out at "end-of-season party." Mike Walker, "Behind the Screens" column, *National Enquirer,* July 20, 1993.

CHAPTER TWELVE: Final Edition

147–48 O'Reilly quits *Inside Edition*. Interviews, John Tomlin, Michael Rose, Carole Cooper, Richard Leibner, Bill O'Reilly.

148   Bob Young refused to talk to me about his experiences with O'Reilly. Apparently, I had made fun in my column of one of his crappy shows after he left *Inside Edition*. I don't even remember doing it, and he wouldn't even tell me

the name of the show I desecrated ten years earlier. "My God," another associate of his at King World said in amazement. "This is a guy who calls in everything to 'Page Six.' He's got balls not to talk to you."

CHAPTER THIRTEEN: Tall Man on Campus

150–52   Kennedy School of Government at Harvard described for me in interviews with Victor S. Navasky, Alex Jones, Marvin Kalb, Steven Singer, Bill O'Reilly.
152–54   "smartest man he knew." Interview, Father Frank Hartmann.
154–55   O'Reilly's graduate thesis on solving the drug problem. Paraphrased for me by O'Reilly.
156–57   O'Reilly meets Maureen. Interviews, Bill O'Reilly, Jan O'Reilly, Maureen O'Reilly, Emily Rooney, Susan Burke Hollo, Andy McGowan, Ted Faraone.
157–58   The wedding. Interviews, Bill O'Reilly, Jeff Cohen, Jan O'Reilly.

PART II: The Factor Factor
CHAPTER FOURTEEN: Roger Discovers Gold

163–64   What Ailes saw in "the unemployed newsman." Interviews, Roger Ailes, Bill O'Reilly.
164   The Keith Hernandez bombshell interview on *Straight Forward,* America's Talking. Interviews, Dave Brown, Roger Ailes, Bill O'Reilly.
165–66   The negotiations: Fox vs. Chris-Craft. Interviews, Bill O'Reilly, Roger Ailes.
166–67   "Ailes . . . and O'Reilly had much in common." Antipathy to research. Interviews, Roger Ailes, Bill O'Reilly.

CHAPTER FIFTEEN: A Star Is Reborn

168–69   "He failed when he first started." Interviews, Roger Ailes, Bill O'Reilly, Dave Brown. Bob Cullinan in *Rolling Stone,* op. cit.
169–72   Early days. Interviews, Bill O'Reilly, Amy Sohnen, Dave Brown, Roger Ailes.
171–72   First guest. The killing of drug czar, General McCaffrey. Interview, Bill O'Reilly.

CHAPTER SIXTEEN: Cracking the O'Reilly Code

174–75   Taking on Larry King. "Suspendermeister" in *New York Observer.* March 22, 2004. Interviews, Roger Ailes, Bill O'Reilly.
175   Passing King in ratings. *Daily Variety,* numerous citations, 2001–2006.
175–77   O'Reilly goes to war against King. "Pitch meeting[s]." Dave Brown, Amy Sohnen, Nate Fredman, Rob Monaco, Bill O'Reilly, Dave Tabacoff.

177–79 Talent booking problems. "Roger Ailes understands why." Interviews, Roger Ailes, Dave Brown, Nate Fredman, Amy Sohnen, Bill O'Reilly, Barney Frank.

180–81 O'Reilly tracking "the numbers." Personal observation in his office, multiple visits. *Daily Variety* stories.

181   Why O'Reilly beats King. Interview, Bill O'Reilly.

181–82 *The Radio Factor* launched, 2002. Statistics from Westwood One syndicator.

182   "O'Reilly is different on radio." Interviews, Dave Tabacoff, Joe Muzio, Herb Meyers, Dennis Ainsworth. "[He] would make a great trial lawyer." Lis Wiehl, describing his prosecutorial style of argument.

182   "He can be a funny guy." On March 11, 2004, Matt Lauer on the *Today* show sought to draw O'Reilly out on one of the world's weighty problems: "Yesterday, the Senate took up the issue of steroids in baseball," began Lauer, who clearly did not approve of their use. "You're on steroids, I heard," O'Reilly interrupted, "aren't you, Matt?"
ML: "You can tell?"
OR: "So you get tested?"
ML: "Yeah, all the time."
OR: "I'll give you a cup right after the show."
ML: "We've got huge deficits. We've got home security. We've got Iraq. Should Congress be taking up steroids in baseball?"
OR: "I think the country is ambidextrous. I think we can do a lot of things at the same time. Should we take up fight fixing? Any kind of cheating in a national sport—of course! You let these people run wild. It's the same message. We have to have people understand that we have rules that have to be followed in society. When discipline breaks down, society breaks down."
That was the essence of his message on the TV and radio shows, the quintessential statement of where O'Reilly is coming from. It seemed to go a mile high over Lauer's well-combed head.
ML: "Do you want Congress to jump in if baseball doesn't get tough?"
OR: "I want John McCain to go over there and slap Barry Bonds's head."
ML: "But if baseball des not crack down enough on its own, should Congress get involved?"
OR: "Yeah, they should force everyone (on steroids) to play for the Mets."

182   "intern listening to Rush Limbaugh." Interview, Bill O'Reilly.

183   "more than 20 million." Transcript. *60 Minutes,* September 26, 2004.

183   "unburdens himself." William McGurn, *Wall Street Journal,* September 15, 2000.

184   O'Reilly as a public speaker. Interview, Don Walker.

184   Merchandise offers from O'Reilly Web site: billoreilly.com

185   "how much money he makes." *Rolling Stone, op.cit.* Interview, Bill O'Reilly.

186 Robert Reich height: Wikipedia.

186–87 Harmon Cove town house. Interview, Bill O'Reilly.

187 "That terrible thing": The overweight comedy star was accused of the rape (with a Coke bottle) and murder of model Virginia Rappe at a wild San Fransico party in 1921 (Simon Louvish, "Man on the Trapeze," p. 323).

189 Groucho Marx swimming pool. Interview, Dave Tabacoff.

189–91 Difference in attitude toward children: boys vs. girls. Interview, Joe Rubino.

193 Description of "editorial packets." Interview, Amy Sohnen.

194–96 Life at home. Interviews, Bill O'Reilly, Maureen O'Reilly, Jan O'Reilly.

196 O'Reilly is an enthusiastic and generous collector. He learned Bruce Feirstein's father was a fan of Harry Truman, and he gifted him a genuine Truman letter. Interview, Bruce Feirstein.

196–97 Kidney stone operation. Interviews, Jan O'Reilly, Bill O'Reilly.

197 Mail count. O'Reilly estimate.

198 War booty in father's navy trunk. Interview, Bill O'Reilly.

198 "I think they're cute," O'Reilly said of the *Mad TV* and *Saturday Night Live* parodies seen frequently by 2004. "Basically, it's here's this O'Reilly guy. 'Here's how he behaves. He's got a huge ego, ha-ha.' I just think it's funny, and I take it as a compliment. I think the guy who does Matthews is much better because he's got Matthews's voice down. These guys don't have my voice down. They're just trying go for broad mannerisms. I'm kind of flattered they even pay attention." In the tight parody race, O'Reilly was ahead of Matthews on *Mad TV*, but behind Matthews and Rush Limbaugh on *Saturday Night Live* (race results as of April 2004). He is equally happy with his contribution to Comedy Central's *The Colbert Report*, without which it wouldn't be possible.

198–99 His reputation for brevity is well-founded. "He always seems to be in a hurry to get them off," said Dr. Abe Chutorian, a dedicated viewer. "The essence of being rude to someone is being in a hurry to get a conversation over. It's hard to imagine him in a soft-spoken voice. The obnoxious, self-righteous, so-full-of-himself O'Reilly seems ingrained in him. If he tried to change, he would look like a fraud. He is who he is."

200–1 Spin Zone analysis based on talks with Tom Snyder, Neil Postman, Victor Navasky, Dennis Ainsworth, Rick MacArthur, Ted Faraone, Dave Tabacoff.

201–3 The No Spin Zone can be seen as a license for running a public torture chamber. Debating techniques discussion based on interviews, Barney Frank, Victor Navasky, David Corn, Michael Kinsley, Dave Tabacoff, Bill O'Reilly.

203 Number of debates. From Bill O'Reilly.

203–4 Bush debate details. Interview, Bill O'Reilly.

204 Goal in interview/debate: unpredictability. Interviews, Bill O'Reilly, Roger Ailes, Dave Tabacoff.

PART III: THE MELTDOWN
CHAPTER SEVENTEEN: Are They Out to Get Him?

208   "Call me Fidel O'Reilly." *The O'Reilly Factor* TV show, September 6, 2005. "roll back prices." Bill O'Reilly column, in *New York Post*, April 28, 2006.

208–9   Shows that failed opposite *The O'Reilly Factor* since 1996: Rob Zimmerman, FNC.

210   "checks and balances deal." Bill O'Reilly column, April 15, 2004.

211   "Dyspeptic discourse." Article, Bruce Kluger, "Skewered by Dean of Mean, Bill O'Reilly," *Los Angeles Times,* February 21, 2003.

211   "inviting target." Interview, Rob Zimmerman.

211   Who bothers attacking Keith Olbermann? Olbermann demurs. "Having spent the last few weeks fending off fake-anthrax letters and daily calls from the *New York Post* gossip page," Olbermann explained in October 2006, "I can assure you, plenty of people attack me."

212   "not playing by the clubhouse rules." Bill O'Reilly, *Who's Looking Out for You?* (2003), p. 80.

212   "fifty-three columns criticizing President Bush." O'Reilly column in *New York Post*, October 21, 2005.

213   "differences with the . . . *Times* as a . . . major news event." Talking Points Memo, *The O'Reilly Factor.* TV show, September 9, 2003.

214   Frank Rich dispute. Article, Nathaniel Popper, "It's a Rich Battle as O'Reilly, *Times* Critic Square Off in Culture War," *Forward*, March 12, 2004. Interviews, Frank Rich, Bill O'Reilly, Victor Navasky.

215–16 "public brawling over the Gibson movie." Interviews, Bill O'Reilly, Frank Rich, Dave Tabacoff.

216   Transcript, Media Matters for America, August 3–4, 2006.

216   Kristoff fights. O'Reilly should go to Darfur. Nicholas Kristoff, *New York Times*, December 11, 2005.

217   The big and powerful, in O'Reilly's view, have no defense against media snipers. It is his passionate defense of the right to be rich, famous, and powerful. On the other hand, O'Reilly attacks Martha Stewart as often as he can. She is big, my wife pointed out, but he doesn't defend her.

CHAPTER EIGHTEEN: O'Reilly Goes to War

218   "nitwit, poseur, or worse." *The No Spin Zone: Confrontations with the Powerful and Famous in America* (2001), p. 176.

218   A deluge of muckraking books on O'Reilly and his Fox News Channel began with Al Franken's *Lies and the Lying Liars Who Tell Them: A Fair and Balanced Look at the Right*, a collection of what he considered O'Reilly's most

embarrassing lies. Then there was Joe Conason's *Big Lies*, David Corn's *The Lies of George W. Bush: Mastering the Politics of Deception*, Eric Alterman's *What Liberal Media? The Truth About Bias and the News*, and Peter Hart's *The Oh Really? Factor: Unspinning Fox News Channel's Bill O'Reilly*.

219   Transcripts for one average night of the six segments on *The Factor* contain 5,750 words (estimate, Kitman). One week of *The Factor* transcripts, as bulky as the *Sunday Times*, weighs 12.4 pounds on average (weighed by Kitman). Add to this all the things he had to say on *The Radio Factor* since 2002. The show runs two unscripted hours a day, largely extemporaneous. During this period he also wrote a weekly contentious newspaper column, and magazine articles. He gave speeches. One hundred twenty-four profiles have been written about him (as of October 2004) in which he had opined profusely for inquiring journalists. He never shuts up.

219   "It's part of his persona." Interview, Peter Hart.

219   Private schools and Harvard. Interview, Bill O'Reilly.

219   "father broke his back." Bill O'Reilly column in *New York Post*, April 7, 2006.

219   Father worked for oil company. Not only that, he even had a pension.

220   "tweener." Interview, Peter Jennings.

220–21   To be fair and balanced, I listened to what newsman/documentary filmmaker Rory O'Connor had to say about the debate on O'Reilly's place in society: "He went to the same high school as me. He was a year ahead at Chaminade. It's not PS 9 in the tough-knocks land of Levittown. There were few attending Chaminade like me. I really felt like an odd duck because I was going to people's homes whose garage was bigger than my house in Queens. If you listen to O'Reilly, you would think he went to a high school in Harlem. O'Reilly is not the only person in the media with the phony Irish Catholic working-class man of the people rep. Chris Matthews does exactly the same thing. Having grown up really working-class Irish Catholic in Queens, I resent these people pretending to be that way and becoming multimillionaires being the authentic voices of the Irish Catholic working class, and it's just not true." Interview, Rory O'Connor.

221   "Was it Westbury or Levittown?" Franken, op. cit., pp. 73–74.

221   "depends on which part of Westbury." Interview, Stanley Cembalist.

221   Levittown divided into four extra postal districts. Interview, Paul Manton, Levittown Historical Society.

221   There goes the neighborhood, the good citizens of Westbury might have said if they had only known Bill O'Reilly was among the flotsam and jetsam that floated into Westbury after the annexation of their Levitt homes. "I gave a speech at Division High in Levittown," O'Reilly was telling me one day after his enemies resuscitated the He's Not From Levittown Theory. "They know who I

am and where I lived, that I am one of them. I'm a Levittown guy. I still go to the Levittown pool. Because my mother still lives there. And to seize upon that to try to make me out to be a charlatan is so dishonest. They're just trying to erode my credibility. All the neighbors get a big kick out of the dispute."

222   O'Reilly home original deed, ——— Page Lane, Levittown, New York, from bank holding mortgage, courtesy of Bill O'Reilly.

222–26 Franken-O'Reilly debate. Interviews, Victor S. Navasky, Evelyn Berezin, Dennis Ainsworth, Herb Meyers, Abe Chutorian, Bill O'Reilly, Roger Ailes, Brian Lamb.

222–26 BookExpo coverage. Bob Minzesheimer, "Insults Thrown Left and Right. O-Reilly-Franken Shouting Match Livens BookExpo." *USA Today*, June 2, 2003.

223   "teed off to the max." *USA Today*, June 2, 2003.

225   *USA Today* found satisfaction in one aspect of the debate. "Unlike the legendary Hemingway encounter with poet Wallace Stevens, no punches were thrown. Both men walked away from the podium without a handshake." *USA Today,* June 2, 2003.

225–26 "Who had won the debate." No doubt in Frank Rich's mind. Frank Rich column, *New York Times,* July 20, 2003.

226   Shut up, he explained. "O'Reilly says 'shut up,'" Shafer wrote, "the way other people say 'um.' . . . Sometimes he says 'shut up' with fury, eyes bulging. When he's being dismissive, he delivers it offhandedly and without real malice. Other times he says it gently with a minxlike twinkle in his eye, signaling to all the world that he is just being frisky." Combing over his list of "shut ups," Shafer found O'Reilly guilty of wanting "specific individuals to shut up." . . . ("He has dodged this program, Alec Baldwin has, for years. Bottom line: If you're going to sling it, Alec, then stand up to some fire. If not, shut up and don't be ridiculous.") . . . He would like all gays and lesbians to zip it—even though he's invited them on his show to talk about . . . homosexuality. . . . ("You can do whatever you want. Just shut up about it. Little kids don't need to know whether you're homosexual, heterosexual, a cross-dresser, whatever." . . . on *The Factor,* September 28, 2000). He's even heaved this impolite language at entire nations, demanding they recuse themselves from the international conversation ("Canada shouldn't have any say about the Guantanamo prisoners at all. I mean, just shut up about it." . . . on *The O'Reilly Factor*, April 16, 2003.

        In the half-decade his top-rated show has been on the air, he's called for the muzzling of practically everybody," wrote Shafer. "At the rate O'Reilly is going, he'll be the only person allowed to speak in a couple of years. Which I suppose is his master plan." *Slate,* August 28, 2003.

226   "Bill's ego gets away." Interview, Rob Zimmerman.

227   Republican. New York *Daily News*, December 6, 2000. Interview, Bill O'Reilly.

228   Hannity was using part of each broadcast in the summer of 2004 to count off the days until the reelection of George Bush. *New York Times*, July 20, 2004.

228–30 O'Reilly positions on issues compiled from interviews, his books, newspaper columns, magazine articles, television shows. Interviews, Bill O'Reilly, Victor Navasky, Rick MacArthur, Roger Ailes, John Blasi, Jeff Cohen, Edgar Royce.

230   Not being able to pigeonhole the loudmouth mad dog O'Reilly ideologically spooks a lot of people. He is not a doctrinaire knee-jerk conservative like Sean the Reliable. He is as likely to defend individual humanists against institutions, as to attack the so-called left-wing elite. He is not one of those people of whom it can be said: "I feel this way because everybody else does." He seems to take each issue, especially tough morality questions, and examine it through his own sometimes foggy glasses. He seems also to understand that no matter how loudly you shout, predictability is ultimately boring. And, as one of his non-fans, *Boston Globe Magazine* observed, "O'Reilly is never boring." *Boston Globe Magazine,* op. cit. Interviews, Howard Schuman, Justin McDevitt.

CHAPTER NINETEEN: Suits Pressed While You Wait

232   "O'Reilly decided to squash the worm." Interview, Bill O'Reilly.

232–33 Letter to Diane Brandi. Interview, Floyd Abrams.

233   Suits involving parody and copyright infringements. Interviews, Victor Navasky, Floyd Abrams. "Don't Use Those Words: Fox News Owns Them." Commentary by Jack M. Balkin, *Los Angeles Times*, August 14, 2003.

233   "dream situation" for Franken. Interview, Larry Arnstein.

234–35 Fox's day in court. Transcript, Southern District Reports, August 22, 2003. Newspaper coverage, *New York Times, New York Post,* New York *Daily News.*

236   O'Reilly walks out on *Fresh Air*. Transcript, *The O'Reilly Factor* TV show. NPR Ombudsmen Jeffrey A. Dvorkin report, on Media Matters, October 15, 2003. Interviews, O'Reilly, others.

237   "downside to being on the defensive all the time." "Bill O'Reilly is turning into a cartoon character, a flipped-out Hulk with steam clouds coming out of his ears," wrote TV critic Matt Zoller Seitz about O'Reilly's increasing involvement in controversial media issues. "O'Reilly's repeated meltdowns in the past few months are making me wonder if he is losing it." Seitz, *The Star-Ledger* of Newark, New Jersey, October 21, 2003.

237   Voice of God. Interview, Glenn Collins.

237–38 Glick-O'Reilly debate. February 3, 2003. Transcripts, *Slate*, oreilly-sucks.com, livejournal.com, *Harper's*, others. Interviews, Rick MacArthur, Victor Navasky, Roger Ailes, Jeffrey Orling, Jamie Kitman, Bill O'Reilly.

"What the leftist press is doing is dishonest and extremely unjust," O'Reilly told me when the dust had settled. "They extrapolate sixty seconds from a five-minute talk to make you look like a fool." *Harper's* claims to have published 84 percent of his discussion with Glick.

239   Grodin quote, Charles Grodin. *I Like It Better When You're Funny: Working in Television and Other Precarious Adventures* (2002).

240   At war with San Francisco. Interview, Howard Ginsberg.

241–42   Olbermann at war with O'Reilly. Story, AP, July 25, 2006. Interviews Glenn Collins, Taya Kitman, Bill O'Reilly.

242–44   O'Reilly one-man war against Canada. Clifford Krauss, "Week in Review," *New York Times,* April 25, 2004. *Toronto Globe and Mail,* April 19, 21, 2004. *The O'Reilly Factor* (TV show) April 21, 29, 2004. Interviews, Abe and Helen Chutorian.

244   Apparently some members of the O'Reilly Brigade waxed poetic on the Canadian-American dispute. "I lost count the number of times I was called 'an a**hole,'" TV critic Doyle wrote. "It was at least forty-three times, anyway. I was called 'a pussy,' a wussy,' 'a pr**ck,' 'a jerk,' a hack,' and 'a creep.' A man in Cleveland not only called me an 'a**hole' but also wished me a 'f***ed-up day.' A lady—and I use the term advisedly—in Colorado wrote to say that all Canadians are 'a**holes' and then ordered me not to visit her state." *Toronto Globe and Mail,* April 21, 2004.

244–45   The B-Bomb. O'Reilly calls for Canada Boycott. Call to arms. *The O'Reilly Factor* (TV show), May 3, 2004.

245   Boycott of France Failure or Success. *Oui:* Interview, Bill O'Reilly. *Non:* *Rolling Stone, op. cit.* Interview, Howard Ginsberg.

245   All of which may explain why Bill O'Reilly is not taking his August vacation in France.

245–46   The mother of all media battles. Letterman gets political with O'Reilly. AP, January 9, 2006. Interviews, Jamie Kitman, Glenn and Sarah Collins.

CHAPTER TWENTY: What Was He Thinking?

247   "unwanted sex chatter." *New York Post,* October 19, 2004. medialifemagazine .com, October 18, 2004, *New York Observer,* October 25, 2004.

247–48   "Steamy soliloquies," thesmokinggun.com.

248–49   Sequence of alleged events. Transcript, Mackris court complaint. *Drudge Report,* October 14, 2004.

249   Mackris background.

249   O'Reilly countersues. Complaint filed in New York State Supreme Court, Nassau County.

251   Laughing stock up. *Borowitz Report,* October 14, 2004.

251   "problem with asserting moral authority." Rebecca Winters, *Time*, October 25, 2004,

252   "First, he had sued, then he went public." *The O'Reilly Factor*, October 13, 2004.

252   Mentions suit once on *Radio Factor*, October 19, 2004.

253   Ratings go up. Medialifemagazine.com.

253   Puzzling aspects of case. Analysis by author and sources.

254   "Hit us up for a lot of money": *New York Post* online edition October 19, 2004.

256   "Lawyers believe that O'Reilly would have won at trial." Beldar blog, October 16, 2004.

257–58 "Not only didn't he implode." Nielsen Media Research in *USA Today*, November 2, 2005.

PART IV: THE LAST HURRAH
CHAPTER TWENTY-ONE: The Future Lies Ahead

261   Will he burn out? Interview, Peter Jennings.

261   "I want to be the top-rated show." Michele Ingrassia, "He's Living the Life of O'Reilly," New York *Daily News*, December 6, 2000.

262   "had no idea the show would become such an icon." Interview, Bill O'Reilly.

262   "I never felt sorry for . . . Lindsay Lohan." Verne Gay, *Newsday*, October 18, 2005.

264   There are those who said he might start out running for a lower office. But why would he want to be in the House of Representatives? Where he is now he gets to talk every day nonstop for two hours on radio and one hour on TV. Why would he want to share the mike with 434 others in the House?

265   "What will become of O'Reilly?" Interviews, Roger Ailes, Victor Navasky, Bill O'Reilly, Peter Jennings, Carol Kitman.

PART V: WHAT SAY YOU?
CHAPTER TWENTY-TWO: The New Journalism

269   "Chris Cuomo must have asked me twenty times: angry guy." Interviews, Bill O'Reilly, Ted Faraone, Roger Ailes.

270   "What was missing from the news . . . was anger." "A lot of people are angry." Interview, Al Levin, Ted Faraone, Dennis Ainsworth, Joe Muzio.

272   "O'Reilly angry to be dismissed as an entertainer." Interviews, Frank Rich. Bill O'Reilly, Roger Ailes.

273   Some people object to O'Reilly news "because it isn't objective." Objectivity in journalism is a sham, a delusion. Interviews, Don Hewett, Tom Snyder, Victor Navasky, Ned Schnurman, Geraldo Rivera, Rick MacArthur, Roger Ailes.

273–74   "Before Cronkite's pure journalism, there was Ed Murrow. Classic example of subjective news/analyisis. Murrow on McCarthy. Other issues Murrow spoke up about. A.M. Sperber, *Murrow: His Life and Times* (1987).

276   O'Reilly as prototype of new kind of journalism. Seed he planted ten years ago bearing fruit. The rise of Brian Williams and Anderson Cooper reporting on Katrina. *The New York Times, USA Today,* Reuven Frank, *The New Leader.*

276   Way to deal with O'Reilly not to shut him down: get more O'Reillys. More news/analysis by author.

277   Will O'Reilly be future or wither away? New age of subjective journalism is the future and past of TV news. News/analysis/opinion by author.

BIBLIOGRAPHY

Alterman, Eric. *What Liberal Media? The Truth About Bias and the News.* New York: Basic Books, 2003.

Arledge, Roone. *Roone: A Memoir.* New York: HarperCollins, 2003.

Arlen, Michael J. *Living-room War.* New York: The Viking Press, 1969.

Auletta, Ken. *Three Blind Mice. How the TV Networks Lost Their Way.* New York: Random House, 1991.

Bernstein, R. B. (Richard). *Thomas Jefferson.* New York: Oxford University Press, 2003.

Block, Mervin. *Rewriting Network News. WordWatching Tips from 345 TV and Radio Scripts.* Chicago: Bonus Books, 1990.

Boyer, Peter J. *Who Killed CBS? The Undoing of America's Number One News Network.* New York: St. Martin's Press, 1989.

Brown, Les. *Les Brown's Encyclopedia of Television.* Washington: Visible Ink Press, 1997.

Conason, Joe. *Big Lies. The Right-Wing Propaganda Machine and How It Distorts the Truth.* New York: Thomas Dunne Books: St. Martin's Press, 2003.

Chenoweth, Neil. *Rupert Murdoch: The Untold Story of the World's Greatest Media Wizard.* New York: Crown Business, 2002.

Conrad, Pam. *Our House (The Stories of Levittown).* New York: Scholastic, 1995.

Colford, Paul D. *The Rush Limbaugh Story: Talent on Loan from God: An Unauthorized Biography.* New York: St. Martin's Press, 1994.

Corcoran, John. *A Few Marbles Left.* Los Angeles: Bonus Books, 2001.

Corn, David. "The Lies of George W. Bush: Mastering the Politics of Deception," Crown Publishers, 2005.

Ferrer, Margaret Lundrigan and Navarra, Tova. *Levittown: The First 50 Years.* Dover, N.H.: Arcadia, 1997.

Franken, Al. *Lies And the Lying Liars Who Tell Them: A Fair and Balanced Look at the Right.* New York: Dutton, 2003.

Gans, Herbert J. *The Levittowners. Ways of Life and Politics in a New Suburban Community.* New York: Vintage Books, 1969.

Grodin, Charles. *I Like It Better When You're Funny: Working in Television and Other Precarious Adventures.* New York: Random House, 2002.

Hack, Richard. *Clash of the Titans*. New York: New Millennium, 2003.

Halberstam, David. *The Fifties*. New York: Ballantine Books, 1994.

Hart, Peter, and Fairness & Accuracy in Reporting (FAIR). *The Oh Really? Factor: Unspinning Fox News Channel's Bill O'Reilly*. New York: Seven Stories Press, 2003.

Jackson, Kenneth T. *Crabgrass Frontier: The Suburbanization of the United States*. New York: Oxford University Press, 1985.

Joyce, Ed. *Prime Times, Bad Times: A Personal Drama of Network Television*. New York: Doubleday, 1988.

Kearns, Burt. *Tabloid Baby*. Nashville, Tennessee: Celebrity Books, 1999.

Kitman, Marvin. *The Marvin Kitman TV Show: Encyclopedia Televisiana*. New York: Outerbridge & Lazard/E. P. Dutton, 1972.

Kitman, Marvin. *I Am a VCR: The Kitman Tapes*. New York: Random House, 1988.

Kurtz, Howard. *Hot Air: All Talk, All the Time. An Inside Look at the Performers and the Pundits*. New York: Times Books/Random House, 1996.

Lattimore, Owen. *Ordeal By Slander*. New York: Carroll & Graf, 2002.

Meara, Mary Jane Frances Cavolina; Stone, Jeffrey, Allen Joseph; Kelly, Maureen Anne Teresa, and David, Richard Glen Michael. *Growing Up Catholic. An Infinitely Funny Guide for the Faithful, the Fallen, and Everyone In-Between*. Garden City: Dolphin/Doubleday, 1985.

Navasky, Victor S. *A Matter of Opinion*. New York: Farrar, Straus and Giroux, 2005.

O'Reilly, Bill. *Those Who Trespass: A Novel of Murder and Television*. Baltimore: Bancroft Press, 1998.

O'Reilly, Bill. *The O'Reilly Factor: The Good, the Bad, and the Completely Ridiculous in American Life*. New York, Broadway Books, 2000.

O'Reilly, Bill. *The No Spin Zone: Confrontations with the Powerful and Famous in America*. New York: Broadway Books, 2001.

O'Reilly, Bill. *Who's Looking Out for You?* New York: Broadway Books, 2003.

O'Reilly, Bill, and Charles Flowers. *The O'Reilly Factor for Kids. A Survival Guide for America's Families*. New York: HarperEntertainment, 2004.

Schieffer, Bob. *This Just In: What I Couldn't Tell You on TV*. New York: G. P. Putnam's Sons, 2003.

Schonfeld, Reese. *Me and Ted Against the World: The Unauthorized Story of the Founding of CNN*. New York: Cliff Street/HarperCollins, 2001.

Schott, Ben. *Schott's Original Miscellany*. New York: Bloomsbury, 2002.

Shawcross, William. *Murdoch: The Making of a Media Empire*. New York: Touchstone, 1997.

Sperber, A. M. *Murrow: His Life and Times*. New York: Bantam Books, 1987.

Tannen, Deborah. *The Argument Culture (Stopping America's War of Words)*. New York: Balantine Books, 1998.

Westin, Av. *Newswatch. How TV Decides the News*. New York: Simon & Schuster, 1982.

INDEX

Blair, Jayson, 213

Blasi, John, 20, 24, 36, 54

Blitzer, Wolf, 211

BookExpo America Convention (Los
    Angeles, California, 2003),
    222–223, 236

Borowitz, Andy, 250

Boston, Massachusetts, 106–114,
    119–121

Boston Globe (newspaper), 107, 108, 110,
    112, 113, 116, 191

Boston Herald (newspaper), 108, 211–212

Boston Phoenix (newspaper), 70

Boston University, 69–72, 121

Brandi, Dianne, 232–233

Brando, Marlon, 15

Brandt, Arnold, 194

Brennan, Peter, 134, 135

Brill's Content (magazine), 212

Brinkley, David, 265

Broadcasting Magazine, 75

Brockovitch, Erin, 178

Brokaw, Tom, 1, 121, 166–167

Brown, Dave, 164, 179, 198

Buchanan, Pat, 4–5, 264

Burke, Susan, 108, 110, 125

Bush, George H. W., 238

Bush, George W., 154, 222, 223, 226, 249
    Gergen, David, 4
    New York Times (newspaper), 212
    O'Reilly, Bill, 181, 203–204
    Rather, Dan, 1

Bush, Jeb, 227

Bush administration, 4

Butterfield, Fox, 70

cable television news. *See* television news;
    specific cable networks

Cahill Gordon & Reindel (law firm),
    232–233

Callahan, Charlie, 59

Canada, 242–245

Capital Gang, The (TV show), 4

capital punishment, 227–228

Carey, Drew, 182

Carey, Hugh, 99–100

Carnes, Jennifer King, 62

Carroll, E. Jean, 199

Carson, Johnny, 49, 134

Carter administration, 4, 238

Carville, James, 5, 183, 225

Cashman, Edward, 200

Castaway Cowboys (film), 85

CBS Evening News, 102, 104, 121,
    273–275

CBS television network, 1, 2, 3, 87,
    93–101, 106, 124, 128, 151, 251,
    271, 273

Cembalist, Stanley, 221

Central Intelligence Agency (CIA), 87,
    238

Chambers, Robert, 134

Chancellor, John, 121

Chandler, Bob, 98

Chao, Stephen, 6

Charlie's Angels (film), 178

Cheney, Dick, 222, 223, 232

Chicago Tribune (newspaper), 191

Chin, Denny, 234–235

Chirac, Jacques, 245

Chris-Craft company, 165

Chung, Connie, xiii

Clinton, Hillary, 179, 228, 264

Clinton, William J., 4, 171, 228, 230

Clooney, George, 179

CNN television network, xiii, 5, 131,
    180, 181, 208–209, 226, 242, 248

Cohen, Jeff, 17, 18, 19, 25, 68, 89, 90,
    157, 158

Cohen, Steve, 99–100

Colapinto, John, 85

Collins, Glenn, 237